THE
JESUS
I NEVER KNEW

D0752809

DISAPPOINTMENT
WITH GOD

Resources by Philip Yancey

The Jesus I Never Knew

What's So Amazing About Grace?

The Bible Jesus Read

Reaching for the Invisible God

Where Is God When It Hurts?

Disappointment with God

The Student Bible, General Edition (with Tim Stafford)

Meet the Bible (with Brenda Quinn)

Church: Why Bother?

Finding God in Unexpected Places

I Was Just Wondering

Soul Survivor

Rumors of Another World

Prayer

Books by Philip Yancey and Dr. Paul Brand

Fearfully and Wonderfully Made

In His Image

The Gift of Pain

THE JESUS I NEVER KNEW

PHILIP YANCEY

DISAPPOINTMENT WITH GOD

ZONDERVAN.com/
AUTHORTRACKER
follow your favorite authors

ZONDERVAN®

The Jesus I Never Knew/Disappointment with God
Copyright © 2007 by Philip Yancey

The Jesus I Never Knew
Copyright © 1995 by Philip Yancey

Disappointment with God
Copyright © 1988 by Philip Yancey
First paperback edition 1992

Requests for information should be addressed to:
Zondervan, Grand Rapids, Michigan 49530

ISBN-10: 0-310-60959-3
ISBN-13: 978-0-310-60959-9

Printed in the United States of America

07 08 09 10 11 12 13 • 21 20 19 18 17 16 15 14 13 12 11 10 9 8 7 6 5 4 3 2 1

CONTENTS

THE JESUS I NEVER KNEW

DISAPPOINTMENT WITH GOD

———∞∞∞———

PART FOUR—TURNING IT OVER: THE SPIRIT

BOOK II: SEEING IN THE DARK

THE
JESUS
I NEVER KNEW

Thanks ...

To the class I taught, and was taught by, at LaSalle Street Church in Chicago.

To Tim Stafford, Bud Ogle, and Walter Wangerin Jr., whose perceptive comments caused me to rewrite this book several more times than I would have on my own.

To Verlyn Verbrugge, for his careful technical editing on matters of biblical accuracy.

To my editor John Sloan, who patiently endured, and helped improve, all those drafts.

PART ONE
WHO HE WAS

THE JESUS
I THOUGHT I KNEW

Suppose we hear an unknown man spoken of by many men. Suppose we were puzzled to hear that some men said he was too tall and some too short; some objected to his fatness, some lamented his leanness; some thought him too dark, and some too fair. One explanation . . . would be that he might be an odd shape. But there is another explanation. He might be the right shape. . . . Perhaps (in short) this extraordinary thing is really the ordinary thing; at least the normal thing, the centre.

G. K. CHESTERTON

THE JESUS
I THOUGHT I KNEW

---✦---

I first got acquainted with Jesus when I was a child, singing "Jesus Loves Me" in Sunday school, addressing bedtime prayers to "Dear Lord Jesus," watching Bible Club teachers move cutout figures across a flannelgraph board. I associated Jesus with Kool-Aid and sugar cookies and gold stars for good attendance.

I remember especially one image from Sunday school, an oil painting that hung on the concrete block wall. Jesus had long, flowing hair, unlike that of any man I knew. His face was thin and handsome, his skin waxen and milky white. He wore a robe of scarlet, and the artist had taken pains to show the play of light on its folds. In his arms, Jesus cradled a small sleeping lamb. I imagined myself as that lamb, blessed beyond all telling.

Recently, I read a book that the elderly Charles Dickens had written to sum up the life of Jesus for his children. In it, the portrait emerges of a sweet Victorian nanny who pats the heads of boys and girls and offers such advice as, "Now, children, you must be nice to your mummy and daddy." With a start I recalled the Sunday school image of Jesus that I grew up with: someone kind and reassuring, with no sharp edges at all—a Mister Rogers before the age of children's television. As a child I felt comforted by such a person.

Later, while attending a Bible college, I encountered a different image. A painting popular in those days depicted Jesus, hands outstretched, suspended in a Dalí-like pose over the United Nations building in New York City. Here was the cosmic Christ, the One in whom all things inhere, the still point of the turning world. This world figure had come a long way from the lamb-toting shepherd of my childhood.

Still, students spoke of the cosmic Jesus with a shocking intimacy. The faculty urged us to develop a "personal relationship with Jesus Christ," and in chapel services we hymned our love for him in most familiar terms. One song told about walking beside him in a garden with dew still on the roses. Students testifying about their faith casually dropped in phrases like "The Lord told me...." My own faith hung in a kind of skeptical suspension during my time there. I was wary, confused, questioning.

Looking in retrospect on my years at Bible college, I see that, despite all the devotional intimacies, Jesus grew remote from me there. He became an object of scrutiny. I memorized the list of thirty-four specific miracles in the Gospels but missed the impact of just one miracle. I learned the Beatitudes yet never faced the fact that none of us—I above all—could make sense of those mysterious sayings, let alone live by them.

A little later, the decade of the 1960s (which actually reached me, along with most of the church, in the early 1970s) called everything into question. Jesus freaks—the very term would have been an oxymoron in the tranquil 1950s—suddenly appeared on the scene, as if deposited there by extraterrestrials. No longer were Jesus' followers well-scrubbed representatives of the middle class; some were unkempt, disheveled radicals. Liberation theologians began enshrining Jesus on posters in a troika along with Fidel Castro and Che Guevara.

It dawned on me that virtually all portrayals of Jesus, including the Good Shepherd of my Sunday school and the United Nations Jesus of my Bible college, showed him wearing a mustache and beard, both of which were strictly banned from the Bible college. Questions now loomed that had never occurred to me in childhood. For example, How would telling people to be nice to one another get a man crucified? What government would execute Mister Rogers or Captain Kangaroo? Thomas Paine said that no religion could be truly divine which has in it any doctrine that offends the sensibilities of a little child. Would the cross qualify?

In 1971 I first saw the movie *The Gospel According to St. Matthew*, directed by Italian filmmaker Pier Paolo Pasolini. Its release had scandalized not only the religious establishment, who barely recognized the Jesus on-screen, but also the film community, who knew Pasolini as an outspoken homosexual and Marxist. Pasolini wryly dedicated the film to Pope John XXIII, the man indirectly responsible for its creation. Trapped in an enormous traffic jam during a papal visit to Florence, Pasolini had checked into a hotel room where, bored, he picked up a copy of the New Testament from the bedside table and read through Matthew. What he discovered in those pages so startled him that he determined to make a film using no text but the actual words from Matthew's gospel.

Pasolini's film captures well the reappraisal of Jesus that took place in the 1960s. Shot in southern Italy on a tight budget, it evokes in chalky whites and dusty grays something of the Palestinian surroundings Jesus lived in. The Pharisees wear towering headpieces, and Herod's soldiers faintly resemble Fascist *squadristi*. The disciples act like bumbling raw recruits, but Jesus himself, with a steady gaze and a piercing intensity, seems fearless. The parables and other sayings, he fires in clipped phrases over his shoulder as he dashes from place to place.

The impact of Pasolini's film can only be understood by one who passed through adolescence during that tumultuous period. Back then it had the power to hush scoffing crowds at art theaters. Student radicals realized they were not the first to proclaim a message that was jarringly antimaterialistic, antihypocritical, pro-peace, and pro-love.

For me, the film helped to force a disturbing revaluation of my image of Jesus. In physical appearance, Jesus favored those who would have been kicked out of Bible college and rejected by most churches. Among his contemporaries he somehow gained a reputation as "a wine-bibber and a glutton." Those in authority, whether religious or political, regarded him as a troublemaker, a disturber of the peace. He spoke and acted like a revolutionary, scorning fame, family, property, and other traditional measures of success. I could not dodge the fact that the words in Pasolini's film were taken entirely from Matthew's gospel, yet their message clearly did not fit my prior conception of Jesus.

About this same time a Young Life worker named Bill Milliken, who had founded a commune in an inner-city neighborhood, wrote *So Long, Sweet Jesus.* The title of that book gave words to the change at work inside me. In those days I was employed as the editor of *Campus Life* magazine, an official publication of Youth For Christ. *Who was this Christ, after all?* I wondered. As I wrote, and edited the writing of others, a tiny dybbuk of doubt hovered just to my side. *Do you really believe that? Or are you merely dispensing the party line, what you're paid to believe? Have you joined the safe, conservative establishment—modern versions of the groups who felt so threatened by Jesus?*

As often as not I avoided writing directly about Jesus.

When I switched on my computer this morning, Microsoft Windows flashed the date, implicitly acknowledging that, whatever you may believe about it, the birth of Jesus was so important that it split history into two parts. Everything that has ever happened on this planet falls into a category of before Christ or after Christ.

Richard Nixon got carried away with excitement in 1969 when Apollo astronauts first landed on the moon. "It's the greatest day since Creation!" crowed the president, until Billy Graham solemnly reminded him of Christmas and Easter. By any measure of history Graham was right. This Galilean, who in his lifetime spoke to fewer people than would fill just one of the many stadia Graham has filled, changed the world more than any other person. He introduced a new force field into history, and now holds the allegiance of a third of all people on earth.

Today, people even use Jesus' name to curse by. How strange it would sound if, when a businessman missed a golf putt, he yelled, "Thomas Jefferson!" or if a plumber screamed "Mahatma Gandhi!" when his pipe wrench mashed a finger. We cannot get away from this man Jesus.

THE JESUS I THOUGHT I KNEW

"More than 1900 years later," said H. G. Wells, "a historian like myself, who doesn't even call himself a Christian, finds the picture centering irresistibly around the life and character of this most significant man. . . . The historian's test of an individual's greatness is 'What did he leave to grow?' Did he start men to thinking along fresh lines with a vigor that persisted after him? By this test Jesus stands first." You can gauge the size of a ship that has passed out of sight by the huge wake it leaves behind.

And yet I am not writing a book about Jesus because he is a great man who changed history. I am not tempted to write about Julius Caesar or the Chinese emperor who built the Great Wall. I am drawn to Jesus, irresistibly, because he positioned himself as the dividing point of life—my life. "I tell you, whoever acknowledges me before men, the Son of Man will also acknowledge him before the angels of God," he said. According to Jesus, what I think about him and how I respond will determine my destiny for all eternity.

Sometimes I accept Jesus' audacious claim without question. Sometimes, I confess, I wonder what difference it should make to my life that a man lived two thousand years ago in a place called Galilee. Can I resolve this inner tension between doubter and lover?

I tend to write as a means of confronting my own doubts. My book titles—*Where Is God When It Hurts*, *Disappointment with God*—betray me. I return again and again to the same questions, as if fingering an old wound that never quite heals. Does God care about the misery down here? Do we really matter to God?

Once, for a two-week period, I was snowbound in a mountain cabin in Colorado. Blizzards closed all roads and, somewhat like Pasolini, I had nothing to do but read the Bible. I went through it slowly, page by page. In the Old Testament I found myself identifying with those who boldly stood up to God: Moses, Job, Jeremiah, Habakkuk, the psalmists. As I read, I felt I was watching a play with human characters who acted out their lives of small triumph and large tragedy onstage, while periodically calling to an unseen Stage Manager, "You don't know what it's like out here!" Job was most brazen, flinging to God this accusation: "Do you have eyes of flesh? Do you see as a mortal sees?"

Every so often I could hear the echo of a booming voice from far offstage, behind the curtain. "Yeah, and you don't know what it's like back here either!" it said, to Moses, to the prophets, most loudly to Job. When I got to the Gospels, however, the accusing voices stilled. God, if I may use such language, "found out" what life is like in the confines of planet earth. Jesus got acquainted with grief in person, in a brief, troubled life not far from the dusty plains where Job had travailed. Of the many reasons for Incarnation, surely one was to answer Job's accusation: Do you have eyes of flesh? For a time, God did.

If only I could hear the voice from the whirlwind and, like Job, hold a conversation with God himself! I sometimes think. And perhaps that is why I now choose to write about Jesus. God is not mute: the Word spoke, not out of a whirlwind, but out of the human larynx of a Palestinian Jew. In Jesus, God lay down on the dissection table, as it were, stretched out in cruciform posture for the scrutiny of all skeptics who have ever lived. Including me.

The vision of Christ that thou dost see
Is my vision's greatest enemy:
Thine has a great hook nose like thine,
Mine has a snub nose like to mine. . . .
Both read the Bible day and night,
But thou read'st black where I read white.
WILLIAM BLAKE

As I think about Jesus, an analogy from Karl Barth comes to mind. A man stands by a window gazing into the street. Outside, people are shading their eyes with their hands and looking up into the sky. Because of the overhang of the building though, the man cannot see what it is they are pointing toward. We who live two thousand years after Jesus have a viewpoint not unlike the man standing by the window. We hear the shouts of exclamation. We study the gestures and words in the Gospels and the many books they have spawned. Yet no amount of neck-craning will allow us a glimpse of Jesus in the flesh.

For this reason, as William Blake's poem expresses so well, sometimes those of us who look for Jesus cannot see past our own noses. The Lakota tribe, for example, refers to Jesus as "the buffalo calf of God." The Cuban government distributes a painting of Jesus with a carbine slung over his shoulder. During the wars of religion with France, the English used to shout, "The pope is French but Jesus Christ is English!"

Modern scholarship further muddies the picture. If you peruse the academic books available at a seminary bookstore you may encounter Jesus as a political revolutionary, as a magician who married Mary Magdalene, as a Galilean charismatic, a rabbi, a peasant Jewish Cynic, a Pharisee, an anti-Pharisee Essene, an eschatological prophet, a "hippie in a world of Augustan yuppies," and as the hallucinogenic leader of a sacred mushroom cult. Serious scholars write these works, with little sign of embarrassment.*

Athletes come up with creative portrayals of Jesus that elude modern scholarship. Norm Evans, former Miami Dolphins lineman, wrote in his book *On God's Squad*, "I guarantee you Christ would be the toughest guy who ever played this game.... If he were alive today I would picture a six-foot-six-inch 260-pound defensive tackle who would always make the big plays and would be hard to keep out of the backfield for offensive linemen like myself." Fritz Peterson, former New York Yankee, more easily fancies Jesus in a baseball uniform: "I firmly believe that if Jesus Christ was sliding into second base, he would knock the second baseman into left field to break up the double play. Christ might not throw a spitball, but he would play hard within the rules."

In the midst of such confusion, how do we answer the simple question, "Who was Jesus?" Secular history gives few clues. In a delicious irony, the figure who has changed history more than any other

---

*The U.S. public tends to ignore such trendy portrayals. A recent Gallup survey revealed that 84 percent of Americans believe Jesus Christ was God or the Son of God. Overwhelmingly Americans believe that Jesus was sinless, brave, and emotionally stable. By lesser margins they regard him as easy to understand (!), physically strong and attractive, practical, warm, and accepting.

managed to escape the attention of most scholars and historians of his own time. Even the four men who wrote the Gospels omitted much that would interest modern readers, skipping over nine-tenths of his life. Since none devotes a word to physical description, we know nothing about Jesus' shape or stature or eye color. Details of his family life are so scant that scholars still debate whether or not he had brothers and sisters. The facts of biography considered essential to modern readers simply did not concern the gospel writers.

Before beginning this book I spent several months in three seminary libraries—one Catholic, one liberal Protestant, one conservative evangelical—reading about Jesus. It was daunting in the extreme to walk in the first day and see not just shelves but entire walls devoted to books about Jesus. A scholar at the University of Chicago estimates that more has been written about Jesus in the last twenty years than in the previous nineteen centuries. I felt almost as if the hyperbolic comment at the end of John's gospel had come true: "Jesus did many other things as well. If every one of them were written down, I suppose that even the whole world would not have room for the books that would be written."

The agglomeration of scholarship began to have a numbing effect on me. I read scores of accounts of the etymology of Jesus' name, discussions of what languages he spoke, debates about how long he lived at Nazareth or Capernaum or Bethlehem. Any true-to-life image receded into a fuzzy, indistinct blur. I had a hunch that Jesus himself would be appalled by many of the portrayals I was reading.

At the same time, with great consistency I found that whenever I returned to the Gospels themselves the fog seemed to lift. J. B. Phillips wrote, after translating and paraphrasing the Gospels, "I have read, in Greek and Latin, scores of myths, but I did not find the slightest flavour of myth here.... No man could have set down such artless and vulnerable accounts as these unless some real Event lay behind them."

Some religious books have about them the sour smell of propaganda—but not the Gospels. Mark records what may be the most important event in all history, an event that theologians strive to interpret with words like "propitiation, atonement, sacrifice," in one sentence: "With a loud cry, Jesus breathed his last." Odd, unpredictable scenes show up, such as Jesus' family and neighbors trying to put him away under suspicion of insanity. Why include such scenes if you are writing hagiography? Jesus' most devoted followers usually come off as scratching their heads in wonderment—*Who is this guy?*—more baffled than conspiratorial.

Jesus himself, when challenged, did not offer airtight proofs of his identity. He dropped clues here and there, to be sure, but he also said, after appealing to the evidence, "Blessed is he who takes no offense at me." Reading the accounts, it is hard to find anyone who does not at some point or another take offense. To a remarkable degree the Gospels throw the decision back to the reader. They operate more like a "whodunit" (or as Alister McGrath has pointed out, a "whowashe") detective story than like a connect-the-dots drawing. I found fresh energy in this quality of the Gospels.

It occurs to me that all the contorted theories about Jesus that have been spontaneously generating since the day of his death merely confirm the awesome risk God took when he stretched himself out on the dissection table—a risk he seemed to welcome. Examine me. Test me. You decide.

———

The Italian movie *La Dolce Vita* opens with a shot of a helicopter ferrying a giant statue of Jesus to Rome. Arms outstretched, Jesus hangs in a sling, and as the helicopter passes over the landscape, people begin to recognize him. "Hey, it's Jesus!" shouts one old farmer, hopping off his tractor to race across the field. Nearer Rome, bikini-clad girls sunbathing around a swimming pool wave a friendly greeting, and the helicopter pilot swoops in for a closer look. Silent, with an almost doleful expression on his face, the concrete Jesus hovers incongruously above the modern world.

My search for Jesus took off in a new direction when the filmmaker Mel White loaned me a collection of fifteen movies on the life of Jesus. They ranged from *King of Kings*, the 1927 silent classic by Cecil B. DeMille, to musicals such as *Godspell* and *Cotton Patch Gospel* to the strikingly modern French-Canadian treatment *Jesus of Montreal*.

I reviewed these films carefully, outlining them scene by scene. Then, for the next two years, I taught a class on the life of Jesus, using the movies as a springboard for our discussion.

The class worked like this. As we came to a major event in Jesus' life, I would scout through the various films and from them select seven or eight treatments that seemed notable. As class began, I would show the two- to four-minute clips from each film, beginning with the comical and stiff renditions and working toward profound or evocative treatments. We found that the process of viewing the same event through the eyes of seven or eight filmmakers helped to strip away the patina of predictability that had built up over years of Sunday school and Bible reading. Obviously, some of the film interpretations had to be wrong—they blatantly contradicted each other—but which ones? What really happened? After reacting to the film clips we turned to the gospel accounts, and the discussion took off.

This class met at LaSalle Street Church, a lively congregation in downtown Chicago, which included Ph.D.'s from Northwestern as well as homeless men who used the hour in a warm room as a chance to catch up on sleep. Thanks largely to the class, I gradually underwent a transformation in how I viewed Jesus. Walter Kasper has said, "Extreme notions ... see God dressed as a Father Christmas, or slipping into human nature like someone putting on dungarees in order to repair the world after a breakdown. The biblical and church doctrine that Jesus was a complete man with a human intellect and human freedom, does not seem to prevail in the average Christian head." It did not prevail in my head, I admit, until I taught the class at LaSalle Street Church and sought to encounter the historical person Jesus.

Essentially, the films helped restore Jesus' humanity for me. The creeds repeated in churches tell about Christ's eternal preexistence and glorious afterlife, but largely ignore his earthly career. The Gospels themselves were written years after Jesus' death, from the far side of Easter, reporting on events as distant from the authors as the Korean War is from us today. The films helped me get further back, closer to a sense of Jesus' life as seen by his contemporaries. What would it have been like to hang on the edges of the crowd? How would I have responded to this man? Would I have invited him over for dinner, like

Zacchaeus? Turned away in sadness, like the rich young ruler? Betrayed him, like Judas and Peter? Jesus, I found, bore little resemblance to the Mister Rogers figure I had met in Sunday school, and was remarkably unlike the person I had studied in Bible college. For one thing, he was far less tame. In my prior image, I realized, Jesus' personality matched that of a *Star Trek* Vulcan: he remained calm, cool, and collected as he strode like a robot among excitable human beings on spaceship earth. That is not what I found portrayed in the Gospels and in the better films. Other people affected Jesus deeply: obstinacy frustrated him, self-righteousness infuriated him, simple faith thrilled him. Indeed, he seemed more emotional and spontaneous than the average person, not less. More passionate, not less.

The more I studied Jesus, the more difficult it became to pigeonhole him. He said little about the Roman occupation, the main topic of conversation among his countrymen, and yet he took up a whip to drive petty profiteers from the Jewish temple. He urged obedience to the Mosaic law while acquiring the reputation as a lawbreaker. He could be stabbed by sympathy for a stranger, yet turn on his best friend with the flinty rebuke, "Get behind me, Satan!" He had uncompromising views on rich men and loose women, yet both types enjoyed his company.

One day miracles seemed to flow out of Jesus; the next day his power was blocked by people's lack of faith. One day he talked in detail of the Second Coming; another, he knew neither the day nor hour. He fled from arrest at one point and marched inexorably toward it at another. He spoke eloquently about peacemaking, then told his disciples to procure swords. His extravagant claims about himself kept him at the center of controversy, but when he did something truly miraculous he tended to hush it up. As Walter Wink has said, if Jesus had never lived, we would not have been able to invent him.

Two words one could never think of applying to the Jesus of the Gospels: boring and predictable. How is it, then, that the church has tamed such a character—has, in Dorothy Sayers' words, "very efficiently pared the claws of the Lion of Judah, certified Him as a fitting household pet for pale curates and pious old ladies"?

Pulitzer prize-winning historian Barbara Tuchman insists on one rule in writing history: no "flash-forwards." When she was writing about the Battle of the Bulge in World War II, for example, she resisted the temptation to include "Of course we all know how this turned out" asides. In point of fact, the Allied troops involved in the Battle of the Bulge did *not* know how the battle would turn out. From the look of things, they could well be driven right back to the beaches of Normandy where they had come from. A historian who wants to retain any semblance of tension and drama in events as they unfold dare not flash-forward to another, all-seeing point of view. Do so, and all tension melts away. Rather, a good historian re-creates for the reader the conditions of the history being described, conveying a sense that "you were there."

That, I concluded, is the problem with most of our writing and thinking about Jesus. We read the Gospels through the flash-forward lenses of church councils like Nicea and Chalcedon, through the church's studied attempts to make sense of him.

Jesus was a human being, a Jew in Galilee with a name and a family, a person who was in a way just like everyone else. Yet in another way he was something different than anyone who had ever lived on earth before. It took the church five centuries of active debate to agree on some sort of epistemological balance between "just like everyone else" and "something different." For those of us raised in the church, or even raised in a nominally Christian culture, the balance inevitably tilts toward "something different." As Pascal said, "The Church has had as much difficulty in showing that Jesus Christ was man, against those who denied it, as in showing that he was God; and the probabilities were equally great."

Let me make it clear that I affirm the creeds. But in this book I hope to go back beyond those formulations. I hope, as far as is possible, to look at Jesus' life "from below," as a spectator, one of the many who followed him around. If I were a Japanese filmmaker, given $50 million and no script but the Gospels' text, what kind of film would I make? I hope, in Luther's words, to "draw Christ as deep as possible into the flesh."

26

In the process, sometimes I have felt like a tourist walking around a great monument, awed and overwhelmed. I circle the monument of Jesus inspecting its constituent parts—the birth stories, the teachings, the miracles, the enemies and followers—in order to reflect on and try to comprehend the man who has changed history.

Other times I have felt like an art restorer stretched out on the scaffolding of the Sistine Chapel, swabbing away the grime of history with a moistened Q-tip. If I scrub hard enough, will I find the original beneath all those layers?

In this book I attempt to tell the story of Jesus, not my own story. Inevitably, though, a search for Jesus turns out to be one's own search. No one who meets Jesus ever stays the same. I have found that the doubts that afflict me from many sources—from science, from comparative religion, from an innate defect of skepticism, from aversion to the church—take on a new light when I bring those doubts to the man named Jesus. To say more at this stage, in this first chapter, would cause me to break Barbara Tuchman's cherished principle.

BIRTH:
THE VISITED PLANET

———— ∞∞ ————

The God of power, as he did ride
In his majestick robes of glorie
Resolv'd to light; and so one day
He did descend, undressing all the way.

GEORGE HERBERT

BIRTH:
THE VISITED PLANET

———∞∞∞———

Sorting through the stack of cards that arrived at our house last Christmas, I note that all kinds of symbols have edged their way into the celebration. Overwhelmingly, the landscape scenes render New England towns buried in snow, usually with the added touch of a horse-drawn sleigh. On other cards, animals frolic: not only reindeer, but also chipmunks, raccoons, cardinals, and cute gray mice. One card shows an African lion reclining with a foreleg draped affectionately around a lamb.

Angels have made a huge comeback in recent years, and Hallmark and American Greetings now feature them prominently, though as demure, cuddly-looking creatures, not the type who would ever need to announce "Fear not!" The explicitly religious cards (a distinct minority) focus on the holy family, and you can tell at a glance these folks are different. They seem unruffled and serene. Bright gold halos, like crowns from another world, hover just above their heads.

Inside, the cards stress sunny words like love, goodwill, cheer, happiness, and warmth. It is a fine thing, I suppose, that we honor a sacred holiday with such homey sentiments. And yet when I turn to the gospel accounts of the first Christmas, I hear a very different tone and sense mainly disruption at work.

I recall watching an episode of the TV show *Thirtysomething* in which Hope, a Christian, argues with her Jewish husband, Michael, about the holidays. "Why do you even bother with Hanukkah?" she asks. "Do you really believe a handful of Jews held off a huge army by using a bunch of lamps that miraculously wouldn't run out of oil?"

Michael exploded. "Oh, and Christmas makes more sense? Do you really believe an angel appeared to some teenage girl who then got pregnant without ever having had sex and traveled on horseback to Bethlehem where she spent the night in a barn and had a baby who turned out to be the Savior of the world?"

Frankly, Michael's incredulity seems close to what I read in the Gospels. Mary and Joseph must face the shame and derision of family and neighbors, who react, well, much like Michael ("Do you really believe an angel appeared …").

Even those who accept the supernatural version of events concede that big trouble will follow: an old uncle prays for "salvation from our enemies and from the hand of all who hate us"; Simeon darkly warns the virgin that "a sword will pierce your own soul too"; Mary's hymn of thanksgiving mentions rulers overthrown and proud men scattered.

In contrast to what the cards would have us believe, Christmas did not sentimentally simplify life on planet earth. Perhaps this is what I sense when Christmas rolls around and I turn from the cheeriness of the cards to the starkness of the Gospels.

Christmas art depicts Jesus' family as icons stamped in gold foil, with a calm Mary receiving the tidings of the Annunciation as a kind of benediction. But that is not at all how Luke tells the story. Mary was "greatly troubled" and "afraid" at the angel's appearance, and when the angel pronounced the sublime words about the Son of the Most High whose kingdom will never end, Mary had something far more mundane on her mind: *But I'm a virgin!*

Once, a young unmarried lawyer named Cynthia bravely stood before my church in Chicago and told of a sin we already knew about: we had seen her hyperactive son running up and down the aisles every

Sunday. Cynthia had taken the lonely road of bearing an illegitimate child and caring for him after his father decided to skip town. Cynthia's sin was no worse than many others, and yet, as she told us, it had such conspicuous consequences. She could not hide the result of that single act of passion, sticking out as it did from her abdomen for months until a child emerged to change every hour of every day of the rest of her life. No wonder the Jewish teenager Mary felt greatly troubled: she faced the same prospects even without the act of passion.

In the modern United States, where each year a million teenage girls get pregnant out of wedlock, Mary's predicament has undoubtedly lost some of its force, but in a closely knit Jewish community in the first century, the news an angel brought could not have been entirely welcome. The law regarded a betrothed woman who became pregnant as an adulteress, subject to death by stoning.

Matthew tells of Joseph magnanimously agreeing to divorce Mary in private rather than press charges, until an angel shows up to correct his perception of betrayal. Luke tells of a tremulous Mary hurrying off to the one person who could possibly understand what she was going through: her relative Elizabeth, who miraculously got pregnant in old age after another angelic annunciation. Elizabeth believes Mary and shares her joy, and yet the scene poignantly highlights the contrast between the two women: the whole countryside is talking about Elizabeth's healed womb even as Mary must hide the shame of her own miracle.

In a few months, the birth of John the Baptist took place amid great fanfare, complete with midwives, doting relatives, and the traditional village chorus celebrating the birth of a Jewish male. Six months later, Jesus was born far from home, with no midwife, extended family, or village chorus present. A male head of household would have sufficed for the Roman census; did Joseph drag his pregnant wife along to Bethlehem in order to spare her the ignominy of childbirth in her home village?

C. S. Lewis has written about God's plan, "The whole thing narrows and narrows, until at last it comes down to a little point, small as the point of a spear—a Jewish girl at her prayers." Today as I read the accounts of Jesus' birth I tremble to think of the fate of the world resting on the responses of two rural teenagers. How many times did Mary review the angel's words as she felt the Son of God kicking against the walls of her uterus? How many times did Joseph second-guess his own encounter with an angel—*just a dream?*—as he endured the hot shame of living among villagers who could plainly see the changing shape of his fiancée?

We know nothing of Jesus' grandparents. What must they have felt? Did they respond like so many parents of unmarried teenagers today, with an outburst of moral fury and then a period of sullen silence until at last the bright-eyed newborn arrives to melt the ice and arrange a fragile family truce? Or did they, like many inner-city grandparents today, graciously offer to take the child under their own roof?

Nine months of awkward explanations, the lingering scent of scandal—it seems that God arranged the most humiliating circumstances possible for his entrance, as if to avoid any charge of favoritism. I am impressed that when the Son of God became a human being he played by the rules, harsh rules: small towns do not treat kindly young boys who grow up with questionable paternity.

Malcolm Muggeridge observed that in our day, with family-planning clinics offering convenient ways to correct "mistakes" that might disgrace a family name, "It is, in point of fact, extremely improbable, under existing conditions, that Jesus would have been permitted to be born at all. Mary's pregnancy, in poor circumstances, and with the father unknown, would have been an obvious case for an abortion; and her talk of having conceived as a result of the intervention of the Holy Ghost would have pointed to the need for psychiatric treatment, and made the case for terminating her pregnancy even stronger. Thus our generation, needing a Savior more, perhaps, than any that has ever existed, would be too humane to allow one to be born."

The virgin Mary, though, whose parenthood was unplanned, had a different response. She heard the angel out, pondered the repercussions, and replied, "I am the Lord's servant. May it be to me as you have said." Often a work of God comes with two edges, great joy and great pain, and in that matter-of-fact response Mary embraced both. She was the first person to accept Jesus on his own terms, regardless of the personal cost.

When the Jesuit missionary Matteo Ricci went to China in the sixteenth century, he brought along samples of religious art to illustrate the Christian story for people who had never heard it. The Chinese readily adopted portraits of the Virgin Mary holding her child, but when he produced paintings of the crucifixion and tried to explain that the God-child had grown up only to be executed, the audience reacted with revulsion and horror. They much preferred the Virgin and insisted on worshiping her rather than the crucified God.

As I thumb once more through my stack of Christmas cards, I realize that we in Christian countries do much the same thing. We observe a mellow, domesticated holiday purged of any hint of scandal. Above all, we purge from it any reminder of how the story that began at Bethlehem turned out at Calvary.

In the birth stories of Luke and Matthew, only one person seems to grasp the mysterious nature of what God has set in motion: the old man Simeon, who recognized the baby as the Messiah, instinctively understood that conflict would surely follow. "This child is destined to cause the falling and rising of many in Israel, and to be a sign that will be spoken against . . ." he said, and then made the prediction that a sword would pierce Mary's own soul. Somehow Simeon sensed that though on the surface little had changed—the autocrat Herod still ruled, Roman troops were still stringing up patriots, Jerusalem still overflowed with beggars—underneath, everything had changed. A new force had arrived to undermine the world's powers.

At first, Jesus hardly seemed a threat to those powers. He was born under Caesar Augustus, at a time when hope wafted through the Roman Empire. More than any other ruler, Augustus raised the expectations of what a leader could accomplish and what a society could achieve. It was Augustus, in fact, who first borrowed the Greek word for "Gospel" or "Good News" and applied it as a label for the new world order represented by his reign. The empire declared him a god and established rites of worship. His enlightened and stable regime, many believed, would last forever, a final solution to the problem of government.

Meanwhile, in an obscure corner of Augustus's empire the birth of a baby named Jesus was overlooked by the chroniclers of the day. We know about him mainly through four books written years after his death, at a time when less than one-half of one percent of the Roman world had ever heard of him. Jesus' biographers would also borrow the word *gospel*, proclaiming a different kind of new world order altogether. They would mention Augustus only once, a passing reference to set the date of a census that ensured Jesus would be born in Bethlehem.

The earliest events in Jesus' life, though, give a menacing preview of the unlikely struggle now under way. Herod the Great, King of the Jews, enforced Roman rule at the local level, and in an irony of history we know Herod's name mainly because of the massacre of the innocents. I have never seen a Christmas card depicting that state-sponsored act of terror, but it too was a part of Christ's coming. Although secular history does not refer to the atrocity, no one acquainted with the life of Herod doubts him capable. He killed two brothers-in-law, his own wife Mariamne, and two of his own sons. Five days before his death he ordered the arrest of many citizens and decreed that they be executed on the day of his death, in order to guarantee a proper atmosphere of mourning in the country. For such a despot, a minor extermination procedure in Bethlehem posed no problem.

Scarcely a day passed, in fact, without an execution under Herod's regime. The political climate at the time of Jesus' birth resembled that of Russia in the 1930s under Stalin. Citizens could not gather in public meetings. Spies were everywhere. In Herod's mind, the command to slaughter Bethlehem's infants was probably an act of utmost rationality, a rearguard action to preserve the stability of his kingdom against a rumored invasion from another.

In *For the Time Being*, W. H. Auden projects what might have been going on inside Herod's mind as he mused about ordering the massacre:

> Today has been one of those perfect winter days, cold, brilliant, and utterly still, when the bark of a shepherd's dog carries for miles, and the great wild mountains come up quite close to the city walls, and the mind feels intensely awake, and this evening as I stand at this window high up in the citadel there is

nothing in the whole magnificent panorama of plain and mountains to indicate that the Empire is threatened by a danger more dreadful than any invasion of Tartar on racing camels or conspiracy of the Praetorian Guard. . . .

O dear, Why couldn't this wretched infant be born somewhere else?

And so Jesus the Christ entered the world amid strife and terror, and spent his infancy hidden in Egypt as a refugee. Matthew notes that local politics even determined where Jesus would grow up. When Herod the Great died, an angel reported to Joseph it was safe for him to return to Israel, but not to the region where Herod's son Archelaus had taken command. Joseph moved his family instead to Nazareth in the north, where they lived under the domain of another of Herod's sons, Antipas, the one Jesus would call "that fox," and also the one who would have John the Baptist beheaded.

A few years later the Romans took over direct command of the southern province that encompassed Jerusalem, and the cruelest and most notorious of these governors was a man named Pontius Pilate. Well-connected, Pilate had married the granddaughter of Augustus Caesar. According to Luke, Herod Antipas and the Roman governor Pilate regarded each other as enemies until the day fate brought them together to determine the destiny of Jesus. On that day they collaborated, hoping to succeed where Herod the Great had failed: by disposing of the strange pretender and thus preserving the kingdom.

From beginning to end, the conflict between Rome and Jesus appeared to be entirely one-sided. The execution of Jesus would put an apparent end to any threat, or so it was assumed at the time. Tyranny would win again. It occurred to no one that his stubborn followers just might outlast the Roman empire.

※

The facts of Christmas, rhymed in carols, recited by children in church plays, illustrated on cards, have become so familiar that it is easy to miss the message behind the facts. After reading the birth

stories once more, I ask myself, *If Jesus came to reveal God to us, then what do I learn about God from that first Christmas?*
The word associations that come to mind as I ponder that question take me by surprise. Humble, approachable, underdog, courageous—these hardly seem appropriate words to apply to deity.

Humble. Before Jesus, almost no pagan author had used "humble" as a compliment. Yet the events of Christmas point inescapably to what seems like an oxymoron: a humble God. The God who came to earth came not in a raging whirlwind nor in a devouring fire. Unimaginably, the Maker of all things shrank down, down, down, so small as to become an ovum, a single fertilized egg barely visible to the naked eye, an egg that would divide and redivide until a fetus took shape, enlarging cell by cell inside a nervous teenager. "Immensity cloistered in thy dear womb," marveled the poet John Donne. He "made himself nothing . . . he humbled himself," said the apostle Paul more prosaically.

I remember sitting one Christmas season in a beautiful auditorium in London listening to Handel's *Messiah,* with a full chorus singing about the day when "the glory of the Lord shall be revealed." I had spent the morning in museums viewing remnants of England's glory—the crown jewels, a solid gold ruler's mace, the Lord Mayor's gilded carriage—and it occurred to me that just such images of wealth and power must have filled the minds of Isaiah's contemporaries who first heard that promise. When the Jews read Isaiah's words, no doubt they thought back with sharp nostalgia to the glory days of Solomon, when "the king made silver as common in Jerusalem as stones."

The Messiah who showed up, however, wore a different kind of glory, the glory of humility. "'God is great,' the cry of the Moslems, is a truth which needed no supernatural being to teach men," writes Father Neville Figgis. "That *God is little,* that is the truth which Jesus taught man." The God who roared, who could order armies and empires about like pawns on a chessboard, this God emerged in Palestine as a baby who could not speak or eat solid food or control his bladder, who depended on a teenager for shelter, food, and love.

In London, looking toward the auditorium's royal box where the queen and her family sat, I caught glimpses of the more typical way rulers stride through the world: with bodyguards, and a trumpet fanfare, and a flourish of bright clothes and flashing jewelry. Queen Elizabeth II had recently visited the United States, and reporters delighted in spelling out the logistics involved: her four thousand pounds of luggage included two outfits for every occasion, a mourning outfit in case someone died, forty pints of plasma, and white kid leather toilet seat covers. She brought along her own hairdresser, two valets, and a host of other attendants. A brief visit of royalty to a foreign country can easily cost twenty million dollars.

In meek contrast, God's visit to earth took place in an animal shelter with no attendants present and nowhere to lay the newborn king but a feed trough. Indeed, the event that divided history, and even our calendars, into two parts may have had more animal than human witnesses. A mule could have stepped on him. "How silently, how silently, the wondrous gift is given."

For just an instant the sky grew luminous with angels, yet who saw that spectacle? Illiterate hirelings who watched the flocks of others, "nobodies" who failed to leave their names. Shepherds had such a randy reputation that proper Jews lumped them together with the "godless," restricting them to the outer courtyards of the temple. Fittingly, it was they whom God selected to help celebrate the birth of one who would be known as the friend of sinners.

In Auden's poem the wise men proclaim, "O here and now our endless journey stops." The shepherds say, "O here and now our endless journey starts." The search for worldly wisdom has ended; true life has just begun.

Approachable. Those of us raised in a tradition of informal or private prayer may not appreciate the change Jesus wrought in how human beings approach deity. Hindus offer sacrifices at the temple. Kneeling Muslims bow down so low that their foreheads touch the ground. In most religious traditions, in fact, *fear* is the primary emotion when one approaches God.

Certainly the Jews associated fear with worship. The burning bush of Moses, the hot coals of Isaiah, the extraterrestrial visions of Ezekiel—a person "blessed" with a direct encounter with God expected to come away scorched or glowing or maybe half-crippled like Jacob. These were the fortunate ones: Jewish children also learned

39

stories of the sacred mountain in the desert that proved fatal to everyone who touched it. Mishandle the ark of the covenant, and you died. Enter the Most Holy Place, and you'd never come out alive.

Among people who walled off a separate sanctum for God in the temple and shrank from pronouncing or spelling out the name, God made a surprise appearance as a baby in a manger. What can be less scary than a newborn with his limbs wrapped tight against his body? In Jesus, God found a way of relating to human beings that did not involve fear.

In truth, fear had never worked very well. The Old Testament includes far more low points than high ones. A new approach was needed, a New Covenant, to use the words of the Bible, one that would not emphasize the vast gulf between God and humanity but instead would span it.

A friend of mine named Kathy was using a "Can you guess?" game to help her six-year-old learn the different animals. His turn: "I'm thinking of a mammal. He's big and he does magic." Kathy thought for a while and then gave up. "I don't know." "It's Jesus!" said her son in triumph. The answer seemed irreverent at the time, Kathy told me, but later as she thought about it she realized her son had hit upon an unsettling insight into the depths of incarnation: Jesus as a mammal!

I learned about incarnation when I kept a salt-water aquarium. Management of a marine aquarium, I discovered, is no easy task. I had to run a portable chemical laboratory to monitor the nitrate levels and the ammonia content. I pumped in vitamins and antibiotics and sulfa drugs and enough enzymes to make a rock grow. I filtered the water through glass fibers and charcoal, and exposed it to ultraviolet light. You would think, in view of all the energy expended on their behalf, that my fish would at least be grateful. Not so. Every time my shadow loomed above the tank they dove for cover into the nearest shell. They showed me one "emotion" only: fear. Although I opened the lid and dropped in food on a regular schedule, three times a day, they responded to each visit as a sure sign of my designs to torture them. I could not convince them of my true concern.

To my fish I was deity. I was too large for them, my actions too incomprehensible. My acts of mercy they saw as cruelty; my attempts at healing they viewed as destruction. To change their perceptions, I began to see, would require a form of incarnation. I would have to become a fish and "speak" to them in a language they could understand.

A human being becoming a fish is nothing compared to God becoming a baby. And yet according to the Gospels that is what happened at Bethlehem. The God who created matter took shape within it, as an artist might become a spot on a painting or a playwright a character within his own play. God wrote a story, only using real characters, on the pages of real history. The Word became flesh.

Underdog. I wince even as I write the word, especially in connection with Jesus. It's a crude word, probably derived from dogfighting and applied over time to predictable losers and victims of injustice. Yet as I read the birth stories about Jesus I cannot help but conclude that though the world may be tilted toward the rich and powerful, God is tilted toward the underdog. "He has brought down rulers from their thrones but has lifted up the humble. He has filled the hungry with good things but has sent the rich away empty," said Mary in her Magnificat hymn.

Laszlo Tokes, the Romanian pastor whose mistreatment outraged the country and prompted rebellion against the Communist ruler Ceausescu, tells of trying to prepare a Christmas sermon for the tiny mountain church to which he had been exiled. The state police were rounding up dissidents, and violence was breaking out across the country. Afraid for his life, Tokes bolted his doors, sat down, and read again the stories in Luke and Matthew. Unlike most pastors who would preach that Christmas, he chose as his text the verses describing Herod's massacre of the innocents. It was the single passage that spoke most directly to his parishioners. Oppression, fear, and violence, the daily plight of the underdog, they well understood.

The next day, Christmas, news broke that Ceausescu had been arrested. Church bells rang, and joy broke out all over Romania. Another King Herod had fallen. Tokes recalls, "All the events of the Christmas story now had a new, brilliant dimension for us, a dimension of history rooted in the reality of our lives.... For those of us who

41

lived through them, the days of Christmas 1989 represented a rich, resonant embroidery of the Christmas story, a time when the providence of God and the foolishness of human wickedness seemed as easy to comprehend as the sun and the moon over the timeless Transylvanian hills." For the first time in four decades, Romania celebrated Christmas as a public holiday.

Perhaps the best way to perceive the "underdog" nature of the incarnation is to transpose it into terms we can relate to today. An unwed mother, homeless, was forced to look for shelter while traveling to meet the heavy taxation demands of a colonial government. She lived in a land recovering from violent civil wars and still in turmoil— a situation much like that in modern Bosnia, Rwanda, or Somalia. Like half of all mothers who deliver today, she gave birth in Asia, in its far western corner, the part of the world that would prove least receptive to the son she bore. That son became a refugee in Africa, the continent where most refugees can still be found.

I wonder what Mary thought about her militant Magnificat hymn during her harrowing years in Egypt. For a Jew, Egypt evoked bright memories of a powerful God who had flattened a pharaoh's army and brought liberation; now Mary fled there, desperate, a stranger in a strange land hiding from her own government. Could her baby, hunted, helpless, on the run, possibly fulfill the lavish hopes of his people?

Even the family's mother-tongue summoned up memories of their underdog status: Jesus spoke Aramaic, a trade language closely related to Arabic, a stinging reminder of the Jews' subjection to foreign empires.

Some foreign astrologers (probably from the region that is now Iraq) had dropped by to visit Jesus, but these men were considered "unclean" by Jews of the day. Naturally, like all dignitaries they had checked first with the ruling king in Jerusalem, who knew nothing about a baby in Bethlehem. After they saw the child and realized who he was, these visitors engaged in an act of civil disobedience: they deceived Herod and went home another way, to protect the child. They had chosen Jesus' side, against the powerful.

Growing up, Jesus' sensibilities were affected most deeply by the poor, the powerless, the oppressed—in short, the underdogs. Today theologians debate the aptness of the phrase "God's preferential option for the poor" as a way of describing God's concern for the underdog. Since God arranged the circumstances in which to be born on planet earth—without power or wealth, without rights, without justice—his preferential options speak for themselves.

Courageous. In 1993 I read a news report about a "Messiah sighting" in the Crown Heights section of Brooklyn, New York. Twenty thousand Lubavitcher Hasidic Jews live in Crown Heights, and in 1993 many of them believed the Messiah was dwelling among them in the person of Rabbi Menachem Mendel Schneerson.

Word of the Rabbi's public appearance spread like a flash fire through the streets of Crown Heights, and Lubavitchers in their black coats and curly sideburns were soon dashing down the sidewalks toward the synagogue where the Rabbi customarily prayed. Those lucky enough to be connected to a network of beepers got a head start, sprinting toward the synagogue the instant they felt a slight vibration. They jammed by the hundreds into a main hall, elbowing each other and even climbing the pillars to create more room. The hall filled with an air of anticipation and frenzy normally found at a championship sporting event, not a religious service.

The Rabbi was ninety-one years old. He had suffered a stroke the year before and had not been able to speak since. When the curtain finally pulled back, those who had crowded into the synagogue saw a frail old man in a long beard who could do little but wave, tilt his head, and move his eyebrows. No one in the audience seemed to mind, though. "Long live our master, our teacher, and our rabbi, King, Messiah, forever and ever!" they sang in unison, over and over, building in volume until the Rabbi made a small, delphic gesture with his hand, and the curtain closed. They departed slowly, savoring the moment, in a state of ecstasy.*

When I first read the news account I nearly laughed out loud. Who are these people trying to kid—a nonagenarian mute Messiah in Brooklyn? And then it struck me: I was reacting to Rabbi Schneer-

---

*Rabbi Schneerson died in June 1994. Now many Lubavitchers are anticipating his bodily resurrection.

son exactly as people in the first century had reacted to Jesus. A Messiah from Galilee? A carpenter's kid, no less?

The scorn I felt as I read about the Rabbi and his fanatical followers gave me a clue to the responses Jesus faced throughout his life. His neighbors asked, "Isn't his mother's name Mary, and aren't his brothers James, Joseph, Simon, and Judas? Where did this man get this wisdom and these miraculous powers?" Other countrymen scoffed, "Nazareth! Can anything good come from there?" His own family tried to put him away, believing he was out of his mind. The religious experts sought to kill him. As for the whipsaw commoners, one moment they judged him "demon-possessed and raving mad," the next they forcibly tried to crown him king.

It took courage, I believe, for God to lay aside power and glory and to take a place among human beings who would greet him with the same mixture of haughtiness and skepticism that I felt when I first heard about Rabbi Schneerson of Brooklyn. It took courage to risk descent to a planet known for its clumsy violence, among a race known for rejecting its prophets. What more foolhardy thing could God have done?

The first night in Bethlehem required courage as well. How did God the Father feel that night, helpless as any human father, watching his Son emerge smeared with blood to face a harsh, cold world? Lines from two different Christmas carols play in my mind. One, "The little Lord Jesus, no crying he makes," seems to me a sanitized version of what took place in Bethlehem. I imagine Jesus cried like any other baby the night he entered the world, a world that would give him much reason to cry as an adult. The second, a line from "O Little Town of Bethlehem," seems as profoundly true today as it did two thousand years ago: "The hopes and fears of all the world do rest on thee tonight."

"Alone of all creeds, Christianity has added courage to the virtues of the Creator," said G. K. Chesterton. The need for such courage began with Jesus' first night on earth and did not end until his last.

<hr />

There is one more view of Christmas I have never seen on a Christmas card, probably because no artist, not even William Blake, could do it justice. Revelation 12 pulls back the curtain to give us a glimpse of Christmas as it must have looked from somewhere far beyond Andromeda: Christmas from the angels' viewpoint.

The account differs radically from the birth stories in the Gospels. Revelation does not mention shepherds and an infanticidal king; rather, it pictures a dragon leading a ferocious struggle in heaven. A woman clothed with the sun and wearing a crown of twelve stars cries out in pain as she is about to give birth. Suddenly the enormous red dragon enters the picture, his tail sweeping a third of the stars out of the sky and flinging them to the earth. He crouches hungrily before the woman, anxious to devour her child the moment it is born. At the last second the infant is snatched away to safety, the woman flees into the desert, and all-out cosmic war begins.

Revelation is a strange book by any measure, and readers must understand its style to make sense of this extraordinary spectacle. In daily life two parallel histories occur simultaneously, one on earth and one in heaven. Revelation, however, views them together, allowing a quick look behind the scenes. On earth a baby was born, a king got wind of it, a chase ensued. In heaven the Great Invasion had begun, a daring raid by the ruler of the forces of good into the universe's seat of evil.

John Milton expressed this point of view majestically in *Paradise Lost* and *Paradise Regained*, poems which make heaven and hell the central focus and earth a mere battleground for their clashes. The modern author J. B. Phillips also attempted such a point of view, on a much less epic scale, and last Christmas I turned to Phillips's fantasy to try to escape my earthbound viewpoint.

In Phillips's version, a senior angel is showing a very young angel around the splendors of the universe. They view whirling galaxies and blazing suns, and then flit across the infinite distances of space until at last they enter one particular galaxy of 500 billion stars.

> As the two of them drew near to the star which we call our sun and to its circling planets, the senior angel pointed to a small and rather insignificant sphere turning very slowly on its axis. It looked as dull as a dirty tennis-ball to the little angel, whose mind was filled with the size and glory of what he had seen.

45

"I want you to watch that one particularly," said the senior angel, pointing with his finger.

"Well, it looks very small and rather dirty to me," said the little angel. "What's special about that one?"

When I read Phillips's fantasy, I thought of the pictures beamed back to earth from the Apollo astronauts, who described our planet as "whole and round and beautiful and small," a blue-green-and-tan globe suspended in space. Jim Lovell, reflecting on the scene later, said, "It was just another body, really, about four times bigger than the moon. But it held all the hope and all the life and all the things that the crew of Apollo 8 knew and loved. It was the most beautiful thing there was to see in all the heavens." That was the viewpoint of a human being.

To the little angel, though, earth did not seem so impressive. He listened in stunned disbelief as the senior angel told him that this planet, small and insignificant and not overly clean, was the renowned Visited Planet.

"Do you mean that our great and glorious Prince ... went down in Person to this fifth-rate little ball? Why should He do a thing like that?" ...

The little angel's face wrinkled in disgust. "Do you mean to tell me," he said, "that He stooped so low as to become one of those creeping, crawling creatures of that floating ball?"

"I do, and I don't think He would like you to call them 'creeping, crawling creatures' in that tone of voice. For, strange as it may seem to us, He loves them. He went down to visit them to lift them up to become like Him."

The little angel looked blank. Such a thought was almost beyond his comprehension.

It is almost beyond my comprehension too, and yet I accept that this notion is the key to understanding Christmas and is, in fact, the touchstone of my faith. As a Christian I believe that we live in parallel worlds. One world consists of hills and lakes and barns and politicians and shepherds watching their flocks by night. The other consists of angels and sinister forces and somewhere out there places called heaven and hell. One night in the cold, in the dark, among the wrinkled hills of Bethlehem, those two worlds came together at a dramatic point of intersection. God, who knows no before or after, entered time and space. God, who knows no boundaries took on the shocking confines of a baby's skin, the ominous restraints of mortality.

"He is the image of the invisible God, the firstborn over all creation," an apostle would later write; "He is before all things, and in him all things hold together." But the few eyewitnesses on Christmas night saw none of that. They saw an infant struggling to work never-before-used lungs.

Could it be true, this Bethlehem story of a Creator descending to be born on one small planet? If so, it is a story like no other. Never again need we wonder whether what happens on this dirty little tennis ball of a planet matters to the rest of the universe. Little wonder a choir of angels broke out in spontaneous song, disturbing not only a few shepherds but the entire universe.

BACKGROUND:
JEWISH ROOTS AND SOIL

This again is a great contradiction: though he was a Jew, his followers were not Jews.

VOLTAIRE

BACKGROUND: JEWISH ROOTS AND SOIL

———∞∞∞———

As a boy growing up in a WASP community in Atlanta, Georgia, I did not know a single Jew. I pictured Jews as foreigners with thick accents and strange hats who lived in Brooklyn or some such faraway place where they all studied to become psychiatrists and musicians. I knew the Jews had something to do with World War II, but I had heard little about the Holocaust. Certainly these people had no relation to my Jesus.

Not until my early twenties did I befriend a Jewish photographer who disabused me of many notions about his race. One night when we stayed up late talking, he described what it was like to lose twenty-seven members of his family to the Holocaust. Later, he acquainted me with Elie Wiesel, Chaim Potok, Martin Buber, and other Jewish writers, and after these encounters I began reading the New Testament through new eyes. How could I have missed it! Jesus' true-blue Jewishness leaps out from Matthew's very first sentence, which introduces him as "the son of David, son of Abraham."

In church we affirmed Jesus as "the only-begotten Son of God, begotten of his Father before all worlds . . . Very God of Very God." Those creedal statements, though, are light-years removed from the Gospels' account of Jesus growing up in a Jewish family in the agricultural town of Nazareth. I later learned that not even converted

Jews—who might have rooted Jesus more solidly in Jewish soil—were invited to the Council of Chalcedon that composed the creed. We Gentiles face the constant danger of letting Jesus' Jewishness, and even his humanity, slip away.

In historical fact, we are the ones who have co-opted *their* Jesus. As I got to know Jesus, the realization sank in that he probably did not spend his life among Jews in the first century merely to save Americans in the twentieth. Alone of all people in history, he had the privilege of choosing where and when to be born, and he chose a pious Jewish family living in a backwater protectorate of a pagan empire. I can no more understand Jesus apart from his Jewishness than I can understand Gandhi apart from his Indianness. I need to go back, way back, and picture Jesus as a first-century Jew with a phylactery on his wrist and Palestinian dust on his sandals.

Martin Buber said, "We Jews know [Jesus] in a way—in the impulses and emotions of his essential Jewishness—that remains inaccessible to the Gentiles subject to him." He is right, of course. To know Jesus' story I must, in the same way I get to know anyone else's story, learn something of his culture, family, and background.

Following this principle, Matthew opens his gospel not as I might be tempted to begin, with a teaser on "How this book will change your life," but rather with a dry list of names, the genealogy of Jesus. Matthew chose a representative sampling from forty-two generations of Jews in order to establish Jesus' royal bloodline. Much like the shabby descendants of deposed European royalty, the peasant family of Joseph and Mary could trace their lineage back to some impressive ancestors, including Israel's greatest king, David, and its original founder, Abraham.*

---

*Matthew's list of names also lets some skeletons out of the closet. Consider the women mentioned (a rarity in Jewish genealogies). At least three of the four were foreigners, which may have been Matthew's way of hinting that Jesus held out universal promise. The Jewish Messiah had gentile blood!

Tamar, a childless widow, had to dress like a prostitute and seduce her father-in-law in order to produce her contribution to Jesus' line. Rahab did not merely pre-

Jesus grew up during a time of resurgent "Jewish pride." In a backlash against the pressure to embrace Greek culture, families had recently begun adopting names that harked back to the times of the patriarchs and the Exodus from Egypt (not unlike ethnic Americans who choose African or Hispanic names for their children). Thus Mary was named for Miriam, the sister of Moses, and Joseph was named after one of the twelve sons of Jacob, as were Jesus' four brothers.

Jesus' own name comes from the word *Joshua*—"he shall save"—a common name in those days. (As major-league baseball rosters reveal, the name Jesus remains popular among Latin Americans.) Its very ordinariness, not unlike "Bob" or "Joe" today, must have grated on Jewish ears in the first century as they listened to Jesus' words. Jews did not pronounce the Honorable Name of GOD, save for the high priest one day a year, and even today Orthodox Jews carefully spell out G_D. For people raised in such a tradition, the idea that an ordinary person with a name like Jesus could be the Son of God and Savior of the world seemed utterly scandalous. Jesus was a man, for goodness' sake, Mary's boy.

Signs of Jesus' Jewishness surface throughout the Gospels. He was circumcised as a baby. Significantly, the one scene included from Jesus' childhood shows his family attending an obligatory festival in Jerusalem, several days' journey from their home. As an adult Jesus worshiped in the synagogue and temple, followed Jewish customs, and spoke in terms his fellow Jews would understand. Even his controversies with other Jews, such as the Pharisees, underscored the fact that they expected him to share their values and act more like them.

As the German theologian Jürgen Moltmann has pointed out, if Jesus had lived during the Third Reich, very likely he would have been branded like other Jews and shipped to the gas chambers. A pogrom of his own time, Herod's massacre of infants, was specifically targeted against Jesus.

---

tend, but actually made her living as a prostitute. And "Uriah's wife," or Bathsheba, was the object of David's lust, which led to the most famous royal scandal of the Old Testament. These shady ancestors show that Jesus entered human history in the raw, a willing descendant of its shame. In contrast, Herod the Great, reigning king at Jesus' birth, had his genealogical records destroyed out of vanity because he wanted no one to compare his background with others'.

A rabbi friend mentioned to me that Christians perceive Jesus' cry from the cross, "My God, my God why have you forsaken me?" as a profound moment of struggle between Father and Son; Jews, however, hear those words as the death cry of yet another Jewish victim. Jesus was not the first and certainly not the last Jew to cry out words from the Psalms at a time of torture.

Yet a strange reversal occurred within a few generations of Jesus' life. With rare exceptions, Jews stopped following him and the church became thoroughly Gentile. What happened? It seems clear to me that Jesus failed to meet the expectations of Messiah the Jews were awaiting.

It would be impossible to exaggerate the import of the word *Messiah* among faithful Jews. The Dead Sea Scrolls discovered in 1947 confirm that the Qumram community imminently expected a Messiah-like figure, setting aside an empty seat for him each day at the sacred meal. Audacious as it may be to dream that a tiny province wedged in among great powers would produce a worldwide ruler, nonetheless Jews believed just that. They staked their future on a king who would lead their nation back to glory.

During Jesus' lifetime, revolt was in the air. Pseudo-messiahs periodically emerged to lead rebellions, only to be crushed in ruthless crackdowns. To take just one example, a prophet known as "the Egyptian" attracted multitudes into the wilderness where he proclaimed that at his command the walls of Jerusalem would fall; the Roman governor sent a detachment of soldiers after them and killed four thousand of the rebels.

When another report spread that the long-awaited prophet had turned up in the desert, crowds flocked to see the wild man dressed in camel skin. "I am not the Christ [Messiah]," insisted John the Baptist, who then proceeded to raise hopes even higher by speaking in exalted terms of one who would soon appear. John's question of Jesus, "Are you the one who was to come, or shall we expect someone else?" was in a real sense the question of the age, whispered everywhere.

Every Hebrew prophet had taught that someday God would install his kingdom on earth, and that is why rumors about the "Son of David" so inflamed Jewish hopes. God would prove in person that he had not forsaken them. He would, as Isaiah had cried, "rend the heavens and come down, that the mountains would tremble before you! . . . come down to cause the nations to quake before you."

But let us be honest. When the one John pointed to arrived on the scene, neither the mountains trembled nor the nations quaked. Jesus did not come close to satisfying the lavish hopes of the Jews. The opposite happened: within a generation Roman soldiers razed Jerusalem to the ground. The young Christian church accepted the destruction of the temple as a sign of the end of the covenant between God and Israel, and after the first century very few Jews converted to Christianity. Christians appropriated Jewish Scriptures, renaming them "Old Testament," and put an end to most Jewish customs.

Rejected by the church, blamed for Jesus' death, some Jews began a counter-campaign against the Christians. They spread a rumor that Jesus was the illegitimate offspring of Mary's liaison with a Roman soldier, and wrote a cruel parody of the Gospels. Jesus was hanged on the eve of Passover, said one report, because "he hath practiced sorcery and beguiled and led astray Israel." The man whose birth angels celebrated with a proclamation of peace on earth became the great divide of human history.

⁂

A few years ago I met with ten Christians, ten Jews, and ten Muslims in New Orleans. The psychiatrist and author M. Scott Peck had invited us there to see if we could overcome our differences enough to produce some sort of community. Each faith held a worship service—Muslims on Friday, Jews on Saturday, Christians on Sunday—which the others were invited to observe. The services had striking similarities and reminded us how much the three faiths have in common. Perhaps the intensity of feeling among the three traditions stems from a common heritage: family disputes are always the stubbornest, and civil wars the bloodiest.

I learned a new word in New Orleans: *supersessionism*. The Jews resented the notion that Christian faith had superseded Judaism. "I feel like a curiosity of history, as if my religion should be put in a nursing home," said one. "It grates on me to hear the term 'Old Testament God' or even 'Old' Testament, for that matter." Christians had also taken over the word Messiah, or at least its Greek equivalent, "Christ." One rabbi told of growing up in the only Jewish household in a small Virginia town. Each year the Christians asked his father, a respected member of the community (and, as a Jew, impartial in judgment), to rank the displays of Christmas lights and decide which houses deserved prizes. As a young boy, this rabbi drove with his father past every house in town, staring with longing and incomprehension at the bright displays of *Christ*-mas lights: literally, "Messiah lights."

I had not realized that Muslims look on both faiths with a supersessionist attitude. As they see it, just as Christianity grew out of and incorporated parts of Judaism, Islam grew out of and incorporated parts of both religions. Abraham was a prophet, Jesus was a prophet, but Muhammad was The Prophet. The Old Testament has a place, as does the New Testament, but the Qur'an is "the final revelation." Hearing my own faith talked about in such paternalistic terms gave me insight into how Jews have felt for two millennia.

I also realized, after listening to three faiths articulate their differences, how deep is the divide that Jesus introduced. The Muslim worship service consisted mostly of reverential prayers to the Almighty. The Jewish service incorporated readings from Psalms and the Torah and some warmhearted singing. Any of those elements can be found in a Christian service. What divided us from the others was the celebration of the Lord's Supper. "This is my body, broken for you," our leader read, before distributing the bread—Christ's body, the divergence point.

When Muslims conquered Asia Minor they converted many Christian churches into mosques, carving this stern inscription for the admonition of any remaining Christians: "God did not beget and is not begotten." The same phrase could be painted on synagogue walls. The great divide of history traces back to Bethlehem and Jerusalem. Was Jesus really Messiah, the Son of God? As the Jews in New

Orleans explained, a Messiah who dies at the age of thirty-three, a nation that goes downhill after its Savior's death, a world that grows more fractured, not less—these facts do not seem to add up for the members of Jesus' own race.

Nevertheless, despite two thousand years of the great divide, despite all that has taken place in this century of violent anti-Semitism, interest in Jesus is resurging among the Jews. In 1925, when the Hebrew scholar Joseph Klausner decided to write a book about Jesus, he could find only three full-length treatments of Jesus' life by contemporary Jewish scholars. Now there are hundreds, including some of the most illuminating studies available. Modern Israeli schoolchildren learn that Jesus was a great teacher, perhaps the greatest Jewish teacher, who was subsequently "co-opted" by the Gentiles.

Is it possible to read the Gospels without blinders on? Jews read with suspicion, preparing to be scandalized. Christians read through the refracted lenses of church history. Both groups, I believe, would do well to pause and reflect on Matthew's first words, "A record of the genealogy of Jesus Christ, son of David, son of Abraham." The son of David speaks of Jesus' messianic line, which Jews should not ignore; "a title which he would not deny to save his life cannot have been without significance for him," notes C. H. Dodd. The son of Abraham speaks of Jesus' Jewish line, which we Christians dare not ignore either. Jaroslav Pelikan writes,

> Would there have been such anti-Semitism, would there have been so many pogroms, would there have been an Auschwitz, if every Christian church and every Christian home had focused its devotion and icons of Mary not only as Mother of God and Queen of Heaven but as the Jewish maiden and the new Miriam, and on icons of Christ not only as a Pantocrator but as *Rabbi Jeshua bar-Joseph*, Rabbi Jesus of Nazareth?

Growing up, I did not know a single Jew. I do now. I know something of their culture. The close ties that keep sacred holidays alive even for families who no longer believe in their meaning. The passionate arguments that at first intimidated me but soon attracted me as a style of personal engagement. The respect, even reverence, for legalism amid a society that mainly values autonomy. The tradition of scholarship that has helped sustain a culture despite others' relentless attempts to obliterate it. The ability to link arms and dance and sing and laugh even when the world offers scant reason for celebration. This was the culture Jesus grew up in, a Jewish culture. Yes, he changed it, but always from his starting point as a Jew. Now when I find myself wondering what Jesus was like as a teenager, I think of Jewish boys I know in Chicago. And when the thought jars me, I remember that in his own day Jesus got the opposite reaction. A Jewish teenager, surely—but the Son of God?

Not only did Jesus choose a race, he also chose a time and place in which to be born. History became, in Bonhoeffer's phrase, "the womb of the birth of God." Why that particular history? I sometimes wonder why Jesus did not come in modern times, when he could have taken advantage of mass communications. Or back in Isaiah's day, when expectations for the Messiah also ran high and Israel was still an independent nation. What about the first century made it the right time to ease God into the world?

Every age has its prevailing mood: the sunny confidence of the nineteenth century, the violent chaos of the twentieth. In the era of Jesus' birth, at the height of the Roman Empire, hope and optimism held sway. As in the Soviet Union before its breakup or the British Empire in Queen Victoria's day, Rome kept peace at the point of a sword, but by and large even the conquered peoples cooperated. Except in Palestine, that is.

Anticipation soared for "a new order of the ages" at the time of Jesus' birth. The Roman poet Virgil coined that phrase, sounding like an Old Testament prophet as he declared that "a new human race is descending from the heights of heaven," a change that would come about due to "the birth of a child, with whom the iron age of humanity will end and the golden age begin." Virgil wrote these messianic words not about Jesus, however, but about Caesar Augustus, the "present deity," the "restorer of the world," who had managed to reunite the empire after the civil war sparked by Julius Caesar's assassination.

To loyal Roman subjects Augustus offered peace, security, and entertainment: in two words, bread and circuses. The Pax Romana assured that citizens had protection from outside enemies and enjoyed the benefits of Roman justice and civil government. Meanwhile, a Greek soul filled the Roman body politic. People throughout the empire dressed like the Greeks, built their buildings in the Greek style, played Greek sports, and spoke the Greek language. Except in Palestine.

Palestine, the one lump the anaconda could not digest, exasperated Rome to no end. Contrary to Roman tolerance for many gods, the Jews held tenaciously to the notion of one God, their God, who had revealed to them a distinct culture as the Chosen People. William Barclay describes what happened when these two societies collided. "It is the simple historical fact that in the thirty years from 67 to 37 B.C. before the emergence of Herod the Great, no fewer than one hundred and fifty thousand men perished in Palestine in revolutionary uprisings. There was no more explosive and inflammable country in the world than Palestine."

Jews resisted Hellenization (imposed Greek culture) as fiercely as they fought the Roman legions. Rabbis kept this aversion alive by reminding Jews of the attempts by a Seleucid madman named Antiochus to Hellenize the Jews more than a century before. Antiochus had compelled young boys to undergo reverse circumcision operations so they could appear nude in Greek athletic contests. He flogged an aged priest to death for refusing to eat pig's flesh, and butchered a mother and her seven children for not bowing down to an image. In a heinous act that became known as the "abomination of desolation," he invaded the Most Holy Place of the temple, sacrificed an unclean pig on the altar in honor of the Greek god Zeus, and smeared the sanctuary with its blood.

Antiochus's campaign failed miserably, driving Jews to an open revolt led by the Maccabeans. (Jews still celebrate Hanukkah in memory of this victory.) For nearly a century, in fact, the Maccabeans held off foreign invaders, until the Roman juggernaut rolled into Palestine. It took thirty years for Roman armies to quash all signs of rebellion; then they installed the local strongman Herod as their puppet "King of the Jews." As Herod watched the Romans killing women and children in their houses, markets, and even in the temple, he asked a general, "Would the Romans deprive the city of all its inhabitants and possessions and leave me a king of the wilderness?" Almost. By the time Herod ascended the throne, not only Jerusalem but the entire country lay in ruins. Herod the Great still reigned when Jesus was born. Comparatively, Palestine stayed quiet under his iron thumb, for the long wars had drained both the spirit and resources of the Jews. An earthquake in 31 B.C. killed 30,000 people and much livestock, leading to more destitution. The Jews called such tragedies "pangs of the Messiah" and pled with God for a deliverer.

It is difficult to find a modern parallel, now that the Soviet empire has collapsed, to the brittle situation the Jews faced under Roman rule. Tibet under China perhaps? The blacks in South Africa before they gained freedom from minority rule? The most provocative suggestion comes from visitors to modern Israel, who cannot help noticing the similar plights of Galilean Jews in Jesus' day and Palestinians in modern times. Both served the economic interests of their richer neighbors. Both lived in small hamlets, or refugee camps, in the midst of a more modern and alien culture. Both were subject to curfews, crackdowns, and discrimination.

As Malcolm Muggeridge observed in the 1970s, "The role of the Roman legionnaires had been taken over by the Israeli army. Now it was the Arabs who were in the position of a subject people; entitled, like the Jews in Jesus' lifetime, to attend their mosques and practise their religion, but otherwise treated like second-class citizens."

Both groups, modern Palestinians and Galilean Jews, also share a susceptibility to hotheads who would call them to armed revolt. Think of the modern Middle East with all its violence, intrigues, and squabbling parties. Into such an incendiary environment, Jesus was born.

The journey from Judea to Galilee in springtime is a journey from brown to green, from an arid, rocky terrain to some of the lushest fields in the Mediterranean basin. Fruits and vegetables grow in abundance, fishermen work the Sea of Galilee, and beyond rolling hills to the west lies the shimmering blue of the Mediterranean itself. Jesus' hometown of Nazareth, so obscure that it does not make the list of sixty-three Galilean towns mentioned in the Talmud, sits on a hillside 1,300 feet above sea level. The view from a ridge allows a sweeping panorama all the way from Mt. Carmel by the ocean to the snowy peak of Mt. Hermon to the north.

With fertile land, beautiful vistas, and moderate climate, Galilee had its attractions, and clearly Jesus enjoyed his childhood there. The wildflowers and weeds growing among the crops, the laborious method of separating wheat and chaff, the fig trees and grapevines dotting the hillsides, the fields white unto harvest—all these would show up later in his parables and sayings. Just as telling, some obvious features of Galilee did not show up. A mere three miles north, in easy view of Nazareth, sat the gleaming city of Sepphoris, just then in the process of being rebuilt. Jesus' neighbors—perhaps his own father— were employed in building trades there.

For most of Jesus' life, construction crews worked on this beautiful Greco-Roman metropolis, which featured colonnaded streets, a forum, a palace, a bath and gymnasium, and luxurious villas, all constructed in white limestone and colored marble. In an imposing theater that seated four thousand, Greek actors, or *hypocritēs,* entertained the multinational crowds. (Jesus would later borrow the word to describe one who played a false role in public.) During Jesus' lifetime Sepphoris served as Galilee's capital, second in importance only to Jerusalem in all of Palestine. Not once, however, do the Gospels record that Jesus visited or even mentioned the city. Nor did he visit Tiberias, Herod's winter resort town situated nearby on the shore of Lake Galilee. He gave centers of wealth and political power a wide berth.

Although Herod the Great managed to make Galilee the most prosperous province in Palestine, only a few reaped the benefits. Landless peasants mainly served the interests of wealthy landlords (another fact that would surface in Jesus' parables). An illness or back-to-back seasons of bad weather would bring disaster to most families. We know that Jesus was raised in poverty: his family could not afford a lamb for the sacrifice at the temple and offered instead a pair of doves or two young pigeons.

Galilee had a reputation as a breeding ground for revolutionaries. In 4 B.C., around the time of Jesus' birth, a rebel broke into the arsenal in Sepphoris and looted it to arm his followers. Roman troops recaptured and burned the town—which explains why it had to be rebuilt—crucifying two thousand Jews who had participated in the uprising. Ten years later another rebel, named Judas, incited a revolt, urging his countrymen to pay no taxes to the pagan Roman emperor. He helped found the Zealot party which would harass Rome for the next six decades. Two of Judas's sons would be crucified after Jesus' death, and his last son would ultimately capture the stronghold of Masada from the Romans, vowing to defend it until every last Jew had died. In the end, 960 Jewish men, women, and children took their own lives rather than fall captive to the Romans. Galileans were freedom-lovers to the core.

For all its prosperity and political activism, Galilee got little respect from the rest of the country. It was the farthest province from Jerusalem and the most backward culturally. Rabbinic literature of the time portrays Galileans as bumpkins, fodder for ethnic jokes. Galileans who learned Hebrew pronounced it so crudely that they were not called on to read the Torah in other synagogues. Speaking the common language of Aramaic in a slipshod way was a telltale sign of Galilean roots (as Simon Peter would one day find out, betrayed in a courtyard by his rural accent). The Aramaic words preserved in the Gospels show that Jesus, too, spoke in that northern dialect, no doubt encouraging skepticism about him. "How can the Christ come from Galilee?" "Nazareth! Can anything good come from there?"

Other Jews regarded Galilee as lax about spiritual matters as well. One Pharisee, after eighteen fruitless years there, lamented, "Galilee, Galilee, you hate the Torah!" Nicodemus, who stuck up for Jesus, was silenced by the rebuke, "Are you from Galilee, too? Look into it, and you will find that a prophet does not come out of Galilee." Jesus' own brothers encouraged him, "You ought to leave here and go to Judea." From the perspective of the religious power base in Jerusalem, Galilee seemed a most unlikely place for the Messiah to arise.

As I read the Gospels, I try to project myself back into those times. How would I have responded to oppression? Would I strive to be a model citizen and keep out of trouble, to live and let live? Would I be tempted by fiery insurrectionists like the Zealots? Would I fight back in more devious ways, by avoiding taxes perhaps? Or would I throw my energies into a religious movement and shun political controversies? What kind of Jew would I have made in the first century? Eight million Jews lived in the Roman Empire then, just over a quarter of them in Palestine itself,* and sometimes they stretched Roman forbearance to the breaking point. Romans branded Jews "atheists" for their refusal to honor Greek and Roman gods, and regarded them as social misfits because of their peculiar customs: Jews refused to eat the "unclean" food of their neighbors, eschewed all business on Friday evenings and Saturdays, and disdained civic office. Nevertheless, Rome had granted Judaism legal status.

In many ways the plight of Jewish leaders resembled that of the Russian churches under Stalin. They could cooperate, which meant submitting to government interference, or they could go their own way, which meant harsh persecution. Herod the Great fit the Stalin pattern well, keeping the religious community in a state of suspicion and terror through his network of spies. "His High Priests he changed as he might change his clothes," complained one Jewish writer.

In response, the Jews splintered into parties that followed different paths of collaboration or separatism. These were the parties who would follow Jesus around, listening to him, testing him, taking his measure.

The Essenes were the most separate of all. Pacifistic, they did not actively resist Herod or the Romans, but rather withdrew into monkish communities in the caves of a barren desert. Convinced that the Roman invasion had come as a punishment for their failure to keep the Law, they devoted themselves to purity. The Essenes took ritual baths every day, maintained a strict diet, did not defecate on the Sabbath, wore no jewelry, took no oaths, and held all material goods in common. They hoped their faithfulness would encourage the advent of the Messiah.

---

*Due largely to the Holocaust, the number of Jews is approximately the same nineteen centuries later, and the same proportion lives in Palestine.

Zealots, representing a different strategy of separatism, advocated armed revolt to throw out impure foreigners. One branch of the Zealots specialized in acts of political terrorism against the Romans while another operated as a kind of "morals police" to keep fellow Jews in line. In an early version of ethnic cleansing, the Zealots declared that anyone who married into another race should be lynched. During Jesus' years of ministry, observers surely would have noted that his group of disciples included Simon the Zealot. On the other hand, Jesus' social contacts with Gentiles and foreigners, not to mention parables like the Good Samaritan, would have driven the jingoistic Zealots to fury.

At the other extreme, collaborationists tried to work within the system. The Romans had granted limited authority to a Jewish council called the Sanhedrin, and in return for their privileges the Sanhedrin cooperated with Romans in scouting out any sign of insurrection. It was in their best interests to prevent uprisings and the harsh reprisals they would surely bring.

The Jewish historian Josephus tells of a mentally ill peasant who would cry out "Woe to Jerusalem!" in the midst of popular festivals, agitating the crowds. The Sanhedrin tried punishing him, to no avail, so they turned him over to the Roman governor for a proper flogging. He was flayed to the bone and peace was restored. In the same vein, the Sanhedrin sent representatives to examine John the Baptist and Jesus. Did they represent a true threat to the peace? If so, should they be turned in to the Romans? Caiphas, the high priest, perfectly captured the collaborationist point of view: "It is better for you that one man die for the people than that the whole nation perish."

Sadducees were the most blatant collaborationists. They had first Hellenized under the Greeks, and then cooperated in turn with Maccabeans, Romans, and now Herod. Humanistic in theology, the Sadducees did not believe in an afterlife or divine intervention on this earth. What happens, happens, and since there is no future system of reward and punishment, a person might as well enjoy the limited time on earth. From the palatial homes and silver and gold kitchen utensils that archaeologists have uncovered, it appears that Sadducees enjoyed life very well indeed. Of all parties in Palestine, the mandarin Sadducees had the most to lose from any threat to the status quo.

Pharisees, the popular party of the middle class, often found themselves on the fence, vacillating between separatism and collaboration. They held to high standards of purity, particularly on such matters as Sabbath observance, ritual cleanliness, and the exact time of feast days. They treated nonobservant Jews "as Gentiles," shutting them out of local councils, boycotting their businesses, and ostracizing them from meals and social affairs. Yet the Pharisees had already suffered their share of persecution: in one instance eight hundred Pharisees were crucified on a single day. Although they believed passionately in the Messiah, Pharisees hesitated to follow too quickly after any impostor or miracle worker who might bring disaster on the nation.

The Pharisees picked their battles carefully, putting their lives on the line only when necessary. Once, Pontius Pilate spurned a prior agreement with the Jews that Roman troops would not enter Jerusalem carrying standards that bore an image ("icon") of the emperor. The Pharisees regarded this act as idolatry. In protest a crowd of Jews, mostly Pharisees, stood outside Pilate's palace for five days and nights in a kind of sit-down strike, weeping and begging him to change. Pilate ordered them to the hippodrome, where soldiers lay in ambush, and threatened to put to death any who did not cease their begging. As one, they fell on their faces, bared their necks, and announced they were prepared to die rather than have their laws broken. Pilate backed down.

⁂

As I consider each one of these groups, I conclude that most likely I would have ended up in the party of Pharisees. I would have admired their pragmatic approach to the ruling government, balanced by their willingness to stand up for principle. Orderly people, the Pharisees produced good citizens.* Radicals like the Essenes and

---

*Scholars have debated why the Gospels record so much conflict between Jesus and the Pharisees, when actually he had more in common with them than with the Sadducees, Essenes, or Zealots. One explanation is that the Gospels were written several decades after Jesus' death. By then Jerusalem had been destroyed and the other parties had virtually disappeared. Understandably, the gospel writers focused on the sole surviving threat to Christians, the Pharisees.

Zealots would have made me nervous; the Sadducees I would have scorned as opportunists. Thus as a sympathizer of the Pharisees, I would have stood on the edge of Jesus' audience, watching him deal with the burning issues of the day.

Would Jesus have won me over? Much as I wish, I cannot easily answer that question. At one time or another, Jesus managed to confound and alienate each of the major groups in Palestine. He held out a third way, neither separation nor collaboration, radically changing the emphasis from the kingdom of Herod or Caesar to the kingdom of God.

Looking back now, it may seem difficult to sort out the nuances that divided one party from another, or to understand why controversy flared over minor aspects of Jesus' teaching. For all their differences, though, Essenes, Zealots, Pharisees, and even Sadducees shared one goal: to preserve what was distinctively Jewish, no matter what. To that goal, Jesus represented a threat, and I'm sure I would have perceived that threat.

The Jews were, in effect, erecting a fence around their culture in hopes of saving their tiny nation of high ideals from the pagans around them. Could God liberate them from Rome as he had once liberated them from Egypt? One tradition promised that if all Israel repented for an entire day, or if Israel kept two Sabbaths perfectly, then redemption by the Messiah would soon follow. Something of a spiritual revival was under way, spurred by a splendid new temple. Constructed on a huge platform that dominated the entire city of Jerusalem, the temple had become the focal point of national pride and hope for the future.

It was against this background that I, like other Jews, would have judged Jesus' statements about legalism, about Sabbath-keeping, and about the temple. How could I reconcile my respect for family values with a comment like, "If anyone comes to me and does not hate his father and mother, his wife and children, his brothers and sisters ... he cannot be my disciple"? What could Jesus possibly mean? Similarly, to official Sanhedrin ears, a reported comment like "I am able to destroy the temple of God and rebuild it in three days" was no idle boast but a form of blasphemy and even treason, striking against the very thing that held Jews together. Jesus' offer to forgive a person's sin seemed to them as bizarrely inappropriate as a private individual today offering to issue someone a passport or a building permit. Who did he think he was, preempting the entire temple system?

As it turned out, Jewish fears about cultural suicide proved entirely justified. Not Jesus, but other charismatic figures would lead revolts that finally, in A.D. 70, provoked Rome to destroy the temple and level Jerusalem. The city would later be rebuilt as a Roman colony, with a temple to the god Jupiter occupying the site of the demolished Jewish temple. Jews were forbidden to enter the city on pain of death. Rome set in motion an exile that would not end until our own generation, and it changed the face of Judaism forever.

CHAPTER 4

TEMPTATION: SHOWDOWN IN THE DESERT

———— ◍ ————

Love consents to all and commands only those who consent. Love is abdication. God is abdication.

SIMONE WEIL

TEMPTATION:
SHOWDOWN IN THE DESERT

———∞∞∞———

The Gospels assert that Jesus, the Jew who grew up in rural Galilee, was none other than God's own Son, dispatched from heaven to lead the fight against evil. With that mission in view, certain questions about Jesus' priorities immediately come to mind. At the top of the list, natural disasters: If Jesus had the power to cure illness and raise the dead, why not tackle a few macro-problems like earthquakes and hurricanes, or perhaps the whole sinister swarm of mutating viruses that plague the earth?

Philosophers and theologians blame many of the rest of earth's ills on the consequences of human freedom, which raises a whole new set of questions. Do we in fact enjoy too much freedom? We have the freedom to harm and kill each other, to fight global wars, to despoil our planet. We are even free to defy God, to live without restraints as though the other world did not exist. At the least, Jesus could have devised some irrefutable proof to silence all skeptics, tilting the odds decisively in God's favor. As it is, God seems easy to ignore or deny.

Jesus' first "official" act as an adult, when he went into the wilderness to meet the accuser face-to-face, gave him the occasion to address these problems. Satan himself tempted the Son of God to change the rules and achieve his goals by a dazzling, shortcut method. More than

71

Jesus' character was at stake on the sandy plains of Palestine; human history hung in the balance.

﹉

When John Milton wrote a sequel to his epic *Paradise Lost*, he made the Temptation, not the crucifixion, the hinge event in Jesus' effort to regain the world. In a garden, a man and woman had fallen for Satan's promise of a way to rise above their assigned state. Millennia later, another representative—the Second Adam, in Paul's phrase—faced a similar test, though curiously inverted. *Can you be like God?* the serpent had asked in Eden; *Can you be truly human?* asked the tempter in the desert.

As I read the Temptation story it occurs to me that, in the absence of eyewitnesses, all details must have come from Jesus himself. For some reason, Jesus felt obliged to disclose to his disciples this moment of struggle and personal weakness. I presume the Temptation was a genuine conflict, not a role Jesus acted out with a prearranged outcome. The same tempter who had found a fatal spot of vulnerability in Adam and Eve aimed his thrust against Jesus with deadly accuracy.

Luke sets the stage with a tone of understated drama. "Jesus, full of the Holy Spirit, returned from the Jordan and was led by the Spirit in the desert, where for forty days he was tempted by the devil. He ate nothing during those days, and at the end of them he was hungry." Like single combat warriors, two giants of the cosmos converged on a scene of desolation. One, just beginning his mission in enemy territory, arrived in a badly weakened state. The other, confident and on home turf, seized the initiative.

I puzzle over certain details of the Temptation. Satan asked Jesus to turn a stone into bread, offered him all the kingdoms of the world, and urged him to jump from a high place in order to test God's promise of physical safety. Where is the evil in these requests? The three temptations seem like Jesus' prerogatives, the very qualities to be expected in a Messiah. Would not Jesus go on to multiply bread for five thousand, a far more impressive display? He would also conquer death and rise again to become King of Kings. The three temptations do not seem evil in themselves—and yet clearly something pivotal happened in the desert.

The British poet Gerard Manley Hopkins presents the Temptation as something of a get-acquainted session between Jesus and Satan. In the dark about the Incarnation, Satan did not know for certain whether Jesus was an ordinary man or a theophany or perhaps an angel with limited powers like himself. He challenged Jesus to perform miracles as a means of scouting his adversary's powers. Martin Luther goes further, speculating that throughout his life Jesus "conducted himself so humbly and associated with sinful men and women, and as a consequence was not held in great esteem," on account of which "the devil overlooked him and did not recognize him. For the devil is farsighted; he looks only for what is big and high and attaches himself to that; he does not look at that which is low down and beneath himself."

In the gospel accounts, the single combat warriors treat each other with a kind of wary respect, like two boxers circling one another in the ring. For Jesus, the greatest strain was probably a willingness to put up with the Temptation in the first place. Why not simply destroy the tempter, saving human history from his evil plague? Jesus demurred.

For his part, Satan offered to trade away his dominion over the world in exchange for the satisfaction of prevailing over the Son of God. Although Satan posed the tests, in the end it was he who flunked them. In two tests he merely asked Jesus to prove himself; by the third he was demanding worship, something God would never accede to.

The Temptation unmasked Satan, while God remained masked. *If you are God,* said Satan, *then dazzle me. Act like God should act.* Jesus replied, *Only God makes those decisions, therefore I do nothing at your command.*

⸺

In Wim Wender's elegant films about angels (*Wings of Desire*; *Faraway, So Close*), celestial beings discuss together in childlike wonder what it must be like to drink coffee and digest food, to experience warmth and pain, to sense a skeleton moving as you walk, to feel the touch of another human being, to say "Ah!" and "Oh!" because not everything is known in advance, to live by minutes and hours and thus to encounter *now* instead of just forever. At the age of thirty or so, when Jesus first squared off with Satan in the desert, he had realized all those "advantages" of being human. He lived comfortably inside his suit of skin.

As I look back on the three temptations, I see that Satan proposed an enticing improvement. He tempted Jesus toward the good parts of being human without the bad: to savor the taste of bread without being subject to the fixed rules of hunger and of agriculture, to confront risk with no real danger, to enjoy fame and power without the prospect of painful rejection—in short, to wear a crown but not a cross. (The temptation that Jesus resisted, many of us, his followers, still long for.)

Apocryphal gospels, judged spurious by the church, suggest what it might have looked like had Jesus succumbed to Satan's temptations. These fantastic accounts show the child Jesus making clay sparrows that he could bring to life with a puff of breath, and dropping dried fish into water to see them miraculously start swimming. He turned his playmates into goats to teach them a lesson, and made people go blind or deaf just for the thrill of healing them. The apocryphal gospels are the second-century counterparts to modern comic books about Superboy and Batgirl. Their value lies mainly in the contrast they form with the actual Gospels, which reveal a Messiah who did not use miraculous powers to benefit himself. Beginning with the Temptation, Jesus showed a reluctance to bend the rules on earth.

Malcolm Muggeridge, while filming a documentary in Israel, found himself musing on the Temptation:

> Curiously enough, just at the right moment to begin filming, when the shadows were long enough and the light not too weak, I happened to notice near by a whole expanse of stones, all identical, and looking uncommonly like loaves well baked and brown. How easy for Jesus to have turned these stone loaves into edible ones, as, later, he would turn water into wine at a wedding feast! And, after all, why not? The Roman authorities distributed free bread to promote Caesar's kingdom, and Jesus could do the same to promote his. . . .

Jesus had but to give a nod of agreement and he could have constructed Christendom, not on four shaky Gospels and a defeated man nailed on a Cross, but on a basis of sound socio-economic planning and principles.... Every utopia could have been brought to pass, every hope have been realized and every dream been made to come true. What a benefactor, then, Jesus would have been. Acclaimed, equally, in the London School of Economics and the Harvard Business School; a statue in Parliament Square, and an even bigger one on Capitol Hill and in the Red Square.... Instead, he turned the offer down on the ground that only God should be worshipped.

As Muggeridge sees it, the Temptation revolved around the question uppermost in the minds of Jesus' countrymen: What should the Messiah look like? A People's Messiah who could turn stones into bread to feed the multitudes? A Torah Messiah, standing tall at the lofty pinnacle of the temple? A King Messiah, ruling over not just Israel but all the kingdoms of earth? In short, Satan was offering Jesus the chance to be the thundering Messiah we think we want. Certainly, I recognize in Muggeridge's description the Messiah I think I want.

We want anything but a Suffering Messiah—and so did Jesus, at one level. Satan hit closest to home with his suggestion that Jesus throw himself from a high place to test God's care. That temptation would surface again. Once, in a flash of anger Jesus gave Peter a strong rebuke. "Out of my sight, Satan!" he said. "You do not have in mind the things of God, but the things of men." Peter had recoiled at Jesus' prediction of suffering and death—"Never, Lord! This shall never happen to you!"—and that instinctively protective reaction had hit a nerve. In Peter's words, Jesus heard again the allure of Satan tempting him toward an easier way.

Nailed to the cross, Jesus would hear the last temptation repeated as a taunt. A criminal scoffed, "Aren't you the Christ? Save yourself and us." Spectators took up the cry: "Let him come down from the cross, and we will believe in him.... Let God rescue him now if he wants him." But there was no rescue, no miracle, no easy, painless path. For Jesus to save others, quite simply, he could not save himself. That fact, he must have known as he faced Satan in the desert.

My own temptations tend to involve common vices such as lust and greed. As I reflect on Jesus' temptations, though, I realize they centered on his reason for coming to earth, his "style" of working. Satan was, in effect, dangling before Jesus a speeded-up way of accomplishing his mission. He could win over the crowds by creating food on demand and then take control of the kingdoms of the world, all the while protecting himself from danger. "Why move thy feet so slow to what is best?" Satan jeered in Milton's version.

I first found this insight in the writings of Dostoevsky, who made the Temptation scene the centerpiece of his great novel *The Brothers Karamazov*. The agnostic brother Ivan Karamazov writes a poem called "The Grand Inquisitor" set in sixteenth-century Seville at the height of the Inquisition. In the poem, a disguised Jesus visits the city at a time when heretics are daily being burned at the stake. The Grand Inquisitor, a cardinal, "an old man, almost ninety, tall and erect, with a withered face and sunken eyes," recognizes Jesus and has him thrown into prison. There, the two visit in a scene intentionally reminiscent of the Temptation in the desert.

The Inquisitor has an accusation to make: by turning down the three temptations, Jesus forfeited the three greatest powers at his disposal, "miracle, mystery, and authority." He should have followed Satan's advice and performed the miracles on demand in order to increase his fame among the people. He should have welcomed the offer of authority and power. Did Jesus not realize that people want more than anything else to worship what is established beyond dispute? "Instead of taking possession of men's freedom, you increased it, and burdened the spiritual kingdom of mankind with its sufferings forever. You desired man's free love, that he should follow you freely, enticed and taken captive by you."

By resisting Satan's temptations to override human freedom, the Inquisitor maintains, Jesus made himself far too easy to reject. He surrendered his greatest advantage: the power to compel belief. Fortunately, continues the sly Inquisitor, the church recognized the error and corrected it, and has been relying on miracle, mystery, and authority ever since. For this reason, the Inquisitor must execute Jesus one more time, lest he hinder the church's work.

The scene from *Karamazov* has added poignancy because at the time of its composition, communist revolutionaries were organizing themselves in Russia. As Dostoevsky noted, they too would borrow techniques from the church. They promised to turn stones into bread and to guarantee safety and security for all citizens in exchange for one simple thing: their freedom. Communism would become the new church in Russia, one likewise founded on miracle, mystery, and authority.

More than a century after Dostoevsky wrote this chilling dialogue about power and freedom, I had the opportunity to visit his homeland and observe in person the results of seven decades of Communist rule. I went in November of 1991, when the Soviet empire was crumbling, Mikhail Gorbachev was giving way to Boris Yeltsin, and the entire nation was trying to rediscover itself. The iron grasp of power had loosened, and people were now reveling in the freedom to say whatever they wished.

I remember vividly a meeting with the editors of *Pravda*, formerly the official mouthpiece of the Communist Party. *Pravda* as much as any institution had slavishly served the Communist "church." Now, though, *Pravda*'s circulation was falling dramatically (from eleven million to 700,000) in concert with communism's fall from grace. The editors of *Pravda* seemed earnest, sincere, searching—and shaken to the core. So shaken that they were now asking advice from emissaries of a religion their founder had scorned as "the opiate of the people."

The editors remarked wistfully that Christianity and communism have many of the same ideals: equality, sharing, justice, and racial harmony. Yet they had to admit the Marxist pursuit of that vision had produced the worst nightmares the world has ever seen. Why?

"We don't know how to motivate people to show compassion," said the editor-in-chief. "We tried raising money for the children of Chernobyl, but the average Russian citizen would rather spend his money on drink. How do you reform and motivate people? How do you get them to be good?"

Seventy-four years of communism had proved beyond all doubt that goodness could not be legislated from the Kremlin and enforced at the point of a gun. In a heavy irony, attempts to compel morality tend to produce defiant subjects and tyrannical rulers who lose their moral core. I came away from Russia with the strong sense that we Christians would do well to relearn the basic lesson of the Temptation. Goodness cannot be imposed externally, from the top down; it must grow internally, from the bottom up.

The Temptation in the desert reveals a profound difference between God's power and Satan's power. Satan has the power to coerce, to dazzle, to force obedience, to destroy. Humans have learned much from that power, and governments draw deeply from its reservoir. With a bullwhip or a billy club or an AK-47, human beings can force other human beings to do just about anything they want. Satan's power is external and coercive.

God's power, in contrast, is internal and noncoercive. "You would not enslave man by a miracle, and craved faith given freely, not based on miracle," said the Inquisitor to Jesus in Dostoevsky's novel. Such power may seem at times like weakness. In its commitment to transform gently from the inside out and in its relentless dependence on human choice, God's power may resemble a kind of abdication. As every parent and every lover knows, love can be rendered powerless if the beloved chooses to spurn it.

"God is not a Nazi," said Thomas Merton. Indeed God is not. The Master of the universe would become its victim, powerless before a squad of soldiers in a garden. God made himself weak for one purpose: to let human beings choose freely for themselves what to do with him.*

—∞—

Søren Kierkegaard wrote about God's light touch: "Omnipotence which can lay its hand so heavily upon the world can also make its touch so light that the creature receives independence." Sometimes, I concede, I wish that God used a heavier touch. My faith suffers from too much freedom, too many temptations to disbelieve. At times I

---

*In Dorothy Sayers' play *The Man Born to Be King*, King Herod tells the Magi, "You cannot rule men by love. When you find your king, tell him so. Only three things will govern a people—fear and greed and the promise of security." King Herod understood the management principles Satan operates by, the same ones Jesus declined in the wilderness.

want God to overwhelm me, to overcome my doubts with certainty, to give final proofs of his existence and his concern.

I want God to take a more active role in human affairs as well. If God had merely reached down and flicked Saddam Hussein off the throne, how many lives would have been saved in the Gulf War? If God had done the same with Hitler, how many Jews would have been spared? Why must God "sit on his hands"?

I want God to take a more active role in my personal history too. I want quick and spectacular answers to my prayers, healing for my diseases, protection and safety for my loved ones. I want a God without ambiguity, One to whom I can point for the sake of my doubting friends.

When I think these thoughts, I recognize in myself a thin, hollow echo of the challenge that Satan hurled at Jesus two thousand years ago. God resists those temptations now as Jesus resisted them on earth, settling instead for a slower, gentler way. In George MacDonald's words,

> Instead of crushing the power of evil by divine force; instead of compelling justice and destroying the wicked; instead of making peace on earth by the rule of a perfect prince; instead of gathering the children of Jerusalem under His wings whether they would or not, and saving them from the horrors that anguished His prophetic soul—He let evil work its will while it lived; He contented Himself with the slow unencouraging ways of help essential; making men good; casting out, not merely controlling Satan....
>
> To love righteousness is to make it grow, not to avenge it.... He resisted every impulse to work more rapidly for a lower good.

"O Jerusalem, Jerusalem," Jesus cried, in the scene MacDonald alludes to, "how often I have longed to gather your children together, as a hen gathers her chicks under her wings, but you were not willing." The disciples had proposed that Jesus call down fire on unrepentant cities; in contrast, Jesus uttered a cry of helplessness, an astonishing "if only" from the lips of the Son of God. He would not force himself on those who were not willing.

The more I get to know Jesus, the more impressed I am by what Ivan Karamazov called "the miracle of restraint." The miracles Satan suggested, the signs and wonders the Pharisees demanded, the final proofs I yearn for—these would offer no serious obstacle to an omnipotent God. More amazing is his *refusal* to perform and to overwhelm. God's terrible insistence on human freedom is so absolute that he granted us the power to live as though he did not exist, to spit in his face, to crucify him. All this Jesus must have known as he faced down the tempter in the desert, focusing his mighty power on the energy of restraint.

I believe God insists on such restraint because no pyrotechnic displays of omnipotence will achieve the response he desires. Although power can force obedience, only love can summon a response of love, which is the one thing God wants from us and the reason he created us. "I, when I am lifted up from the earth, will draw all men to myself," Jesus said. In case we miss the point John adds, "He said this to show the kind of death he was going to die." God's nature is self-giving; he bases his appeal on sacrificial love.

I remember one afternoon in Chicago sitting in an outdoor restaurant listening to a broken man relate the story of his prodigal son. Jake, the son, could not keep a job. He wasted all his money on drugs and alcohol. He rarely called home, and brought little joy and much grief to both parents. Jake's father described to me his feeling of helplessness in words not unlike those Jesus used about Jerusalem. "If only I could bring him back, and shelter him and try to show how much I love him," he said. He paused to gain control of his voice, then added, "The strange thing is, even though he rejects me, Jake's love means more to me than that of my other three, responsible children. Odd, isn't it? That's how love is."

I sense in that final four-word sentence more insight into the mystery of God's restraint than I have found in any book of theodicy. Why does God content himself with the slow, unencouraging way of making righteousness grow rather than avenging it? *That's how love is.* Love has its own power, the only power ultimately capable of conquering the human heart.

Though rebuffed in all three temptations, Satan may well have departed from the confrontation wearing a smirk. Jesus' steadfast refusal to play by Satan's rules meant that Satan himself could continue playing by those rules. He still had the kingdoms of the world at his disposal, after all, and now he had learned a lesson about God's restraint. Restraint by God creates opportunity for those opposed to God.

Other skirmishes would come, of course. Jesus would forcibly cast out demons, but the Spirit he replaced them with was far less possessive and depended always on the will of the one possessed. Occasions for mischief abounded: Jesus admitted as much in his analogy of the kingdom of God growing up in the midst of evil, like wheat among the weeds.

From Satan's perspective, the Temptation offered a new lease on life. The kids from *Lord of the Flies* could roam the island awhile longer, apparently free of adult authority. Furthermore, God could be blamed for what went wrong. If God insisted on sitting on his hands while devilment like the Crusades and the Holocaust went on, why not blame the Parent, not the kids?

It occurs to me that by turning down the temptations in the desert, Jesus put God's own reputation at risk. God has promised to restore earth to perfection one day, but what about the meantime? The swamp of human history, the brutality even of church history, the apocalypse to come—are all these worth the divine restraint? To put it bluntly, is human freedom worth the cost?

No one who lives in the midst of the restoration process, not at its end, can answer that question fairly. All I can do is recall that Jesus, a single combat warrior facing Evil head-on with the power to destroy it, chose a different way. For him, preserving the free will of a notoriously flawed species seemed worth the cost. The choice could not have been easy, for it involved his own pain as well as his followers'.

As I survey the rest of Jesus' life, I see that the pattern of restraint established in the desert persisted throughout his life. I never sense Jesus twisting a person's arm. Rather, he stated the consequences of a choice, then threw the decision back to the other party. He answered

THE JESUS I NEVER KNEW

a wealthy man's question with uncompromising words and then let him walk away. Mark pointedly adds this comment: "Jesus looked at him and loved him." Jesus had a realistic view of how the world would respond to him: "Because of the increase of wickedness, the love of most will grow cold."

We sometimes use the term "savior complex" to describe an unhealthy syndrome of obsession over curing others' problems. The true Savior, however, seemed remarkably free of such a complex. He had no compulsion to convert the entire world in his lifetime or to cure people who were not ready to be cured. In Milton's words, Jesus "held it more humane, more heavenly first / By winning words to conquer willing hearts, / And make persuasion do the work of fear."

In short, Jesus showed an incredible respect for human freedom. When Satan asked for the chance to test Peter and sift him as wheat, even then Jesus did not refuse the request. His response: "I have prayed for you, Simon, that your faith may not fail." When the crowds turned away and many disciples deserted him, Jesus said to the Twelve, almost plaintively, "You do not want to leave too, do you?" As his life moved toward doom in Jerusalem, he exposed Judas but did not try to prevent his evil deed—that, too, a consequence of restraint.

"Take up your *cross* and follow me," Jesus said, in the least manipulative invitation that has ever been given.

———

This quality of restraint in Jesus—one could almost call it a divine shyness—took me by surprise. I realized, as I absorbed the story of Jesus in the Gospels, that I had expected from him the same qualities I had met in the southern fundamentalist church of my childhood. There, I often felt the victim of emotional pressures. Doctrine was dished out in a "Believe and don't ask questions!" style. Wielding the power of miracle, mystery, and authority, the church left no place for doubt. I also learned manipulative techniques for "soul-winning," some of which involved misrepresenting myself to the person I was talking to. Yet now I am unable to find any of these qualities in the life of Jesus.

If I read church history correctly, many other followers of Jesus have yielded to the very temptations he resisted. Dostoevsky shrewdly replayed the Temptation scene in the torture cell of the Grand Inquisitor. How could a church founded by the One who withstood the Temptation carry out an Inquisition of forced belief that lasted half a millennium? Meanwhile, in a milder Protestant version in the city of Geneva, officials were making attendance at church compulsory and refusal to take the Eucharist a crime. Heretics there, too, were burned at the stake.

To its shame, Christian history reveals unrelieved attempts to improve on the way of Christ. Sometimes the church joins hands with a government that offers a shortcut path to power. "The worship of success is generally *the* form of idol worship which the devil cultivates most assiduously," wrote Helmut Thielicke about the German church's early infatuation with Adolf Hitler. "We could observe in the first years after 1933 the almost suggestive compulsion that emanates from great successes and how, under the influence of these successes, men, even Christians, stopped asking in whose name and at what price...."

Sometimes the church grows its own mini-Hitlers, men with names like Jim Jones and David Koresh, who understand all too well the power represented in miracle, mystery, and authority. And sometimes the church simply borrows the tools of manipulation perfected by politicians, salesmen, and advertising copywriters.

I am quick to diagnose these flaws. Yet when I turn from church history and examine myself, I find that I too am vulnerable to the Temptation. I lack the willpower to resist shortcut solutions to human needs. I lack the patience to allow God to work in a slow, "gentlemanly" way. I want to seize control myself, to compel others to help accomplish the causes I believe in. I am willing to trade away certain freedoms for the guarantee of safety and protection. I am willing to trade away even more for the chance to realize my ambitions.

When I feel those temptations rising within me, I return to the story of Jesus and Satan in the desert. Jesus' resistance against Satan's temptations preserved for me the very freedom I exercise when I face my own temptations. I pray for the same trust and patience that Jesus showed. And I rejoice that, as Hebrews said, "We do not have a high priest who is unable to sympathize with our weaknesses, but we have one who has been tempted in every way, just as we are—yet without sin. . . . Because he himself suffered when he was tempted, he is able to help those who are being tempted."

CHAPTER 5

PROFILE: WHAT WOULD I HAVE NOTICED?

———∞∞∞———

Everything in Christ astonishes me. His spirit overawes me, and his will confounds me. Between him and whoever else in the world, there is no possible term of comparison. He is truly a being by himself. . . . I search in vain in history to find the similar to Jesus Christ, or anything which can approach the gospel. Neither history, nor humanity, nor the ages, nor nature, offer me anything with which I am able to compare it or to explain it. Here everything is extraordinary.

NAPOLEON

CHAPTER 5

PROFILE: WHAT WOULD I HAVE NOTICED?

———— ∽∾∽ ————

The Apostles' Creed hustles through Jesus' life in one paragraph, beginning with his birth and skipping immediately to his death, descent into hell, and ascent into heaven. Wait a minute—isn't something missing? What happened in the interval between his being born of the Virgin Mary and his suffering under Pontius Pilate? Somehow everything Jesus said and did in thirty-three years on earth gets swept aside in the rush to interpret his life. How did he spend his time here?

Memories from Sunday school actually detract from my efforts to picture Jesus' everyday life, for he was rendered in lifeless flannelboard scenes. There he is teaching. That's him holding a lamb. Now he's talking with a Samaritan woman and, look, another conversation with a man named Nicodemus. The closest thing to action came when the disciples in their miniature sailboats bobbed across the blue flannelboard sea. I remember one scene of Jesus standing in the temple with a whip in his hand, but it matched nothing else I had learned about him. I certainly never saw him at a party. I may have learned facts about Jesus' life in Sunday school, but as a person he remained remote and two-dimensional.

Movies about Jesus helped bring him to life for me. Some of them, such as *Jesus of Nazareth* by Zeffirelli, take great pains to recreate settings faithful to the gospel accounts. Unlike the placid flannelgraph scenes, the movies show Jesus in action, surrounded by unruly spectators who jostle each other for a better view and press their demands on him.

As I watch these movies, and then return to the Gospels, I try to place myself in my familiar role as a journalist, or at least the first-century equivalent. I stand on the margins, listening and taking notes, intent to capture something of Jesus in my reports, while at the same time aware he is having an effect on me personally. What do I see? What impresses me? Disturbs me? How can I convey him to my readers?

I cannot begin where I normally begin in reporting on a person, by describing what my subject looked like. No one knows. The first semi-realistic portraits of Jesus did not come until the fifth century, and these were pure speculation; until then the Greeks had portrayed him as a young, beardless figure resembling the god Apollo.

In 1514 someone forged a document under the name of Publius Lentulus, the Roman governor who succeeded Pontius Pilate, which contained this description of Jesus:

> He is a tall man, well shaped and of an amiable and reverend aspect; his hair is of a color that can hardly be matched, falling into graceful curls ... parted on the crown of his head, running as a stream to the front after the fashion of the Nazarites; his forehead high, large and imposing; his cheeks without spot or wrinkle, beautiful with a lovely red; his nose and mouth formed with exquisite symmetry; his beard, and of a color suitable to his hair, reaching below his chin and parted in the middle like a fork; his eyes bright blue, clear and serene....

I recognize that Jesus from the oil paintings hanging on the concrete-block walls of my childhood church. The forger gave himself away, however, with his next sentence: "No man has seen him laugh." Was he reading the same Gospels that I read, documents that say not a word about Jesus' physical appearance yet depict him performing his first miracle at a wedding, giving playful nicknames to his disciples, and somehow gaining a reputation as a "gluttonous man and a wine-bibber"? When the pious criticized his disciples for their lax-ity in spiritual disciplines, Jesus replied, "How can the guests of the bridegroom fast while he is with them?" Of all the images he could have chosen for himself, Jesus settled on that of the groom whose radiance cheers up the entire wedding party.

I once showed to a class several dozen art slides portraying Jesus in a variety of forms—African, Korean, Chinese—and then asked the class to describe what they thought Jesus looked like. Virtually every-one suggested he was tall (unlikely for a first-century Jew), most said handsome, and no one said overweight. I showed a BBC film on the life of Christ that featured a pudgy actor in the title role, and some in the class found it offensive. We prefer a tall, handsome, and, above all, slender Jesus.

One tradition dating back to the second century suggested Jesus was a hunchback. In the Middle Ages, Christians widely believed that Jesus had suffered from leprosy. Most Christians today would find such notions repulsive and perhaps heretical. Was he not a perfect specimen of humanity? Yet in all the Bible I can find only one physi-cal description of sorts, a prophecy written hundreds of years before Christ's birth. Here is Isaiah's portrayal, in the midst of a passage that the New Testament applies to the life of Jesus:

> Just as there were many who were appalled at him—his appearance was so disfigured beyond that of any man and his form marred beyond human likeness.... He had no beauty or majesty to attract us to him, nothing in his appearance that we should desire him. He was despised and rejected by men, a man of sorrows, and familiar with suffering. Like one from whom men hide their faces he was despised, and we esteemed him not.

Because of the Gospels' silence, we cannot answer with certainty the basic question of what Jesus looked like. That is a good thing, I believe. Our glamorized representations of Jesus say more about us than about him. He had no supernatural glow about him: John the Baptist admitted he never would have recognized Jesus apart from special revelation. According to Isaiah, we cannot point to his beauty or majesty or anything else in his appearance to explain his attraction. The key lies elsewhere.

I move beyond physical appearance to consider what Jesus was like as a person. How would he have scored on a personality profile test?

The personality that emerges from the Gospels differs radically from the image of Jesus I grew up with, an image I now recognize in some of the older Hollywood films about Jesus. In those films, Jesus recites his lines evenly and without emotion. He strides through life as the one calm character among a cast of flustered extras. Nothing rattles him. He dispenses wisdom in flat, measured tones. He is, in short, the Prozac Jesus.

In contrast, the Gospels present a man who has such charisma that people will sit three days straight, without food, just to hear his riveting words. He seems excitable, impulsively "moved with compassion" or "filled with pity." The Gospels reveal a range of Jesus' emotional responses: sudden sympathy for a person with leprosy, exuberance over his disciples' successes, a blast of anger at coldhearted legalists, grief over an unreceptive city, and then those awful cries of anguish in Gethsemane and on the cross. He had nearly inexhaustible patience with individuals but no patience at all with institutions and injustice.

I once attended a men's movement retreat designed to help men "get in touch with their emotions" and break out of restrictive stereotypes of masculinity. As I sat in a small group, listening to other men tell of their struggles to express themselves and to experience true intimacy, I realized that Jesus lived out an ideal for masculine fulfillment that nineteen centuries later still eludes most men. Three times, at least, he cried in front of his disciples. He did not hide his fears or hesitate to ask for help: "My soul is overwhelmed with sorrow to the point of death," he told them in Gethsemane; "Stay here and keep watch with me." How many strong leaders today would make themselves so vulnerable?

Unlike most men I know, Jesus also loved to praise other people. When he worked a miracle, he often deflected credit back on the recipient: "Your faith has healed you." He called Nathanael "a true Israelite, in whom there is nothing false." Of John the Baptist, he said there was none greater born of women. Volatile Peter he renamed "the Rock." When a cringing woman offered him an extravagant act of devotion, Jesus defended her against critics and said the story of her generosity would be told forever.

The Gospels show that Jesus quickly established intimacy with the people he met. Whether talking with a woman at a well, a religious leader in a garden, or a fisherman by a lake, he cut instantly to the heart of the matter, and after a few brief lines of conversation these people revealed to Jesus their innermost secrets. People of his day tended to keep rabbis and "holy men" at a respectful distance, but Jesus drew out something else, a hunger so deep that people crowded around him just to touch his clothes.

Novelist Mary Gordon mentions Jesus' sensitivity to women and children as one of the main qualities that attracted her: "Surely, He is the only affectionate hero in literature. Who can imagine an affectionate Odysseus, Aeneas?" To Jesus' aside to the daughters of Jerusalem, "Alas for women with child in those days," Gordon responds, "I knew I wanted children; I felt those words were for me. Now I think: how many men would take into consideration the hardships of pregnancy and nursing?"

Jesus did not mechanically follow a list of "Things I Gotta Do Today," and I doubt he would have appreciated our modern emphasis on punctuality and precise scheduling. He attended wedding feasts that lasted for days. He let himself get distracted by any "nobody" he came across, whether a hemorrhaging woman who shyly touched his robe or a blind beggar who made a nuisance of himself. Two of his most impressive miracles (the raising of Lazarus and of Jairus's daughter) took place because he arrived too late to heal the sick person.

Jesus was "the man for others," in Bonhoeffer's fine phrase. He kept himself free—free for the other person. He would accept almost anybody's invitation to dinner, and as a result no public figure had a more diverse list of friends, ranging from rich people, Roman centurions, and Pharisees to tax collectors, prostitutes, and leprosy victims. People *liked* being with Jesus; where he was, joy was.

And yet, for all these qualities that point toward what psychologists like to call self-actualization, Jesus broke the mold. As C. S.

Lewis puts it, "He was not at all like the psychologist's picture of the integrated, balanced, adjusted, happily married, employed, popular citizen. You can't really be very well 'adjusted' to your world if it says you 'have a devil' and ends by nailing you up naked to a stake of wood."

Like most of Jesus' contemporaries, no doubt I would have balked at the odd combination of extravagant claims coming from an ordinary-looking Jewish man. He claimed to be the Son of God, and yet he ate and drank like other men, and even got tired and lonely. What kind of creature was he?

In some ways Jesus seemed to feel "at home" here, and in other ways he felt unequivocally "not at home." I think of the single scene preserved from his adolescence, when he disappeared in Jerusalem and got scolded by his mother. The cryptic record of her Jewish-mother response, "Son, why have you treated us like this?" probably does not do justice to the scene—his parents had, after all, been searching for three days. Jesus replied, "Why were you searching for me? Didn't you know I had to be in my Father's house?" Already a cleft, a conflict of loyalties, was dividing Jesus and his family.

Living on a planet of free will and rebellion, Jesus often must have felt "not at home." At such times he went aside and prayed, as if to breathe pure air from a life-support system that would give him the strength to continue living on a polluted planet. Yet he did not always get formulaic answers to his prayers. Luke reports that he prayed all night before choosing the twelve disciples—even so, the group included a traitor. In Gethsemane he prayed at first that the cup of suffering be taken from him, but of course it was not. That scene in the garden shows a man desperately "not at home," yet resisting all temptations toward supernatural rescue.

For me, one scene in the Gospels brings together the "at home" and "not at home" nature of Jesus. A storm blew up on the Sea of Galilee, nearly capsizing the boat in which Jesus lay sleeping. He stood up and yelled into the wind and spray, "Quiet! Be still!" The disciples shrank back in terror. What kind of person could shout to the weather as if correcting an unruly child?

The display of power in the midst of a storm helped convince the disciples that Jesus was unlike any other man. Yet it also hints at the depths of Incarnation. "God is vulnerable," said the philosopher Jacques Maritain. Jesus had, after all, fallen asleep from sheer fatigue. Moreover, the Son of God was, but for this one instance of miracle, one of its victims: the creator of rain clouds was rained on, the maker of stars got hot and sweaty under the Palestine sun. Jesus subjected himself to natural laws even when, at some level, they went against his desires ("If it is possible, may this cup be taken from me"). He would live, and die, by the rules of earth.

He comes as yet unknown into a hamlet of Lower Galilee. He is watched by the cold, hard eyes of peasants living long enough at subsistence level to know exactly where the line is drawn between poverty and destitution. He looks like a beggar, yet his eyes lack the proper cringe, his voice the proper whine, his walk the proper shuffle. He speaks about the rule of God, and they listen as much from curiosity as anything else. They know all about rule and power, about kingdom and empire, but they know it in terms of tax and debt, malnutrition and sickness, agrarian oppression and demonic possession. What, they really want to know, can this kingdom of God do for a lame child, a blind parent, a demented soul screaming its tortured isolation among the graves that mark the edges of the village? (John Dominic Crossan)

Jesus' neighbors soon found out what he could do for them. He made the lame child walk and the blind parent see, and exorcised demons from the demented soul among the graves. When Jesus inaugurated his ministry of healing and teaching, his neighbors scratched their heads and asked, flabbergasted, "Isn't he Mary's boy, Joseph the carpenter's son? Where did he get such wisdom and such miraculous power?"

Initially, for perhaps a year, Jesus met with great success. So many people flocked to him that he sometimes had to flee to a boat offshore. Without doubt it was the physical healings that first put him on the map. The Jews, who believed the Devil caused illness and thus holy men could be channels for God's intervention, had a long history of miracle workers. (One named Honi lived just before Jesus' time and is mentioned by the historian Josephus.) Jesus apparently knew of some rivals, for he subdued his disciples' impulse to condemn them.

About a third of the Gospels' stories about Jesus involve physical healings, and by journalistic instinct I probably would have investigated these stories, searching out medical records and interviewing the families of those who claimed a miracle. The healings were diverse and fit no real pattern. At least one person Jesus healed long-distance; some were instant and some gradual; many required the healed person to follow specific instructions.

I would have noticed in Jesus a curious ambivalence about miracles. On the one hand, Jesus healed in spontaneous response to human need: he saw a suffering person before him, felt compassion, and healed the person. Not once did he turn down a direct request for help. On the other hand, Jesus certainly did not advertise his powers. He condemned the "wicked and adulterous generation" who clamored for signs and, just as he had in the desert, resisted all temptation toward spectacle. Mark records seven separate occasions when Jesus instructed a person he had healed, "Tell no one!" In regions where people had no faith, he did no miracles.

Probably I would have speculated about what a man with such powers might have accomplished in Rome, Athens, or Alexandria. Jesus' brothers proposed that at the least he should concentrate his work in Jerusalem, Israel's capital. Jesus himself, though, preferred to keep out of the spotlight. Distrusting crowds and public opinion, he spent most of his time in towns of small size and little importance.

Despite his ambivalence, Jesus did not hesitate to use the miracles as proof of who he was: "Believe me when I say that I am in the Father and the Father is in me; or at least believe on the evidence of the miracles themselves," he told his disciples. And when his cousin John the Baptist, languishing in a jail cell, entertained doubts about whether Jesus was indeed the Messiah, Jesus gave John's disciples this message (as paraphrased by Frederick Buechner):

> You go tell John what you've seen around here. Tell him there are people who have sold their seeing-eye dogs and taken up bird-watching. Tell him there are people who've traded in aluminum walkers for hiking boots. Tell him the down-and-out have turned into the up-and-coming and a lot of dead-beats are living it up for the first time in their lives.

If I had sought a one-word label to describe Jesus to his contemporaries, I would have chosen the word *rabbi*, or teacher. In the United States now I know of no parallels to Jesus' life. Surely his style had little in common with that of modern mass evangelists, with their tents and stadia, their advance teams and billboards and direct-mail campaigns, their electronically enhanced presentations. His little band of followers, possessing no permanent base of operations, wandered from town to town without much discernible strategy.

"Foxes have holes and birds of the air have nests, but the Son of Man has no place to lay his head," Jesus said. Were they living in modern times, with the crackdown on homelessness, Jesus and his disciples would likely be harassed by police and forced to move on. Ancient times, though, knew many such teachers (there was actually a school of philosophers called the Peripatetics based on this common style of wisdom-sharing on the run).

In India I had the chance to observe in person something like the life Jesus led. There, Christian evangelists follow in the path of itinerant Hindu and Buddhist "holy men." Some hang around train stations, introducing themselves to waiting travelers and asking if they want to know more about God. Some walk from town to town, accompanied by their disciples. Others invite disciples to meet with them in *ashrams*, where together they worship and study the Scriptures.

The group Jesus led functioned with no headquarters or other property and apparently no officers except a treasurer (Judas). Financially, it seems, they barely scraped by. In order to scrounge up money for taxes, Jesus sent Peter fishing. He borrowed a coin to make a point about Caesar and had to borrow a donkey the one time he opted against traveling on foot. As his disciples walked through fields they pulled off the heads of standing grain to eat the raw kernels, taking advantage of Mosaic laws that made allowances for the poor. When Jesus met with influential people like Nicodemus or the rich young ruler it never seemed to occur to him that a person with money and influence could be of potential use.

How did Jesus support himself? In the Middle East of that day, teachers lived off the gifts of appreciative listeners. Luke points out that certain women who had been healed by Jesus—including the wife of Herod's finance minister!—helped provide for him. Touchingly, some of these women made the long and dangerous journey from Galilee to Jerusalem at the time of the Passover Feast, and stayed by Jesus at the cross after his closest disciples had deserted him.

By any account, Jesus was a master teacher. Followers were drawn by the magnetic power of his words which, in poet John Berryman's description, were "short, precise, terrible, and full of refreshment." Jesus gave his most enduring lessons on the spot, in spontaneous response to questions. A woman had seven successive husbands: Whose wife will she be in the life to come? Is it lawful to pay taxes to pagan authorities? What must I do to inherit eternal life? Who is the greatest in the kingdom of heaven? How can a man be born when he is old?

Jaroslav Pelikan tells of an old rabbi asked by his pupil, "Why is it that you rabbis so often put your teaching in the form of a question?" The rabbi shot back, "So what's wrong with a question?" Very often Jesus too deflected the question back in Socratic style, pressing the seeker toward a crisis point. His answers cut to the heart of the question and to the hearts of his listeners. I doubt I would have left any encounter with Jesus feeling smug or self-satisfied.

I would have marveled at Jesus' parables, a form that became his trademark. Writers ever since have admired his skill in communicating profound truth through such everyday stories. A scolding woman wears down the patience of a judge. A king plunges into an ill-planned war. A group of children quarrel in the street. A man is mugged and left for dead by robbers. A single woman who loses a penny acts as if she has lost everything. There are no fanciful creatures and sinuous plots in Jesus' parables; he simply describes the life around him.

The parables served Jesus' purposes perfectly. Everyone likes a good story, and Jesus' knack for storytelling held the interest of a mostly illiterate society of farmers and fishermen. Since stories are easier to remember than concepts or outlines, the parables also helped preserve his message: years later, as people reflected on what Jesus had taught, his parables came to mind in vivid detail. It is one thing to talk in abstract terms about the infinite, boundless love of God. It is quite another to tell of a man who lays down his life for friends, or of a heartsick father who scans the horizon every night for some sign of a wayward son.

Jesus came to earth "full of grace and truth," says the gospel of John, and that phrase makes a good summary of his message. First, grace: in contrast to those who tried to complicate the faith and petrify it with legalism, Jesus preached a simple message of God's love. For no reason—certainly not because we deserve it—God has decided to extend to us love that comes free of charge, no strings attached, "on the house."

In a rabbinic story of the time, the owner of a farm went into town to hire temporary workers for the harvest. The day wore on, and as late as the eleventh hour he recruited one last batch of workers, who had a mere hour remaining to prove their worth. In the familiar version of the story, the latecomers made up for lost time by working so hard that the foreman decided to reward them with a whole day's pay. Jesus' version, though, says nothing about the diligence of the workers. He accents instead the generosity of the employer—God—who lavishes his grace on veterans and newcomers alike. No one gets cheated and everyone gets rewarded, far beyond what they deserve.

Despite this emphasis on grace, no one could accuse Jesus of watering down the holiness of God. I would likely have stumbled over the truth that Jesus proclaimed, a truth more uncompromising by far than that taught by the strictest rabbis of his day. Contemporary teachers strove to "not impose a restriction upon the community unless the majority of the community will be able to stand it." Jesus had no such reticence. He broadened murder to include anger, adultery to include lust, theft to include coveting. "Be perfect, therefore, as your heavenly Father is perfect," he said, setting down an ethical standard that no one could reach.

As Elton Trueblood has observed, all the major symbols that Jesus used had a severe, even offensive quality: the yoke of burden, the cup of suffering, the towel of servanthood, and finally the cross of execution. "Count the cost," Jesus said, giving fair warning to any who dared follow him.

A modern rabbi named Jacob Neusner, the world's preeminent scholar on Judaism of the early Christian era, devoted one of his five hundred books (*A Rabbi Talks with Jesus*) to the question of how he would have responded to Jesus. Neusner has great respect for Jesus and for Christianity, and he admits that such teaching as the Sermon on the Mount leaves him "impressed—and moved." It would have quickened enough interest, he says, that he likely would have joined the crowd who followed Jesus from place to place, feasting on his wisdom.

Ultimately, though, Neusner concludes he would have parted company with the rabbi from Nazareth. "Jesus takes an important step—in the wrong direction," he says, by moving the emphasis from "us" as a Jewish community to an "I." Neusner could not go along with the shift from the Torah to Jesus himself as the central authority. "At issue is the figure of Jesus, not the teachings at all. . . . In the end the master, Jesus, makes a demand that only God makes." Respectfully, Neusner turns away, unable to make that leap of faith.

Neusner is right that Jesus' content hardly fit the pattern of other rabbis, not to mention wandering masters such as Confucius or Socrates. He was not so much seeking truth as pointing to it, by pointing to himself. In Matthew's words, "he taught as one who had authority, and not as their teachers of the law." The scribes endeavored to offer no personal opinions, rather basing their remarks on the Scriptures and approved commentaries. Jesus had many personal opinions, and used Scripture as the commentary. "You have heard that it was said . . . but I tell you . . ." went his commanding refrain. *He* was the source, and as he spoke he made no distinction between his own words and God's. His listeners understood the implication clearly, even in rejecting it. "This fellow is blaspheming!" they said.

Fearless, Jesus never backed away from a conflict. He took on hecklers and scoffers of every stripe. Once, he stood down a mob intent on stoning an adulterous woman. Another time, when guards went to seize him, they returned to the temple empty-handed: "No one ever spoke the way this man does," they said, awed by his presence. Jesus even gave direct orders to demons: "Be quiet!" "You deaf and dumb spirit, I command you, come out of him and never enter him again!" (Interestingly, the demons never failed to recognize him as the "holy one of God" or "son of the Most High"; it was human beings who questioned his identity.)

Jesus' statements about himself (I and the Father are one; I have the power to forgive sins; I will rebuild the temple in three days) were unprecedented and got him into constant trouble. Indeed, his teaching was so entwined with his person that many of his words could not have outlived him; the grand claims died with him on the cross. Disciples who had followed him as a master returned to their former lives, muttering sadly, "We had hoped that he was the one who was going to redeem Israel." It took the Resurrection to turn the proclaimer of truth into the one proclaimed.

I have placed myself on the edges of the crowd in Jesus' day, as a sincere seeker captivated by the rabbi but reluctant to commit to him. If I turn my attention from Jesus himself to the constellation of people surrounding me, I would see several groupings of onlookers forming concentric rings around him.

Farthest away, in the outer circle, are the groundlings, curiosity-seekers and others who, like me, are trying to figure out Jesus. The very presence of this multitude serves to protect Jesus: grumbling that "the whole world has gone after him," his enemies hesitate to seize him. In the early days especially, Jewish patriots hang out as well, eager for Jesus to announce a revolt against Rome. I note that Jesus never caters to this outer group. Yet he does preach to them, and that in itself distinguishes him from the Essenes and other sects, who reserve their meetings for initiates only.

Closer in, I spot a group of maybe a hundred sincere followers. Many of these traveling companions, I know, have joined up after John the Baptist's arrest—John's disciples complained that "everyone" was going over to Jesus. Spurning popularity, Jesus directs most of his comments not to the masses but to these serious seekers. He constantly pushes them toward a deeper level of commitment, with strong words that would bring anyone up short. You cannot serve two masters, he says. Forsake the love of money and the pleasures the world has to offer. Deny yourself. Serve others. Take up your cross.

That last phrase is no idle metaphor: along the roads of Palestine, Romans regularly nail up the worst criminals as an object lesson to the Jews. What kind of image could these words of "invitation" summon up in his followers' minds? Is he to lead a procession of martyrs? Apparently so. Jesus repeats one saying more than any other: "Whoever finds his life will lose it, and whoever loses his life for my sake will find it."

I have heard the closest ring of followers, the Twelve, boast that they welcome such a sacrifice. "You don't know what you are asking," Jesus replied. "Can you drink the cup I am going to drink?" "We can," they insist in their naïveté.

*

I sometimes ask myself if I would have wanted to join the Twelve. No matter. Unlike other rabbis, Jesus handpicked his inner circle of disciples, rather than letting them choose him. Such was Jesus' magnetism that it took only a few phrases to persuade them to leave their jobs and families to join him. Two sets of brothers—James and John, and Peter and Andrew—worked as partners on fishing boats, and when he called them they abandoned the business (ironically, after Jesus gave them their most successful fishing day ever). All but Judas Iscariot come from Jesus' home province of Galilee; Judas hails from Judea, which shows how Jesus' reputation has spread across the country.

I would have puzzled over the strange mixture represented by the Twelve. Simon the Zealot belongs to the party violently opposing Rome, while Matthew the tax collector has recently been employed by Rome's puppet ruler. No scholars like Nicodemus or wealthy patrons like Joseph of Arimethea have made it into the Twelve. One must look hard to detect any strong leadership abilities.

In my observation, in fact, the disciples' most obvious trait seems to be their denseness. "Are you so dull?" Jesus asks, and again, "How long shall I put up with you?" While he is trying to teach them servant leadership, they are squabbling about who deserves the most favored position. Their gnomic faith exasperates Jesus. After every miracle, they fret anxiously about the next. Can he feed five thousand—what about four thousand? Much of the time a fog of incomprehension separates the Twelve from Jesus.

Why does Jesus invest so much in these apparent losers? To answer that, I turn to Mark's written account, which mentions Jesus' motives in choosing the Twelve: "that they might be with him and that he might send them out to preach."

That they might be with him. Jesus never tried to hide his loneliness and his dependence on other people. He chose his disciples not as servants but as friends. He shared moments of joy and grief with them, and asked for them in times of need. They became his family, his substitute mother and brothers and sisters. They gave up everything for him, as he had given up everything for them. He loved them, plain and simple.

That he might send them out. From his very first invitation to the Twelve, Jesus had in mind what would transpire one day on Calvary. He knew his time on earth was short, and the ultimate success of his mission depended not just on what he accomplished in a few years but on what the Twelve—then eleven, soon to be thousands and then millions—would do after he had left.

Oddly, as I look back on Jesus' time from the present perspective, it is the very ordinariness of the disciples that gives me hope. Jesus does not seem to choose his followers on the basis of native talent or perfectibility or potential for greatness. When he lived on earth he surrounded himself with ordinary people who misunderstood him, failed to exercise

101

much spiritual power, and sometimes behaved like churlish schoolchildren. Three followers in particular (the brothers James and John, and Peter) Jesus singled out for his strongest reprimands—yet two of these would become the most prominent leaders of the early Christians.

I cannot avoid the impression that Jesus prefers working with unpromising recruits. Once, after he had sent out seventy-two disciples on a training mission, Jesus rejoiced at the successes they reported back. No passage in the Gospels shows him more exuberant. "At that time Jesus, full of joy through the Holy Spirit, said, 'I praise you, Father, Lord of heaven and earth, because you have hidden these things from the wise and learned, and revealed them to little children. Yes, Father, for this was your good pleasure.'" From such a ragtag band Jesus founded a church that has not stopped growing in nineteen centuries.

PART TWO

WHY HE CAME

BEATITUDES:
LUCKY ARE THE UNLUCKY

A saint is one who exaggerates what the world neglects.

G. K. CHESTERTON

CHAPTER 6

BEATITUDES:
LUCKY ARE THE UNLUCKY

⸺⟨≋⟩⸺

The Sermon on the Mount haunted my adolescence. I would read a book like Charles Sheldon's *In His Steps*, solemnly vow to act "as Jesus would act," and turn to Matthew 5–7 for guidance. What to make of such advice! Should I mutilate myself after a wet dream? Offer my body to be pummeled by the motorcycle-riding "hoods" in school? Tear out my tongue after speaking a harsh word to my brother?

Once, I became so convicted about my addiction to material things that I gave away to a friend my prized collection of 1,100 baseball cards, including an original 1947 Jackie Robinson and a Mickey Mantle rookie card. Anticipating a divine reward for this renunciation, instead I had to endure the monumental injustice of watching my friend auction off the entire collection at a huge profit. "Blessed are those who are persecuted because of righteousness," I consoled myself.

Now that I am an adult, the crisis of the Sermon on the Mount still has not gone away. Though I have tried at times to dismiss it as rhetorical excess, the more I study Jesus, the more I realize that the statements contained here lie at the heart of his message. If I fail to understand this teaching, I fail to understand him.

Jesus delivered the famous sermon at a time when his popularity was soaring. Crowds pursued him wherever he went, obsessed with one question: *Has the Messiah come at last?* On this unusual occasion

Jesus skipped the parables and granted his audience a full-blown "philosophy of life," somewhat like a candidate unveiling a new political platform. What a platform.

When time came to teach the Beatitudes to my class at LaSalle Street Church in Chicago, I followed my regular routine of previewing the movies about Jesus. Since I drew from fifteen different movies, the task of locating and viewing all the right portions consumed several hours of my time each week, much of it spent waiting for the VCR to fast-forward or reverse to the appropriate scenes. To relieve boredom while the VCR whirred and clicked its way to the right places, I had CNN playing on the TV monitor in the foreground. As the machine sped, say, to the eight-minute-twenty-second mark of Cecil B. DeMille's *King of Kings*, I caught up on news from around the world. Then I hit the "play" button and was transported back into first-century Palestine.

A lot was happening in the world in 1991 the week I taught the Beatitudes. In a ground campaign that lasted a scant one hundred hours, allied forces had achieved a stunning victory over Iraq in the Gulf War. Like most Americans, I could hardly believe the long-feared war had ended so quickly, with so few American casualties. As my VCR searched through the celluloid frames of Jesus in the background, various commentators on-screen were illustrating with charts and maps exactly what had transpired in Kuwait. Then came General Norman Schwarzkopf.

CNN announced an interruption in scheduled programming: they would shift to live coverage of the morning-after press conference by the commander of allied forces. For a time I tried to continue preparing for my class. I watched five minutes of Pasolini's version of Jesus delivering the Beatitudes, then several minutes of General Schwarzkopf's version of allied troops bearing down on Kuwait City. Soon I abandoned the VCR altogether—Stormin' Norman proved entirely too engaging. He told of the "end run" around Iraq's elite Republican Guard, of a decoy invasion by sea, of the allied capability of marching all the way to Baghdad unopposed. He credited the Kuwaitis, the British, the Saudis, and every other participant in the multinational force. A general confident in his mission and immensely proud of the soldiers who had carried it out, Schwarzkopf gave a bravura performance. I remember thinking, *That's exactly the person you want to lead a war.*

The briefing ended, CNN switched to commercials, and I returned to the VCR tapes. Max von Sydow, a blond, pasty Jesus, was giving an improbable rendition of the Sermon on the Mount in *The Greatest Story Ever Told.* "Blessed . . . are . . . the . . . poor . . . in spirit," he intoned in a slow, thick Scandinavian accent, "for . . . theirs . . . is . . . the . . . kingdom . . . of . . . heaven." I had to adjust to the languid pace of the movie compared to General Schwarzkopf's briefing, and it took a few seconds for the irony to sink in: I had just been watching the Beatitudes in reverse!

Blessed are the strong, was the general's message. Blessed are the triumphant. Blessed are the armies wealthy enough to possess smart bombs and Patriot missiles. Blessed are the liberators, the conquering soldiers.

The bizarre juxtaposition of two speeches gave me a feeling for the shock waves the Sermon on the Mount must have caused among its original audience, Jews in first-century Palestine. Instead of General Schwarzkopf, they had Jesus, and to a downtrodden people yearning for emancipation from Roman rule, Jesus gave startling and unwelcome advice. If an enemy soldier slaps you, turn the other cheek. Rejoice in persecution. Be grateful for your poverty.

The Iraqis, chastened on the battlefield, got a nasty measure of revenge by setting fire to Kuwait's oil fields; Jesus enjoined not revenge but love for one's enemies. How long would a kingdom founded on such principles survive against Rome?

"Happy are the bombed-out and the homeless," Jesus might as well have said. "Blessed are the losers and those grieving for fallen comrades. Blessed are the Kurds still suffering under Iraqi rule." Any Greek scholar will tell you the word "blessed" is far too sedate and beatific to carry the percussive force Jesus intended. The Greek word conveys something like a short cry of joy, "Oh, you lucky person!"

"How lucky are the unlucky!" Jesus said in effect.

A few years after the Gulf War episode, I received an invitation to the White House. President Bill Clinton, alarmed about his low standing among evangelical Christians, summoned twelve of us to a private breakfast in order to hear our concerns. Each of us would have five minutes to say whatever we wanted the president and vice-president to hear. The question, "What would Jesus say in such a setting?" crossed my mind, and I realized with a start that the only time Jesus met with powerful political leaders, his hands were tied and his back was clotted with blood. Church and state have had an uneasy relationship ever since.

I turned to the Beatitudes and found myself startled anew. What if I translated their message into contemporary terms?

Mr. President, first I want to advise you to stop worrying so much about the economy and jobs. A lower Gross National Product is actually good for the country. Don't you understand that the poor are the fortunate ones? The more poor we have in the U.S., the more blessed we are. Theirs is the kingdom of heaven.

And don't devote so much time to health care. You see, Mr. President, those who mourn are blessed too, for they'll be comforted.

I know you've heard from the Religious Right about the increasing secularization of our country. Prayer is no longer allowed in schools, and protesters against abortion are subject to arrest. Relax, sir. Government oppression gives Christians an opportunity to be persecuted, and therefore blessed. Thank you for the expanded opportunities.

I did not deliver such a speech to President Clinton, choosing instead to represent the immediate concerns of American Christians, but I did come away from the experience puzzled afresh. What meaning can the Beatitudes have for a society that honors the self-assertive, confident, and rich? Blessed are the happy and the strong, we believe. Blessed are those who hunger and thirst for a good time, who look out for Number One.

Some psychologists and psychiatrists, following Freud's lead, point to the Beatitudes as proof of Jesus' imbalance. Said one distinguished British psychologist, in a speech prepared for the Royal Society of Medicine,

> The spirit of self-sacrifice which permeates Christianity, and is so highly prized in the Christian religious life, is masochism moderately indulged. A much stronger expression of it is to be found in Christ's teaching in the Sermon on the Mount. This blesses the poor, the meek, the persecuted; exhorts us not to resist evil but to offer the second cheek to the smiter; and to do good to them that hate you and forgive men their trespasses. All this breathes masochism.

Which is it, masochism or profound wisdom? Anyone who responds with a quick and easy answer probably has not taken the Beatitudes seriously enough.

To put the issue bluntly, are the Beatitudes true? If so, why doesn't the church encourage poverty and mourning and meekness and persecution instead of striving against them? What is the real meaning of the Beatitudes, this cryptic ethical core of Jesus' teaching?

If I had been sitting in the audience when Jesus first delivered the Beatitudes, I believe I would have left the event feeling confused or outraged, not comforted. Nineteen centuries later, I still struggle to make sense of them. Yet now, especially as I think back on my teenage days of frenzied legalism, I can see that my understanding has developed in stages.

I am not, and may never be, ready to declare, "This is what the Beatitudes mean." But gradually, almost osmotically, I have come to recognize them as important truths. To me, they apply on at least three levels.

Dangled Promises. In my first stage of understanding, I regarded the Beatitudes as a sop Jesus threw to the unfortunates: "Well, since you aren't rich, and your health is failing, and your face is wet with tears, I'll toss out a few nice phrases to make you feel better."

Later, as cynicism faded and my faith strengthened, I came to see them as genuine promises central to Jesus' message.

Unlike medieval kings who threw coins to the masses (or modern politicians who make promises to the poor just before elections), Jesus had the ability to offer his audience lasting, even eternal rewards. Alone of all people on earth, Jesus had actually lived "on the other side," and he who came down from heaven knew well that the spoils of the kingdom of heaven can easily counterbalance whatever misery we might encounter in this life. Those who mourn *will be* comforted; the meek *will inherit the earth*; the hungry *will be filled*; the pure *will see God*. Jesus could make such promises with authority, for he had come to establish God's kingdom that would rule forever.

One summer I met with a group of Wycliffe Bible Translators at their austere headquarters in the Arizona desert. Many lived in mobile homes, and we convened in a concrete-block building with a metal roof. I was impressed with the dedication of these professional linguists who were preparing for a life of poverty and hardship in remote outposts. They loved to sing one song especially: "So send I you, to labor unrewarded, to serve unpaid, unloved, unsought, unknown...." Listening to them, the thought occurred to me that the song has it slightly wrong: these missionaries were not planning to labor unrewarded. Rather, they endured certain hardships with the prospect of other rewards in mind. They served God, trusting in turn that God would make it worth their while—if not here, then in eternity.

In the mornings, before the sun rose too high above the hilltops, I went jogging along dirt roads that coiled among the stalky stands of saguaro cacti. Wary of rattlesnakes and scorpions, I mostly kept my head down looking at the road, but one morning on a new route I glanced up to see a shimmering resort looming before me, almost like a mirage. I jogged closer and discovered two Olympic swimming pools, aerobic workout rooms, a cinder jogging trail, lush gardens, a baseball diamond, soccer fields, and horse stables. The facilities, I learned, belonged to a famous eating disorder clinic that caters to movie stars and athletes. The clinic features the latest twelve-step program techniques, has a staff well stocked with Ph.D.'s and M.D.'s, and charges its clients about $300 per day.

I jogged slowly back to the jumble of houses and buildings at the Wycliffe base, keenly aware of their contrast to the gleaming architecture of the eating disorder clinic. One institution endeavored to save souls, to prepare people to serve God here and in eternity; the other endeavored to save bodies, to prepare people to enjoy this life. It seemed obvious which institution the world honors.

In the Beatitudes, Jesus honored people who may not enjoy many privileges in this life. To the poor, the mourners, the meek, the hungry, the persecuted, the poor in heart, he offered assurance that their service would not go unrecognized. They would receive ample reward. "Indeed," wrote C. S. Lewis, "if we consider the unblushing promises of reward and the staggering nature of the rewards promised in the Gospels, it would seem that Our Lord finds our desires, not too strong, but too weak. We are half-hearted creatures, fooling about with drink and sex and ambition when infinite joy is offered us, like an ignorant child who wants to go on making mud pies in a slum because he cannot imagine what is meant by the offer of a holiday at the sea."

I know that among many Christians an emphasis on future rewards has fallen out of fashion. My former pastor Bill Leslie used to observe, "As churches grow wealthier and more successful, their preference in hymns changes from 'This world is not my home, I'm just a passin' through' to 'This is my father's world.'" In the United States, at least, Christians have grown so comfortable that we no longer identify with the humble conditions Jesus addressed in the Beatitudes— which may explain why they sound so strange to our ears.

Yet, as C. S. Lewis reminds us, we dare not discount the value of future rewards. One need only listen to the songs composed by American slaves to realize this consolation of belief. "Swing low, sweet chariot, comin' for to carry me home." "When I get to heaven, goin' to put on my robe, goin' to shout all over God's heaven." "We'll soon be free, we'll soon be free, when the Lord will call us home." If the slave masters had written these songs for the slaves to sing, they would be an obscenity; rather, they come from the mouths of the slaves themselves, people who had little hope in this world but abiding hope in a world to come. For them, all hope centered in Jesus. "Nobody knows the trouble I see, nobody knows but Jesus." "I'm gonna' lay all my troubles on Jesus' shoulder."

I no longer scorn the eternal rewards mentioned in the Beatitudes as "pie in the sky." What good does it do to hope for future rewards? What good did it do Terry Waite to believe that he would not spend the rest of his life chained to a door in a filthy Beirut apartment, but that a world of family and friends and mercy and love and music and food and good books awaited him if he could just find the strength to hang on a little longer? What good did it do the slaves to believe that God was not satisfied with a world that included back-breaking labor and masters armed with bullwhips and lynching ropes? To believe in future rewards is to believe that the long arm of the Lord bends toward justice, to believe that one day the proud will be overthrown and the humble raised up and the hungry filled with good things.

The prospect of future rewards in no way cancels out our need to fight for justice now, in this life. Yet it is a plain fact of history that for convicts in the Soviet Gulag and slaves in America and Christians in Roman cages awaiting their turn with the wild beasts, the promise of reward was a source not of shame but of hope. It keeps you alive. It allows you to believe in a just God after all. Like a bell tolling from another world, Jesus' promise of rewards proclaims that no matter how things appear, there is no future in evil, only in good.

My wife, Janet, worked with senior citizens near a Chicago housing project judged the poorest community in the United States. About half her clients were white, half were black. All of them had lived through harsh times—two world wars, the Great Depression, social upheavals—and all of them, in their seventies and eighties, lived in awareness of death. Yet Janet noted a striking difference in the way the whites and the blacks faced death. There were exceptions, of course, but the trend was this: many of the whites became increasingly fearful and anxious. They complained about their lives, their families, and their deteriorating health. The blacks, in contrast, maintained a good humor and triumphant spirit even though they had more apparent reason for bitterness and despair.

What caused the difference in outlooks? Janet concluded the answer was hope, a hope that traced directly to the blacks' bedrock belief in heaven. If you want to hear contemporary images of heaven, attend a few black funerals. With characteristic eloquence, the preachers paint word pictures of a life so serene and sensuous that everyone in the congregation starts fidgeting to go there. The mourners feel grief, naturally, but in its proper place: as an interruption, a temporary setback in a battle whose end has already been determined.

I am convinced that for these neglected saints, who learned to anticipate and enjoy God in spite of the difficulties of their lives on earth, heaven will seem more like a long-awaited homecoming than a visit to a new place. In their lives, the Beatitudes have become true. To people who are trapped in pain, in broken homes, in economic chaos, in hatred and fear, in violence—to these, Jesus offers a promise of a time, far longer and more substantial than this time on earth, of health and wholeness and pleasure and peace. A time of reward.

The Great Reversal. Over time I learned to respect, and even long for, the rewards Jesus promised. Even so, these rewards lay somewhere in the future, and dangled promises do not satisfy immediate needs. Along the way, I have also come to believe that the Beatitudes describe the present as well as the future. They neatly contrast how to succeed in the kingdom of heaven as opposed to the kingdom of this world.

J. B. Phillips rendered the Beatitudes that apply in the kingdom of this world:

Happy are the "pushers": for they get on in the world.
Happy are the hard-boiled: for they never let life hurt them.
Happy are they who complain: for they get their own way
in the end.
Happy are the blasé: for they never worry over their sins.
Happy are the slave-drivers: for they get results.
Happy are the knowledgeable men of the world: for they know
their way around.
Happy are the trouble-makers: for they make people take notice
of them.*

*Indeed, it appears that Jesus adapted a form of proverbs common in his day to make the opposite point. According to Walter Kasper, Greek and Jewish wisdom

Modern society lives by the rules of survival of the fittest. "The one who dies with the most toys wins," reads one bumper sticker. So does the nation with the best weapons and the largest gross national product. The owner of the Chicago Bulls gave a compact summary of the rules governing the visible world on the occasion of Michael Jordan's (temporary) retirement. "He's living the American Dream," said Jerry Reinsdorf. "The American Dream is to reach a point in your life where you don't have to do anything you don't want to do and can do everything that you do want to do."

That may be the American Dream, but it decidedly is not Jesus' dream as revealed in the Beatitudes. The Beatitudes express quite plainly that God views this world through a different set of lenses. God seems to prefer the poor and those who mourn to the Fortune 500 and supermodels who frolic on the beach. Oddly, God may prefer South Central L. A. to Malibu Beach, and Rwanda to Monte Carlo. In fact, one could almost subtitle the Sermon on the Mount not "survival of the fittest" but "triumph of the victims."

Various scenes in the Gospels give a good picture of the kind of people who impressed Jesus. A widow who placed her last two cents in the offering. A dishonest tax collector so riddled with anxiety that he climbed a tree to get a better view of Jesus. A nameless, nondescript child. A woman with a string of five unhappy marriages. A blind beggar. An adulteress. A man with leprosy. Strength, good looks, connections, and the competitive instinct may bring a person success in a society like ours, but those very qualities may block entrance to the kingdom of heaven. Dependence, sorrow, repentance, a longing to change—these are the gates to God's kingdom.

"Blessed are the poor in spirit," said Jesus. One commentary translates that "Blessed are the desperate." With nowhere else to turn, the desperate just may turn to Jesus, the only one who can offer the deliverance they long for. Jesus really believed that a person who is poor in spirit, or mourning, or persecuted, or hungry and thirsty for righteousness has a peculiar "advantage" over the rest of us. Maybe,

literature describes as blessed the man who has obedient children, a good wife, faithful friends, is successful, and so forth. Jesus added a contrarian twist to what the audience expected.

just maybe, the desperate person will cry out to God for help. If so, that person is truly blessed.

Catholic scholars coined the phrase "God's preferential option for the poor" to describe a phenomenon they found throughout both the Old and New Testaments: God's partiality toward the poor and the disadvantaged. *Why would God single out the poor for special attention over any other group?* I used to wonder. What makes the poor deserving of God's concern? I received help on this issue from a writer named Monika Hellwig, who lists the following "advantages" to being poor:

1. The poor know they are in urgent need of redemption.
2. The poor know not only their dependence on God and on powerful people but also their interdependence with one another.
3. The poor rest their security not on things but on people.
4. The poor have no exaggerated sense of their own importance, and no exaggerated need of privacy.
5. The poor expect little from competition and much from cooperation.
6. The poor can distinguish between necessities and luxuries.
7. The poor can wait, because they have acquired a kind of dogged patience born of acknowledged dependence.
8. The fears of the poor are more realistic and less exaggerated, because they already know that one can survive great suffering and want.
9. When the poor have the Gospel preached to them, it sounds like good news and not like a threat or a scolding.
10. The poor can respond to the call of the Gospel with a certain abandonment and uncomplicated totality because they have so little to lose and are ready for anything.

In summary, through no choice of their own—they may urgently wish otherwise—poor people find themselves in a posture that befits the grace of God. In their state of neediness, dependence, and dissatisfaction with life, they may welcome God's free gift of love.

As an exercise I went back over Monika Hellwig's list, substituting the word "rich" for "poor," and changing each sentence to its opposite. "The rich do not know they are in urgent need of redemption. . . . The rich rest their security not on people but on things. . . ." (Jesus did something similar in Luke's version of the Beatitudes, but that portion gets much less attention: "But woe to you who are rich, for you have already received your comfort. . . .")

Next, I tried something far more threatening: I substituted the word "I." Reviewing each of the ten statements, I asked myself if my own attitudes more resembled those of the poor or of the rich. Do I easily acknowledge my needs? Do I readily depend on God and on other people? Where does my security rest? Am I more likely to compete or cooperate? Can I distinguish between necessities and luxuries? Am I patient? Do the Beatitudes sound to me like good news or like a scolding?

As I did this exercise I began to realize why so many saints voluntarily submit to the discipline of poverty. Dependence, humility, simplicity, cooperation, and a sense of abandon are qualities greatly prized in the spiritual life, but extremely elusive for people who live in comfort. There may be other ways to God but, oh, they are hard—as hard as a camel squeezing through the eye of a needle. In the Great Reversal of God's kingdom, prosperous saints are very rare.

I do not believe the poor to be more virtuous than anyone else (though I have found them more compassionate and often more generous), but they are less likely to *pretend* to be virtuous. They have not the arrogance of the middle class, who can skillfully disguise their problems under a facade of self-righteousness. They are more naturally dependent, because they have no choice; they must depend on others simply to survive.

I now view the Beatitudes not as patronizing slogans, but as profound insights into the mystery of human existence. God's kingdom turns the tables upside down. The poor, the hungry, the mourners, and the oppressed truly are blessed. Not because of their miserable states, of course—Jesus spent much of his life trying to remedy those miseries. Rather, they are blessed because of an innate advantage they hold over those more comfortable and self-sufficient. People who are rich, successful, and beautiful may well go through life relying on their natural gifts. People who lack such natural advantages, hence underqualified for success in the kingdom of this world, just might turn to God in their time of need.

Human beings do not readily admit desperation. When they do, the kingdom of heaven draws near.

Psychological Reality. More recently, I have come to see a third level of truth in the Beatitudes. Not only did Jesus offer an ideal for us to strive toward, with appropriate rewards in view; not only did he turn the tables on our success-addicted society; he also set forth a plain formula of psychological truth, the deepest level of truth that we can know on earth.

The Beatitudes reveal that what succeeds in the kingdom of heaven also benefits us most in this life here and now. It has taken me many years to recognize this fact, and only now am I beginning to understand the Beatitudes. They still jar me every time I read them, but they jar me because I recognize in them a richness that unmasks my own poverty.

Blessed are the poor in spirit . . . Blessed are the meek. A book like Paul Johnson's *Intellectuals* sets out in convincing detail what all of us know to be true: the people we laud, strive to emulate, and feature on the covers of popular magazines are not the fulfilled, happy, balanced persons we might imagine. Although Johnson's subjects (Ernest Hemingway, Bertrand Russell, Jean-Paul Sartre, Edmund Wilson, Bertolt Brecht, et al.) would be judged successful by any modern standard, it would be difficult to assemble a more miserable, egomaniacal, abusive company.

My career as a journalist has afforded me opportunities to interview "stars," including NFL football greats, movie actors, music performers, bestselling authors, politicians, and TV personalities. These are the people who dominate the media. We fawn over them, poring over the minutiae of their lives: the clothes they wear, the food they eat, the aerobic routines they follow, the people they love, the toothpaste they use. Yet I must tell you that, in my limited experience, I have found Paul Johnson's principle to hold true: our "idols" are as miserable a group of people as I have ever met. Most have troubled or broken marriages. Nearly all are incurably dependent on psychotherapy. In a heavy irony, these larger-than-life heroes seem tormented by self-doubt.

I have also spent time with people I call "servants." Doctors and nurses who work among the ultimate outcasts, leprosy patients in rural India. A Princeton graduate who runs a hotel for the homeless in Chicago. Health workers who have left high-paying jobs to serve in a backwater town of Mississippi. Relief workers in Somalia, Sudan, Ethiopia, Bangladesh, and other repositories of human suffering. The Ph.D.s I met in Arizona, who are now scattered throughout jungles of South America translating the Bible into obscure languages.

I was prepared to honor and admire these servants, to hold them up as inspiring examples. I was not prepared to envy them. Yet as I now reflect on the two groups side by side, stars and servants, the servants clearly emerge as the favored ones, the graced ones. Without question, I would rather spend time among the servants than among the stars: they possess qualities of depth and richness and even joy that I have not found elsewhere. Servants work for low pay, long hours, and no applause, "wasting" their talents and skills among the poor and uneducated. Somehow, though, in the process of losing their lives they find them.

The poor in spirit and the meek are indeed blessed, I now believe. Theirs is the kingdom of heaven, and it is they who will inherit the earth.

Blessed are the pure in heart. During a period of my life when I was battling sexual temptation, I came across an article that referred me to a thin book, *What I Believe,* by the French Catholic writer François Mauriac. It surprised me that Mauriac, an old man, devoted considerable space to a discussion of his own lust. He explained, "Old age risks being a period of redoubled testing because the imagination in an old man is substituted in a horrible way for what nature refuses him."

I knew that Mauriac understood lust. *Viper's Tangle* and *A Kiss for the Leper,* novels which helped win him the Nobel prize in literature, portray lust, repression, and sexual anger as well as anything I have ever read. For Mauriac, sexual temptation was a familiar battleground.

Mauriac dismissed most of the arguments in favor of sexual purity that he had been taught in his Catholic upbringing. "Marriage will cure lust": it did not for Mauriac, as it has not for so many others, because lust involves the attraction of unknown creatures and the taste for adventure and chance meetings. "With self-discipline you can master lust": Mauriac found that sexual desire is like a tidal wave powerful enough to bear away all the best intentions. "True fulfillment can only be found in monogamy": this may be true, but it certainly does not *seem* true to someone who finds no slackening of sexual urges even in monogamy. Thus he weighed the traditional arguments for purity and found them wanting.

Mauriac concluded that self-discipline, repression, and rational argument are inadequate weapons to use in fighting the impulse toward impurity. In the end, he could find only one reason to be pure, and that is what Jesus presented in the Beatitudes: "Blessed are the pure in heart, for they will see God." In Mauriac's words, "Impurity separates us from God. The spiritual life obeys laws as verifiable as those of the physical world.... Purity is the condition for a higher love—for a possession superior to all possessions: that of God. Yes, this is what is at stake, and nothing less."

Reading François Mauriac's words did not end my struggle with lust. But I must say beyond all doubt that I have found his analysis to be true. The love God holds out to us requires that our faculties be cleansed and purified before we can receive a higher love, one attainable in no other way. That is the motive to stay pure. By harboring lust, I limit my own intimacy with God.

The pure in heart are truly blessed, for they will see God. It is as simple, and as difficult, as that.

Blessed are the merciful. I learned the truth of this Beatitude from Henri Nouwen, a priest who used to teach at Harvard University. At the height of his career, Nouwen moved from Harvard to a community called Daybreak, near Toronto, in order to take on the demanding chores required by his friendship with a man named Adam. Nouwen now ministers not to intellectuals but to a young man who is considered by many a useless person who should have been aborted. Nouwen describes his friend:

Adam is a 25-year-old man who cannot speak, cannot dress or undress himself, cannot walk alone, cannot eat without much help. He does not cry or laugh. Only occasionally does he make eye contact. His back is distorted. His arm and leg movements are twisted. He suffers from severe epilepsy and, despite heavy medication, sees few days without grand-mal seizures. Sometimes, as he grows suddenly rigid, he utters a howling groan. On a few occasions I've seen one big tear roll down his cheek.

It takes me about an hour and a half to wake Adam up, give him his medication, carry him into his bath, wash him, shave him, clean his teeth, dress him, walk him to the kitchen, give him his breakfast, put him in his wheelchair and bring him to the place where he spends most of the day with therapeutic exercises.

On a visit to Nouwen in Toronto, I watched him perform that routine with Adam, and I must admit I had a fleeting doubt as to whether this was the best use of his time. I have heard Henri Nouwen speak, and have read many of his books. He has much to offer. Could not someone else take over the menial task of caring for Adam? When I cautiously broached the subject with Nouwen himself, he informed me that I had completely misinterpreted what was going on. "I am not giving up anything," he insisted. "It is *I*, not Adam, who gets the main benefit from our friendship."

Then Nouwen began listing for me all the benefits he has gained. The hours spent with Adam, he said, have given him an inner peace so fulfilling that it makes most of his other, more high-minded tasks seem boring and superficial by contrast. Early on, as he sat beside that helpless child-man, he realized how marked with rivalry and competition, how obsessive, was his drive for success in academia and Christian ministry. Adam taught him that "what makes us human is not our mind but our heart, not our ability to think but our ability to love." From Adam's simple nature, he had glimpsed the "emptiness" necessary before one can be filled by God—the kind of emptiness that desert monks achieved only after much searching and discipline.

All during the rest of our interview, Henri Nouwen circled back to my question, as if he could not believe I could ask such a thing. He kept thinking of other ways he had benefited from his relationship with Adam. Truly, he was enjoying a new kind of spiritual peace, acquired not within the stately quadrangles of Harvard, but by the bedside of incontinent Adam. I left Daybreak convicted of my own spiritual poverty, I who so carefully arrange my writer's life to make it efficient and single-focused. The merciful are indeed blessed, I learned, for they will be shown mercy.

Blessed are the peacemakers . . . Blessed are those who are persecuted for the sake of righteousness. This truth came to me in a roundabout way. The great novelist Leo Tolstoy tried to follow it, but his irascible temper kept getting in the way of peacemaking. Tolstoy did write eloquently about the Sermon on the Mount, however, and half a century later a Hindu ascetic named Mohandas Gandhi read *The Kingdom of God Is Within You* by Tolstoy and decided to live by the literal principles of the Sermon on the Mount.

The movie *Gandhi* contains a fine scene in which Gandhi tries to explain his philosophy to the Presbyterian missionary Charlie Andrews. Walking together in a South African city, the two suddenly find their way blocked by young thugs. The Reverend Andrews takes one look at the menacing gangsters and decides to run for it. Gandhi stops him. "Doesn't the New Testament say if an enemy strikes you on the right cheek you should offer him the left?" Andrews mumbles that he thought the phrase was used metaphorically. "I'm not so sure," Gandhi replies. "I suspect he meant you must show courage—be willing to take a blow, several blows, to show you will not strike back nor will you be turned aside. And when you do that it calls on something in human nature, something that makes his hatred decrease and his respect increase. I think Christ grasped that and I have seen it work."

Years later an American minister, Martin Luther King Jr., studied Gandhi's tactics and decided to put them into practice in the United States. Many blacks abandoned King over the issue of nonviolence and drifted toward "black power" rhetoric. After you've been hit on the head with a policeman's nightstick for the dozenth time and received yet another jolt from a jailer's cattle prod, you begin to question the effectiveness of nonviolence. But King himself never wavered.

As riots broke out in places like Los Angeles, Chicago, and Harlem, King traveled from city to city trying to cool tempers, forcefully reminding demonstrators that moral change is not accomplished through immoral means. He had learned that principle from the Sermon on the Mount and from Gandhi, and almost all his speeches reiterated the message. "Christianity," he said, "has always insisted that the cross we bear precedes the crown we wear. To be a Christian one must take up his cross, with all its difficulties and agonizing and tension-packed content, and carry it until that very cross leaves its mark upon us and redeems us to that more excellent way which comes only through suffering."

Martin Luther King Jr. had some weaknesses, but one thing he got right. Against all odds, against all instincts of self-preservation, he stayed true to the principle of peacemaking. He did not strike back. Where others called for revenge, he called for love. The civil rights marchers put their bodies on the line before sheriffs with nightsticks and fire hoses and snarling German shepherds. That, in fact, was what brought them the victory they had been seeking so long. Historians point to one event as the single moment in which the movement attained a critical mass of public support for its cause. It occurred on a bridge outside Selma, Alabama, when Sheriff Jim Clark turned his policemen loose on unarmed black demonstrators. The American public, horrified by the scene of violent injustice, at last gave assent to passage of a civil rights bill.

I grew up in Atlanta, across town from Martin Luther King Jr., and I confess with some shame that while he was leading marches in places like Selma and Montgomery and Memphis, I was on the side of the white sheriffs with the nightsticks and German shepherds. I was quick to pounce on his moral flaws and slow to recognize my own blind sin. But because he stayed faithful, by offering his body as a target but never as a weapon, he broke through my moral calluses.

The real goal, King used to say, was not to defeat the white man, but "to awaken a sense of shame within the oppressor and challenge his false sense of superiority. . . . The end is reconciliation; the end is redemption; the end is the creation of the beloved community." And that is what Martin Luther King Jr. finally set into motion, even in racists like me.

King, like Gandhi before him, died a martyr. After his death, more and more people began adopting the principle of nonviolent protest as a way to demand justice. In the Philippines, after Benigno Aquino's martyrdom, ordinary people brought down a government by gathering in the streets to pray; army tanks rolled to a stop before the kneeling Filipinos as if blocked by an invisible force. Later, in the remarkable year of 1989, in Poland, Hungary, Czechoslovakia, East Germany, Bulgaria, Yugoslavia, Romania, Mongolia, Albania, the Soviet Union, Nepal, and Chile, more than half a billion people threw off the yoke of oppression through nonviolent means. In many of these places, especially the nations of Eastern Europe, the Christian church led the way. Protesters marched through the streets carrying candles, singing hymns, and praying. As in Joshua's day, the walls came tumbling down.

Peacemakers will be called sons and daughters of God. Blessed also are those who are persecuted because of righteousness, for theirs is the kingdom of heaven.

Blessed are those who mourn. Because I have written books with titles like *Where Is God When It Hurts?* and *Disappointment with God,* I have spent time among mourners. They intimidated me at first. I had few answers for the questions they were asking, and I felt awkward in the presence of their grief. I remember especially one year when, at the invitation of a neighbor, I joined a therapy group at a nearby hospital. This group, called Make Today Count, consisted of people who were dying, and I accompanied my neighbor to their meetings for a year.

Certainly I cannot say that I "enjoyed" the gatherings; that would be the wrong word. Yet the meetings became for me one of the most meaningful events of each month. In contrast to a party, where participants try to impress each other with signs of status and power, in this group no one was trying to impress. Clothes, fashions, apartment furnishings, job titles, new cars—what do these things mean to people who are preparing to die? More than any other people I had met, the Make Today Count group members concentrated on ultimate issues. I found myself wishing that some of my shallow, hedonistic friends would attend a meeting.

Later, when I wrote about what I had learned from grieving and suffering people, I began hearing from strangers. I have three folders, each one several inches thick, filled with these letters. They are among my most precious possessions. One letter, twenty-six pages long, was written on blue-lined note paper by a mother sitting in a lounge outside a room where surgeons were operating on her four-year-old daughter's brain tumor. Another came from a quadriplegic who "wrote" by making puffs of air into a tube, which a computer translated into letters on a printer.

Many of the people who have written me have no happy endings to their stories. Some still feel abandoned by God. Few have found answers to the "Why?" questions. But I have seen enough grief that I have gained faith in Jesus' promise that those who mourn will be comforted.

I know two small-scale ministries, run from private homes, that have developed out of grief. The first came into being when a woman in California discovered that her son, the apple of her eye, was dying of AIDS. She got little sympathy and support from her church and community because of the young man's homosexuality. She felt so alone and needy that she decided to start a newsletter that now brings together a network of parents of gay people. Although she offers little professional help and promises no magic cures, now hundreds of other parents view this courageous woman as a lifesaver.

Another woman, in Wisconsin, lost her only son in a Marine Corps helicopter crash. For years she could not escape the dark cloud of grief. She kept her son's room intact just as he had left it. Eventually, she began to notice how frequently helicopter crashes were reported on the news. She kept thinking of other families facing tragedies like hers, and wondering whether she could do something to help. Now, whenever a military helicopter crashes, she sends a packet of letters and helpful materials to an officer in the Defense Department who forwards the packet on to the affected family. About half of them strike up a regular correspondence, and in her retirement this Wisconsin woman directs her own "community of suffering." The activity has not solved the grief for her son, of course, but it has given her a sense of meaning, and she no longer feels helpless against that grief.

There is no more effective healer, I have found, than what Henri Nouwen calls "a wounded healer." Blessed are those who mourn, for they will be comforted.

Blessed are those who hunger and thirst for righteousness. In a sense, everyone I have mentioned in this litany of the Beatitudes manifests this final promise of Jesus. The "servants" who invest their lives among the poor and needy, François Mauriac striving to stay pure, Henri Nouwen bathing and dressing Adam, Martin Luther King Jr. and the disciples of nonviolence, mothers of gay men and Marine pilots who reach out beyond their grief—all these are responding to pangs of hunger and thirst for righteousness. All of them have received a reward, not only in the life to come, but in this life as well.

An Albanian nun spent sixteen years in an exclusive convent teaching geography to the wealthiest Bengali and British daughters of Calcutta. One day, on a railway trip to the Himalayas, she heard a voice calling her to change paths and minister to the poorest of the poor. Can anyone really doubt that Mother Teresa has found more personal fulfillment in her latter occupation than in her former? I have seen this principle borne out in saints and in ordinary people so often that I now easily understand why the Gospels repeat the one saying of Jesus more than any other: "Whoever wants to save his life will lose it, but whoever loses his life for my sake will find it."

Jesus came, he told us, not to destroy life but that we may have it more abundantly, "life ... to the full." Paradoxically, we get this abundant life in ways we may not have counted on. We get it by investing in others, by taking courageous stands for justice, by ministering to the weak and needy, by pursuing God and not self. I would not dare feel pity for any of the people I have just mentioned, though all have lived with hardship. For all their "sacrifices," they seem to me more fully alive, not less. Those who hunger and thirst for righteousness get filled.

In the Beatitudes, strange sayings that at first glance seem absurd, Jesus offers a paradoxical key to abundant life. The kingdom of heaven, he said elsewhere, is like a treasure of such value that any shrewd investor would "in his joy" sell all he has in order to buy it. It represents value far more real and permanent than anything the world has to offer, for this treasure will pay dividends both here on earth and also in the life to come. Jesus places the emphasis not on what we give up but on what we receive. Is it not in our own self-interest to pursue such a treasure?

127

When I first heard the Beatitudes, they sounded to me like impossible ideals given by some dreamy mystic. Now, though, I see them as truths proclaimed by a realist every bit as pragmatic as General Norman Schwarzkopf. Jesus knew how life works, in the kingdom of heaven as well as the kingdom of this world. In a life characterized by poverty, mourning, meekness, a hunger for righteousness, mercy, purity, peacemaking, and persecution, Jesus himself embodied the Beatitudes. Perhaps he even conceived the Beatitudes as a sermon to himself as well as to the rest of us, for he would have much opportunity to practice these hard truths.

CHAPTER 7

MESSAGE:
A SERMON OF OFFENSE

⚯

The test of observance of Christ's teachings is our consciousness of our failure to attain an ideal perfection. The degree to which we draw near this perfection cannot be seen; all we can see is the extent of our deviation.

LEO TOLSTOY

MESSAGE:
A SERMON OF OFFENSE

⎯⎯⎯ ⚬⚬⚬ ⎯⎯⎯

The Beatitudes represent only the first step toward understanding the Sermon on the Mount. Long after I came to recognize the enduring truth of the Beatitudes, I still brooded over the uncompromising harshness of the rest of Jesus' sermon. Its absolutist quality left me gasping. "Be perfect, therefore, as your heavenly Father is perfect," Jesus said, his statement tucked almost casually between commands to love enemies and give away money. Be perfect like God? Whatever did he mean?

I cannot easily dismiss this extremism, because it turns up elsewhere in the Gospels. When a rich man asked Jesus what he should do to ensure eternal life, Jesus told him to give his money away—not 10 percent or 18.5 percent or even 50 percent, but all of it. When a disciple asked if he should forgive his brother seven times, Jesus replied, "I tell you, not seven times, but seventy-seven times." Other religions taught variations of the "Golden Rule," but stated in a more limited, negative form: "Don't do to others what you wouldn't want them to do to you." Jesus expanded the Rule into its unbounded form, "In everything, do to others what you would have them do to you."

Has anyone ever lived a life as perfect as God's? Has anyone ever followed the Golden Rule? How can we even respond to such impossible ideals? We humans prefer common sense and balance, something closer to Aristotle's Golden Mean than Jesus' Golden Rule.

A friend of mine named Virginia Stem Owens assigned the Sermon on the Mount to her composition class at Texas A&M University, asking the students to write a short essay. She had expected them to have a basic respect for the text, since the Bible Belt extends right across Texas, but her students' reactions soon disabused her of that notion. "In my opinion religion is one big hoax," wrote one. "There is an old saying that 'you shouldn't believe everything you read' and it applies in this case," wrote another.

Virginia recalled her own introduction to the Sermon on the Mount in Sunday school, where pastel poster illustrations showed Jesus sitting on a green hillside surrounded by eager, pink children. It never occurred to her to react with anger or disgust. Her students thought otherwise:

> The stuff the churches preach is extremely strict and allows for almost no fun without thinking it is a sin or not.

> I did not like the essay "Sermon on the Mount." It was hard to read and made me feel like I had to be perfect and no one is.

> The things asked in this sermon are absurd. To look at a woman is adultery. That is the most extreme, stupid, unhuman statement that I have ever heard.

"At this point," Virginia wrote about the experience, "I began to be encouraged. There is something exquisitely innocent about not realizing you shouldn't call Jesus stupid. . . . This was the real thing, a pristine response to the gospel, unfiltered through a two-millennia cultural haze. . . . I find it strangely heartening that the Bible remains offensive to honest, ignorant ears, just as it was in the first century. For me, that somehow validates its significance. Whereas the scriptures almost lost their characteristically astringent flavor during the past century, the current widespread biblical illiteracy should catapult us into a situation more nearly approximating that of their original, first-century audience."

Offensive, astringent—yes, these are apt words to apply to the Sermon on the Mount. As I viewed fifteen movie treatments of the scene, only one seemed to capture anything like the offense of the original. A low-budget BBC production entitled *Son of Man* sets the Sermon on the Mount against a background of chaos and violence. Roman soldiers have just invaded a Galilean village to exact vengeance for some trespass against the empire. They have strung up Jewish men of fighting age, shoved their hysterical wives to the ground, even speared babies in order to "teach these Jews a lesson." Into that tumultuous scene of blood and tears and keening for the dead strides Jesus with eyes ablaze.

I tell you: Love your enemies and pray for those that persecute you.

An eye for an eye, a tooth for a tooth, right? So our forefathers said. Love your kinsmen, hate your enemies, right? But I say it's easy to love your own brother, to love those who love you. Even tax collectors do that! You want me to congratulate you for loving your own kinsmen? No, Love your *enemy*.

Love the man who would kick you and spit at you. Love the soldier who would drive his sword in your belly. Love the brigand who robs and tortures you.

Listen to me! Love your enemy! If a Roman soldiers hits you on the left cheek, offer him the right one. If a man in authority orders you to walk one mile, walk two miles. If a man sues you for your coat, give him the shirt off your back.

Listen! I tell you, it is hard to follow me. What I'm saying to you hasn't been said since the world began!

You can imagine the villagers' response to such unwelcome advice. The Sermon on the Mount did not puzzle them; it infuriated them.

⁂

Early in the Sermon on the Mount, Jesus addressed head-on a question that worried most of his listeners: Was he a revolutionary or an authentic Jewish prophet? Here is Jesus' own description of his relationship to the Torah:

Do not think that I have come to abolish the Law or the Prophets; I have not come to abolish them but to fulfill them. . . .

For I tell you that unless your righteousness surpasses that of the Pharisees and the teachers of the law, you will certainly not enter the kingdom of heaven.

That last statement surely made the crowd sit up and take notice. Pharisees and teachers of the law competed with one another in strictness. They had atomized God's law into 613 rules—248 commands and 365 prohibitions—and bolstered these rules with 1,521 emendations. To avoid breaking the third commandment, "You shall not misuse the name of the LORD," they refused to pronounce God's name at all. To avoid sexual temptation they had a practice of lowering their heads and not even looking at women (the most scrupulous of these were known as "bleeding Pharisees" because of frequent collisions with walls and other obstacles). To avoid defiling the Sabbath they outlawed thirty-nine activities that might be construed as "work." How could an ordinary person's righteousness ever *surpass* that of such professional holy men?

The Sermon on the Mount details exactly what Jesus meant, and this explication is what seemed so absurd to twentieth-century students at Texas A&M as well as first-century Jews in Palestine. Using the Torah as a starting point, Jesus pushed the law in the same direction, further than any Pharisee had dared push it, further than any monk has dared live it. The Sermon on the Mount introduced a new moon in the moral universe that has exerted its own force of gravity ever since.

Jesus made the law impossible for anyone to keep and then charged us to keep it. Consider some examples.

Every human society in history has had a law against murder. There are variations, of course: the U.S. allows killing in self-defense or in unusual circumstances such as spouse abuse. But no society has come up with anything like Jesus' enlarged definition of murder: "I tell you that anyone who is angry with his brother will be subject to judgment. . . . anyone who says 'You fool!' will be in danger of the fire of hell." Growing up with an older brother, I fretted over this verse. Can two brothers weather the storms of adolescence without relying on words such as "stupid" and "fool"?

Every society also has taboos against sexual promiscuity. Today at least one college requires male students to ask females' permission for each stage of sexual contact. Meanwhile, some feminist groups are trying to forge a legal link between pornography and crimes against women. But no society has ever proposed a rule as strict as Jesus': "I tell you that anyone who looks at a woman lustfully has already committed adultery with her in his heart. If your right eye causes you to sin, gouge it out and throw it away. It is better for you to lose one part of your body than for your whole body to be thrown into hell."

I have heard calls for castration of serial rapists, but never have I heard a proposal for facial mutilation on account of lust. Indeed, lust in America is an established national pastime, celebrated in ads for blue jeans and beer, in the annual *Sports Illustrated* swimming suit issue, and in the twenty million copies of pornographic magazines sold each month. When presidential candidate Jimmy Carter tried to explain this verse in a *Playboy* magazine interview, the press reacted with what John Updike described as "nervous hilarity." "How strangely on modern ears," said Updike, "falls the notion that lust—sexual desire that wells up in us as involuntarily as saliva—in itself is wicked!"

As for divorce, in Jesus' day the Pharisees heatedly debated how to interpret the Old Testament rules. The prominent rabbi Hillel taught that a man could divorce his wife if she did anything at all to displease him, even something as trivial as burning his food; a husband needed only to pronounce "I divorce you" three times to make the divorce final. Jesus countered, "I tell you that anyone who divorces his wife, except for marital unfaithfulness, causes her to become an adulteress, and anyone who marries the divorced woman commits adultery."

Finally, Jesus spelled out the principle of nonviolence. Who could even survive with the rule Jesus laid down: "Do not resist an evil person. If someone strikes you on the right cheek, turn to him the other also. And if someone wants to sue you and take your tunic, let him have your cloak as well."

I stare at these and the other strict commands of the Sermon on the Mount and ask myself how to respond. Does Jesus really expect me to give to every panhandler who crosses my path? Should I abandon all insistence on consumer rights? Cancel my insurance policies and trust God for the future? Discard my television to avoid temptations to lust? How can I possibly translate such ethical ideals into my everyday life?

I once went on a reading binge in search of the "key" to understanding the Sermon on the Mount, and it brought some consolation to learn I was not the first to flounder over its high ideals. Throughout church history, people have found canny ways to reconcile Jesus' absolute demands with the grim reality of human delinquency.

Thomas Aquinas divided Jesus' teaching into Precepts and Counsels, which in more modern language we might rename Requirements and Suggestions. Precepts encompassed universal moral laws like the Ten Commandments. But for the more idealistic commands, such as Jesus' statements about anger and lust, Aquinas applied a different standard: though we should accept them as a good model and strive to fulfill them, they have not the moral force of Precepts. The Roman Catholic Church later codified Aquinas's distinctions into lists of "mortal" and "venial" sins.

Martin Luther interpreted the Sermon on the Mount in light of Jesus' formula "Give to Caesar what is Caesar's and to God what is God's." Christians maintain a dual citizenship, he said: one in the kingdom of Christ and one in the kingdom of the world. The extremism in the Sermon on the Mount applies absolutely to Christ's kingdom, but not to the world's. Take the commands to "Love your enemies" and "Do not resist an evil person"; of course these do not apply to the state! In order to prevent anarchy, a government must resist evil and repel enemies. Therefore, a Christian should learn to separate the office from the person: a Christian soldier, say, must carry out orders to fight and kill even while following Christ's law of love for enemies in his heart.

In Luther's day, various Anabaptist movements chose a radically different approach. All such attempts to water down Jesus' straightforward commands are misguided, they said. Had not the early church cited Christ's command to "love your enemies" more often than any other during its first four centuries? Simply read the Sermon on the Mount. Jesus does not differentiate between Precepts and Counsels, or the office and the person. He says don't resist an evil person, don't take oaths, give to the needy, love your enemies. We should follow his commands in the most literal way possible. For this reason some groups vowed to hold no personal property. Others, like the Quakers, refused to take oaths or doff their hats to a public official, and opposed having an army or even a police force. Subsequently, thousands of Anabaptists were killed in Europe, England, and Russia; many of the survivors made their way across the ocean to America, where they attempted to found colonies and communes based on the principles of the Sermon on the Mount.*

In nineteenth-century America a theological movement emerged with a new spin on the Sermon on the Mount. Dispensationalism explained such teaching as the last vestige of the age of Law, soon to be displaced by the age of Grace after Jesus' death and resurrection. Hence we need not follow its strict commands. The popular Scofield Bible described the sermon as "pure law" but with "beautiful moral application to the Christian."

Still another interpretation came from Albert Schweitzer, who saw the Sermon on the Mount as a set of interim demands for unusual times. Convinced that the world would soon end in the apocalypse, Jesus was setting into motion a kind of "martial law." Since the world did not end, we must now view his instructions differently.

Assiduously I studied all these movements, trying to understand the Sermon on the Mount from their vantage point—and, I must admit, trying to find a way to wriggle out from under its stern demands. Each school of thought contributed important insights, yet each also seemed to have a blind spot. Like most of the good doctor's elucidations, Aquinas's categories of Precepts and Counsels made fine common sense, but his was not a distinction Jesus made. Jesus seemed rather to equate the Precept "Do not commit adultery" with the Counsel " . . . anyone who looks at a woman lustfully has already committed adultery with her in his heart." Luther's solution seemed ingenious and wise, but World War II demonstrated the schizophrenic abuse it may allow. Many Lutheran Christians served in Hitler's army with a clear conscience: "just following orders," they carried out the office of the state while maintaining an inner allegiance to Christ.

---

*In response to Anabaptists, Luther scornfully wrote about a Christian who let lice nibble on him because he would not kill the vermin and thus risk defying the command "Resist not evil."

As for Anabaptists and other literalists, their nonviolent response to persecution stands as one of the shining moments in church history. Yet they themselves admitted their failure to fulfill literally every command in the Sermon on the Mount. Quakers, for example, found ways to circumvent the rules in order to help the cause of the American Revolution. And what of Jesus' unbending statements against anger and lust? Origen had taken the warning against lust to its literal extreme many centuries before, but the church, horrified, then banned his solution of castration.

Dispensationalists and apocalyptists found clever ways to dodge the harder requirements of Jesus' sermon, but they seemed to me just that: ways to dodge. Jesus himself gave no indication that his commands applied only for a short period or in special circumstances. He delivered them with authority ("But I say unto you . . .") and severity ("Anyone who breaks one of the least of these commandments and teaches others to do the same will be called least in the kingdom of heaven . . .").

No matter how hard I tried, I could not find an easy way around or through the Sermon on the Mount. Like a low-grade case of depression, my cognitive dissonance over Jesus' words kept me in a state of spiritual restlessness. If the Sermon on the Mount sets forth God's standard of holiness, I concluded, then I may as well resign from the start. The Sermon on the Mount did not help me improve; it simply revealed all the ways I had not.

―――

Ultimately I found a key to understanding the Sermon on the Mount, not in the writings of great theologians but in a more unlikely place: the writings of two nineteenth-century Russian novelists. From them I have gained my own view of the Sermon on the Mount and its mosaic of law and grace, consisting of one-half Tolstoy and one-half Dostoevsky.*

---

*In the early 1970s Malcolm Muggeridge was surprised to hear that members of the intellectual elite in the Soviet Union were experiencing a spiritual revival. Anatoli Kuznetsov, living in exile in England, told him there was scarcely a single

From Tolstoy I learned a deep respect for God's inflexible, absolute Ideal. The ethical ideals Tolstoy encountered in the Gospels attracted him like a flame, though his failure to live up to those ideals ultimately consumed him. Like the Anabaptists, Tolstoy strove to follow the Sermon on the Mount literally, and his intensity soon caused his family to feel like victims of his quest for holiness. For instance, after reading Jesus' command to the rich man to give away everything, Tolstoy decided to free serfs, give away his copyrights, and dispose of his vast estate. He wore peasant clothes, made his own shoes, and began working in the fields. His wife, Sonya, seeing the family's financial security about to vaporize, protested petulantly until he made some concessions.

As I read Tolstoy's diaries, I see flashbacks of my own lunges toward perfectionism. The diaries record many struggles between Tolstoy and his family, but many more between Tolstoy and himself. In an attempt to reach perfection he kept devising new lists of rules. He gave up hunting, smoking, drinking, and meat. He drafted "Rules for developing the emotional will. Rules for developing lofty feelings and eliminating base ones." Yet he could never achieve the self-discipline necessary to keep the rules. More than once, Tolstoy took a public vow of chastity and asked for separate bedrooms. He could never keep the vow for long, and much to his shame, Sonya's sixteen pregnancies broadcast to the world that inability.

Sometimes Tolstoy managed to accomplish great good. For example, after a long hiatus he wrote one last novel, *Resurrection*, at the age of seventy-one, in support of the Doukhobors—an Anabaptist group undergoing persecution by the tsar—donating all proceeds to finance their emigration to Canada. And, as I have mentioned, Tolstoy's philosophy of nonviolence, lifted directly from the Sermon on the Mount, had an impact that long outlived him, in ideological descendants like Gandhi and Martin Luther King Jr.

---

writer or artist or musician in the U.S.S.R. who was not exploring spiritual issues. Muggeridge said, "I asked him [Kuznetsov] how this could have happened, given the enormous anti-religious brainwashing job done on the citizenry, and the absence of all Christian literature, including the Gospels. His reply was memorable; the authorities, he said, forgot to suppress the works of Tolstoy and Dostoevsky, the most perfect expositions of the Christian faith of modern times."

For every Gandhi stirred by such high-minded ideals, though, there is a critic or biographer repelled by how miserably Tolstoy himself failed to meet those ideals. Frankly, he failed to practice what he preached. His wife put it well (in an obviously biased account):

> There is so little genuine warmth about him; his kindness does not come from his heart, but merely from his principles. His biographies will tell of how he helped the laborers to carry buckets of water, but no one will ever know that he never gave his wife a rest and never—in all these thirty-two years—gave his child a drink of water or spent five minutes by his bedside to give me a chance to rest a little from all my labors.

Tolstoy's ardent strides toward perfection never resulted in any semblance of peace or serenity. Up to the moment of his death the diaries and letters kept circling back to the rueful theme of failure. When he wrote about his religious faith, or attempted to live out that faith, the antagonism between the real and the ideal haunted him like a dybbuk. Too honest for self-deception, he could not silence the conscience that convicted him because he knew his conscience to be true.

Leo Tolstoy was a deeply unhappy man. He fulminated against the corrupt Russian Orthodox Church of his day and earned their excommunication. His schemes for self-improvement all foundered. He had to hide all the ropes on his estate and put away his guns in order to resist the temptation toward suicide. In the end, Tolstoy fled from his fame, his family, his estate, his identity; he died like a vagrant in a rural railroad station.

What, then, do I learn from the tragic life of Leo Tolstoy? I have read many of his religious writings, and without fail I come away inspired by his penetrating insight into God's Ideal. I have learned that, contrary to those who say the gospel solves our problems, in many ways—justice issues, money issues, race issues—the gospel actually adds to our burdens. Tolstoy saw this, and never lowered the ideals of the gospel. A man willing to free his serfs and give away his possessions in simple obedience to Christ's command is not easy to dismiss. If only he could live up to those ideals—if only I could live up to them.

To his critics Tolstoy replied, Don't judge God's holy ideals by my inability to meet them. Don't judge Christ by those of us who imperfectly bear his name. One passage especially, taken from a personal letter, shows how Tolstoy responded to such critics toward the end of his life. It stands as a summary of his spiritual pilgrimage, at once a ringing affirmation of the truth that he believed with all his heart and a plangent appeal for grace that he never fully realized.

"What about you, Lev Nikolayevich, you preach very well, but do you carry out what you preach?" This is the most natural of questions and one that is always asked of me; it is usually asked victoriously, as though it were a way of stopping my mouth. "You preach, but how do you live?" And I answer that I do not preach, that I am not able to preach, although I passionately wish to. I can preach only through my actions, and my actions are vile. . . . And I answer that I am guilty, and vile, and worthy of contempt for my failure to carry them out.

At the same time, not in order to justify, but simply in order to explain my lack of consistency, I say: "Look at my present life and then at my former life, and you will see that I do attempt to carry them out. It is true that I have not fulfilled one thousandth part of them [Christian precepts], and I am ashamed of this, but I have failed to fulfill them not because I did not wish to, but because I was unable to. Teach me how to escape from the net of temptations that surrounds me, help me and I will fulfill them; even without help I wish and hope to fulfill them.

"Attack me, I do this myself, but attack *me* rather than the path I follow and which I point out to anyone who asks me where I think it lies. If I know the way home and am walking along it drunkenly, is it any less the right way because I am staggering from side to side! If it is not the right way, then show me another way; but if I stagger and lose the way, you must help me, you must keep me on the true path, just as I am ready to support you. Do not mislead me, do not be glad that I have got lost, do not shout out joyfully: 'Look at him! He said he was going home, but there he is crawling into a bog!' No, do not gloat, but give me your help and support."

I feel sad as I read Tolstoy's religious writings. The X-ray vision into the human heart that made him a great novelist also made him a tortured Christian. Like a spawning salmon, he fought upstream all his life, in the end collapsing from moral exhaustion.

Yet I also feel grateful to Tolstoy, for his relentless pursuit of authentic faith has made an indelible impression upon me. I first came across his novels during a period when I was suffering the delayed effects of "biblical child abuse." The churches I grew up in contained too many frauds, or at least that is how I saw it in the arrogance of youth. When I observed the huge gap between the ideals of the gospel and the flaws of its followers, I was sorely tempted to abandon those ideals as hopelessly unattainable.

Then I discovered Tolstoy. He was the first author who, for me, accomplished that most difficult of tasks: to make Good as believable and appealing as Evil. I found in his novels, fables, and short stories a Vesuvian source of moral power. Unfailingly, he raised my sights.

A. N. Wilson, a biographer of Tolstoy, remarks that Tolstoy suffered from a "fundamental theological inability to understand the Incarnation. His religion was ultimately a thing of Law rather than of Grace, a scheme for human betterment rather than a vision of God penetrating a fallen world." With crystalline clarity Tolstoy could see his own inadequacy in the light of God's Ideal. But he could not take the further step of trusting God's grace to overcome that inadequacy.

Shortly after reading Tolstoy I discovered his countryman Fyodor Dostoevsky. These two, the most famous and accomplished of all Russian writers, lived and worked during the same period of history. Oddly, they never met, and perhaps it was just as well—they were opposites in every way. Where Tolstoy wrote bright, sunny novels, Dostoevsky wrote dark and brooding ones. Where Tolstoy worked out ascetic schemes for self-improvement, Dostoevsky periodically squandered his health and fortune on alcohol and gambling. Dostoevsky got many things wrong, but he got one thing right: His novels communicate grace and forgiveness with a Tolstoyan force.

Early in his life, Dostoevsky underwent a virtual resurrection. He had been arrested for belonging to a group judged treasonous by Tsar

Nicholas I, who, to impress upon the young parlor radicals the gravity of their errors, sentenced them to death and staged a mock execution. The conspirators were dressed in white death gowns and led to a public square where a firing squad awaited them. Blindfolded, robed in white burial shrouds, hands bound tightly behind them, they were paraded before a gawking crowd and then tied to posts. At the very last instant, as the order, "Ready, aim!" was heard and rifles were cocked and lifted upward, a horseman galloped up with a pre-arranged message from the tsar: he would mercifully commute their sentences to hard labor.

Dostoevsky never recovered from this experience. He had peered into the jaws of death, and from that moment life became for him precious beyond all calculation. "Now my life will change," he said; "I shall be born again in a new form." As he boarded the convict train toward Siberia, a devout woman handed him a New Testament, the only book allowed in prison. Believing that God had given him a second chance to fulfill his calling, Dostoevsky pored over that New Testament during his confinement. After ten years he emerged from exile with unshakable Christian convictions, as expressed in one famous passage, "If anyone proved to me that Christ was outside the truth . . . then I would prefer to remain with Christ than with the truth."

Prison offered Dostoevsky another opportunity as well. It forced him to live at close quarters with thieves, murderers, and drunken peasants. His shared life with these people later led to unmatched characterizations in his novels, such as that of the murderer Raskolnikov in *Crime and Punishment*. Dostoevsky's liberal view of the inherent goodness in humanity shattered in collision with the granitic evil he found in his cellmates. Yet over time he also glimpsed the image of God in even the lowest of prisoners. He came to believe that only through being loved is a human being capable of love; "We love because he [God] first loved us," as the apostle John says.

I encountered grace in the novels of Dostoevsky. *Crime and Punishment* portrays a despicable human being who commits a despicable crime. Yet grace enters Raskolnikov's life as well, through the person of the converted prostitute Sonia, who follows him all the way to Siberia and leads him to redemption. *The Brothers Karamazov*, perhaps the greatest novel ever written, draws a contrast between Ivan the brilliant agnostic and his devout brother Alyosha. Ivan can critique the failures of humankind and every political system devised to deal with those failures, but he can offer no solutions. Alyosha has no solutions for the intellectual problems Ivan raises, but he has a solution for humanity: love. "I do not know the answer to the problem of evil," said Alyosha, "but I do know love." Finally, in the magical novel *The Idiot*, Dostoevsky presents a Christ figure in the form of an epileptic prince. Quietly, mysteriously, Prince Myshkin moves among the circles of Russia's upper class, exposing their hypocrisy while also illuminating their lives with goodness and truth.

Taken together, these two Russians became for me, at a crucial time in my Christian pilgrimage, spiritual directors. They helped me come to terms with a central paradox of the Christian life. From Tolstoy I learned the need to look inside, to the kingdom of God that is within me. I saw how miserably I had failed the high ideals of the gospel. But from Dostoevsky I learned the full extent of grace. Not only the kingdom of God is within me; Christ himself dwells there. "Where sin increased, grace increased all the more," is how Paul expressed it in Romans.

There is only one way for any of us to resolve the tension between the high ideals of the gospel and the grim reality of ourselves: to accept that we will never measure up, but that we do not have to. We are judged by the righteousness of the Christ who lives within, not our own. Tolstoy got it halfway right: anything that makes me feel comfort with God's moral standard, anything that makes me feel, "At last I have arrived," is a cruel deception. But Dostoevsky got the other half right: anything that makes me feel discomfort with God's forgiving love is also a cruel deception. "There is now no condemnation for those who are in Christ Jesus": that message, Leo Tolstoy never fully grasped.

Absolute ideals and absolute grace: after learning that dual message from Russian novelists, I returned to Jesus and found that it suffuses his teaching throughout the Gospels and especially in the Sermon on the Mount. In his response to the rich young ruler, in the parable of the Good Samaritan, in his comments about divorce, money, or any other moral issue, Jesus never lowered God's Ideal. "Be perfect, therefore, as your heavenly Father is perfect," he said. "Love the Lord your God with all your heart and with all your soul and with all your mind." Not Tolstoy, not Francis of Assisi, not Mother Teresa, not anyone has completely fulfilled those commands.

Yet the same Jesus tenderly offered absolute grace. Jesus forgave an adulteress, a thief on the cross, a disciple who had denied ever knowing him. He tapped that traitorous disciple, Peter, to found his church and for the next advance turned to a man named Saul, who had made his mark persecuting Christians. Grace is absolute, inflexible, all-encompassing. It extends even to the people who nailed Jesus to the cross: "Father, forgive them, for they do not know what they are doing" were among the last words Jesus spoke on earth.

For years I had felt so unworthy before the absolute ideals of the Sermon on the Mount that I had missed in it any notion of grace. Once I understood the dual message, however, I went back and found that the message of grace gusts through the entire speech. It begins with the Beatitudes—Blessed are the poor in spirit, those who mourn, the meek; blessed are the desperate—and it moves toward the Lord's Prayer: "Forgive us our debts ... deliver us from the evil one." Jesus began this great sermon with gentle words for those in need and continued on with a prayer that has formed a model for all twelve-step groups. "One day at a time," say the alcoholics in AA; "Give us this day our daily bread," say the Christians. Grace is for the desperate, the needy, the broken, those who cannot make it on their own. Grace is for all of us.

For years I had thought of the Sermon on the Mount as a blueprint for human behavior that no one could possibly follow. Reading it again, I found that Jesus gave these words not to cumber us, but to tell us what *God* is like. The character of God is the urtext of the Sermon on the Mount. Why should we love our enemies? Because our clement Father causes his sun to rise on the evil and the good. Why be perfect? Because God is perfect. Why store up treasures in heaven? Because the Father lives there and will lavishly reward us. Why live without fear and worry? Because the same God who clothes the lilies and the grass of the field has promised to take care of us. Why pray?

If an earthly father gives his son bread or fish, how much more will the Father in heaven give good gifts to those who ask him.

How could I have missed it? Jesus did not proclaim the Sermon on the Mount so that we would, Tolstoy-like, furrow our brows in despair over our failure to achieve perfection. He gave it to impart to us God's Ideal toward which we should never stop striving, but also to show that none of us will ever reach that Ideal. The Sermon on the Mount forces us to recognize the great distance between God and us, and any attempt to reduce that distance by somehow moderating its demands misses the point altogether.

The worst tragedy would be to turn the Sermon on the Mount into another form of legalism; it should rather put an end to all legalism. Legalism like the Pharisees' will always fail, not because it is too strict but because it is not strict enough. Thunderously, inarguably, the Sermon on the Mount proves that before God we all stand on level ground: murderers and temper-throwers, adulterers and lusters, thieves and coveters. We are all desperate, and that is in fact the only state appropriate to a human being who wants to know God. Having fallen from the absolute Ideal, we have nowhere to land but in the safety net of absolute grace.

MISSION:
A REVOLUTION OF GRACE

The quality of mercy is not strained.
It droppeth as the gentle rain from heaven . . .
And earthly power doth then show likest God's
When mercy seasons justice.

SHAKESPEARE, THE MERCHANT OF VENICE

MISSION:
A REVOLUTION OF GRACE

———— ∞∞ ————

As my class in Chicago read the Gospels and watched movies about Jesus' life, we noticed a striking pattern: the more unsavory the characters, the more at ease they seemed to feel around Jesus. People like these found Jesus appealing: a Samaritan social outcast, a military officer of the tyrant Herod, a quisling tax collector, a recent hostess to seven demons.

In contrast, Jesus got a chilly response from more respectable types. Pious Pharisees thought him uncouth and worldly, a rich young ruler walked away shaking his head, and even the open-minded Nicodemus sought a meeting under the cover of darkness.

I remarked to the class how strange this pattern seemed, since the Christian church now attracts respectable types who closely resemble the people most suspicious of Jesus on earth. What has happened to reverse the pattern of Jesus' day? Why don't sinners *like* being around us?

I recounted a story told me by a friend who works with the down-and-out in Chicago. A prostitute came to him in wretched straits, homeless, her health failing, unable to buy food for her two-year-old daughter. Her eyes awash with tears, she confessed that she had been renting out her daughter—two years old!—to men interested in kinky sex, in order to support her own drug habit. My friend could hardly bear hearing the sordid details of her story. He sat in silence, not knowing what to say. At last he asked if she had ever thought of going to a church for help. "I will never forget the look of pure astonishment that crossed her face," he later told me. "'Church!' she cried. 'Why would I ever go there? They'd just make me feel even worse than I already do!'"

Somehow we have created a community of respectability in the church, I told my class. The down-and-out, who flocked to Jesus when he lived on earth, no longer feel welcome. How did Jesus, the only perfect person in history, manage to attract the notoriously imperfect? And what keeps us from following in his steps today?

Someone in the class suggested that legalism in the church had created a barrier of strict rules that made non-Christians feel uncomfortable. The class discussion abruptly lurched in a new direction, as survivors of Christian colleges and fundamentalist churches began swapping war stories. I told of my own bemusement in the early seventies when the redoubtable Moody Bible Institute, located just four blocks down the street from our church, was banning all beards, mustaches, and hair below the ears of male students—though each day students filed past a large oil painting of Dwight L. Moody, hirsute breaker of all three rules.

Everyone laughed. Everyone except Greg, that is, who fidgeted in his seat and smoldered. I could see his face flush red, then blanch with anger. Finally Greg raised his hand, and rage and indignation spilled out. He was almost stammering. "I feel like walking out of this place," he said, and all of a sudden the room hushed. "You criticize others for being Pharisees. I'll tell you who the real Pharisees are. They're *you* [he pointed at me] and the rest of you people in this class. You think you're so high and mighty and mature. I became a Christian because of Moody Church. You find a group to look down on, to feel more spiritual than, and you talk about them behind their backs. That's what a Pharisee does. You're all Pharisees."

All eyes in the class turned to me for a reply, but I had none to offer. Greg had caught us red-handed. In a twist of spiritual arrogance, we were now looking down on other people for being Pharisees. I glanced at the clock, hoping for a reprieve. No such luck: It showed fifteen minutes of class time remaining. I waited for a flash of inspiration, but none came. The silence grew louder. I felt embarrassed and trapped.

Then Bob raised his hand. Bob was new to the class, and until the day I die I will always be grateful to him for rescuing me. He began softly, disarmingly, "I'm glad you didn't walk out, Greg. We need you here. I'm glad you're here, and I'd like to tell you why I come to this church.

"Frankly, I identify with the Chicago prostitute Philip mentioned. I was addicted to drugs, and in a million years it wouldn't have occurred to me to approach a church for help. Every Tuesday, though, this church lets an Alcoholics Anonymous chapter meet in the basement room we're sitting in right now. I started attending that group, and after a while I decided a church that welcomes an AA group— cigarette butts, coffee spills, and all—can't be too bad, so I made a point to visit a service.

"I've got to tell you, the people upstairs were threatening to me at first. They seemed like they had it all together while I was barely hanging on. People here dress pretty casually, I guess, but the best clothes I owned were blue jeans and T-shirts. I managed to swallow my pride, though, and started coming on Sunday mornings as well as Tuesday nights. People didn't shun me. They reached out to me. It's here that I met Jesus."

As if someone had opened an air lock, all tension discharged from the room during Bob's speech of simple eloquence. Greg relaxed, I mumbled an apology for my own Pharisaism, and the class ended on a note of unity. Bob had brought us back to common ground, as sinners equally desperate in our need of God.

What would it take, I asked in closing, for church to become a place where prostitutes, tax collectors, and even guilt-tinged Pharisees would gladly gather?

Jesus was the friend of sinners. They liked being around him and longed for his company. Meanwhile, legalists found him shocking, even revolting. What was Jesus' secret that we have lost?

"You can know a person by the company he keeps," the proverb goes. Imagine the consternation of people in first-century Palestine who tried to apply that principle to Jesus of Nazareth. The Gospels mention eight occasions when Jesus accepted an invitation to dinner. Three of these (the wedding at Cana, hospitality by Mary and Martha, and the interrupted meal in Emmaus after his resurrection) were normal social occasions among friends. The other five, however, defy all rules of social propriety.

Once, Jesus dined with Simon the Leper. Because of my work with Dr. Paul Brand, a leprosy specialist, I too have dined with leprosy patients, and I can tell you that two thousand years of medical progress have done little to lessen the social stigma of the disease. One refined, educated man in India told me of the day he sat weeping in a car outside a church as his daughter got married within. He dared not show his disfigured face, lest all the guests leave. Nor could he host the traditional wedding banquet, for who would enter the home of a leper?

In Palestine, stern laws enforced the stigma against leprosy: the afflicted had to live outside city walls and yell "Unclean!" when they approached anyone. Yet Jesus ignored those rules and reclined at the table of a man who wore that stigma as part of his name. To make matters worse, during the course of the meal a disreputable woman poured expensive perfume on Jesus' head. According to Mark, Judas Iscariot left the meal in disgust and went straight to the chief priests to betray Jesus.

In a different scene with some striking parallels, Jesus shared a meal with another man named Simon, and here too a woman anointed Jesus with perfume, wiping his feet with her hair and her tears. This Simon, though, being a proper Pharisee, recoiled at the indiscretion. Jesus gave a searing reply that helps explain why he preferred the company of "sinners and tax collectors" over outstanding citizens like Simon:

> Do you see this woman? I came into your house. You did not give me any water for my feet, but she wet my feet with her tears and wiped them with her hair. You did not give me a kiss, but this woman, from the time I entered, has not stopped kissing my feet. You did not put oil on my head, but she has poured perfume on my feet. Therefore, I tell you, her many sins have been forgiven—for she loved much. But he who has been forgiven little loves little.

At least one other time Jesus accepted hospitality from a prominent Pharisee. Like double agents, the religious leaders were following him around and inviting him to meals while scrutinizing his every move. Provocatively, despite it being the Sabbath, Jesus healed a man from dropsy, and then he drew a stinging contrast between the social-climbing banquets of the Pharisees and God's banquet spread for "the poor, the crippled, the blind and the lame." The Gospels record no other meals with prominent citizens, and I can easily understand why: Jesus hardly made for a soothing dinner guest.*

The last two meals we know about took place in the homes of "publicans," or tax collectors, a class of people unpopular in any age but especially so in Jesus' day. They collected taxes on a commission basis, pocketing whatever profits they could extort from the locals, and most Jews viewed them as traitors serving the Roman Empire. The word *publican* became synonymous with robber, brigand, murderer, and reprobate. Jewish courts considered a tax collector's evidence as invalid, and his money could not be accepted as alms for the poor or used in exchange since it had been acquired by such despicable means.

Pointedly, Jesus invited himself to the homes of both tax collectors. When he noticed the ostracized Zacchaeus, so short he had to climb a tree to see Jesus, he called the man down and asked to stay at his house. The crowd muttered disapproval, but Jesus shrugged off their complaints: "For the Son of Man came to seek and to save what was lost." Another such reprobate, Levi, Jesus met at a booth in the very act of collecting the hated taxes. "It is not the healthy who need a doctor, but the sick," he told the crowd that time.

Reading about Jesus' assorted dinner companions, I search for a clue that might explain why Jesus made one group (sinners) feel so comfortable and the other group (pious) feel so uncomfortable. I find such a clue in one more scene from the Gospels that brings together Pharisees and a blatant sinner simultaneously. The Pharisees have

---

*Pharisees thought of their dining table as a kind of "little temple," which explains why they refused to dine with Gentiles or sinners. Perhaps Jesus understood his dining table as a little temple as well, which explains why he ate with such a motley assortment of dining companions. The great banquet, he proclaimed, is now open to all, not merely those who have been through proper purification.

caught a woman in the very act of adultery, a crime that calls for the death penalty. What would Jesus have them do? they ask, hoping to trap him in a conflict between morality and mercy.

Jesus pauses, writes on the ground for a moment, then says to the accusers, "If any one of you is without sin, let him be the first to throw a stone at her." When all of them have filed away, Jesus turns to the cringing woman. "Where are they? Has no one condemned you?" he asks. "Then neither do I condemn you. Go now and leave your life of sin."

This tense scene reveals a clear principle in Jesus' life: he brings to the surface repressed sin, yet forgives any freely acknowledged sin. The adulteress went away forgiven, with a new lease on life; the Pharisees slunk away, stabbed to the heart.

Perhaps prostitutes, tax collectors, and other known sinners responded to Jesus so readily because at some level they knew they were wrong and to them God's forgiveness looked very appealing. As C. S. Lewis has said, "Prostitutes are in no danger of finding their present life so satisfactory that they cannot turn to God: the proud, the avaricious, the self-righteous, are in that danger."

Jesus' message met a mixed response among first-century Jews, many of whom preferred the style of John the Baptist, with his insect diet and his stern message of judgment and wrath, to Jesus' message of grace and a banquet spread for all. I can understand this odd preference for the law because of the legalistic environment I grew up in. Grace was slippery, evanescent, hard to get my mind around. Sin was concrete, visible, an easy target to pounce on. Under law, I always knew where I ranked.

Wendy Kaminer, a modern Jew trying to comprehend Christianity, confesses that "as an article of faith, this doctrine of salvation by grace and grace alone is remarkably unappealing to me. It takes, I think, remarkable disregard for justice to idealize a God who so values belief over action. I prefer the God who looks down upon us (in a very old joke) and says, 'I wish they'd stop worrying about whether or not I exist and start obeying my commandments.'"

In truth we Christians, too, may find it easier to follow a God who simply says, "Start obeying my commandments."

Jews in Jesus' day envisioned a ladder reaching higher and higher towards God, a hierarchy expressed in the very architecture of the temple. Gentiles and "half-breeds" like the Samaritans were permitted only in the outer Court of the Gentiles; a wall separated them from the next partition, which admitted Jewish women. Jewish men could proceed one stage further, but only priests could enter the sacred areas. Finally, only one priest, the high priest, could enter the Most Holy Place, and that just once a year on the day of Yom Kippur.

The society was, in effect, a religious caste system based on steps toward holiness, and the Pharisees' scrupulosity reinforced the system daily. All their rules on washing hands and avoiding defilement were an attempt to make themselves acceptable to God. Had not God set forth lists of desirable (spotless) and undesirable (flawed, unclean) animals for use in sacrifice? Had not God banned sinners, menstruating women, the physically deformed, and other "undesirables" from the temple? The Qumram community of the Essenes made a firm rule, "No madman, or lunatic, or simpleton, or fool, no blind man, or maimed, or lame, or deaf man, and no minor, shall enter into the Community."

In the midst of this religious caste system, Jesus appeared. To the Pharisees' dismay he had no qualms about socializing with children or sinners or even Samaritans. He touched, or was touched by, the "unclean": those with leprosy, the deformed, a hemorrhaging woman, the lunatic and possessed. Although Levitical laws prescribed a day of purification after touching a sick person, Jesus conducted mass healings in which he touched scores of sick people; he never concerned himself with the rules of defilement after contact with the sick or even the dead.

To take just one example of the revolutionary changes Jesus set in motion, consider Jesus' attitude toward women. In those days, at every synagogue service Jewish men prayed, "Blessed art thou, O Lord, who hast not made me a woman." Women sat in a separate section, were not counted in quorums, and were rarely taught the Torah. In social life, few women would talk to men outside of their families, and a woman was to touch no man but her spouse. Yet Jesus associated freely with women and taught some as his disciples. A Samaritan woman who had been through five husbands, Jesus tapped to lead a spiritual revival (notably, he began the conversation by asking *her* for help). A prostitute's anointing, he accepted with gratitude. Women traveled with his band of followers, no doubt stirring up much gossip. Women populated Jesus' parables and illustrations, and frequently he did miracles on their behalf. According to biblical scholar Walter Wink, Jesus violated the mores of his time in every single encounter with women recorded in the four Gospels. Truly, as Paul would later say, in Christ "There is neither Jew nor Greek, slave nor free, male nor female. . . ."*

Indeed, for women and other oppressed people, Jesus turned upside down the accepted wisdom of the day. Pharisees believed that touching an unclean person polluted the one who touched. But when Jesus touched a person with leprosy, Jesus did not become soiled—the leprous became clean. When an immoral woman washed Jesus' feet, *she* went away forgiven and transformed. When he defied custom to enter a pagan's house, the pagan's servant was healed. In word and in deed Jesus was proclaiming a radically new gospel of grace: to get clean a person did not have to journey to Jerusalem, offer sacrifices, and undergo purification rituals. All a person had to do was follow Jesus. As Walter Wink puts it, "The contagion of holiness overcomes the contagion of uncleanness."

---

*Dorothy Sayers expands the point: "Perhaps it is no wonder that the women were first at the Cradle and last at the Cross. They had never known a man like this Man—there had never been such another. A prophet and teacher who never nagged at them, who never flattered or coaxed or patronized; who never made arch jokes about them, never treated them either as 'The women, God help us!' or 'The ladies, God bless them!'; who rebuked without querulousness and praised without condescension; who took their questions and arguments seriously, who never mapped out their sphere for them, never urged them to be feminine or jeered at them for being female; who had no ax to grind and no uneasy male dignity to defend; who took them as he found them and was completely unselfconscious.

"There is no act, no sermon, no parable in the whole Gospel that borrows its pungency from female perversity; nobody could possibly guess from the words of Jesus that there was anything 'funny' about woman's nature.

"But we might easily deduce it from His contemporaries, and from His prophets before Him, and from His Church to this day."

In short, Jesus moved the emphasis from God's holiness (exclusive) to God's mercy (inclusive). Instead of the message "No undesirables allowed," he proclaimed, "In God's kingdom there are no undesirables." By going out of his way to meet with Gentiles, eat with sinners, and touch the sick, he extended the realm of God's mercy. To Jewish leaders, Jesus' actions jeopardized the very existence of their religious caste system—no wonder the Gospels mention more than twenty occasions when they conspired against Jesus.

One of Jesus' stories, contrasting a pious Pharisee with a remorseful tax collector, captures the inclusive gospel of grace in a nutshell. The Pharisee, who fasted twice a week and tithed on schedule, piously thanked God that he was above robbers, evildoers, and adulterers—and far above the tax collector standing to the side. The tax collector, too humiliated even to raise his eyes to heaven, prayed the simplest prayer possible, "God, have mercy on me, a sinner." Jesus drew the conclusion, "I tell you that this man, rather than the other, went home justified before God."

Can we infer from Jesus' story that behavior does not matter, that there is no moral difference between a disciplined legalist and a robber, evildoer, and adulterer. Of course not. Behavior matters in many ways; it simply is not how to get accepted by God. The skeptic A. N. Wilson comments on Jesus' parable of the Pharisee and tax collector, "It is a shocking, morally anarchic story. All that matters in the story appears to be God's capacity to forgive." Precisely.

In his own social interactions, Jesus was putting into practice "the great reversal" heralded in the Beatitudes. Normally in this world we look up to the rich, the beautiful, the successful. Grace, however, introduces a world of new logic. Because God loves the poor, the suffering, the persecuted, so should we. Because God sees no undesirables, neither should we. By his own example, Jesus challenged us to look at the world through what Irenaeus would call "grace-healed eyes."

Jesus' parables underscored that mission, for often he made the poor and oppressed the heroes of his stories. One such story featured a poor man, Lazarus—the only named person in Jesus' parables—who was being exploited by a rich man. At first the rich man enjoyed sumptuous clothes and food while the beggar Lazarus, covered with scars, lay outside his gate with the dogs. Death, though, stunningly reversed their fortunes. The rich man heard from Abraham, "Son, remember that in your lifetime you received your good things, while Lazarus received bad things, but now he is comforted here and you are in agony."

That trenchant story sank deep into the consciousness of early Christians, many of whom belonged to lower economic classes. Rich and poor Christians struck a bargain: the rich agreed to fund charities in exchange for the poor praying for their souls. Surely God was more inclined toward the prayers of the poor, they reasoned. (Even today at funerals Benedictine monks pray that "Lazarus will know" their fallen colleague, following the tradition that Lazarus, not Peter, guards the entrance into heaven.)

For a while, the church worked hard to follow this new logic, and as a result, early Christians were renowned within the Roman Empire for their support of the poor and suffering. The Christians, unlike their pagan neighbors, readily ransomed their friends from barbarian captors, and when plague hit, the Christians tended their sufferers whereas the pagans abandoned the sick at the first symptoms. For the first few centuries, at least, the church took literally Christ's commands to receive strangers, clothe the naked, feed the hungry, and visit those in prison.*

As I read the stories of Jesus and study the history of the early church, I feel both inspired and troubled. The question I first raised with my class in Chicago returns to convict me. In view of Jesus' clear example, how is it that the church has now become a community of respectability, where the down-and-out no longer feel welcome?

I presently live in Colorado, where I attend a church in which most people come from the same race (white) and the same social class (middle). It startles me to open the New Testament and see in what mixed soil the early church took root. The middle-class church many

---

*According to church historians, this good work continued until the triumph of Constantine, who legalized the faith and established an official imperial church. From that point on the church tended to spiritualize poverty and leave "welfare" to the emperor. Over time the church itself became part of the wealthy establishment.

of us know today bears little resemblance to the diverse group of social rejects described in the Gospels and the book of Acts.

Projecting myself back into Jesus' time, I try to picture the scene. The poor, the sick, the tax collectors, sinners, and prostitutes crowd around Jesus, stirred by his message of healing and forgiveness. The rich and powerful stand on the sidelines, testing him, spying, trying to entrap him. I know these facts about Jesus' time, and yet, from the comfort of a middle-class church in a wealthy country like the U.S., I easily lose sight of the radical core of Jesus' message.

To help correct my vision, I have read sermons that come out of the Christian base communities in the Third World. The gospel through Third World eyes looks very different from the gospel as preached in many U.S. churches. The poor and the unlearned cannot always identify Jesus' mission statement (" ... he has anointed me to preach good news to the poor ... to proclaim freedom for the captives and release for the prisoners ...") as a quotation from Isaiah, but they hear it as good news indeed. They understand the great reversal not as an abstraction but as God's promise of defiant hope and Jesus' challenge to his followers. Regardless of how the world treats them, the poor and the sick have assurance, because of Jesus, that God knows no undesirables.

It took the writings of a Japanese novelist named Shusaku Endo to impress on me that the phenomenon of reversal lay at the very heart of Jesus' mission.

In a country where the church comprises less than one percent of the population, Endo was raised by a devout Christian mother and baptized at the age of eleven. Growing up as a Christian in prewar Japan, he felt a constant sense of alienation and was sometimes bullied by classmates for his association with a "Western" religion. After World War II ended he traveled to France, hoping there to find spiritual soulmates. Again he faced persecution, this time on account of race, not religion. As one of the first Japanese exchange students in an

THE JESUS I NEVER KNEW

Allied country, Endo found himself the target of racial abuse. "Slanty-eyed gook," some called him.

Rejected in his homeland, rejected in his spiritual homeland, Endo underwent a grave crisis of faith. He began visiting Palestine to research the life of Jesus, and while there he made a transforming discovery: Jesus too knew rejection. More, Jesus' life was *defined* by rejection. His neighbors laughed at him, his family questioned his sanity, his closest friends betrayed him, and his countrymen traded his life for that of a terrorist. Throughout his ministry, Jesus gravitated toward the poor and the rejected ones, the riffraff.

This new insight into Jesus hit Endo with the force of revelation. From his faraway vantage point in Japan he had viewed Christianity as a triumphant, Constantinian faith. He had studied the Holy Roman Empire and the glittering Crusades, had admired photos of the grand cathedrals of Europe, had dreamed of living in a nation where one could be a Christian without disgrace. Now, as he studied the Bible, he saw that Christ himself had not avoided "dis-grace." Jesus was the Suffering Servant, as depicted by Isaiah: "despised and rejected by men, a man of sorrows, and familiar with suffering. Like one from whom men hide their faces. . . ." Endo felt that surely this Jesus, if anyone, could understand the rejection he himself was going through.

As Shusaku Endo sees it, Jesus brought the message of mother-love to balance the father-love of the Old Testament.* Of course mercy appears in the Old Testament as well, but it easily gets lost amid the overwhelming emphasis on judgment and law. Addressing a culture raised on those strict demands of the Torah, Jesus told of a God who prefers the pleas of an ordinary sinner to the supplications of a religious professional. He likened God to a shepherd who leaves ninety-nine sheep inside the fence and hunts frantically for one stray; to a father who can't stop thinking about his rebellious ingrate of a son though he has another who's

---

*Therapist Erich Fromm says that a child from a balanced family receives two kinds of love. Mother-love tends to be unconditional, accepting the child no matter what, regardless of behavior. Father-love tends to be more provisional, bestowing approval as the child meets certain standards of behavior. Ideally, says Fromm, a child should receive and internalize both kinds of love. According to Endo, Japan, a nation of authoritarian fathers, has understood the father-love of God, but not the mother-love.

160

respectful and obedient; to a rich host who opens the doors of the banquet hall to a menagerie of bag ladies and bums.

Jesus was often "moved by compassion," and in New Testament times that very word was used maternally to express what a mother feels for her child in her womb. Jesus went out of his way to embrace the unloved and unworthy, the folks who matter not at all to the rest of society—they embarrass us, we wish they'd go away—to prove that even "nobodies" matter infinitely to God. One unclean woman, too shy and full of shame to approach Jesus face-to-face, grabbed his robe, hoping he would not notice. He did notice. She learned, like so many other "nobodies," that you cannot easily escape Jesus' gaze.

Jesus proved in person that God loves people not as a race or species, but as individuals. We *matter* to God. "By loving the unlovable," said Augustine, "You made me lovable."

At times, I do not find it easy to believe in the love of God. I do not live in poverty, like the Christians in the Third World. Nor have I known a life of rejection, like Shusaku Endo. But I have known my share of suffering, a fact of life that cuts across all racial and economic boundaries. Suffering people also need grace-healed eyes.

One terrible week two people called me on successive days to talk about one of my books. The first, a youth pastor in Colorado, had just learned his wife and baby daughter were dying of AIDS. "How can I possibly talk to my youth group about a loving God after what has happened to me?" he asked. The next day I heard from a blind man who, several months before, had invited a recovering drug addict into his home as an act of mercy. Recently he had discovered that the recovering addict was carrying on an affair with his wife, under his own roof. "Why is God punishing me for trying to serve him?" he asked. Just then he ran out of quarters, the phone went dead, and I never heard from the man again.

I have learned not even to attempt an answer to the "Why?" questions. Why did the youth pastor's wife happen to get the one tainted bottle of blood? Why do some good people get persecuted for their deeds while some evil people live to healthy old age? Why do so few of the millions of prayers for physical healing get answered? I do not know.

One question, however, no longer gnaws at me as it once did, a question that I believe lurks behind most of our issues with God: "Does God care?" I know of only one way to answer that question, and it has come through my study of the life of Jesus. In Jesus, God gave us a face, and I can read directly in that face how God feels about people like the youth pastor and the blind man who never gave me his name. By no means did Jesus eliminate all suffering—he healed only a few in one small patch of the globe—but he did signify an answer to the question of whether God cares.

Three times that we know of, suffering drove Jesus to tears. He wept when his friend Lazarus died. I remember one dreadful year when three of my friends died in quick succession. Grief, I found, is not something you get used to. My experience of the first two deaths did nothing to prepare me for the third. Grief hit like a freight train, flattening me. It left me gasping for breath, and I could do nothing but cry. Somehow, I find it comforting that Jesus felt something similar when his friend Lazarus died. That gives a startling clue into how God must have felt about my three friends, whom he also loved.

Another time, tears came to Jesus when he looked out over Jerusalem and realized the fate awaiting that fabled city. He let out a cry of what Shusaku Endo has called mother-love: "O Jerusalem, Jerusalem, you who kill the prophets and stone those sent to you, how often I have longed to gather your children together, as a hen gathers her chicks under her wings, but you were not willing." I sense in that spasm of emotional pain something akin to what a parent feels when a son or daughter goes astray, flaunting freedom, rejecting everything he or she was brought up to believe. Or the pain of a man or woman who has just learned a spouse has left—the pain of a jilted lover. It is a helpless, crushing pain of futility, and it staggers me to realize that the Son of God himself emitted a cry of helplessness in the face of human freedom. Not even God, with all his power, can force a human being to love.

Finally, Hebrews tells us, Jesus "offered up ... loud cries and tears to the one who could save him from death." But of course he was not saved from death. Is it too much to say that Jesus himself asked the question that haunts me, that haunts most of us at one time or another: Does God care? What else can be the meaning of his quotation from that dark psalm, "My God, my God, why have you forsaken me?"

Again, I find it strangely comforting that when Jesus faced pain he responded much as I do. He did not pray in the garden, "Oh, Lord, I am so grateful that you have chosen me to suffer on your behalf. I rejoice in the privilege!" No, he experienced sorrow, fear, abandonment, and something approaching even desperation. Still, he endured because he knew that at the center of the universe lived his Father, a God of love he could trust regardless of how things appeared at the time.

Jesus' response to suffering people and to "nobodies" provides a glimpse into the heart of God. God is not the unmoved Absolute, but rather the Loving One who draws near. God looks on me in all my weakness, I believe, as Jesus looked on the widow standing by her son's bier, and on Simon the Leper, and on another Simon, Peter, who cursed him yet even so was commissioned to found and lead his church, a community that need always find a place for rejects.

MIRACLES: SNAPSHOTS OF THE SUPERNATURAL

The genuine realist, if he is an unbeliever, will always find strength and ability to disbelieve in the miraculous, and if he is confronted with a miracle as an irrefutable fact he would rather disbelieve his own senses than admit the fact. Faith does not . . . spring from the miracle, but the miracle from faith.

FYODOR DOSTOEVSKY

MIRACLES: SNAPSHOTS OF THE SUPERNATURAL

———— ∞∞∞ ————

The atmosphere I grew up in was humid with miracles. Most Sundays people in our church would testify about marvelous answers to prayer they had received the preceding week. God found parking places for mothers who drove their children to the doctor. Lost fountain pens mysteriously reappeared. Tumors shrank away the day before scheduled surgery.

In those days I envisioned Jesus as the Great Magician and, fittingly, the story of his walking on water especially impressed me. If only I could pull off such a stunt in my school, just once! How I would love to fly through the room like an angel, silencing with levitation all who scoffed at me and other religious types. How I would love to walk unscathed through the bullies at the bus stop, as Jesus had walked through an angry crowd in his hometown.

I never managed to fly through the classroom, though, and bullies continued to torment me no matter how hard I prayed. Even the "answers to prayer" confused me. Sometimes, after all, parking places did not open up and fountain pens stayed lost. Sometimes church people lost their jobs. Sometimes they died. A great shadow darkened my own life: my father had died of polio just after my first birthday, despite a round-the-clock prayer vigil involving hundreds of dedicated Christians. Where was God then?

I have spent much of my adult life coming to terms with questions first stirred up during my youth. Prayer, I have found, does not work like a vending machine: insert request, receive answer. Miracles are just that, *miracles*, not "ordinaries" common to daily experience. My view of Jesus too has changed. As I now reflect on his life, miracles play a less prominent role than what I had imagined as a child. Superman, he was not.

Yes, Jesus performed miracles—around three dozen, depending on how you count them—but the Gospels actually downplay them. Often Jesus asked those who had seen a miracle not to tell anyone else. Some miracles, such as the Transfiguration or the raising of a twelve-year-old dead girl, he let only his closest disciples watch, with strict orders to keep things quiet. Though he never denied someone who asked for physical healing, he always turned down requests for a demonstration to amaze the crowds and impress important people. Jesus recognized early on that the excitement generated by miracles did not readily convert into life-changing faith.

Some skeptics, of course, have no place for miracles, and for them any account of a supernatural event must by definition be discarded. The Smithsonian museum in Washington displays a leather-bound book in which Thomas Jefferson pasted all the passages from the Gospels that contain no miraculous element. This was the Bible he read every day toward the end of his life, a more palatable gospel of Jesus the teacher but not the miracle worker.

Thomas Jefferson's approach is a historical echo of what happened in Jesus' own day. Then too rationalists pondered Jesus' teaching and scrutinized his miracles. Sometimes they denied the plain evidence in front of them and sometimes they sought alternative explanations (magic, the Devil's power). Rarely did people find it easy to believe in miracles; they seemed as peculiar in the first century as they would seem if performed today. Then, as now, miracles aroused suspicion, contempt, and only occasionally faith.

Because I accept Jesus as God's Son, who came to earth "trailing clouds of glory," I accept the miracles he performed as a natural complement to his work. Even so, the miracles raise big questions for me. Why are there so few? Why any at all? Why these particular miracles and not others? I am a journalist, not a theologian, so in my search for clues I look at the miracles not in systematic categories but rather as individual scenes, impressionistic snapshots from the life of Jesus.

Jesus' first miracle was perhaps the strangest of all. He never repeated anything quite like it, and the miracle seemed to take Jesus by surprise as much as anyone else.

At the age of thirty or so Jesus showed up at a wedding with his newly formed band of disciples. His mother came too, probably accompanied by other members of the family. In the village life of Galilee, a wedding brought celebration into an otherwise drab existence. The bridegroom and his men made a gala procession through the streets to fetch the bride's party by torchlight, then everyone rushed to the groom's house for a feast worthy of royalty. Think of happy scenes from *Fiddler on the Roof*: of peasant Jewish families dancing across the courtyard in their finest embroidered clothes, of music and laughter, of banquet tables laden with clay platters of food and jugs of wine. The feast might go on for as long as a week, as long as the food and wine and good cheer held out. Truly a wedding was a time of high joy.

Jesus' disciples must have blinked in disbelief at the raucous scene, especially those who had come over to him from John the Baptist with his desert diet and animal-skin clothes. Did these ascetics now dance with the Jewish girls and gorge themselves on culinary delights? Did townsfolk quiz them about the Baptist, the closest thing to a prophet Israel had seen in four hundred years? John's gospel does not say. It only tells us that in a moment of social crisis the whole feast nearly ground to a halt. The wine ran out.

As emergencies go, this one falls well down the list. It caused embarrassment, to be sure, but need a Messiah who had come to heal the sick and liberate the captives concern himself with a social *faux pas*? "Dear woman, why do you involve me?" Jesus replied when his mother mentioned the problem. "My time has not yet come."

We can only guess what went through Jesus' mind during those next few seconds as he weighed Mary's request. If he acted, that would mean his time *had* come, and from that moment on life would change. If word of his powers leaked, he would soon hear pleas from needy people from Tyre to Jerusalem. Crowds would flock: epileptics, paralytics, deaf-mutes, the demon-possessed, not to mention any street beggar who wanted a free glass of wine. Investigators would be dispatched from the capital. A clock would start ticking that would not stop until Calvary.

Then Jesus, the same person who while fasting in the desert a scant time before had rebuffed Satan's challenge to turn stones into bread, reached a decision. For the first but surely not the last time in his public life, he changed his plans to accommodate someone else. "Fill the jars with water," he told the servants. Water went in and miraculously wine—the best wine, the choice wine usually served early on when palates are most discriminating and guests most impressionable—flowed out. The feast kicked into gear again, the host relaxed, the bridal party returned to serious celebrating.

John gives no indication that the guests or even the host knew about the little drama behind the scenes. Mary knew, of course, as did the servants. And Jesus' disciples knew: "He thus revealed his glory and his disciples put their faith in him."

What can we learn from this odd incident? The writers George MacDonald and C. S. Lewis see in it a reminder of God's common grace, focused in this instance in a narrow beam like solar rays through a magnifying glass. Jesus' miracles, they note, do not usually contradict natural law, but rather replicate the normal activity of creation at a different speed and on a smaller scale. "Some of the miracles do locally what God has already done universally," writes Lewis. "God creates the vine and teaches it to draw up water by its roots and, with the aid of the sun, to turn that water into a juice which will ferment and take on certain qualities. Thus every year, from Noah's time till ours, God turns water into wine." Similarly, antibodies and antigens conduct miracles of healing in our bodies every day, but in a slower, less sensational manner than the kinds of healings Jesus would go on to perform.

Yes, but what about the underlying meaning? What did this strange first miracle signify? In a departure from custom, John fails to interpret for us the miraculous "sign," which for him almost always means a symbol, a kind of acted parable. Some commentators see in it a preview of the Last Supper, when Jesus transforms not water into wine but wine into blood, his blood, shed for all humanity. Maybe.

I prefer a more whimsical interpretation. Tellingly, John notes that the wine came from huge (twenty- to thirty-gallon) jugs that stood full of water at the front of the house, vessels that were used by observant Jews to fulfill the rules on ceremonial washing. Even a wedding feast had to honor the burdensome rituals of cleansing. Jesus, perhaps with a twinkle in his eye, transformed those jugs, ponderous symbols of the old way, into wineskins, harbingers of the new. From purified water of the Pharisees came the choice new wine of a whole new era. The time for ritual cleansing had passed; the time for celebration had begun.

Prophets like John the Baptist preached judgment, and indeed many miracles of the Old Testament expressed that sense of stern judgment. Jesus' first miracle, though, was one of tender mercy. The lesson was not lost on the disciples who joined him at the wedding that night in Cana—especially the recent recruits from the Baptist.

⸺

The miracle of changing water into wine, a one-time event, occurred out of the spotlight in an obscure town whose location archaeologists cannot even agree on. Before long, though, Jesus was exercising miraculous powers in broad daylight before enthusiastic crowds. As is true today, the miracles of physical healing captured the most attention, and John 9 tells of one such miracle in Jerusalem, the capital city and heart of opposition to Jesus. John devotes an entire chapter to the story, sketching a classic portrayal of what happens when Jesus disturbs the accepted order.

The story starts where many sick people start, with the question of cause. *Why me? What is God trying to tell me?* In Jesus' day people assumed that tragedy hit people who deserved it.* "There is no death

---

*I have noticed a remarkable change since Jesus' time in how people think about calamity. Nowadays we tend to blame God, both for the cataclysmic (which insurance companies call "acts of God") and for the trivial. At the 1994 Winter

without sin, and there is no suffering without iniquity," taught the Pharisees, who saw the hand of punishment in natural disasters, birth defects, and such long-term conditions as blindness and paralysis. Here is where "the man blind from birth" entered the picture. Steeped in good Jewish tradition, Jesus' disciples debated what could account for such a birth defect. Had the man somehow sinned *in utero*? Or was he suffering the consequences of his parents' sin—a prospect easier to imagine but patently unfair.

Jesus responded by overturning common notions about how God views sick and disabled people. He denied that the man's blindness came from any sin, just as he dismissed the common opinion that tragedies happen to those who deserve them (see Luke 13:1–5). Jesus wanted the sick to know they are especially loved, not cursed, by God. Every one of his miracles of healing, in fact, undercut the rabbinic tradition of "You deserved it."

The disciples were looking backward, to find out "Why?" Jesus redirected their attention forward, answering a different question: "To what end?" His answer: "Neither this man nor his parents sinned, but this happened so that the work of God might be displayed in his life."

What began as a tragic tale of one man's blindness ends as a surreal tale of everyone else's blindness. The man's neighbors make him prove his identity, the Pharisees subject him to formal interrogations, and his own parents (who had been callous enough to let him lead a life of begging, after all) waffle under all the pressure. As for the once-blind man, he has little time for such theoretical musings: "Whether he is a sinner or not, I don't know," he testifies about Jesus. "One thing I do know. I was blind but now I see!"

In Jerusalem, where Jesus had been censured as a heretic, a clear-cut miracle, especially one performed on the Sabbath, posed a grave threat to official doctrine. Although the Pharisees could not disprove

---

Olympics, when speed-skater Dan Janssen scraped the ice and lost the 500-meter race once again, his wife, Robin, cried out instinctively, "Why, God, again? God can't be that cruel!" A few months later a young woman wrote Dr. James Dobson this letter, "Four years ago, I was dating a man and became pregnant. I was devastated! I asked God, 'Why have You allowed this to happen to me?'" Exactly what role, I cannot help but wonder, did God play in an ice-skater losing control on a turn and a young couple losing control on a date?

the miracle—a blind beggar was now looking them in the eye and taunting them in open court—in the end they clung to their time-worn theories of punishment. "You were steeped in sin at birth; how dare you lecture us!" they snapped at the man. Theological blinders do not easily fall off.

The response to this miracle, as well as most of the others reported in the Gospels, bears out a striking principle of faith: Although faith may produce miracles, miracles do not necessarily produce faith.

You can view disease as a mechanical breakdown of bodily cells, or you can view it in a broader sense as a state of dis-ease involving body, mind, and soul. I learned this from the patients of Dr. Paul Brand, the leprosy specialist whose books I have coauthored. Except in very early stages, the leprosy patient does not feel physical pain. That, in fact, is the problem: after leprosy bacilli deaden nerve cells, patients no longer alert to danger proceed to damage their own bodies. A leprosy patient may walk all day on a sharp metal screw, or use a splintery hammer, or scratch an infected spot on the eyeball. Each of these acts destroys tissue and may eventually lead to loss of limb or vision, but at no point does the leprosy patient *hurt*.

Though they may not hurt, leprosy patients surely *suffer*, as much as any people I have ever known. Almost all the pain they feel comes from outside, the pain of rejection imposed on them by the surrounding community. Dr. Brand told me of one bright young man he was treating in India. In the course of the examination Brand laid his hand on the patient's shoulder and informed him through a translator of the treatment that lay ahead. To his surprise the man began to shake with muffled sobs. "Have I said something wrong?" Brand asked his translator. She quizzed the patient in a spurt of Tamil and reported, "No, doctor. He says he is crying because you put your hand around his shoulder. Until he came here no one had touched him for many years."

In modern Western countries, where leprosy is rare, a new disease has taken over much of its moral and social stigma. "AIDS is the

173

modern-day leprosy," says former Surgeon General C. Everett Koop. "There are people who have the same attitude toward AIDS patients today that many people had toward leprosy patients one hundred years ago." I know of one AIDS patient who traveled eleven hundred miles to be with his family in Michigan for Thanksgiving dinner. He had not seen them in seven years. The parents welcomed him warily, and when dinner was served everyone got a heaping portion of turkey and all the trimmings on the best Wedgewood china plates—except for their son the AIDS patient, who was served on Chinette, with plastic utensils.

Jesus knew all about the social stigma that accompanies a disease like AIDS or leprosy. Levitical laws decreed that a person with leprosy live outside the town, keep a six-foot distance from everyone else, and wear the clothes of a mourner going to a burial service. I can easily imagine indignation rippling through the crowd when one such outcast walked through them, no doubt given a wide berth, and threw himself at the feet of Jesus. "Lord, if you are willing, you can make me clean," he said.

Matthew, Mark, and Luke give varying accounts of the scene, but all three include the same explosive sentence: "Jesus reached out his hand and touched the man." The crowd must have gasped—had not Moses' law forbidden such an act? The leprosy victim may have flinched. For how many months or years had he been deprived of the sensation of warm human flesh against his own? That one touch from Jesus brought his state of dis-ease to an end. Shalom was restored.

Jesus' response to dis-ease set a pattern for the church that formed around him, and Christians proceeded to follow his example of caring for the sick, the poor, and the outcast. In the case of leprosy, although the church sometimes added to the misery with its "curse of God" message, at the same time individuals rose up to lead the way in treatment. Religious orders dedicated themselves to the care of leprosy, and scientific breakthroughs on the disease tended to come from missionaries because they were the only ones willing to work with leprosy patients.* Similarly,

---

*A bizarre belief in the Middle Ages spurred the church's outreach to leprosy patients. Due to a mistranslation by Jerome, church leaders came to believe that Isaiah's description of the Suffering Servant as "afflicted," or "familiar with suffering"

Christians are now involved in ministries to AIDS patients and in hospice, a modern movement devoted to those who have little hope of physical healing but much need for love and care.

Mother Teresa, whose sisters in Calcutta run both a hospice and a clinic for leprosy patients, once said, "We have drugs for people with diseases like leprosy. But these drugs do not treat the main problem, the disease of being *unwanted*. That's what my sisters hope to provide." The sick and the poor, she said, suffer even more from rejection than material want. "An alcoholic in Australia told me that when he is walking along the street he hears the footsteps of everyone coming toward him or passing him becoming faster. Loneliness and the feeling of being unwanted is the most terrible poverty." One need not be a doctor or a miracle worker to meet that need.

A delightful story that directly follows the leprosy healing in the Gospels shows the difference friends can make for an afflicted person. A paralyzed man, who by necessity had to rely on others for food, bathing, and even help with sanitation, now needed assistance in acting on his faith.

I remember my destructive impulses being aroused the first time I heard the story in Sunday school. This paralytic wanted so desperately to meet Jesus that he talked four friends into digging up a roof and lowering him through the hole! The man who had spent his life horizontal would have one moment of vertical fame. Biblical commentators take pains to mention that the thatch and tile roofs of Palestine were much easier to disassemble and repair than the roofs that adorn our houses today. They miss the point: a hole in the roof is hardly the normal way to

---

meant he was actually stricken with leprosy. Thus in the twelfth and thirteenth centuries people jumped to the conclusion that Jesus must have had leprosy. This belief led to a complete reversal of how leprosy was regarded: no longer a curse of God, it was now a "Holy Disease." Crusaders who returned with leprosy were treated with great reverence, and "lazar houses" to treat the disease (named for Lazarus the beggar) sprang up everywhere, nearly two thousand in France alone. This historical movement stands as a novel example of the church following literally Jesus' command to treat "the least of these brothers of mine" as they would treat Christ himself.

enter a house. Moreover, no matter how flimsy the roof, ripping a hole in it will surely disrupt what goes on underneath. Dust flies, bits of straw and clay fall on the guests, noise and chaos interrupt the meeting.*

The crowd whose very presence had created the accessibility problem had two rude shocks. First was the messy way the paralytics' friends solved it. Then came Jesus' completely unexpected reaction. When Jesus saw *their* faith—plural, emphasizing the four friends' role in the healing—he said, "Take heart, son; your sins are forgiven." "Son, be of good cheer," the *King James Version* translates that first phrase. Literally, "Cheer up!"

Apparently, Jesus rather enjoyed the interruption. Outstanding faith never failed to impress him, and certainly the four-man demolition crew had demonstrated that. Yet his response baffled the observers. Who said anything about sins? And who was Jesus to forgive them? In typical fashion, the religious experts started arguing about Jesus' right to forgive sins, all the while ignoring the disabled man lying in the debris.

Jesus hushed the debate with enigmatic words that seem to sum up his general attitude toward physical healing: "Which is easier, to say to the paralytic, 'Your sins are forgiven,' or to say, 'Get up, take your mat and walk'?" Although he let the question hang there for the moment, his entire ministry provides an answer. Physical healing was far easier, without question. As if to prove the point, Jesus merely gave a word and the paralyzed man stood to his feet, rolled up his mat, and walked—or perhaps skipped—home.

Jesus never met a disease he could not cure, a birth defect he could not reverse, a demon he could not exorcise. But he did meet skeptics he could not convince and sinners he could not convert. Forgiveness of sins requires an act of will on the receiver's part, and some

---

*A priest named Donald Senior made an observation about this story that I had never before noticed, concerning the issue of accessibility for the disabled. Senior writes, "Any disabled person can supply lots of stories like this one—entering a church through the sacristy (or, worse, having to be carried up the front steps like a child), coming into a lecture hall by means of a freight elevator and then through the kitchen or utility room before being able to join the 'normal' people who come in the front door."

who heard Jesus' strongest words about grace and forgiveness turned away unrepentant.

"But that you may know that the Son of Man has authority on earth to forgive sins ..." Jesus announced to the skeptics as he healed the man, a clear illustration of the "lower" serving the "higher." Jesus knew that spiritual dis-ease has a more devastating effect than any mere physical ailment. Every healed person ultimately dies—then what? He had not come primarily to heal the world's cells, but to heal its souls.

How easily do we who live in material bodies devalue the world of spirit. It occurs to me that although Jesus spent much time on issues such as hypocrisy, legalism, and pride, I know of no television ministries devoted to healing those "spiritual" problems; yet I know of many that center on physical ailments. Just as I begin feeling smug, however, I remember how easily I feel tormented by the slightest bout with physical suffering, and how seldom I feel tormented by sin.

When it comes to miracles, Jesus has a different set of priorities than most of his followers.

Only one miracle made it into all four Gospels. It transpired on the grassy hills by the shores of the Sea of Galilee at a time when Jesus' popularity—and also his vulnerability—was cresting. Wherever he went, a throng that included many deranged and afflicted trailed behind.

The day before the big miracle, Jesus crossed the lake to elude the masses. Herod had just executed John the Baptist, Jesus' relative, his forerunner and friend, and Jesus needed time alone to grieve. Doubtless, John's death provoked somber thoughts of the fate awaiting him.

Alas, there would be no secluded retreat. A huge swarm of yesterday's multitude made the ten-mile journey around the lake and soon hundreds, even thousands of people clamored around Jesus. "He had compassion on them," says Mark, "because they were like sheep without a shepherd." Instead of spending the day renewing his spirit, Jesus spent it healing the sick, always an energy drain, and speaking to a crowd large enough to fill a modern basketball arena.

The issue of food came up. *What to do? There are at least five thousand men, not to mention the women and children!* Send them away, suggested one disciple. Buy them dinner, said Jesus. *What? Is he kidding? We're talking eight months' wages!*

Then Jesus took command in a way none of them had seen before. Have the people sit down in groups of fifty, he said. It was like a political rally—festive, orderly, hierarchical—exactly what one might expect from a Messiah figure.

Unavoidably, we moderns read Jesus' life backwards, knowing how it turns out. That day, no one but Jesus had a clue. Murmurs rustled through the groups on the packed hillside. *Is he the one? Could it be?* In the wilderness, Satan had dangled before Jesus the prospects of a crowd-pleasing miracle. Now, not to please a crowd but merely to settle their stomachs, Jesus took two salted fish and five small loaves of bread and performed the miracle everyone was waiting for.

Three of the Gospels leave it at that. "They all ate and were satisfied, and the disciples picked up twelve basketfuls of broken pieces of bread and fish," reports Mark with masterful understatement. Only John tells what happened next. Jesus got his time alone, at last. As the disciples rowed back across the lake, fighting a storm all the way, Jesus spent the night on a mountain, alone in prayer. Later that night he rejoined them by walking across the water.

The next morning, in a near-comic chase scene, the crowd commandeered boats and sailed in hot pursuit, like a shoal of fish chasing a curiosity around the lake. After a day to savor one miracle, they were spoiling for more. Jesus detected the mob's true intent: to seize him by force and crown him king. *All the kingdoms of the world I will give you,* Satan had promised.

A conversation ensued between two parties who might as well have been speaking different languages. Jesus was unusually brusque, accusing the crowd of greedy motives, of desiring only food for their bellies. He made provocative statements, such as "I am the bread of life" and "I have come down from heaven." He said incomprehensible things like, " . . . unless you eat the flesh of the Son of Man and drink his blood, you have no life in you."

Like a Greek chorus, the audience gave a dramatic response to each of these tough words. They grumbled. They argued. Not easily would they give up their dream, however. An old Jewish tradition taught that the Messiah would renew Moses' practice of serving manna, and had not Jesus done that very thing the day before? With yesterday's miracle still digesting in their bellies, they asked for yet another miraculous sign. They were addicted.

In the end, Jesus "won" the argument. He was not their kind of Messiah after all: he would not provide bread and circuses on demand. The large, restless crowd filed away, and Jesus' own disciples began grumbling among themselves. "This is a hard teaching. Who can accept it?" they said. Many deserted him, a breakup of disciples mentioned only by John. "You do not want to leave too, do you?" Jesus sadly asked the Twelve.

The feeding of the five thousand illustrates why Jesus, with all the supernatural powers at his command, showed such ambivalence toward miracles. They attracted crowds and applause, yes, but rarely encouraged repentance and long-term faith. He was bringing a hard message of obedience and sacrifice, not a sideshow for gawkers and sensation-seekers.

From that day on, Jesus' teaching had a different twist. As if the back-to-back scenes of acclamation and rejection had clarified his future, he began to talk much more openly about his death. The odd figures of speech he had used against the crowd began to make more sense. The bread of life was not magic, like manna; it came down from heaven in order to be broken, and mixed with blood. He was talking about his own body. In the words of Robert Farrar Capon, "the Messiah was not going to save the world by miraculous, Band-Aid interventions: a storm calmed here, a crowd fed there, a mother-in-law cured back down the road. Rather, it was going to be saved by means of a deeper, darker, left-handed mystery, at the center of which lay his own death."

Jesus passed a kind of test that day on the grassy knoll by the lake. Satan had given him a preview in the desert, but that temptation was more theoretical. This was the real thing, a test of proffered kingship to which he had every right—and which he declined, in favor of a harder, humbler way.

"A wicked and adulterous generation asks for a miraculous sign!" Jesus would say when someone else asked for a display of his powers.

179

And in Jerusalem, the capital, though many people saw the miracles he did and believed in him, "he would not entrust himself to them," for he knew what was in their hearts. A sign is not the same thing as proof; a sign is merely a marker for someone who is looking in the right direction.

⸺

The last great "sign" in John appears in the exact center of his book, chapter 11, and forms a narrative hinge for all that precedes and follows. John points to the miracle involving Lazarus as the event that turned the religious establishment fatally against Jesus. His account also offers a neat summary of what miracles did, and did not, accomplish in Jesus' time on earth.

The story of Lazarus has a unique "staged" quality about it. Usually when Jesus got word of a sick person he responded immediately, sometimes changing plans in order to accommodate the request. This time, after receiving word of the illness of one of his good friends, he lingered in another town for two more days. He did so intentionally, in full knowledge that the delay would result in Lazarus's death. John includes Jesus' cryptic explanation to his disciples, "Lazarus is dead, and for your sake I am glad I was not there, so that you may believe." Deliberately, he let Lazarus die and his family grieve.

In another context Luke contrasts the personality types of Lazarus's two sisters: Martha, the obsessive hostess who scurries about the kitchen, and Mary the contemplative, content to sit at the feet of Jesus. In a time of tragedy, the personality types held true. Martha rushed down the road to meet Jesus' party outside the village. "Lord," she chided him, "if you had been here, my brother would not have died." Some time later Mary caught up and, poignantly, said exactly the same words: "Lord, if you had been here, my brother would not have died."

The sisters' words carry the tone of accusation, the indictment of a God who did not answer prayer. No matter how hard we try, those of us who grieve cannot avoid words like "if only." *If only he had missed that flight. If only she had quit smoking. If only I had taken time to say "Good-bye."*

In this case, Mary and Martha had a clear target for their "if onlys": the Son of God himself, their friend, who could have prevented the death. Lack of faith was not to blame. Martha assured Jesus that she believed in the afterlife, and, remarkably, she even proclaimed Jesus the Messiah, the Son of God. That childlike faith lay at the heart of the issue: Why had Jesus not honored it? Friends and relatives asked curtly, "Could not he who opened the eyes of the blind man have kept this man from dying?"

Martha was crying. Mary was crying. All the mourners were crying. Finally, Jesus himself, "deeply moved in spirit and troubled," broke into tears. John does not say why Jesus wept. Since he had already revealed his plans to raise Lazarus from the dead, he surely did not feel the same grief as the devastated mourners. Still, something got to him. As he approached the tomb, again he felt a spasm, "groaning in spirit" as some translations have it.

Death had never bothered Jesus before. Effortlessly he restored a son to the widow of Nain, stopping a funeral prosession in its tracks. He returned Jairus's daughter to life with an almost playful command, "My child, get up!"—like a parent announcing the end of nap time. With Lazarus's family, though, he seemed troubled, affected, distressed.

Jesus' prayer at the tombside gives a clue: "Father, I thank you that you have heard me. I knew that you always hear me, but I said this for the benefit of the people standing here, that they may believe that you sent me." Nowhere else had Jesus prayed with an over-the-shoulder audience in mind, like a Shakespearean actor who turns to the crowd to deliver an aside. At this moment Jesus seemed self-consciously aware of his dual identity, simultaneously the One who came down from heaven and the Son of Man born on earth.

The public prayer, the loud voice, the gestures—these have all the marks of a spiritual battle under way. Jesus was making a point, working out a "sign" in full public view, and here as nowhere else he acknowledged the in-between state of God's creation. Jesus knew, of course, that Lazarus was now whole and content, in every way better for having shuffled off this mortal coil. Martha and Mary knew as much too, theoretically. But unlike Jesus and unlike Lazarus, they had never heard the sounds of laughter from the other side of death. Belief in God's power and love was for the moment overwhelmed by grief. All they knew was loss, all they felt was pain.

That in-between state of loss and pain perhaps explains the source of Jesus' tears. Greek scholars say that the word translated "deeply moved" conveys more than distress; it implies anger, even rage. At that very moment Jesus himself hung between two worlds. Standing before a tomb stinking of death gave a portent of what lay before him in this damned—literally damned—world. That his own death would also end in resurrection did not reduce the fear or the pain. He was human: he had to pass through Golgotha to reach the other side.

Lazarus's story, seen in full cycle, gives not only a preview of Jesus' future but also a compressed view of the entire planet. All of us live out our days in the in-between time, the interval of chaos and confusion between Lazarus's death and reappearance. Although such a time may be temporary, and may pale into insignificance alongside the glorious future that awaits us, right now it is all we know, and that is enough to bring tears to our eyes—enough to bring tears to Jesus' eyes.

The resurrection of one man, Lazarus, would not solve the dilemma of planet earth. For that, it would take one man's death. John adds the startling, ironic detail that the miracle of Lazarus sealed Jesus' fate. "So from that day on they plotted to take his life." And from that day on, significantly, Jesus' signs and wonders ceased.

As I now read the accounts of selected miracles from Jesus' time, I find in them a very different message.

As a child, I saw the miracles as absolute proofs of Jesus' claims. In the Gospels, however, miracles never offered such certitude even to those who saw the wonders in person. "If they do not listen to Moses and the Prophets, they will not be convinced even if someone rises from the dead," Jesus said of skeptics. Probably Jesus had his own resurrection in mind, but the sequel to Lazarus's story proves the same point: bizarrely, the chief priests sought to cover up the miracle by killing off poor Lazarus again! With hard evidence of a spectacular miracle walking around free in the person of Lazarus, they balefully conspired to destroy that evidence. In no event did the miracles bowl people over and "steamroller" them into belief. Otherwise, there would be no room for faith.

As a child, I saw the miracles as guarantees of personal safety. Did not Jesus promise, " ... not one [sparrow] will fall to the ground apart from the will of your Father"? Later, I learned that this promise appears in the midst of a series of dire warnings to the twelve disciples, in which Jesus predicts their arrest, persecution, and death. According to tradition, the eleven disciples who survived Judas all died martyrs' deaths. Jesus suffered, as did the apostle Paul and most early Christian leaders. Faith is not an insurance policy. Or, as Eddie Askew suggests, maybe it is: insurance does not prevent accidents, but rather gives a secure base from which to face their consequences.

As a child, I strove for ever more faith. Adults urged me to develop faith, and I had few clues as to how to proceed. Reading all the healing stories together, I now detect in the Gospels a kind of "ladder of faith." At the top of the ladder stand those people who impressed Jesus with bold, unshakable faith: a centurion, an impertinent blind beggar, a persistent Canaanite woman. These stories of gristly faith threaten me, because seldom do I have such faith. I am easily discouraged by the silence of God. When my prayers are not answered, I am tempted to give up and not ask again. For this reason, I look down the ladder to find people of lesser faith, and it heartens me to learn that Jesus seemed willing to work with whatever tiny glimmer of faith came to light. I cling to the tender accounts of how Jesus treated the disciples who forsook and then doubted him. The same Jesus who praised the bold faith of those high up the ladder also gently quickened the flagging faith of his disciples. And I take special comfort in the confession of the father of a demon-possessed boy who said to Jesus, "I do believe; help me overcome my unbelief!" Even that wavering man got his request granted.

As a child, I saw miracles everywhere. Now I see them rarely, and they seem ambiguous, susceptible to different interpretations. My childlike vision has doubtless grown cloudy with age, and I feel this as a loss. Yet surely the baffling selectivity of miracles was no easier to understand in Jesus' day than it is today. A man who could walk on water did it only once. What self-restraint! Yes, he brought Lazarus back from death and dried the tears of his sisters—but what about the many other sisters and wives and daughters and mothers who were grieving that day for their own loved ones? When Jesus himself discussed miracles directly, he stressed their *infrequency*.

As a child, I saw miracles as magic. Now, I see them as signs. When John the Baptist languished in prison, Jesus sent him reports of healings and resurrections to prove that he was "the one"; a short time later, though, John himself died at an executioner's hand. Jesus' message to John did nothing to alleviate his physical condition, and we do not know what effect it might have had on his faith. Regardless, the message did express the character of the kingdom Jesus had come to set in motion. It was a kingdom of liberation in which the blind would see, the lame would leap, the deaf would hear, the leprous would be cleansed, and the poor set free. For some (in three dozen miraculous instances that we know of), liberation occurred while Jesus walked the roads of Galilee and Judea. Others have realized liberation through the dedicated service of Jesus' followers. But others, John the Baptist among them, did not achieve such liberation on earth at all.

Why, then, any miracles? Did they make any difference? I readily concede that Jesus, with a few dozen healings and a handful of resurrections from the dead, did little to solve the problem of pain on this planet. That is not why he came. Nevertheless, it was in Jesus' nature to counteract the effects of the fallen world during his time on earth. As he strode through life Jesus used supernatural power to set right what was wrong. Every physical healing pointed back to a time in Eden when physical bodies did not go blind, get crippled, or bleed nonstop for twelve years—and also pointed forward to a time of re-creation to come. The miracles he did perform, breaking as they did the chains of sickness and death, give me a glimpse of what the world was meant to be and instill hope that one day God will right its wrongs. To put it mildly, God is no more satisfied with this earth than we are; Jesus' miracles offer a hint of what God intends to do about it.

Some see miracles as an implausible suspension of the laws of the physical universe. As signs, though, they serve just the opposite function. Death, decay, entropy, and destruction are the true suspensions of God's laws; miracles are the early glimpses of restoration. In the words of Jürgen Moltmann, "Jesus' healings are not supernatural miracles in a natural world. They are the only truly 'natural' things in a world that is unnatural, demonized and wounded."

DEATH:
THE FINAL WEEK

Why did Providence hide its face "at the most critical moment" ... as though voluntarily submitting to the blind, dumb, pitiless laws of nature?

FYODOR DOSTOEVSKY

CHAPTER 10

DEATH: THE FINAL WEEK

———∞∞∞———

The church I grew up in skipped past the events of Holy Week in a rush to hear the cymbal sounds of Easter. We never held a service on Good Friday. We celebrated the Lord's Supper only once per quarter, an awkward ceremony in which solemn ushers monitored the progress of trays bearing thimble-cups and broken Saltine crackers.

Roman Catholics did not believe in the Resurrection, I was told, which explained why Catholic girls wore crosses "with the little man on them." Mass, I learned, they celebrated with burning candles in a kind of cultic ritual, a symptom of their fixation with death. We Protestants were different. We saved our best clothes, our rousing hymns, and our few sanctuary decorations for Easter.

When I began to study theology and church history I found that my church was wrong about the Catholics, who believed in Easter as strongly as we did and in fact wrote many of the creeds best expressing that belief. From the Gospels I also learned that, unlike my church, the biblical record slows down rather than speeds up when it gets to Holy Week. The Gospels, said one early Christian commentator, are chronicles of Jesus' final week with increasingly longer introductions.

Of the biographies I have read, few devote more than ten percent of their pages to the subject's death—including biographies of men like Martin Luther King Jr. and Mahatma Gandhi, who died violent and politically significant deaths. The Gospels, though, devote nearly a third of their length to the climactic last week of Jesus' life. Matthew, Mark, Luke, and John saw death as the central mystery of Jesus.

Only two of the Gospels mention the events of his birth, and all four offer only a few pages on his resurrection, but each chronicler gives a detailed account of the events leading to Jesus' death. Nothing remotely like it had happened before. Celestial beings had slipped in and out of our dimension prior to the Incarnation (remember Jacob's wrestler and Abraham's visitors), and a few humans had even waked from the dead. But when the Son of God died on planet earth—how could it be that a Messiah should face defeat, a God get crucified? Nature itself convulsed at the deed: the ground shook, rocks cracked open, the sky went black.

For several years, as Holy Week approaches, I have read all the gospel accounts together, sometimes back-to-back, sometimes interwoven in a "harmony of the Gospels" format. Each time I feel swept away by the sheer drama. The simple, unadorned rendering has a grinding power, and I can almost hear a bass drum beating dolefully in the background. No miracles break in, no supernatural rescue attempts. This is tragedy beyond Sophocles or Shakespeare.

The might of the world, the most sophisticated religious system of its time allied with the most powerful political empire, arrays itself against a solitary figure, the only perfect man who has ever lived. Though he is mocked by the powers and abandoned by his friends, yet the Gospels give the strong, ironic sense that he himself is overseeing the whole long process. He has resolutely set his face for Jerusalem, knowing the fate that awaits him. The cross has been his goal all along. Now, as death nears, he calls the shots.

One year I came to the gospel narratives just after reading the entire Old Testament. Working my way through the books of history, poetry, and prophecy, I had got to know a God of muscular power. Heads rolled, empires toppled, entire nations disappeared from the earth. Every year the Jews paused as a nation to remember God's great feat of deliverance from Egypt, an event replete with miracles. I felt aftershocks of the Exodus all through the psalms and prophets, cues to a beleaguered tribe that the God who had answered their prayers once might do so again.

With those accounts still ringing in my ears, I arrived at Matthew's scene-by-scene description of Jesus' final week. Once more Jews had gathered in Jerusalem to remember the Exodus and celebrate the Passover. Once more hope sprang eternal: *Messiah has come!* ran one rumor. And then, like an arrow shot into the heart of hope, came Jesus' betrayal, trial, and death.

How can we who know the outcome in advance ever recapture the dire end-of-the-world feeling that descended upon Jesus' followers? Over the centuries the story has grown familiar, and I cannot comprehend, much less re-create, the impact of that final week on those who lived through it. I will merely record what stands out to me as I review the Passion story one more time.

Triumphal Entry. All four Gospels mention this event, which at first glance seems the one departure from Jesus' aversion to acclaim. Crowds spread clothes and tree branches across the road to show their adoration. "Blessed is the king who comes in the name of the Lord!" they cried. Though Jesus usually recoiled from such displays of fanaticism, this time he let them yell. To indignant Pharisees he explained, "I tell you, if they keep quiet, the stones will cry out."

Was the prophet from Galilee now being vindicated in Jerusalem? "Look how the whole world has gone after him!" exclaimed the Pharisees in alarm. At that moment, with several hundred thousand pilgrims assembled in Jerusalem, it looked for all the world as if the King had arrived in force to claim his rightful throne.

I remember as a child riding home from Palm Sunday service, absentmindedly tearing apart the palm fronds, skimming ahead in the Sunday school quarterly to the next week's topic. It made no sense. With such a throng throwing themselves at his feet one week, how did Jesus get arrested and killed the next?

Now when I read the Gospels I see undercurrents that help explain the shift. On Palm Sunday a group from Bethany surrounded him, still exultant over the miracle of Lazarus. No doubt pilgrims from Galilee, who knew him well, comprised another large portion of the crowd. Matthew points out that further support came from the blind, the lame, and the children. Beyond that constituency, however, lurked danger. Religious authorities resented Jesus, and Roman legions brought in to control the festival crowds would heed the Sanhedrin's assessment of who might present a threat to order.

Jesus himself had mixed feelings during the clamorous parade. Luke reports that as he approached the city he began to weep. He knew how easily a mob could turn. Voices who shout "Hosanna!" one week can shriek "Crucify him!" the next.

The triumphal entry has about it an aura of ambivalence, and as I read all the accounts together, what stands out to me now is the slapstick nature of the affair. I imagine a Roman officer galloping up to check on the disturbance. He has attended processions in Rome, where they do it right. The conquering general sits in a chariot of gold, with stallions straining at the reins and wheel spikes flashing in the sunlight. Behind him, officers in polished armor display the banners captured from vanquished armies. At the rear comes a ragtag procession of slaves and prisoners in chains, living proof of what happens to those who defy Rome.

In Jesus' triumphal entry, the adoring crowd makes up the ragtag procession: the lame, the blind, the children, the peasants from Galilee and Bethany. When the officer looks for the object of their attention he spies a forlorn figure, *weeping*, riding on no stallion or chariot but on the back of a baby donkey, a borrowed coat draped across its backbone serving as his saddle.

Yes, there was a whiff of triumph on Palm Sunday, but not the kind of triumph that might impress Rome and not the kind that impressed crowds in Jerusalem for long either. What manner of king was this?

The Last Supper. Every time I read John's account I am startled by its "modern" tone. Here, as nowhere else, a writer of the Gospels provides a realistic, slow-motion portrayal. John quotes long stretches of dialogue and notes the emotional interplay between Jesus and his disciples. We have, in John 13–17, an intimate memoir of Jesus' most anguished night on earth.

There were many surprises in store for the disciples that evening as they moved through the Passover ritual, laden with symbolism. When Jesus read aloud the story of the Exodus, the disciples' minds may have understandably substituted "Rome" for "Egypt." What better plan than for God to duplicate that tour de force at such a moment, with all the pilgrims congregated in Jerusalem. Jesus' sweeping pronouncement excited their wildest dreams: "I confer on you a kingdom," he said magisterially, and "I have overcome the world."

As I read John's account, I keep coming back to a peculiar incident that interrupts the progress of the meal. "Jesus knew that the Father had put all things under his power," John begins with a flourish and then adds this incongruous completion: "so he got up from the meal, took off his outer clothing, and wrapped a towel around his waist." In the garb of a slave, he then bent over and washed the grime of Jerusalem from the disciples' feet.

What a strange way for the guest of honor to act during a final meal with his friends. What incomprehensible behavior from a ruler who would momentarily announce, "I confer on you a kingdom." In those days, foot washing was considered so degrading that a master could not require it of a Jewish slave. Peter blanched at the provocation.

The scene of the foot washing stands out to author M. Scott Peck as one of the most significant events of Jesus' life. "Until that moment the whole point of things had been for someone to get on top, and once he had gotten on top to stay on top or else attempt to get farther up. But here this man already on top—who was rabbi, teacher, master—suddenly got down on the bottom and began to wash the feet of his followers. In that one act Jesus symbolically overturned the whole social order. Hardly comprehending what was happening, even his own disciples were almost horrified by his behavior."

Jesus asked us his followers to do three things to remember him. He asked us to baptize others, just as he had been baptized by John. He asked to us remember the meal he shared that very evening with the disciples. Finally, he asked us to wash one another's feet. The church has always honored two of those commands, although with much dispute about what they mean and how best to fulfill them. But today we tend to associate the third, foot washing, with small denominations tucked away in the hills of Appalachia. Only a few denominations carry on the practice of foot washing; for the rest, the whole notion seems primitive, rural, unsophisticated. One can debate about whether Jesus intended his command only for the twelve disciples or for all of us to come, but there is no evidence that the Twelve followed instructions either.

Later that same evening a dispute arose among the disciples as to which of them was considered to be greatest. Pointedly, Jesus did not deny the human instinct of competition and ambition. He simply redirected it: "the greatest among you should be like the youngest, and the one who rules like the one who serves." That is when he proclaimed, "I confer on you a kingdom"—a kingdom, in other words, based on service and humility. In the foot washing, the disciples had seen a living tableau of what he meant. Following that example has not gotten any easier in two thousand years.

Betrayal. In the midst of this intimate evening with his closest friends, Jesus dropped a bombshell: One of the twelve men gathered around him would, that night, betray him to the authorities. The disciples "stared at one another, at a loss to know which of them he meant," and began to interrogate each other.

Jesus had hit a nerve. "Surely not I?" the disciples responded in turn, exposing their underlying doubts. Betrayal was no new thought. In conspiratorial Jerusalem, who knows how many disciples had been approached by Jesus' enemies, probing for access. The Last Supper itself was shrouded in danger, the upstairs room arranged clandestinely with a mystery man carrying a jar of water.

A few moments after Jesus' bombshell, Judas quietly left the room, arousing no suspicion. Naturally the group's treasurer may have to excuse himself to purchase supplies or perhaps run an errand of charity.

The name "Judas," once common, has all but disappeared. No parent wants to name a child after the most notorious traitor in history. And yet now, to my own surprise, as I read the gospel accounts it is Judas's *ordinariness*, not his villainy, that stands out. He, like other disciples, had been handpicked by Jesus after a long night of prayer. As treasurer, he obviously held the others' trust. Even at the Last Supper he sat in an honored place near Jesus. The Gospels contain no hint that Judas had been a "mole" infiltrating the inner circle to plan this perfidy.

How, then, could Judas betray the Son of God? Even as I ask the question I think of the remaining disciples fleeing from Jesus in Gethsemane and of Peter swearing, "I don't know the man!" when pressured in a courtyard and of the Eleven stubbornly refusing to believe reports of Jesus' resurrection. Judas's act of betrayal differed in degree, but not in kind, from many other disloyalties.

Curious as to how Hollywood would render the act of betrayal, I watched fifteen movie treatments of Judas. Theories abounded. According to some, he was money hungry. Others showed him as fearful, deciding to strike a deal as Jesus' enemies closed in. Some portrayed him as disillusioned—why did Jesus cleanse the sacred temple with a whip instead of raising an army against Rome? Perhaps he had grown annoyed at Jesus' "softness": like militants in modern Palestine or Northern Ireland, Judas had no patience for a slow, nonviolent revolution. Or, on the contrary, was he hoping to force Jesus' hand? If Judas arranged an arrest, surely that would prompt Jesus to declare himself and install his kingdom.

Hollywood prefers casting Judas as a complex, heroic rebel; the Bible states simply, "Satan entered into him" as he left the table to do the deed. In any event, Judas's disenchantment differed, again, only in degree from what other disciples had felt. When it became clear that Jesus' kind of kingdom led to a cross, not a throne, each one of them slunk away into the darkness.

Judas was not the first or the last person to betray Jesus, merely the most famous. Shusaku Endo, the Christian novelist in Japan, centered many of his novels on the theme of betrayal. *Silence*, his best known, tells of Japanese Christians who recanted their faith under persecution by the shoguns. Endo had read many thrilling stories about the Christian martyrs, but none about the Christian traitors. How could he? None had been written. Yet, to Endo, the most powerful message of Jesus was his unquenchable love even for—*especially* for—people who betrayed him. When Judas led a lynch mob into the garden, Jesus addressed him as "Friend." The other disciples deserted him but still he loved them. His nation had him executed; yet while stretched out naked in the posture of ultimate disgrace, Jesus roused himself for the cry, "Father, forgive them. . . ."

I know of no more poignant contrast between two human destinies than that of Peter and Judas. Both assumed leadership within the group of Jesus' disciples. Both saw and heard wondrous things. Both went through the same dithery cycle of hope, fear, and disillusionment. As the stakes increased, both denied their Master. There, the similarity breaks off. Judas, remorseful but apparently unrepentant, accepted the logical consequences of his deed, took his own life, and went down as the greatest traitor in history. He died unwilling to receive what Jesus had come to offer him. Peter, humiliated but still open to Jesus' message of grace and forgiveness, went on to lead a revival in Jerusalem and did not stop until he had reached Rome.

Gethsemane. From an upstairs room in Jerusalem, stuffy with the smells of lamb, bitter herbs, and sweaty bodies, Jesus and his band of eleven arose and headed for the cool, spacious olive groves in a garden called Gethsemane. Spring was in full bloom, the night air fragrant with blossoms. Reclining under the moon and stars in a peaceful setting outside the bustle of the city, the disciples quickly drifted asleep.

Jesus, however, felt no such peace. "He began to be sorrowful and troubled," says Matthew. He felt "deeply distressed," adds Mark. Both writers record his plaintive words to the disciples: "My soul is overwhelmed with sorrow to the point of death. Stay here and keep watch with me." Often Jesus had gone off by himself to pray, sometimes sending the disciples away in a boat so he could spend the night alone with the Father. This night, though, he needed their presence.

By instinct, we humans want someone by our side in the hospital the night before surgery, in the nursing home as death looms near, in any great moment of crisis. We need the reassuring touch of human presence—solitary confinement is the worst punishment our species has devised. I detect in the Gospels' account of Gethsemane a profound depth of loneliness that Jesus had never before encountered.

Perhaps if women had been included in the Last Supper, Jesus would not have spent those hours alone. Jesus' mother, presciently, had come to Jerusalem—her first mention in the Gospels since early in her son's ministry. The same women who would stand by the cross, and wrap his stiff body, and hurry to the tomb at daybreak surely would have sat with him in the garden, held his head, wiped away his tears. But only male friends accompanied Jesus. Drowsy with dinner and wine, they slept while Jesus endured the crucible, alone.

When the disciples failed him, Jesus did not try to conceal the hurt: "Could you not keep watch for one hour?" His words suggest something more ominous than loneliness. Is it possible that for the first time ever he did not want to be alone with the Father?

A great struggle was under way, and the Gospels describe Jesus' torment in a way quite unlike Jewish and Christian stories of martyrdom. "Take this cup from me," he pled. These were no pious, formal prayers: "being in anguish, he prayed more earnestly, and his sweat was like drops of blood falling to the ground." What was the struggle, exactly? Fear of pain and death? Of course. Jesus no more relished the prospects than you or I do. But there was more at work as well, a new experience for Jesus that can only be called God-forsakenness. At its core Gethsemane depicts, after all, the story of an unanswered prayer. The cup of suffering was not removed.

The world had rejected Jesus: proof came in the torchlight parade then snaking through the pathways of the garden. Soon the disciples would forsake him. During the prayers, the anguished prayers that met a stone wall of no response, it surely must have felt as if God, too, had turned away.

John Howard Yoder speculates on what might have happened if God had intervened to grant the request "Take this cup from me." Jesus was by no means powerless. If he had insisted on his will and not the

Father's, he could have called down twelve legions of angels (72,000) to fight a Holy War on his behalf. In Gethsemane, Jesus relived Satan's temptation in the desert. Either time he could have solved the problem of evil by force, with a quick stab of the accuser in the desert or a fierce battle in the garden. There would be no church history—no church, for that matter—as all human history would come to a halt and the present age would end. All this lay within Jesus' power if he merely said the word, skipped the personal sacrifice, and traded away the messy future of redemption. No kingdom would advance like a mustard seed; the kingdom would rather descend like a hailstorm.

Yet, as Yoder reminds us, the cross, the "cup" that now seemed so terrifying, was the very reason Jesus had come to earth. "Here at the cross is the man who loves his enemies, the man whose righteousness is greater than that of the Pharisees, who being rich became poor, who gives his robe to those who took his cloak, who prays for those who despitefully use him. The cross is not a detour or a hurdle on the way to the kingdom, nor is it even the way to the kingdom; it is the kingdom come."

After several hours of torturous prayer, Jesus came to a resolution. His will and the Father's converged. "Did not the Christ have to suffer these things?" is how he would later put it. He woke his slumberous friends one last time and marched boldly through the darkness toward the ones intent on killing him.

The Trials. These days television programs and bestselling novels make familiar the once-arcane world of legal procedure. For those who desire greater realism, a cable channel broadcasts live the grisliest murder trials and sexiest harassment cases. Time after time the American public has watched with fascination as lawyers craft clever defenses to get famous people off the hook when everyone watching knows the defendants are guilty as sin.

In a span of less than twenty-four hours, Jesus faced as many as six interrogations, some conducted by the Jews and some by the Romans. In the end an exasperated governor pronounced the harshest verdict permitted under Roman law. As I read the trial transcripts, Jesus' *defenselessness* stands out. Not a single witness rose to his defense. No leader had the nerve to speak out against injustice. Not even Jesus tried to defend himself. Throughout, God the Father said not a word.

The trial sequence has a "pass-the-buck" quality. No one seems willing to accept full responsibility for executing Jesus, yet everyone wants him disposed of. Scholars have written thousands of words to determine precisely what share of the blame for Jesus' death belongs to Rome and what share to the Jews.* In fact, both parties participated in the decision. Focusing on all the irregularities in the trials risks missing the main point: Jesus posed a genuine threat to the establishment in Jerusalem.

As a charismatic leader with a large following, Jesus had long aroused the suspicion of Herod in Galilee and the Sanhedrin in Jerusalem. They misunderstood the nature of his kingdom, it is true, but shortly before his arrest Jesus had indeed used force to drive moneychangers out of the temple. To a puppet Sanhedrin government intent on keeping "peace at any cost" for their Roman masters, such an event raised alarm. In addition, a rumor had spread that Jesus claimed he could destroy the temple and rebuild it in three days. Jewish leaders had trouble getting witnesses to agree on the exact wording of Jesus' statement, but their alarm is understandable. Imagine the reaction today if an Arab ran through the streets of New York City shouting, "The World Trade Center will blow up, and I can rebuild it in three days."

---

*To hold the Jewish race as a whole responsible for Jesus' death is one of the great slanders of history. No one thinks of holding modern Italians responsible for what *their* forebears did nineteen centuries ago. Joseph Klausner writes, "The Jews, *as a nation*, were far less guilty of the death of Jesus than the Greeks, as a nation, were guilty of the death of Socrates; but who now would think of avenging the blood of Socrates the Greek upon his countrymen, the present Greek race? Yet these nineteen hundred years past, the world has gone on avenging the blood of Jesus the Jew upon his countrymen, the Jews, who have already paid the penalty, and still go on paying the penalty in rivers and torrents of blood." This despite the fact that Jesus said he had come to "the lost sheep of Israel," and despite the fact that almost all of the first Christians were Jews.

To the priests and the pious, these political threats paled before the reports of Jesus' religious claims. The Pharisees had often blanched at Jesus' boldness in unilaterally forgiving sins and in calling God his own Father. His seeming disregard for the Sabbath scandalized them; Moses' law made Sabbath-breaking a capital offense. Jesus represented a threat to the Law, the sacrificial system, the temple, kosher food regulations, and the many distinctions between clean and unclean.

Finally, at the trial, the high priest appealed to the solemn Oath of the Testimony—"I charge you under oath by the living God"—to ask a question that Jesus as the defendant was required by law to answer. "Tell us if you are the Christ [Messiah], the Son of God." At last Jesus broke his silence: "Yes, it is as you say."

The accused went on to speak in exalted terms of the Son of Man coming on the clouds of heaven. It was too much. To a faithful Jew, Jesus' words sounded blasphemous by any stretch of justice. "Why do we need any more witnesses?" said the high priest, tearing his clothes.

There was only one alternative to blasphemy and the death sentence it carried: that Jesus' words were true and he really was the Messiah. How could that be? Bound, surrounded by armed guards, the very picture of helplessness, Jesus looked to be the least Messiah-like figure in all of Israel.

Blasphemy meant little to the Romans, though, who preferred to stay aloof from local religious disputes. On the way to the Roman judges, the implications of the *Messiah* claim changed from blasphemy to sedition. The word did mean king, after all, and Rome had no tolerance for any agitator who professed such a title.

Before Herod, the same ruler who had hacked off the head of John the Baptist and had long wanted to examine Jesus in person, Jesus maintained a serene silence. Only Pilate could get any kind of confession out of him. "Are you the king of the Jews?" Pilate asked. Once again Jesus, hands tied behind his back, face puffy with sleeplessness, soldiers' palm prints impressed on his cheeks, replied simply, "Yes, it is as you say."

Many times before, Jesus had turned down the chance to declare himself. When healed people, disciples, and even demons recognized him as Messiah, he had hushed them up. In the days of popularity, when crowds chased him around the lake like fanatics pursuing a celebrity, he had fled. When these fans caught him, eager to coronate him on the spot, he preached a sermon so troublesome that all but a few turned away.

Only on this day, first before the religious establishment and then before the political, only when his claims would seem the height of absurdity, did he admit to who he was. "The Son of God," he told the religious powers, who had him in their grasp. "A king," he told a Roman governor, who must have laughed aloud. A pitiful specimen, he probably reminded Pilate of one of Rome's deranged who claimed to be Caesar.

Weak, rejected, doomed, utterly alone—only then did Jesus think it safe to reveal himself and accept the title "Christ." As Karl Barth comments, "He does not confess his Messiahship until the moment when the danger of founding a religion is finally past."

Such a notion was an offense, Paul would later say. A stumbling block—the kind of rock tossed aside as useless, a nuisance on the construction site. But such a rock can form, with God's kind of power, the cornerstone of a new kingdom.

Calvary. In a memoir of the years before World War II, Pierre Van Paassen tells of an act of humiliation by Nazi storm troopers who had seized an elderly Jewish rabbi and dragged him to headquarters. In the far end of the same room, two colleagues were beating another Jew to death, but the captors of the rabbi decided to have some fun with him. They stripped him naked and commanded that he preach the sermon he had prepared for the coming Sabbath in the synagogue. The rabbi asked if he could wear his yarmulke, and the Nazis, grinning, agreed. It added to the joke. The trembling rabbi proceeded to deliver in a raspy voice his sermon on what it means to walk humbly before God, all the while being poked and prodded by the hooting Nazis, and all the while hearing the last cries of his neighbor at the end of the room.

When I read the gospel accounts of the imprisonment, torture, and execution of Jesus, I think of that naked rabbi standing humiliated in a police station. Even after watching scores of movies on the subject, and reading the Gospels over and over, I still cannot fathom the indignity, the *shame* endured by God's Son on earth, stripped naked, flogged, spat on, struck in the face, garlanded with thorns.

Jewish leaders as well as Romans intended the mockery to parody the crime for which the victim had been condemned. *Messiah, huh? Great, let's hear a prophecy.* Wham. *Who hit you, huh?* Thunk. *C'mon, tell us, spit it out, Mr. Prophet. For a Messiah, you don't know much, do you? You say you're a king? Hey, Captain, get a load of this. We have us a regular king here, don't we. Well, then, let's all kneel down before hizzoner. What's this? A king without a crown? Oh, that will never do. Here, Mr. King, we'll fix you a crown, we will.* Crunch. *How's that? A little crooked? I'll fix that. Hey, hold still! My, look how modest we are. Well, how about a robe then—something to cover that bloody mess on your back. What happened, did your majesty have a little tumble?*

It went like that all day long, from the bullying game of Blind Man's Bluff in the high priest's courtyard, to the professional thuggery of Pilate's and Herod's guards, to the catcalls of spectators turned out to jeer the criminals stumbling up the long road to Calvary, and finally to the cross itself where Jesus heard a stream of taunts from the ground below and even from the cross alongside. *You call yourself a Messiah? Well, then come down from that cross. How you gonna save us if you can't even save yourself?*

I have marveled at, and sometimes openly questioned, the self-restraint God has shown throughout history, allowing the Genghis Khans and the Hitlers and the Stalins to have their way. But nothing—nothing—compares to the self-restraint shown that dark Friday in Jerusalem. With every lash of the whip, every fibrous crunch of fist against flesh, Jesus must have mentally replayed the Temptation in the wilderness and in Gethsemane. Legions of angels awaited his command. One word, and the ordeal would end.

"The idea of the cross should never come near the bodies of Roman citizens," said Cicero; "it should never pass through their thoughts, eyes or ears." For the Romans, crucifixion was the cruelest form of capital punishment, reserved for murder, slave revolts, and other heinous crimes in the colonies. Roman citizens were beheaded, not crucified. Jews shared their revulsion—"anyone who is hung on a tree is under God's curse," said Deuteronomy—and preferred stoning when they had authority to carry out executions.

Evangelists, archaeologists, and medical experts have described the grim details of crucifixion so thoroughly that I see no need to iterate them here. Besides, if the "seven last words of Christ" are any indication, Jesus himself had other things on his mind than the pain. The closest to a physical complaint was his cry, "I thirst!" and even then he turned down the vinegar wine offered as an anesthetic. (The irony of one who had made gallons of wine for a wedding party, who had spoken of living water that would quench all thirst forever, dying with a swollen tongue and the sour smell of spilled vinegar on his beard.)

As always, Jesus was thinking about others. He forgave the men who had done the deed. He arranged care for his mother. He welcomed a shriven thief into paradise.

The Gospels record different snatches of conversation from Calvary, and only two agree on Jesus' very last words. Luke has him saying, "Father, into your hands I commit my spirit," a final act of trust before he died. John has the cryptic summation of his entire mission to earth, "It is finished." But Matthew and Mark have the most mysterious saying of all, the woeful quotation, "My God, my God, why have you forsaken me?"*

This time only, of all his prayers in the Gospels, Jesus used the formal, distant word "God" rather than "Abba" or "Father." He was quoting from a psalm, of course, but he was also expressing a grave sense of estrangement. Some inconceivable split had opened up in the Godhead. The Son felt abandoned by the Father.

"The 'hiddenness' of God perhaps presses most painfully on those who are in another way nearest to Him, and therefore God Himself, made man, will of all men be by God most forsaken," wrote C. S. Lewis. No doubt he is right. It matters little if I am rebuffed by the checkout girl at the supermarket or even by a neighbor two blocks down the street. But if my wife, with whom I've spent my entire adult life, suddenly cuts off all communication with me—that matters.

No theologian can adequately explain the nature of what took place within the Trinity on that day at Calvary. All we have is a cry of pain from a child who felt forsaken. Did it help that Jesus had antici-

---

*Commentators have observed that the record in Matthew and Mark is one of the strongest proofs that we have an authentic account of what took place on Calvary. For what reason would the founders of a new religion put such despairing words in the mouth of their dying hero—unless that's precisely what he said.

pated that his mission on earth would include such a death? Did it help Isaac to know his father Abraham was just following orders when he tied him to the altar? What if no angel had appeared and Abraham had plunged a knife into the heart of his son, his only son, whom he loved? What then? That is what happened on Calvary, and to the Son it felt like abandonment.

We are not told what God the Father cried out at that moment. We can only imagine. The Son became "a curse for us," said Paul in Galatians, and "God made him who had no sin to be sin for us," he wrote the Corinthians. We know how God feels about sin; the sense of abandonment likely cut both ways.

Dorothy Sayers writes, "He is the only God who has a date in history.... There is no more astonishing collocation of phrases than that which, in the Nicene Creed, sets these two statements flatly side by side: 'Very God of Very God ... He suffered under Pontius Pilate.' All over the world, thousands of times a day, Christians recite the name of a rather undistinguished Roman proconsul ... merely because that name fixes within a few years the date of the death of God."

Despite the shame and sadness of it all, somehow what took place on a hill called Calvary became arguably the most important fact of Jesus' life—for the writers of the Gospels and Epistles, for the church, and, as far as we can speculate on such matters, for God as well.

It took time for the church to come to terms with the ignominy of the cross. Church fathers forbade its depiction in art until the reign of the Roman emperor Constantine, who had seen a vision of the cross and who also banned it as a method of execution.* Thus not until the fourth century did the cross become a symbol of the faith. (As C. S.

---

*According to historian Michael Grant, Constantine had little interest in the person of Jesus himself and found the crucifixion an embarrassment. In a remarkable irony, seeing "the Cross not so much as an emblem of suffering but as a magic totem confirming his own victoriousness," Constantine transformed the cross from a symbol of sacrificial love and humiliation into a symbol of triumph: he had it painted on the shields of his soldiers.

Lewis points out, the crucifixion did not become common in art until all who had seen a real one died off.)

Now, though, the symbol is everywhere: artists beat gold into the shape of the Roman execution device, baseball players cross themselves before batting, and candy confectioners even make chocolate crosses for the faithful to eat during Holy Week. Strange as it may seem, Christianity has become a religion of the cross—the gallows, the electric chair, the gas chamber, in modern terms.

Normally we think of someone who dies a criminal's death as a failure. Yet the apostle Paul would later reflect about Jesus, "Having disarmed the powers and authorities, he made a public spectacle of them, triumphing over them by the cross." What could he mean?

On one level I think of individuals in our own time who disarm the powers. The racist sheriffs who locked Martin Luther King Jr. in jail cells, the Soviets who deported Solzhenitsyn, the Czechs who imprisoned Václav Havel, the Filipinos who murdered Benigno Aquino, the South African authorities who imprisoned Nelson Mandela—all these thought they were solving a problem, yet instead all ended up unmasking their own violence and injustice. Moral power can have a disarming effect.

When Jesus died, even a gruff Roman soldier was moved to exclaim, "Surely this man was the Son of God!" He saw the contrast all too clearly between his brutish colleagues and their victim, who forgave them in his dying gasp. The pale figure nailed to a crossbeam revealed the ruling powers of the world as false gods who broke their own lofty promises of piety and justice. Religion, not irreligion, accused Jesus; the law, not lawlessness, had him executed. By their rigged trials, their scourgings, their violent opposition to Jesus, the political and religious authorities of that day exposed themselves for what they were: upholders of the status quo, defenders of their own power only. Each assault on Jesus laid bare their illegitimacy.

Thieves crucified on either side of Jesus showed two possible responses. One mocked Jesus' powerlessness: *A Messiah who can't even save himself?* The other recognized a different kind of power. Taking the risk of faith, he asked Jesus to "remember me when you come into your kingdom." No one else, except in mockery, had addressed Jesus as a king. The dying thief saw more clearly than anyone else the nature of Jesus' kingdom.

In a sense, the paired thieves present the choice that all history has had to decide about the cross. Do we look at Jesus' powerlessness as an example of God's impotence or as proof of God's love? The Romans, bred on power deities like Jupiter, could recognize little godlikeness in a crumpled corpse hanging on a tree. Devout Jews, bred on stories of a power Jehovah, saw little to be admired in this god who died in weakness and in shame. As Justin Martyr's "Dialogue with the Jew Tryphon" shows, Jesus' death on a cross made a decisive case against his Messiahship for the Jews; crucifixion had fulfilled the curse of the law.

Even so, over time it was the cross on the hill that changed the moral landscape of the world. M. Scott Peck writes,

> I cannot be any more specific about the methodology of love than to quote these words of an old priest who spent many years in the battle: "There are dozens of ways to deal with evil and several ways to conquer it. All of them are facets of the truth that the only ultimate way to conquer evil is to let it be smothered within a willing, living human being. When it is absorbed there like blood in a sponge or a spear into one's heart, it loses its power and goes no further."
>
> The healing of evil—scientifically or otherwise—can be accomplished only by the love of individuals. A willing sacrifice is required ... I do not know how this occurs. But I know that it does ... Whenever this happens there is a slight shift in the balance of power in the world.

The balance of power shifted more than slightly that day on Calvary because of who it was that absorbed the evil. If Jesus of Nazareth had been one more innocent victim, like King, Mandela, Havel, and Solzhenitsyn, he would have made his mark in history and faded from the scene. No religion would have sprung up around him. What changed history was the disciples' dawning awareness (it took the Resurrection to convince them) that God himself had chosen the way of weakness. The cross redefines God as One who was willing to relinquish power for the sake of love. Jesus became, in Dorothy Sölle's phrase, "God's unilateral disarmament."

Power, no matter how well-intentioned, tends to cause suffering. Love, being vulnerable, absorbs it. In a point of convergence on a hill called Calvary, God renounced the one for the sake of the other.

RESURRECTION:
A MORNING BEYOND BELIEF

———∽∾∾∽———

I find that Holy Week is draining; no matter how many times I have lived through his crucifixion, my anxiety about his resurrection is undiminished—I am terrified that, this year, it won't happen; that, that year, it didn't. Anyone can be sentimental about the Nativity; any fool can feel like a Christian at Christmas. But Easter is the main event; if you don't believe in the resurrection, you're not a believer.

JOHN IRVING, A PRAYER FOR OWEN MEANY

CHAPTER 11

RESURRECTION:
A MORNING BEYOND BELIEF

⸻ ᴓᴓᴓ ⸻

In early childhood I associated Easter with death, not resurrection, because of what happened one sunny Easter Sunday to the only cat I ever owned. Boots was a six-week-old kitten, solid black except for white "boots" on each of her legs, as if she had daintily stepped in a shallow dish of paint. She lived in a cardboard box on the screened porch and slept on a pillow stuffed with cedar shavings. My mother, insisting that Boots must learn to defend herself before sampling the huge outdoors, had fixed a firm date of Easter Sunday for the kitten's big test.

At last the day arrived. Georgia sunshine had already coaxed spring into full bloom. Boots sniffed her first blade of grass that day, batted at her first daffodil, and stalked her first butterfly, leaping high in the air and missing. She kept us joyously entertained until neighbor kids came over for an Easter egg hunt.

When our next-door playmates arrived, the unthinkable happened. Their pet Boston terrier Pugs, following them into our yard, spied Boots, let out a low growl, and charged. I screamed, and we all ran toward Boots. Already Pugs had the tiny kitten in its mouth, shaking it like a sock. We kids encircled the scene, shrieking and jumping up and down to scare Pugs off. Helpless, we watched a whirl of flashing teeth and flying tufts of fur. Finally Pugs dropped the limp kitten on the grass and trotted off.

I could not have articulated it at the time, but what I learned that Easter under the noonday sun was the ugly word *irreversible*. All afternoon I prayed for a miracle. *No! It can't be! Tell me it's not true!* Maybe Boots would come back—hadn't the Sunday school teacher told such a story about Jesus? Or maybe the whole morning could somehow be erased, rewound, and played over again minus that horrid scene. We could keep Boots on the screen porch forever, never allowing her outside. Or we could talk our neighbors into building a fence for Pugs. A thousand schemes ran through my mind over the next days until reality won out and I accepted at last that Boots was dead. Irreversibly dead.

From then on, Easter Sundays in my childhood were stained by the memory of that death in the grass. As the years increased, I would learn much more about the word irreversible.

Not so long ago, as I have mentioned, three of my friends died in quick succession. One, a retired man in excellent health, fell over dead in a parking lot after dining out with his wife. Another, a young woman of forty, died in flames on the way to a church missions conference when a tanker truck rear-ended her car in the fog. A third, my friend Bob, died scuba diving at the bottom of Lake Michigan. Life came to a halt three times that year. I spoke at all three funerals, and each time as I struggled with what to say the old, ugly word *irreversible* came flooding back, with greater force than I had ever known. Nothing I could say, nothing I could do would accomplish what I wanted above all else: to get my friends back.

On the day Bob made his last dive I was sitting, oblivious, in a café at the University of Chicago, reading *My Quest for Beauty* by Rollo May. In that book the famous therapist recalls scenes from his lifelong search for beauty, especially a visit to Mt. Athos, a peninsula of monasteries attached to Greece. There, he happened to stumble upon an all-night celebration of Greek Orthodox Easter. Incense hung in the air. The only light came from candles. At the climax of that service, the priest gave everyone three Easter eggs, splendidly decorated and wrapped in a veil. "Christos Anesti!" he said—"Christ is Risen!" Each person present, including Rollo May, replied according to custom, "He is risen indeed!"

Rollo May writes, "I was seized then by a moment of spiritual reality: what would it mean for our world if He had truly risen?" I read that passage just before returning home to learn that Bob had died, and Rollo May's question kept floating around in my mind, hauntingly, after I heard the terrible news. What did it mean for our world that Christ had risen?

In the cloud of grief over Bob's death, I began to see the meaning of Easter in a new light. As a five-year-old on Easter Sunday I had learned the harsh lesson of irreversibility. Now, as an adult, I saw that Easter actually held out the awesome promise of reversibility. Nothing—no, not even death—was final. Even that could be reversed.

When I spoke at Bob's funeral, I rephrased Rollo May's question in the terms of our particular grief. What would it mean for us if Bob rose again? We were sitting in a chapel, numbed by three days of sorrow, death bearing down upon us like a crushing weight. How would it be to walk outside to the parking lot and there, to our utter astonishment, find Bob. *Bob!* With his bounding walk, his crooked grin, his clear gray eyes. It could be no one else but Bob, alive again!

That image gave me a hint of what Jesus' disciples felt on the first Easter. They too had grieved for three days. On Sunday they heard a new, euphonious sound, clear as a bell struck in mountain air. Easter hits a new note of hope and faith that what God did once in a graveyard in Jerusalem, he can and will repeat on grand scale. For Bob. For us. For the world. Against all odds, the irreversible will be reversed.

The first Christians staked everything on the Resurrection, so much so that the apostle Paul told the Corinthians, "And if Christ has not been raised, our preaching is useless and so is your faith." Did it really happen, this event apart from which our faith is useless? How can we be sure?

People who discount the resurrection of Jesus tend to portray the disciples in one of two ways: either as gullible rubes with a weakness for ghost stories, or as shrewd conspirators who conceived a resurrection plot as a way to jump-start their new religion. The Bible paints a distinctly different picture.

As for the first theory, the Gospels portray Jesus' followers themselves as the ones most leery of rumors about a risen Jesus. One disciple especially, "doubting Thomas," has gained the reputation as a skeptic, but in truth all the disciples showed a lack of faith. None of them believed the wild report the women brought back from the empty tomb; "nonsense" they called it. Even after Jesus appeared to them in person, says Matthew, "some doubted." The eleven, whom Jesus had to rebuke for a stubborn refusal to believe, can hardly be called gullible.

The alternative, a conspiracy theory, falls apart on close examination for, if the disciples had set out to concoct a seamless cover-up story, they failed miserably. Chuck Colson, who participated in a feckless conspiracy after the Watergate break-in, says that cover-ups only work if all participants maintain a unified front of assurance and competence. That, the disciples surely did not do.

The Gospels show the disciples cringing in locked rooms, terrified that the same thing that happened to Jesus might happen to them. Too afraid even to attend Jesus' burial, they left it to a couple of women to care for his body. (Ironically, for Jesus had fought Sabbath restrictions against works of mercy, the dutiful women waited until Sunday morning to finish the embalming process.) The disciples seemed utterly incapable of faking a resurrection or risking their lives by stealing a body; nor did it occur to them in their state of despair.

According to all four Gospels, women were the first witnesses of the resurrection, a fact that no conspirator in the first century would have invented. Jewish courts did not even accept the testimony of female witnesses. A deliberate cover-up would have put Peter or John or, better yet, Nicodemus in the spotlight, not built its case around reports from women. Since the Gospels were written several decades after the events, the authors had plenty of time to straighten out such an anomaly—unless, of course, they were not concocting a legend but recording the plain facts.

A conspiracy also would have tidied up the first witnesses' stories. Were there two white-clad figures or just one? Why did Mary Magdalene mistake Jesus for a gardener? Was she alone or with

Salome and another Mary? Accounts of the discovery of the empty tomb sound breathless and fragmentary. The women were "afraid yet filled with joy," says Matthew; "trembling and bewildered," says Mark. Jesus makes no dramatic, well-orchestrated entrance to quell all doubts; the early reports seem wispy, mysterious, confused. Surely conspirators could have done a neater job of depicting what they would later claim to be the hinge event of history.

In short, the Gospels do not present the resurrection of Jesus in the manner of apologetics, with arguments arranged to prove each main point, but rather as a shocking intrusion that no one was expecting, least of all Jesus' timorous disciples. The first witnesses reacted as any of us would react—as I would react if I answered the doorbell and suddenly saw my friend Bob standing on my front porch: with fear and great joy. Fear is the reflexive human response to an encounter with the supernatural. The fear, though, was overpowered by joy because the news they heard was news too good to be true yet news so good it had to be true. Jesus was alive! Dreams of a Messiah came surging back as the women ran, on legs of fear and joy, to tell the disciples the news.

There actually was a conspiracy, of course, one set in motion not by Jesus' disciples but by the authorities who had to deal with the embarrassing fact of the empty tomb. They could have put a stop to all the wild rumors about a resurrection merely by pointing to a sealed tomb or producing a body. But the seal was broken and the body missing, hence the need for an official plot. Even as the women ran to report their discovery, soldiers were rehearsing an alibi, their role in the scheme of damage-control.

Soldiers standing guard outside Jesus' tomb were the only eyewitnesses of the greatest miracle in history. Matthew says that when the earth quaked and an angel appeared, bright as lightning, they shook and became like dead men.* But here is an astounding fact: later

---

*The Resurrection actually constituted an act of civil disobedience, since it involved breaking Pilate's seal and striking down the official guards. In this case, triumphing over the powers meant active resistance.

The apocryphal Gospel of Peter gives a fanciful version of what took place at the tomb. Two figures descended in a cloud of light, so luminous that many eyewitnesses gathered round to watch. The stone rolled away all by itself, and the two that afternoon the soldiers who had seen proof of the resurrection with their own eyes changed their story to a lie, parroting the priests' line that "His disciples came during the night and stole him away while we were asleep." The alibi had obvious weaknesses (a huge stone rolled away without disturbing sleep? And how could they identify the disciples if asleep?), but at least it kept the guards out of trouble.

Like everything else in Jesus' life, the resurrection drew forth contrasting responses. Those who believed were transformed; infused with hope and courage, they went out to change the world. Those who did not believe found ways to ignore strong evidence. Jesus had predicted as much: "If they do not listen to Moses and the Prophets, they will not be convinced even if someone rises from the dead."

We who read the Gospels from the other side of Easter, who have the day printed on our calendars, forget how *hard* it was for the disciples to believe. In itself the empty tomb did not convince them: that fact only demonstrated "He is not here," not "He is risen." Convincing these skeptics would require intimate, personal encounters with the one who had been their Master for three years, and over the next six weeks Jesus provided exactly that.

Author Frederick Buechner is struck by the unglamorous quality of Jesus' appearances after resurrection Sunday. There were no angels in the sky singing choruses, no kings from afar bearing gifts. Jesus showed up in the most ordinary circumstances: a private dinner, two men walking along a road, a woman weeping in a garden, some fishermen working a lake.

I see in the appearances a whimsical quality, as if Jesus is enjoying the bird-like freedom of his resurrection body. Luke, for example, gives a touching account of Jesus' sudden arrival alongside two forlorn followers on a road to Emmaus. They know about the women's

---

glowing figures emerged from the tomb supporting a third figure, followed by a magical cross. The heads of the two "reached into heaven ... but of him that was led by them ... it overpassed the heavens." It is this kind of sensationalism that the authentic Gospels conspicuously avoid.

discovery of the empty tomb, and Peter's eyewitness confirmation. But who can believe such rumors? Is not death by definition irreversible? "We had hoped that he was the one who was going to redeem Israel," one of them says with obvious disappointment.

A short time later, at mealtime, the stranger makes a riveting gesture, breaking bread, and a link snaps into pace. It is Jesus who has been walking beside them and now sits at their table! Most strangely, the instant they recognize their guest, he disappears.

When the two rush back to Jerusalem, they find the Eleven meeting behind locked doors. They spill out their incredible story, which corroborates what Peter has already learned: Jesus is out there somewhere, alive. Without warning, even as the doubters argue the point, Jesus himself shows up in their midst. *I am no ghost*, he declares. *Touch my scars. It is I myself!* Even then the doubts persist, until Jesus volunteers to eat a piece of broiled fish. Ghosts don't eat fish; a mirage cannot cause food to disappear.

Life continues in that vein for nearly six weeks: Jesus is there, then he's gone. The appearances are not spectral, but flesh-and-blood encounters. Jesus can always prove his identity—no other living person bears the scars of crucifixion—yet often the disciples fail to recognize him right away. Painstakingly, he condescends to meet the level of their skepticism. For suspicious Thomas, it means a personal invitation to finger the scars. For the humiliated Peter, it means a bittersweet scene of rehabilitation in front of six friends.

The appearances, approximately a dozen, show a definite pattern: Jesus visited small groups of people in a remote area or closeted indoors. Although these private rendezvous bolstered the faith of those who already believed in Jesus, as far as we know not a single unbeliever saw Jesus after his death.

Reading the accounts of execution and resurrection back-to-back, I have sometimes wondered why Jesus did not make even more appearances. Why limit visitations to his friends? Why not reappear on Pilate's porch or before the Sanhedrin, this time with a withering blast against those who had condemned him? Perhaps a clue to strategy can be found in his words to Thomas, on the day Thomas's skepticism melted away forever. "Because you have seen me, you have believed; blessed are those who have not seen and yet have believed." In the six-week interlude between Resurrection and Ascension, Jesus, if one may use such language, "broke his own rules" about faith. He made his identity so obvious that no disciple could ever deny him again (and none did). In a word, Jesus overwhelmed the witnesses' faith: anyone who saw the resurrected Jesus lost the freedom of choice to believe or disbelieve. Jesus was now irrefutable. Even Jesus' brother James, always a holdout, capitulated after one of the appearances—enough so that he became a leader of the church in Jerusalem and, according to Josephus, died as one of the early Christian martyrs.

"Because you have seen me, you have believed," said Jesus. These privileged few could hardly disbelieve. But what about the others? Very soon, as Jesus well knew, his personal appearances would come to a halt, leaving only "those who have not seen." The church would stand or fall based on how persuasive these eyewitnesses would be for all—including us today—who have not seen. Jesus had six weeks in which to establish his identity for all time.

That Jesus succeeded in changing a snuffling band of unreliable followers into fearless evangelists, that eleven men who had deserted him at death now went to martyrs' graves avowing their faith in a resurrected Christ, that these few witnesses managed to set loose a force that would overcome violent opposition first in Jerusalem and then in Rome—this remarkable sequence of transformation offers the most convincing evidence for the Resurrection. What else explains the whiplash change in men known for their cowardice and instability?

Others—at least fifteen Jews within a hundred years of Jesus—had made Messiah claims, only to flare and then fade like a dying star. Fanatic loyalty to Jesus, though, did not end with his death. Something had happened, something beyond all precedent. Surely the disciples would not lay down their lives for the sake of a cobbled-together conspiracy theory. Surely it would have been easier, and more natural, to honor a dead Jesus as one of the martyr-prophets whose tombs were so venerated by the Jews.

One need only read the Gospels' descriptions of disciples huddling behind locked doors and then proceed to the descriptions in Acts of the same men proclaiming Christ openly in the streets and in jail cells to perceive the seismic significance of what took place on Easter Sunday. The Resurrection is the epicenter of belief. It is, says C. H. Dodd, "not a belief that grew up within the church; it is the belief around which the church itself grew up, and the 'given' upon which its faith was based." Novelist John Updike states the same truth more poetically:

> Make no mistake: if He rose at all
> it was as His body;
> if the cells' dissolution did not reverse, the molecules
> reknit, the amino acids rekindle,
> the Church will fall.

"Blessed are those who have not seen and yet have believed," Jesus said to doubting Thomas after silencing his doubts with tangible proof of the Easter miracle. Except for the five hundred or so people to whom the resurrected Jesus appeared, every Christian who has ever lived falls into the category of "blessed." I ask myself, *Why do I believe?*—I, who resemble Thomas more than any other disciple in my skepticism and slowness to accept what cannot be proved beyond doubt.

I have weighed the arguments in favor of the resurrection, and they are indeed impressive. The English journalist Frank Morison dealt with most of these arguments in the classic *Who Moved the Stone?* Although Morison had set out to discount the resurrection as a myth, the evidence convinced him otherwise. Yet I also know that many intelligent people have looked at the same evidence and found it impossible to believe. Although much about the Resurrection invites belief, nothing compels it. Faith requires the possibility of rejection, or it is not faith. What, then, gives me Easter faith?

One reason I am open to belief, I admit, is that at a very deep level I want the Easter story to be true. Faith grows out of a subsoil of yearning, and something primal in human beings cries out against the reign of death. Whether hope takes the form of Egyptian pharaohs stashing their jewels and chariots in pyramids, or the modern American obsession with keeping bodies alive until the last possible nanosecond and then preserving them with embalming fluids in double-sealed caskets, we humans resist the idea of death having a final say. We want to believe otherwise. I remember the year I lost my three friends. Above all else, I want Easter to be true because of its promise that someday I will get my friends back. I want to abolish that word *irreversible* forever.

I suppose you could say I want to believe in fairy tales. I am not alone. Has any age not produced fairy tales? We first hear them in our cribs from parents and grandparents, and repeat them to our children who will tell them to their children, and on it goes. Even in this scientific age, some of the highest-grossing movies are variations of fairy tales: *Star Wars*, *Aladdin*, *The Lion King*. Astonishingly in light of human history, most fairy tales have a happy ending. That old instinct, hope, billows up. Like life, fairy tales include much struggle and pain, yet even so they manage to resolve in a way that replaces tears with smiles. Easter does that too, and for this as well as many other reasons, it rings true.*

The crowd at Jesus' crucifixion challenged him to prove himself by climbing down from the cross, but not one person thought of what actually would happen: that he would die and then come back. Once the scenario played out, though, to those who knew Jesus best it made perfect sense. The style fit God's pattern and character. God has always chosen the slow and difficult way, respecting human freedom regardless of cost. "God did not abolish the fact of evil: He transformed it," wrote Dorothy Sayers. "He did not stop the crucifixion: He rose from the dead." The hero bore all consequences, yet somehow triumphed.

I believe in the Resurrection primarily because I have gotten to know God. I know that God is love, and I also know that we human beings want to keep alive those whom we love. I do not let my friends die; they live on in my memory and my heart long after I have stopped seeing them. For whatever reason—human freedom lies at the core, I

---

*J. R. R. Tolkien, perhaps this century's greatest creator of fairy tales, often faced the charge that fantasy is an "escapist" way of shifting attention away from the pressures of the "real world." His reply was simple: Everything depends on that from which one is escaping. We view the flight of a deserter and the escape of a prisoner very differently. "Why should a man be scorned if, finding himself in prison, he tries to get out and go home?"

imagine—God allows a planet where a man dies scuba diving in the prime of life and a woman dies in a fiery crash on the way to a church missions conference. But I believe—if I did not believe this, I would not believe in a loving God—that God is not satisfied with such a blighted planet. Divine love will find a way to overcome. "Death, be not proud," wrote John Donne: God will not let death win.

One detail in the Easter stories has always intrigued me: Why did Jesus keep the scars from his crucifixion? Presumably he could have had any resurrected body he wanted, and yet he chose one identifiable mainly by scars that could be seen and touched. Why?

I believe the story of Easter would be incomplete without those scars on the hands, the feet, and the side of Jesus. When human beings fantasize, we dream of pearly straight teeth and wrinkle-free skin and sexy ideal shapes. We dream of an unnatural state: the perfect body. But for Jesus, being confined in a skeleton and human skin *was* the unnatural state. The scars are, to him, an emblem of life on our planet, a permanent reminder of those days of confinement and suffering.

I take hope in Jesus' scars. From the perspective of heaven, they represent the most horrible event that has ever happened in the history of the universe. Even that event, though—the crucifixion— Easter turned into a memory. Because of Easter, I can hope that the tears we shed, the blows we receive, the emotional pain, the heartache over lost friends and loved ones, all these will become memories, like Jesus' scars. Scars never completely go away, but neither do they hurt any longer. We will have re-created bodies, a re-created heaven and earth. We will have a new start, an Easter start.

There are two ways to look at human history, I have concluded. One way is to focus on the wars and violence, the squalor, the pain and tragedy and death. From such a point of view, Easter seems a fairy-tale exception, a stunning contradiction in the name of God. That gives some solace, although I confess that when my friends died, grief was so overpowering that any hope in an after-life seemed somehow thin and insubstantial.

There is another way to look at the world. If I take Easter as the starting point, the one incontrovertible fact about how God treats those whom he loves, then human history becomes the contradiction and Easter a preview of ultimate reality. Hope then flows like lava beneath the crust of daily life.

This, perhaps, describes the change in the disciples' perspective as they sat in locked rooms discussing the incomprehensible events of Easter Sunday. In one sense nothing had changed: Rome still occupied Palestine, religious authorities still had a bounty on their heads, death and evil still reigned outside. Gradually, however, the shock of recognition gave way to a long slow undertow of joy. If God could do that . . .

PART THREE

WHAT HE LEFT BEHIND

CHAPTER 12

ASCENSION: A BLANK BLUE SKY

———∞∞∞———

But God's own descent
Into flesh was meant
As a demonstration . . .
Spirit enters flesh and for all it's worth
Charges into earth in birth after birth
Ever fresh and fresh.

ROBERT FROST

ASCENSION:
A BLANK BLUE SKY

Sometimes I think about how different the world would be had Jesus not resurrected from the dead. Although the disciples would not risk their lives trumpeting a new faith in the streets of Jerusalem, neither would they forget him. They had given three years to Jesus. He may not be the Messiah (not without Easter), but he had impressed them as the wisest teacher ever and had demonstrated powers that no one could explain.

After time, as emotional wounds began to heal, the disciples would seek some way to memorialize Jesus. Perhaps they would collect his sayings in a written form akin to one of our Gospels, though with the more sensational claims excised. Or, along with Jews from that period who were honoring other martyr-prophets, they might build a monument to Jesus' life. If so, we who live in modern times could still visit that monument and learn about the carpenter/philosopher from Nazareth. We could sift through his sayings, taking or leaving whatever we liked. Worldwide, Jesus would be esteemed in the same way Confucius or Socrates is esteemed.

In many respects I would find an unresurrected Jesus easier to accept. Easter makes him dangerous. Because of Easter I have to listen to his extravagant claims and can no longer pick and choose from his sayings. Moreover, Easter means he must be loose out there somewhere. Like the disciples, I never know where Jesus might turn up, how he might speak to me, what he might ask of me. As Frederick Buechner says, Easter means "we can never nail him down, not even if the nails we use are real and the thing we nail him to is a cross."

Easter puts Jesus' life in a whole new light. Apart from Easter I would think it a tragedy that Jesus died young after a few short years of ministry. What a waste for him to leave so soon, having affected so few people in such a small part of the world! Yet, viewing that same life through the lens of Easter, I see that was Jesus' plan all along. He stayed just long enough to gather around him followers who could carry the message to others. Killing Jesus, says Walter Wink, was like trying to destroy a dandelion seed-head by blowing on it.

When Jesus returned after death to vaporize all doubts among the remnant of believers, he tarried a mere forty days before vanishing for good. The time between Resurrection and Ascension was an interlude, nothing more.

If Easter Sunday was the most exciting day of the disciples' lives, for Jesus it was probably the day of Ascension. He the Creator, who had descended so far and given up so much, was now heading home. Like a soldier returning across the ocean from a long and bloody war. Like an astronaut shedding his spacesuit to gulp in the familiar atmosphere of earth. Home at last.

Jesus' prayer at the Last Supper with his disciples reveals something of this point of view. "I have brought you glory on earth by completing the work you gave me to do," Jesus prayed, "And now, Father, glorify me in your presence with the glory I had with you before the world began." Before the world began! Like an old man reminiscing— no, like an ageless God reminiscing—Jesus, who sat in a stuffy room in Jerusalem, was letting his mind wander back to a time before the Milky Way and Andromeda. On an earthly night dark with fear and menace, Jesus was making preparations to return home, to assume again the glory he had set aside.

On the day Jesus ascended, the disciples stood around dumbfounded, like children who have lost their parent. Two angels sent to calm them asked the obvious question, "Men of Galilee, why do you stand here looking into the sky?" The sky was blank, empty. Still they stood and gazed, not knowing how to go on or what to do next.

So many times in the course of writing this book I have felt like one of those disciples, peering intently at a blank blue sky. I look for some sign of Jesus, some visual clue. When I glance around me at the church he left behind, I want to avert my eyes. Like the disciples' eyes, mine ache for a pure glimpse of the One who ascended. Why, I ask again, did he have to leave?

But as I go back through the Gospels, trying to envision how Jesus himself viewed his time on earth, it seems obvious he planned this departure from the beginning. Nothing pleased Jesus more than the successes of his disciples; nothing disturbed him more than their failures. He had come to earth with the goal of leaving again, after transferring his mission to others. The angels' gentle rebuke might as well have been his own: "Why do you stand here looking into the sky?"

The first time Jesus sent the disciples out alone, he warned them about opposition that would likely take the form of floggings and public torture. "I am sending you out like sheep among wolves," he said. Reading these dire warnings, I cannot push from my mind a harrowing scene from Shusako Endo's novel *Silence*. A Portuguese missionary priest, bound, is forced to watch as samurai guards torture Japanese Christians, one by one, and throw them into the sea. The samurai swear they will keep on killing Christians until the priest renounces his faith. "He had come to this country to lay down his life for other men, but instead of that the Japanese were laying down their lives one by one for him."

What was it like for Jesus, who saw with piercing vision the terrible consequences of what he had set loose in the world, not only for himself but for the huddled few around him, his best friends in all the world? "Brother will betray brother to death, and a father his child ... All men will hate you because of me. ..."

I struggle to reconcile that point of view—a parent consigning her children to the gangs, a general ordering his troops into the line of fire—with what took place at the Last Supper. There, as Jesus disclosed plans for his departure in terms no one could mistake, he said,

"But I tell you the truth: It is for your good that I am going away." All along he had planned to depart in order to carry on his work in other bodies. Their bodies. Our bodies. The new body of Christ.

At the time the disciples had no idea what Jesus meant. *How can it be good that he is going away?* They ate the "body, broken for you" without comprehending the drastic change, that the mission God had assigned to the Son, the Son was now entrusting to them. "As you sent me into the world, I have sent them into the world," Jesus prayed.

Jesus left few traces of himself on earth. He wrote no books or even pamphlets. A wanderer, he left no home or even belongings that could be enshrined in a museum. He did not marry, settle down, and begin a dynasty. We would, in fact, know nothing about him except for the traces he left in human beings. That was his design. The law and the prophets had focused like a beam of light on the One who was to come, and now that light, as if hitting a prism, would fracture and shoot out in a human spectrum of waves and colors.

Six weeks later, the disciples would find out what Jesus had meant by the words *for your good.* As Augustine put it, "You ascended from before our eyes, and we turned back grieving, only to find you in our hearts."

Would it be too much to say that, ever since the Ascension, Jesus has sought other bodies in which to begin again the life he lived on earth? The church serves as an extension of the Incarnation, God's primary way of establishing presence in the world. We are "AfterChrists," in Gerard Manley Hopkins's coinage:

> ... *for Christ plays in ten thousand places,*
> *Lovely in eyes, and lovely in limbs not his*
> *To the Father through the features of men's faces.*

The church is where God lives. What Jesus brought to a few—healing, grace, the good-news message of God's love—the church can now bring to all. That was the challenge, or Great Commission, that Jesus gave just before vanishing from the numbed disciples' sight. "Unless a kernel of wheat falls to the ground and dies," he had explained earlier,

"it remains only a single seed. But if it dies, it produces many seeds."
Propagation by the dandelion method.

Such is the theory, at least. In truth, I must, though, place myself with the disciples who watch with jaws agape as Jesus lifts into the air like some wingless creature defying gravity. "Lord, are you at this time going to restore the kingdom to Israel?" they have just asked—and now this. He's gone! I sympathize with their bewilderment, because I too yearn for a power-Messiah to impose order on a world of evil and violence and poverty. Living two millennia after the disciples, I look back and marvel at how little difference the church has made in such a world. Why did Jesus leave us alone to fight the battles? How can it be good that he went away?

I have concluded, in fact, that the Ascension represents my greatest struggle of faith—not whether it happened, but why. It challenges me more than the problem of pain, more than the difficulty of harmonizing science and the Bible, more than belief in the Resurrection and other miracles. It seems odd to admit such a notion—I have never read a book or article conceived to answer doubts about the Ascension—yet for me what has happened since Jesus' departure strikes at the core of my faith. Would it not have been better if the Ascension had never happened? If Jesus had stayed on earth, he could answer our questions, solve our doubts, mediate our disputes of doctrine and policy.

I find it much easier to accept the fact of God incarnating in Jesus of Nazareth than in the people who attend my local church—and in me. Yet that is what we are asked to believe; that is how we are asked to live. The New Testament declares that the future of the cosmos is being determined by the church (see Romans 8:19–21; Ephesians 3:10). Jesus played his part and then left. Now it is up to us.

"It is a serious thing," wrote C. S. Lewis, "to live in a society of possible gods and goddesses, to remember that the dullest and most uninteresting person you talk to may one day be a creature which, if you saw it now, you would be strongly tempted to worship, or else a horror and a corruption such as you now meet, if at all, only in a nightmare. All day long we are, in some degree, helping each other to one or another of these destinations."

Ancient religions, such as the Roman paganism of Jesus' day, believed that the actions of gods in the heavens above affected the earth below. If Zeus got angry, thunderbolts shot out. Like kids dropping rocks off highway bridges onto the cars below, the gods rained cataclysm onto the earth. "As above, so below," went the ancient formula. Jesus, though, inverted that formula: "As below, so above." "He who listens to you listens to me," Jesus told his followers; "he who rejects you rejects me." A believer prays, and heaven responds; a sinner repents, and the angels rejoice; a mission succeeds, and Satan falls like lightning; a believer rebels, and the Holy Spirit is grieved. What we humans do here decisively affects the cosmos.

I believe these things, and yet somehow I keep "forgetting" them. I forget that my prayers matter to God. I forget that I am helping my neighbors to their eternal destinations. I forget that the choices I make today bring delight—or grief—to the Lord of the Universe. I live in a world of trees and telephones and fax machines, and the reality of this material universe tends to overwhelm my faith in a spiritual universe suffusing it all. I look into the blank blue sky and see nothing.

By ascending, Jesus took the risk of being forgotten.

Not long ago, as I was reading through Matthew, I noticed with a start that Jesus himself foresaw the very predicament of being forgotten. Four parables toward the end of Matthew, among the last that Jesus gave, have a common theme lurking in the background. An owner leaves his house vacant, an absentee landlord puts his servant in charge, a bridegroom arrives so late the guests grow drowsy and fall asleep, a master distributes talents among his servants and takes off— all these circle around the theme of the departed God.

In effect, Jesus' stories anticipated the central question of the modern era: "Where is God now?" The modern answer, from the likes of Nietzsche, Freud, Marx, Camus, and Beckett, is that the landlord has abandoned us, leaving us free to set our own rules. *Deus absconditus*. In places like Auschwitz and Rwanda, we have seen living versions of those parables, graphic examples of how some will act when they stop believing in a sovereign landlord. If there is no God, as Dostoevsky said, then anything is permissible.

Reading on, I came to one more parable, the Sheep and the Goats, probably the last one Jesus taught.

> When the Son of Man comes in his glory, and all the angels with him, he will sit on his throne in heavenly glory. All the nations will be gathered before him, and he will separate the people one from another as a shepherd separates the sheep from the goats. He will put the sheep on his right and the goats on his left.
>
> Then the King will say to those on his right, "Come, you who are blessed by my Father; take your inheritance, the kingdom prepared for you since the creation of the world. For I was hungry and you gave me something to eat, I was thirsty and you gave me something to drink, I was a stranger and you invited me in, I needed clothes and you clothed me, I was sick and you looked after me, I was in prison and you came to visit me."
>
> Then the righteous will answer him, "Lord, when did we see you hungry and feed you, or thirsty and give you something to drink? When did we see you a stranger and invite you in, or needing clothes and clothe you? When did we see you sick or in prison and go to visit you?"
>
> The King will reply, "I tell you the truth, whatever you did for one of the least of these brothers of mine, you did for me."
>
> Then he will say to those on his left, "Depart from me, you who are cursed, into the eternal fire prepared for the devil and his angels. For I was hungry and you gave me nothing to eat, I was thirsty and you gave me nothing to drink, I was a stranger and you did not invite me in, I needed clothes and you did not clothe me, I was sick and in prison and you did not look after me."
>
> They also will answer, "Lord, when did we see you hungry or thirsty or a stranger or needing clothes or sick or in prison, and did not help you?"
>
> He will reply, "I tell you the truth, whatever you did not do for one of the least of these, you did not do for me."
>
> Then they will go away to eternal punishment, but the righteous to eternal life.

I knew this last parable well. It is as potent and disturbing as anything Jesus ever said. But I had never before noticed its logical connection with the four parables that precede it.

In two ways the parable of the Sheep and the Goats directly addresses the question raised by the others: the issue of the absentee landlord, the missing God. First, it gives a glimpse of the landlord's return on judgment day, when there will be hell to pay—literally. The departed One will return, this time in power and in glory, to settle accounts for all that has happened on earth. "Men of Galilee," said the angels, "why do you stand here looking into the sky? This same Jesus, who has been taken from you into heaven, will come back in the same way you have seen him go into heaven."

Second, the parable refers to the meantime, the centuries-long interval we live in now, the time when God seems absent. The answer to that most modern question is at once profound and shocking. God has not absconded at all. Rather, he has taken on a disguise, a most unlikely disguise of the stranger, the poor, the hungry, the prisoner, the sick, the ragged ones of earth: "I tell you the truth, whatever you did for one of the least of these brothers of mine, you did it for me." If we cannot detect God's presence in the world, it may be that we have been looking in the wrong places.

Commenting on this passage, the great American theologian Jonathan Edwards said that God has designated the poor as his "receivers." Since we cannot express our love by doing anything to profit God directly, God wants us to do something profitable for the poor, who have been delegated the task of receiving Christian love.

One night I was absently flipping the channels of television when I came across what seemed to be a children's movie, starring the young Hayley Mills. I settled back and watched the plot unfold. She and two friends, while playing in a country barn, stumbled across a vagrant (Alan Bates) sleeping in the straw. "Who are you?" Mills demanded. The vagrant jerked awake and, seeing the children, muttered, "Jesus Christ!"

What he meant as an expletive, the children took as the truth. They actually believed the man to be Jesus Christ. For the rest of the movie (*Whistle Down the Wind*), they treated the vagrant with awe, respect, and love. They brought him food and blankets, sat and talked with him, and told him about their lives. In time their tenderness transformed the vagrant, an escaped convict who had never before known such mercy.

234

Mills's mother, who wrote the story, intended it as an allegory of what might happen if all of us took literally Jesus' words about the poor and the needy. By serving them, we serve Jesus. "We are a contemplative order," Mother Teresa told a rich American visitor who could not comprehend her fierce commitment to the dregs of Calcutta. "First we meditate on Jesus, and then we go out and look for him in disguise."

As I reflected on the last parable in Matthew 25, I became aware that many of my own questions of God are actually boomerang questions that come right back to me. Why does God allow babies to be born in Brooklyn ghettoes and by a river of death in Rwanda? Why does God allow prisons and homeless shelters and hospitals and refugee camps? Why did Jesus not clean up the world's messes in the years he lived here?

According to this parable, Jesus knew that the world he left behind would include the poor, the hungry, the prisoners, the sick. The decrepit state of the world did not surprise him. He made plans to cope with it: a long-range plan and a short-range plan. The long-range plan involves his return, in power and great glory, to straighten out planet earth. The short-range plan means turning it over to the ones who will ultimately usher in the liberation of the cosmos. He ascended so that we would take his place.

"Where is God when it hurts?" I have often asked. The answer is another question, "Where is the church when it hurts?"

That last question, of course, is the problem of history in a nutshell, and also the reason why I say the Ascension represents my greatest struggle of faith. When Jesus departed, he left the keys of the kingdom in our fumbling hands.

All through my own quest for Jesus has run a counterpoint theme: my need to strip away layers of dust and grime applied *by the church itself*. In my case the image of Jesus was obscured by the racism, intolerance, and petty legalism of fundamentalist churches in the South. A Russian or a European Catholic confronts a very different restoration process. "For not only dust, but also too much gold can cover up the true figure," wrote the German Hans Küng about his own search. Many, far too many, abandon the quest entirely; repelled by the church, they never make it to Jesus.

"What a pity that so hard on the heels of Christ come the Christians," observes Annie Dillard. Her statement reminds me of a T-shirt that can be spotted at contemporary political rallies: "Jesus save us ... from your followers." And of a line from the New Zealand film *Heavenly Creatures* in which two girls describe their imaginary kingdom: "It's like heaven only better—there aren't any Christians!"

The problem showed itself early on. Commenting on the church in Corinth, Frederick Buechner writes, "They were in fact Christ's body, as Paul wrote to them here in one of his most enduring metaphors—Christ's eyes, ears, hands—but the way they were carrying on, that could only leave Christ bloodshot, ass-eared, all thumbs, to carry on God's work in a fallen world." In the fourth century an exasperated St. Augustine wrote about the fractious church, "The clouds roll with thunder that the House of the Lord shall be built throughout the earth; and these frogs sit in their marsh and croak—'We are the only Christians!'"

I could fill several pages with such colorful quotations, all of which underscore the risk involved in entrusting God's own reputation to the likes of us. Unlike Jesus, we do not perfectly express the Word. We speak in garbled syntax, stuttering, mixing languages together, putting accent marks in wrong places. When the world looks for Christ it sees, like the cave-dwellers in Plato's allegory, only shadows created by the light, not the light itself.

Why don't we look more like the church Jesus described? Why does the body of Christ so faintly resemble him? If Jesus could foresee such disasters as the Crusades, the Inquisition, the Christian slave trade, apartheid, why did he ascend in the first place?

I cannot provide a confident answer to such questions, for I am part of the problem. Examined closely, my query takes on a distressingly personal cast: Why do *I* so poorly resemble him? I merely offer three observations that help me come to terms with what has transpired since Jesus' ascension.

First, the church has brought light as well as darkness. In the name of Jesus, St. Francis kissed the beggar and took off his robes,

Mother Teresa founded the Home for the Dying, Wilberforce freed the slaves, General Booth established an urban Army of Salvation, and Dorothy Day fed the hungry. Such work continues: as a journalist I have met educators, urban ministers, doctors and nurses, linguists, relief workers, and ecologists serving all over the world for little pay and less fame, all in the name of Jesus. In other ways, Michelangelo, Bach, Rembrandt, the masons of cathedrals, and many like them offered up the best of their creation "for the glory of God alone." God's hands on earth have reached wider since the Ascension.

I see no point in tallying up a balance sheet to weigh the church's failures against its successes. The final word will come from God's own judgment. The first few chapters of Revelation show how realistically God views the church, and yet elsewhere the New Testament makes clear that God takes pleasure in us: we are "peculiar treasures," a "pleasing aroma," "gifts that he delights in." I cannot fathom such statements; I merely accept them on faith. God alone knows what pleases God.

Second, Jesus takes full responsibility for the constituent parts of his body. "You did not choose me, but I chose you," he told his disciples, and these were the very scalawags who so exasperated him and would soon desert him at his hour of greatest need. I think of Peter, whose bluster, love, hot-headedness, misdirected passion, and faithless betrayal preview in embryo form nineteen centuries of church history. On "rocks" like him, Jesus built his church, and he promised that the gates of hell would not prevail against it.[*]

I take hope as I observe Jesus together with his disciples. Never did they disappoint him more than on the night of his betrayal. Yet it was then, says John, that Jesus "showed them the full extent of his love," and then that he conferred on them a kingdom.

Finally, the problem of the church is no different than the problem of one solitary Christian. How can an unholy assortment of men and women be the body of Christ? I answer with a different question:

---

[*]Charles Williams comments that Jesus "does not seem, to judge by his comments on the religious leaders of his day, ever to have hoped much from officers of a church. The most he would do was to promise that the gates of hell should not *prevail* against it. It is about all that, looking on the history of the Church, one can feel they have not done."

How can one sinful man, myself, be accepted as a child of God? One miracle makes possible the other.

I remind myself that the apostle Paul's soaring words about the bride of Christ and the temple of God were addressed to groups of hideously flawed individuals in places like Corinth. "We have this treasure in jars of clay to show that this all-surpassing power is from God and not from us," wrote Paul in one of the most accurate statements ever penned.

The novelist Flannery O'Connor, who could never be accused of glossing over human depravity, once answered a letter from a reader complaining about the state of the church. "All your dissatisfaction with the Church seems to me to come from an incomplete understanding of sin," O'Connor began:

> ... what you seem actually to demand is that the Church put the kingdom of heaven on earth right here now, that the Holy Ghost be translated at once into all flesh. The Holy Spirit rarely shows Himself on the surface of anything. You are asking that man return at once to the state God created him in, you are leaving out the terrible radical human pride that causes death. Christ was crucified on earth and the Church is crucified in time ... The Church is founded on Peter who denied Christ three times and who couldn't walk on the water by himself. You are expecting his successors to walk on the water. All human nature vigorously resists grace because grace changes us and the change is painful. Priests resist it as well as others. To have the Church be what you want it to be would require the continuous miraculous meddling of God in human affairs ...

In two memorable phrases, O'Connor has captured the choices God faced, looking out on human history: to engage in "the continuous miraculous meddling in human affairs" or to allow himself to be "crucified in time" as his Son was on earth. With a few exceptions, God, whose nature is self-giving love, has chosen the second option. Christ bears the wounds of the church, his body, just as he bore the wounds of crucifixion. I sometimes wonder which have hurt worse.

CHAPTER 13

KINGDOM:
WHEAT AMONG THE WEEDS

———⚬⚬⚬———

The human comedy doesn't attract me enough. I am not entirely of this world. . . . I am from elsewhere. And it is worth finding this elsewhere beyond the walls. But where is it?

EUGENE IONESCO

KINGDOM:
WHEAT AMONG THE WEEDS

———⟨∞⟩———

Each fall the childhood church I attended sponsored a prophecy conference. Silver-haired men of national repute would stretch their prophecy charts—stitched bedsheets covered with Day-Glo renditions of beasts and armies—across the platform and expound on "the last days" we were living in.

I listened in fear and fascination as they drew a straight line south from Moscow to Jerusalem and sketched in the movements of million-strong armies who would soon converge on Israel. I learned that the ten members of Europe's Common Market had recently fulfilled Daniel's prophecy about the beast with ten horns. Soon all of us would wear a number stamped on our foreheads, the mark of the beast, and be registered in a computer somewhere in Belgium. Nuclear war would break out and the planet would teeter on the brink of annihilation, until at the last second Jesus himself would return to lead the armies of righteousness.

That scenario seems far less likely now that Russia has declined and the Common Market (now European Union) has expanded beyond ten members. What sticks with me, though, is not so much the particulars of prophecy as their emotional effect on me. I grew up at once terrified and desperately hopeful. In high school I took courses in Chinese and my brother studied Russian so that one of us could communicate with invading armies from either direction. My uncle went further, packing up his family and moving to Australia. Yet in the midst of this terror we also had hope: though I felt certain the world would soon end, nevertheless I banked all my childhood faith on the belief that somehow Jesus would conquer.

Later, as I read church history, I learned that often before—during the first decades of Christianity, the end of the tenth century, the late 1300s, the Napoleonic era, World War I, the Axis of Hitler and Mussolini—visions of the end times had bubbled to the surface. As recently as the 1991 Gulf War, Saddam Hussein was being branded the Antichrist, the new trigger-man for the apocalypse. Each time, Christians went through a passionate cycle of fear, hope, and sheepish disillusionment. The end times had not arrived after all.

I also learned that the Jewish race has repeatedly undergone the exact same cycle, never more poignantly than in the first century A.D. At that time many Jews expected the Messiah to arise and liberate them from the terrors of Rome, a hope that the man from Nazareth at first ignited, and then dashed. To understand Jesus and the mission he left behind after his ascension, I need to return once more to his own era, to place myself again in his time, to listen to him speak on the topic he favored more than any other: the kingdom of God. What he said about God's kingdom in the first century has great relevance to me today in the twentieth.

In Jesus' day, Jews were poring over the same passages from Daniel and Ezekiel that would later figure so prominently in the prophecy conferences of my childhood.* We disagreed on some details—Northern Europe was then a forest full of barbarians not a Common Market, and Russia was unknown—yet our visions of the Messiah matched: we expected a conquering hero. Anyone

---

*The scribes who pored so assiduously over Old Testament prophecies did not recognize Jesus as the fulfillment of those prophecies. Should not their failure to interpret signs of the first coming sound a note of caution to those today who so confidently proclaim signs of the Second Coming?

who declared "The kingdom of God has come upon you!" would surely awaken in his listeners' minds the image of a political leader who would arise, take charge, and defeat the most powerful empire ever known.

In such an environment, Jesus well understood the explosive power of the word *Messiah*. In William Barclay's judgment, "If Jesus had publicly claimed to be Messiah, nothing could have stopped a useless flood tide of slaughter." Although Jesus did not use the title himself, he accepted it when others called him Messiah, and the Gospels show a gradual dawning on his disciples that their teacher was none other than the long-awaited King.

Jesus encouraged such beliefs by using the word that quickened the pulse of his people. "The *kingdom* of heaven is near," he proclaimed in his very first message. Each time he spoke it, that word stirred memories to life: bright banners, glittering armies, the gold and ivory of Solomon's day, the nation of Israel restored. What was about to happen, Jesus said, would far surpass anything from the past: "For I tell you that many prophets and kings wanted to see what you see but did not see it, and to hear what you hear but did not hear it." On another occasion he announced provocatively, "Now one greater than Solomon is here."

Zealots stood at the edge of Jesus' audience, armed and well-organized guerrillas spoiling for a fight against Rome, but to their consternation the signal for revolt never came. In time, Jesus' pattern of behavior disappointed all who sought a leader in the traditional mold. He tended to flee from, rather than cater to, large groups. He insulted the memory of Israel's glory days, comparing King Solomon to a common day lily. The one time a crowd tried to crown him king by force, he mysteriously withdrew. And when Peter finally did wield a sword on his behalf, Jesus healed the victim's wounds.

To the crowds' dismay, it became clear that Jesus was talking about a strangely different kind of kingdom. The Jews wanted what people have always wanted from a visible kingdom: a chicken in every pot, full employment, a strong army to deter invaders. Jesus announced a kingdom that meant denying yourself, taking up a cross, renouncing wealth, even loving your enemies. As he elaborated, the crowd's expectations crumbled.

By the time Jesus was nailed to wooden crossbeams, everyone had lost hope and fallen away. Scholars report that first-century Jews had no concept of a suffering Messiah. As for the Twelve, no matter how often or how plainly Jesus warned them of his impending death, it never sank in. No one could imagine a Messiah dying.

The word *kingdom* meant one thing to Jesus and quite another to the crowd. Jesus was rejected, in large part, because he did not measure up to a national image of what a Messiah was supposed to look like.

A question has long puzzled me. In view of their expectations, why did Jesus keep arousing his followers' hopes with the word *kingdom*? (It appears fifty-three times in Matthew's gospel alone.) He insisted on associating himself with a term that everyone seemed to misunderstand. What did Jesus mean by the *kingdom of God*?

It is a great irony that the one who so failed the expectations of his people became known to all history as a king—so much so that a form of the word became his "last name." Christ, or *Christos* in Greek, translates the Hebrew word *Messiah*, which means anointed and refers to the ancient manner of coronating kings. Now, all of us who call ourselves *Christ*-ians carry an echo of the word that so baffled the people of Jesus' day. I wonder, Do we understand the kingdom of God any better?

Jesus never offered a clear definition of the kingdom; instead he imparted his vision of it indirectly through a series of stories. His choice of images is telling: everyday sketches of farming, fishing, women baking bread, merchants buying pearls.

The kingdom of heaven is like a farmer going out to sow his seed. As every farmer knows, not all the seed you plant ends up yielding crops. Some falls among rocks, some gets eaten by birds and field mice, some gets crowded out by weeds. All this seems natural to a farmer, but heretical to a traditional kingdom-builder. Are not kings judged by their power, their ability to impose their will on a populace, their strength in repelling enemies? Jesus was indicating that the kingdom of God comes with a resistible power. It is humble and unobtrusive and coexistent with evil—a message that surely did not please patriotic Jews intent on revolt.

Consider the mustard seed, a seed so tiny it can fall to the ground and lie unnoticed by human beings and birds alike. Given time, though, the seed may sprout into a bush that overtakes every other plant in the garden, a bush so large and verdant that birds come and nest in its branches. God's kingdom works like that. It begins so small that people scorn it and give it no chance for success. Against all odds, God's kingdom will grow and spread throughout the world, bringing shade to the sick, the poor, the imprisoned, the unloved.

The kingdom of heaven is like a businessman who specializes in rare gems. One day he finds a pearl gorgeous enough to make princesses drool with envy. Recognizing its value, he liquidates his entire business in order to buy it. Although the purchase costs everything he owns, not for a moment does he regret it. He makes the trade with joy, as the crowning achievement of his life: the treasure will outlive him, enduring long after the family name has disappeared. God's kingdom works like that. The sacrifice—deny yourself, take up your cross—turns out to be a shrewd investment, its outcome not remorse but joy beyond all telling.

These are the stories Jesus told. As I review the parables of the kingdom, though, I realize how far my own understanding has drifted from such homespun images. I tend to envision the same kind of kingdom the Jews did: a visible, powerful kingdom. I think of Constantine leading his troops, crosses emblazoned on their armor, with the slogan "By this sign conquer." I think of the armies marching across the bedsheets at the prophecy conferences. Obviously, I need to listen again to Jesus' description of the kingdom of God.

———

Those of us in the twentieth century, an era that has few literal "kings," conceive of kingdoms in terms of power and polarization. We are the children of revolution. Two centuries ago in the U.S. and France the oppressed rose up and overturned the reigning powers.

Later, in places like Russia and China, Marxists led revolts with an ideology that became a kind of religion: they began, in fact, to view all history as an outgrowth of class struggle, or dialectical materialism. "Workers, unite! Throw off your chains!" cried Marx, and so they did for much of our bloody century.

For a period of time I tried to read the Gospels through the eyes of liberation theology. Ultimately I had to conclude that, whatever else it is, the kingdom of God is decidedly not a call to violent revolution. First-century Jews were doubtless looking for such an upheaval. Battle lines were clear: oppressed Jews versus the bad-guy Romans—pagans who collected taxes, trafficked in slaves, regulated religion, and quashed dissent. Under these conditions the Zealots issued a call much like Marx's: "Jews, unite! Throw off your chains!" But Jesus' message of the kingdom had little in common with the politics of polarization.

As I read the Gospels, Jesus seems to speak a two-pronged message. To the oppressors, he had words of warning and judgment. He treated the powers of government with an attitude of mild contempt, dismissing Herod as "that fox" (a Jewish expression for a worthless or insignificant person) and agreeing to pay a temple tax "so that we may not offend them." He placed little store in politics; it was government, after all, that tried to exterminate him.

To the oppressed, his primary audience, Jesus offered a message of comfort and consolation. He called the poor and the persecuted "blessed." Never did he incite the oppressed to rise up and throw off their chains. In words that must have galled the Zealots, he commanded, "Love your enemies." He invoked a different kind of power: love, not coercion.

People who looked to Jesus as their political savior were constantly befuddled by his choice of companions. He became known as a friend of tax collectors, a group clearly identified with the foreign exploiters, not the exploited. Though he denounced the religious system of his day, he treated a leader like Nicodemus with respect, and though he spoke against the dangers of money and of violence, he showed love and compassion toward a rich young ruler and a Roman centurion.

In short, Jesus honored the dignity of people, whether he agreed with them or not. He would not found his kingdom on the basis of race or class or other such divisions. Anyone, even a half-breed with five husbands or a thief dying on a cross, was welcome to join his kingdom. The person was more important than any category or label.

I feel convicted by this quality of Jesus every time I get involved in a cause I strongly believe in. How easy it is to join the politics of polarization, to find myself shouting across the picket lines at the "enemy" on the other side. How hard it is to remember that the kingdom of God calls me to love the woman who has just emerged from the abortion clinic (and, yes, even her doctor), the promiscuous person who is dying of AIDS, the wealthy landowner who is exploiting God's creation. If I cannot show love to such people, then I must question whether I have truly understood Jesus' gospel.

A political movement by nature draws lines, makes distinctions, pronounces judgment; in contrast, Jesus' love cuts across lines, transcends distinctions, and dispenses grace. Regardless of the merits of a given issue—whether a pro-life lobby out of the Right or a peace-and-justice lobby out of the Left—political movements risk pulling onto themselves the mantle of power that smothers love. From Jesus I learn that, whatever activism I get involved in, it must not drive out love and humility, or otherwise I betray the kingdom of heaven.

If I am tempted to see the kingdom of God as one more power structure, I need only turn to the account of the trial in Jerusalem, a scene that brings together the two kingdoms in striking apposition. On that climactic day the rulers of the "kingdom of this world" confronted Jesus and his kingdom face-to-face.

Two kings, Herod and Jesus, personified very different kinds of power. Herod had legions of Roman soldiers to enforce his will, and history records how Herod used his power: he stole his brother's wife, locked up all dissenters, beheaded John the Baptist as a party trick. Jesus too had power, but he used it compassionately, to feed the hungry and heal the sick. Herod had a gold crown, palaces, guards, and all the visible tokens of royalty. For Jesus, the closest thing to a formal coronation, or Messiah's "anointing," occurred in an embarrassing scene when a disreputable woman poured perfume over his head. He got the title "King of the Jews" as a criminal sentence. His "crown," made of thorns, was merely one more source of pain. And though he could have called on a legion of angels for protection, he declined.

Consistently, Jesus refused to use coercive power. He knowingly let one of his disciples betray him and then surrendered himself without protest to his captors. It never ceases to amaze me that Christian hope rests on a man whose message was rejected and whose love was spurned, who was condemned as a criminal and given a sentence of capital punishment.

Despite Jesus' plain example, many of his followers have been unable to resist choosing the way of Herod over that of Jesus. The Crusaders who pillaged the Near East, the conquistadors who converted the New World at the point of a sword, the Christian explorers in Africa who cooperated with the slave trade—we are still feeling aftershocks from their mistakes. History shows that when the church uses the tools of the world's kingdom, it becomes as ineffectual, or as tyrannical, as any other power structure. And whenever the church has intermingled with the state (the Holy Roman Empire, Cromwell's England, Calvin's Geneva), the appeal of the faith suffers as well. Ironically, our respect in the world declines in proportion to how vigorously we attempt to force others to adopt our point of view.

Sheep among wolves, a tiny seed in the garden, yeast in bread dough, salt in meat: Jesus' own metaphors of the kingdom describe a kind of "secret force" that works from within. He said nothing of a triumphant church sharing power with the authorities. The kingdom of God appears to work best as a minority movement, in opposition to the kingdom of this world. When it grows beyond that, the kingdom subtly changes in nature.

For this reason, I must say in an aside, I worry about the recent surge of power among U.S. Christians, who seem to be focusing more and more on political means. Once Christians were ignored or scorned; now they are courted by every savvy politician. Evangelicals especially are identified with a certain political stance, so much so that the news media use the terms "evangelical" and "religious right" interchangeably. When I ask a stranger, "What is an evangelical Christian?" I get an answer something like this: "Someone who supports family values and opposes homosexual rights and abortion."

This trend troubles me because the gospel of Jesus was not primarily a political platform. The issues that confront Christians in a secular society must be faced and addressed and legislated, and a democracy gives Christians every right to express themselves. But we dare not invest so much in the kingdom of this world that we neglect our main task of introducing people to a different kind of kingdom, one based solely on God's grace and forgiveness. Passing laws to enforce morality serves a necessary function, to dam up evil, but it never solves human problems. If a century from now all that historians can say about evangelicals of the 1990s is that they stood for family values, then we will have failed the mission Jesus gave us to accomplish: to communicate God's reconciling love to *sinners*.

Jesus did not say, "All men will know you are my disciples ... if you just pass laws, suppress immorality, and restore decency to family and government," but rather " ... if you love one another." He made that statement the night before his death, a night when human power, represented by the might of Rome and the full force of Jewish religious authorities, collided head-on with God's power. All his life, Jesus had been involved in a form of "culture wars" against a rigid religious establishment and a pagan empire, yet he responded by giving his life for those who opposed him. On the cross, he forgave them. He had come, above all, to demonstrate love: "For God so loved the world that he gave his one and only Son ... "

When the Roman governor Pilate asked Jesus point-blank whether he was king of the Jews, he replied, "My kingdom is not of this world. If it were, my servants would fight to prevent my arrest by the Jews. But now my kingdom is from another place." Allegiance to a kingdom "not of this world" has emboldened Christian martyrs who, ever since the death of their founder, have met resistance from kingdoms that are of this world. Unarmed believers used that text against their Roman persecutors in the Colosseum, Tolstoy used it to undermine the authority of the tsars, and civil rights marchers used it to challenge apartheid laws in the southern United States and in South Africa. It speaks of a reign that transcends the boundaries—and sometimes the laws—of nation and empire.

On another occasion, Jesus was asked by the Pharisees when the kingdom of God would come. He replied, "The kingdom of God does not come with your careful observation, nor will people say, 'Here it is,' or 'There it is,' because the kingdom of God is within you."

Clearly, the kingdom of God operates by a set of rules different from any earthly kingdom's. God's kingdom has no geographical borders, no capital city, no parliament building, no royal trappings that you can see. Its followers live right among their enemies, not separated from them by a border fence or a wall. It lives, and grows, on the inside of human beings.

Those of us who follow Jesus thus possess a kind of dual citizenship. We live in an external kingdom of family and cities and nationhood, while at the same time belonging to the kingdom of God. In his command, "Give to Caesar what is Caesar's, and to God what is God's," Jesus underscored the fundamental tension that can result. For the early Christians, loyalty to God's kingdom sometimes meant a fatal clash with Caesar's visible kingdom. Historian Will Durant, in *The Story of Civilization*, concludes:

> There is no greater drama in human record than the sight of a few Christians, scorned and oppressed by a succession of emperors, bearing all trials with a fierce tenacity, multiplying quietly, building order while their enemies generated chaos, fighting the sword with the word, brutality with hope, and at last defeating the strongest state that history has known. Caesar and Christ had met in the arena, and Christ had won.

We have seen vivid demonstrations of the clash of kingdoms in our own time. In communist countries—Albania, the U.S.S.R., China—the government forced the Christian church to go underground so that it became, quite literally, invisible. In waves of persecution during the 1960s and 1970s, for instance, Chinese believers were fined, imprisoned, and tortured, and local regulations prohibited most religious activities. Yet despite this government oppression, a spiritual revival broke out that could well be the largest in the history of the church. As many as fifty million believers gave their allegiance to an invisible kingdom even as the visible kingdom made them suffer for it.

In fact, problems seem to arise when the church becomes too external, and gets too cozy with government. As one U.S. legislative aide said after a tour of China, "I believe there is a word of caution for us in the apolitical nature of China's underground church. They fervently pray for their leaders but maintain a careful independence. We are privileged to live in a participatory democracy, but having worked in American politics for almost a decade, I have seen more than a few believers trade in their Christian birthright for a mess of earthly pottage. We must continually ask ourselves: Is our first aim to change our government or to see lives in and out of government changed for Christ?"

To rephrase her question, Is our first aim to change the external, political kingdom or to further God's transcendent kingdom? In a nation like the U.S., the two easily get confused.

I grew up in a church that proudly displayed the "Christian flag" next to the Stars and Stripes, and we would pledge allegiance to both. People would apply to the United States passages from the Old Testament that were obviously intended for a time when God worked through a visible kingdom on earth, the nation of Israel. For example, I often heard this verse quoted as a formula for national revival: "If my people, who are called by my name, will humble themselves and pray and seek my face and turn from their wicked ways, then will I hear from heaven and will forgive their sin and will heal their land." The principle may apply in a general way, of course, but the specific national promise was given as part of God's covenant relationship with the ancient Hebrews; its occasion was the dedication of Solomon's temple, God's dwelling place on earth. Have we any reason to assume God has a similar covenant arrangement with the U.S.?

Indeed, have we any indication that God now judges the U.S. or any other country *as a national entity*? Jesus told his parables of the kingdom in part to correct such nationalistic notions. God is working not primarily through nations, but through a kingdom that transcends nations.

As I now reflect on Jesus' stories of the kingdom, I sense that much uneasiness among Christians today stems from a confusion of the two kingdoms, visible and invisible. Each time an election rolls around, Christians debate whether this or that candidate is "God's man" for the White House. Projecting myself back into Jesus' time, I have difficulty imagining him pondering whether Tiberius, Octavius, or Julius Caesar was "God's man" for the empire. The politics of Rome were virtually irrelevant to the kingdom of God.

Nowadays, as the U.S. grows increasingly secularized, it appears that church and state are heading in different directions. The more I understand Jesus' message of the kingdom of God, the less alarm I feel over that trend. Our real challenge, the focus of our energy, should not be to Christianize the United States (always a losing battle) but rather to strive to be God's kingdom in an increasingly hostile world. As Karl Barth said, "[The Church] exists . . . to set up in the world a new sign which is radically dissimilar to [the world's] own manner and which contradicts it in a way which is full of promise."

Ironically, if the United States is truly sliding down a slippery moral slope, that may better allow the church—as it did in Rome and also in China—to set up "a new sign . . . which is full of promise." I would prefer, I must admit, to live in a country where the majority of people follow the Ten Commandments, act with civility toward each other, and bow their heads once a day for a bland, nonpartisan prayer. I feel a certain nostalgia for the social climate of the 1950s in which I grew up. But if that environment does not return, I will not lose any sleep. As America slides, I will work and pray for the kingdom of God to advance. If the gates of hell cannot prevail against the church, the contemporary political scene hardly offers much threat.

In Stuttgart, Germany, in 1933 Martin Buber held a discussion with a New Testament scholar on why he, a Jew who admired Jesus, nevertheless could not accept him. To Christians, he began, Jews must seem stubborn as they steadfastly wait for a Messiah to come. Why not acknowledge Jesus as Messiah? "The church rests on its faith that the Christ has come, and that this is the redemption which God has bestowed on mankind. We, Israel, are not able to believe this.... We know more deeply, more truly, that world history has not been turned upside down to its very foundations—that the world is not redeemed. We *sense* its unredeemedness." Buber's classic statement took on added poignancy in the next few years, for 1933 was the year Adolf Hitler came to power in Germany, putting to rest any doubts about the unredeemed character of the world. How could a true Messiah allow such a world to continue?

The only possible explanation lies in Jesus' teaching that the kingdom of God comes in stages. It is "Now" and also "Not yet," present and also future. Sometimes Jesus stressed the present aspect, as when he said the kingdom is "at hand" or "within you." At other times he suggested the kingdom lay in the future as when he taught his disciples to pray, "Your kingdom come, your will be done, on earth as it is in heaven." Martin Buber is correct to observe that God's will is apparently not being done on earth as it is in heaven. In some important ways, the kingdom has not fully come.

Probably Jesus himself would have agreed with Buber's assessment of the state of the world. "In this world, you will have trouble," he told his disciples. He also warned of impending disasters: "You will hear of wars and rumors of wars, but see to it that you are not alarmed. Such things must happen, but the end is still to come." The presence of evil guarantees that history will be full of strife and that the world will look unredeemed. For a period of time, the kingdom of God must exist alongside an active rebellion against God. God's kingdom advances slowly, humbly, like a secret invasion force operating within the kingdoms ruled by Satan.

As C. S. Lewis expressed it,

> Why is God landing in this enemy-occupied world in disguise and starting a sort of secret society to undermine the devil? Why is He not landing in force, invading it? Is it that He is not strong enough? Well, Christians think He is going to land in force; we do not know when. But we can guess why He is delaying: He wants to give us the chance of joining His side freely.... God will invade. But I wonder whether people who ask God to

interfere openly and directly in our world quite realise what it will be like when He does. When that happens, it is the end of the world. When the author walks on to the stage the play is over.

Jesus' closest disciples had difficulty grasping this double view of the kingdom. After his death and resurrection, when they understood at last that the Messiah had come not as a conquering king but as one clothed in humility and weakness, even then one thought obsessed them: "Lord, are you at this time going to restore the kingdom to Israel?" No doubt they were thinking of a visible kingdom to replace the rule of Rome. Jesus brushed aside the question and commanded them to carry word of him to the ends of the earth. That is when, to their amazement, he ascended out of sight and when, a few moments later, the angels explained, "This same Jesus, who has been taken from you into heaven, *will come back* in the same way you have seen him go into heaven." The kind of kingdom they yearned for would indeed come, but not yet.

I must confess that for many years I avoided thinking about the Second Coming of Jesus—partly, I'm sure, as a reaction to the prophecy mania of my childhood church. The doctrine seemed an embarrassment, the kind of talk that attracted people who believed in flying saucers. I still have little certainty about details of the Second Coming, but I now see it as the necessary culmination of the kingdom of God. To the degree that the church loses faith in Christ's return and contents itself to be a comfortable part of this world and not the advance guard of a kingdom from another world, to that degree we risk losing faith in a sovereign God.

God has put his reputation on the line. The New Testament points to a time when "every knee should bow . . . and every tongue confess that Jesus Christ is Lord." Obviously, that has not yet happened. Several decades after Easter, the apostle Paul spoke of the whole creation groaning in labor pains for a redemption not yet realized. Jesus' first coming did not solve the problems of planet earth, rather it presented a vision of God's kingdom to help break the earthly spell of delusion.

Only at Christ's second coming will the kingdom of God appear in all its fullness. In the meantime we work toward a better future, always glancing back to the Gospels for a template of what that future will be like. Jürgen Moltmann has observed that the phrase "Day of the Lord" in the Old Testament inspired fear; but in the New Testament it inspires confidence, because those authors had come to know the Lord whose Day it was. They now knew what to expect.

When Jesus lived on earth he made the blind to see and the lame to walk; he will return to rule over a kingdom that has no disease or disability. On earth he died and was resurrected; at his return, death will be no more. On earth he cast out demons; at his return, he will destroy the Evil One. On earth he came as a baby born in a manger; he will return as the blazing figure described in the book of Revelation. The kingdom he set in motion on earth was not the end, only the beginning of the end.

Indeed, the kingdom of God will grow on earth as the church creates an alternative society demonstrating what the world is *not*, but one day will be: Barth's prescription of "a new sign which is radically dissimilar to [the world's] own manner and which contradicts it in a way which is full of promise." A society that welcomes people of all races and social classes, that is characterized by love and not polarization, that cares most for its weakest members, that stands for justice and righteousness in a world enamored with selfishness and decadence, a society in which members compete for the privilege of serving one another—this is what Jesus meant by the kingdom of God.

The Four Horsemen of the Apocalypse give a preview of how the world will end: in war, famine, sickness, and death. But Jesus gave a personal preview of how the world will be restored, by reversing the deeds of the Four Horsemen: he made peace, fed the hungry, healed the sick, and brought the dead to life. He made the message of God's kingdom powerful by living it, by bringing it to reality among the people around him. The prophets' fairy-tale predictions of a world free of pain and tears and death referred to no mythical world, but rather to *this* world.

We in the church, Jesus' successors, are left with the task of displaying the signs of the kingdom of God, and the watching world will judge the merits of the kingdom by us. We live in a transition time—a transition from death to life, from human injustice to divine justice, from the old to the new—tragically incomplete yet marked here and there, now and then, with clues of what God will someday achieve in perfection. The reign of God is breaking into the world, and we can be its heralds.

THE DIFFERENCE HE MAKES

———✺———

The other gods were strong; but Thou wast weak;
They rode, but Thou didst stumble to a throne;
But to our wounds only God's wounds can speak,
And not a god has wounds but Thou alone.

EDWARD SHILLITO

CHAPTER 14

THE DIFFERENCE HE MAKES

Scott Peck writes that he first approached the Gospels skepti-cally, suspecting he would find public-relations accounts written by authors who had tied together loose ends and embellished their biographies of Jesus. The Gospels themselves quickly disabused him of that notion.

> I was absolutely thunderstruck by the extraordinary *reality* of the man I found in the Gospels. I discovered a man who was almost continually frustrated. His frustration leaps out of virtually every page: "What do I have to say to you? How many times do I have to say it? What do I have to do to get through to you?" I also discov-ered a man who was frequently sad and sometimes depressed, fre-quently anxious and scared.... A man who was terribly, terribly lonely, yet often desperately needed to be alone. I discovered a man so incredibly real that no one could have made Him up.
>
> It occurred to me then that if the Gospel writers had been into PR and embellishment, as I had assumed, they would have created the kind of Jesus three quarters of Christians still seem to be trying to create ... portrayed with a sweet, unending smile on His face, patting little children on the head, just strolling the earth with this unflappable, unshakable equanimity.... But the Jesus of the Gospels—who some suggest is the best-kept secret of Christianity—did not have much "peace of mind," as we ordi-narily think of peace of mind in the world's terms, and insofar as we can be His followers, perhaps we won't either.

How can we know the "real Jesus" of whom Scott Peck got a glimpse? I have made a conscious attempt to view Jesus "from below," to grasp as best I can what it must have been like to observe in person the extraordinary events unfolding in Galilee and Judea. Like Scott Peck, I too feel thunderstruck by what I have found.

Icons of the Orthodox Church, stained-glass windows in European cathedrals, and Sunday school art in low-church America all depict on flat planes a placid, "tame" Jesus, yet the Jesus I met in the Gospels was anything but tame. His searing honesty made him seem downright tactless in some settings. Few people felt comfortable around him; those who did were the type no one else felt comfortable around. He was notoriously difficult to predict, pin down, or even understand.

I conclude my survey of Jesus with as many questions as answers. I certainly have not succeeded in taming him, for myself, let alone for anyone else. I now have a built-in suspicion against all attempts to categorize Jesus, to box him in. Jesus is radically unlike anyone else who has ever lived. The difference, in Charles Williams' phrase, is the difference between "one who is an example of living and one who is the life itself."

To sum up what I have learned about Jesus, I offer a series of impressions. They do not form a whole picture by any means, but these are the facets of Jesus' life that challenge me and, I suspect, will never cease to challenge me.

A Sinless Friend of Sinners. When Jesus came to earth, demons recognized him, the sick flocked to him, and sinners doused his feet and head with perfume. Meanwhile he offended pious Jews with their strict preconceptions of what God should be like. Their rejection makes me wonder, Could religious types be doing just the reverse now? Could we be perpetuating an image of Jesus that fits our pious expectations but does not match the person portrayed so vividly in the Gospels?

Jesus was the friend of sinners. He commended a groveling tax collector over a God-fearing Pharisee. The first person to whom he openly revealed himself as Messiah was a Samaritan woman who had a history of five failed marriages and was currently living with yet another man. With his dying breath he pardoned a thief who would have zero opportunity for spiritual growth.

Yet Jesus himself was not a sinner. "Unless your righteousness surpasses that of the Pharisees and the teachers of the law, you will certainly not enter the kingdom of heaven," he taught. The Pharisees themselves searched in vain for proof that he had broken the law of Moses. He had defied certain of their traditions, yes, but at his formal trial the only "crime" that stuck was the one he finally acknowledged, his claim to be Messiah.

I view with amazement Jesus' uncompromising blend of graciousness toward sinners and hostility toward sin, because in much of church history I see virtually the opposite. We give lip service to "hate the sin while loving the sinner," but how well do we practice this principle?

The Christian church has always found ways to soften Jesus' strong words on morality. For three centuries Christians tended to take literally his command to "Resist not evil," but eventually the church developed a doctrine of "just war" and even "holy war." At various times small groups of Christians have followed Jesus' words about disposing of wealth, but most of these have lived on the fringe of a wealthy church establishment. Nowadays many of the same Christians who hotly condemn homosexuality, which Jesus did not mention, disregard his straightforward commands against divorce. We keep redefining sin and changing the emphasis.

At the same time, the institutional church expends much energy positioning itself against the sinful world outside. (A term like "Moral Majority" only sounds appealing to someone already included in it.) I recently attended a play based on stories from a support group comprising people with AIDS. The theater director said he decided to stage the play after hearing a local minister state that he celebrated each time he read an obituary of a young single man, believing each death to be yet another sign of God's disapproval. Increasingly, I fear, the church is viewed as an enemy of sinners.

All too often, sinners feel unloved by a church that, in turn, keeps altering its definition of sin—exactly the opposite of Jesus' pattern. Something has gone awry.

In one of his earlier books, *Shame*, Salman Rushdie said that the true battle of history is fought not between rich and poor, socialist and capitalist, or black and white, but between what he termed the epicure and the puritan. The pendulum of society swings back and forth between those who say, "Anything goes," and those who say, "Oh, no you don't!": the Restoration versus Cromwell, the ACLU versus the religious right, modern secularists versus Islamic fundamentalists. As if to prove his point, soon afterward Iran set a million-dollar bounty on Rushdie's head; he had crossed a line.

History gives ample precedent for legalism and also for decadence. But how does one hold to high standards of moral purity while at the same time showing grace to those who fail those standards? How to embrace the sinner without encouraging sin? Christian history offers few facsimiles of the pattern Jesus laid down.

While I was researching the life of Jesus, I also read several lengthy studies of the first three centuries of the faith. The early church began well, placing a high premium on moral purity. Baptismal candidates had to undergo long periods of instruction, and church discipline was rigorously enforced. Sporadic persecution by Roman emperors helped to purge the church of "lukewarm" Christians. Yet even pagan observers were attracted to the way Christians reached out to others by caring for the oppressed and devoting themselves to the sick and the poor.

A major change took place with the emperor Constantine, who first legalized Christianity and made it a state-subsidized religion. At the time his reign appeared to be the faith's greatest triumph, for the emperor was now using state funds to build churches and sponsor theological conferences rather than to persecute Christians. Alas, the triumph did not come without cost: the two kingdoms got confused. The state began appointing bishops and other church offices, and soon a hierarchy grew up that neatly replicated the hierarchy of the empire itself. As for their part, Christian bishops began imposing morality on society at large, not just the church.

Ever since Constantine, the church has faced the temptation of becoming the "morals police" of society. The Catholic Church in the Middle Ages, Calvin's Geneva, Cromwell's England, Winthrop's New

England, the Russian Orthodox Church—each of these has attempted to legislate a form of Christian morality, and each has in its own way found it hard to communicate grace.

I realize, as I look at the life of Jesus, how far we have come from the divine balance he set out for us. Listening to the sermons and reading the writings of the contemporary church in the U.S., I sometimes detect more of Constantine than of Jesus. The man from Nazareth was a sinless friend of sinners, a pattern that should convict us on both counts.

The God-Man. It would be easier, I sometimes think, if God had given us a set of ideas to mull over and kick around and decide whether to accept or reject. He did not. He gave us himself in the form of a person.

"Jesus saves," announce the bumper stickers—imagine how ridiculous it would sound if you substituted Socrates or Napoleon or Marx. The Buddha gave his disciples permission to forget him as long as they honored his teaching and followed his path. Plato said something similar of Socrates. Jesus, though, pointed to himself and said "*I am the way.*"

Looking at Jesus' life primarily "from below," I have not stressed such concepts as preexistence and divine essence and dual nature, which take up so much space in theology books. It required five centuries for the church to work out the details of Jesus' divinity/humanity, and I have deliberately stayed close to the viewpoint presented by Matthew, Mark, Luke, and John, not the interpretive screen provided by the rest of the New Testament and formalized by the councils of Nicea and Chalcedon.

Even so, the Gospels themselves present the mystery of Jesus' dual identity. How did this Galilean Jew with a family and hometown come to be worshiped as "Very God of Very God"? Simple: Read the Gospels, especially John. Jesus accepted Peter's prostrate worship. To a lame man and an adulterous woman and many others he said commandingly, "I forgive your sins." To Jerusalem he remarked, "I am sending you prophets and wise men and teachers," as if he was not a rabbi standing before them but the sovereign God of history. When challenged, Jesus answered bluntly, "I and the Father are one." "Before Abraham was born, *I am*," he said on another occasion, uttering the sacred Hebrew word for God in case they missed the point. Devout Jews did not miss the point; several times they picked up stones to punish him for blasphemy.

Jesus' audacious claims about himself pose what may be the central problem of all history, the dividing point between Christianity and other religions. Although Muslims and, increasingly, Jews respect Jesus as a great teacher and prophet, no Muslim can imagine Mohammed claiming to be Allah any more than a Jew can imagine Moses claiming to be Yahweh. Likewise, Hindus believe in many incarnations but not one Incarnation, while Buddhists have no categories in which to conceive of a sovereign God becoming a human being.

Could Jesus' disciples have back-filled his teaching to include such brazen claims as part of their conspiracy to launch a new religion? Unlikely. The disciples, as we have seen, were inept conspirators, and in fact the Gospels portray them as resistant to the very idea of Jesus' divinity. Every disciple, after all, belonged to the most fiercely monotheistic race on earth. As late as Jesus' last night with them, after they had heard all the claims and seen all the miracles, one of them asked the Teacher, "Show us the Father." Still they could not grasp it. Jesus was never clearer in his response: "Anyone who has seen me has seen the Father."

It is an incontestable fact of history that Jesus' followers, the same ones who were scratching their heads over his words at the Last Supper, a few weeks later were proclaiming him as the "Holy and Righteous One," the "Lord," the "author of life." By the time the Gospels were written they regarded him as the Word who was God, through whom all things were made. In a later letter John took pains to point out "That which was from the beginning, which we have heard, which we have seen with our eyes, which we have looked at and our hands have touched—this we proclaim concerning the Word of life." The book of Revelation describes Jesus as a blazing figure whose face "was like the sun shining in all its brilliance," but always the author connected this Cosmic Christ to the actual Galilean man the disciples had heard and seen and touched.

THE DIFFERENCE HE MAKES

Why would Jesus' disciples invent these notions? Followers of Mohammed or Buddha, willing to lay down their lives for their master, did not make such a jump in logic. Why would Jesus' disciples, so slow to accept it themselves, require of us a belief so difficult to swallow? Why make it harder rather than easier to accept Jesus?

The alternative to a conspiracy theory, regarding Jesus himself as the source of the audacious claims, only magnifies the problem. As I read through the Gospels, I sometimes try to view them as an outsider might, in the same way I read the Qur'an or the *Upanishads*. When I take up that perspective I find myself repeatedly startled, even offended, by the arrogance of one who says, "I am the way, the truth and the life. No one comes to the Father except through me." I can read only a few pages before stumbling across one of these statements that seem outlandishly to undercut all his wise teaching and good deeds. If Jesus is not God, then he is badly deluded.

C. S. Lewis made this point forcefully. "The discrepancy between the depth and sanity and (let me add) *shrewdness* of His moral teaching and the rampant megalomania which must lie behind His theological teaching unless He is indeed God, has never been satisfactorily got over," he wrote in *Miracles*. Lewis phrased the argument more colorfully in a famous passage in *Mere Christianity*: "A man who was merely a man and said the sort of things Jesus said would not be a great moral teacher. He would either be a lunatic—on the level with the man who says he is a poached egg—or else he would be the Devil of Hell. You must make your choice. Either this man was, and is, the Son of God; or else a madman or something worse."

I remember reading that quote from *Mere Christianity* in college and thinking it a gross exaggeration. I knew many people who respected Jesus as a great moral teacher but judged him neither the Son of God nor a lunatic. That was, in fact, my own view at the time. As I have studied the Gospels, though, I have come to agree with Lewis. Jesus never temporized or waffled about his identity. He was either the Son of God sent to save the world or an impostor deserving of crucifixion. The people of his day understood the binary choice precisely.

265

I now see that Jesus' entire life stands or falls on his claim to be God. I cannot trust his promised forgiveness unless he has the authority to back up such an offer. I cannot trust his words about the other side ("I go to prepare a place for you ...") unless I believe what he said about having come from the Father and returning to the Father. Most important, unless he was in some way God, I must view the cross as an act of divine cruelty rather than sacrificial love.

Sidney Carter wrote this disturbing poem:

> *But God is up in heaven*
> *And he doesn't do a thing,*
> *With a million angels watching,*
> *And they never move a wing....*
> *It's God they ought to crucify*
> *Instead of you and me,*
> *I said to this Carpenter*
> *A-hanging on the tree.*

Theologically, the only answer to Carter's accusation is the mysterious doctrine that, in Paul's words, "God was in Christ reconciling the world to himself." In an incomprehensible way, God personally experienced the cross. Otherwise, Calvary would go down in history as a form of cosmic child abuse, rather than a day we call Good Friday.*

Portrait of God. George Buttrick, former chaplain at Harvard, recalls that students would come into his office, plop down on a chair and declare, "I don't believe in God." Buttrick would give this disarming reply: "Sit down and tell me what kind of God you don't believe in. I probably don't believe in that God either." And then he would talk about Jesus, the corrective to all our assumptions about God.

---

*In Frederick Buechner's words, "What is new about the New Covenant, therefore, is not the idea that God loves the world enough to bleed for it but the claim that here he is actually putting his money where his mouth is. Like a father saying about his sick child, 'I'd do anything to make you well,' God finally calls his own bluff and does it. Jesus Christ is what God does, and the cross where he did it is the central symbol of New Covenant faith."

Books of theology tend to define God by what he is not: God is *im*mortal, *in*visible, *in*finite. But what is God like, positively? For the Christian, Jesus answers such all-important questions. The apostle Paul boldly called Jesus "the image of the invisible God." Jesus was God's exact replica: "For God was pleased to have all his fullness dwell in him."

God is, in a word, Christlike. Jesus presents a God with skin on whom we can take or leave, love or ignore. In this visible, scaled-down model we can discern God's features more clearly.

I must admit that Jesus has revised in flesh many of my harsh and unpalatable notions about God. *Why am I a Christian?* I sometimes ask myself, and to be perfectly honest the reasons reduce to two: (1) the lack of good alternatives, and (2) Jesus. Brilliant, untamed, tender, creative, slippery, irreducible, paradoxically humble—Jesus stands up to scrutiny. He is who I want my God to be.

Martin Luther encouraged his students to flee the hidden God and run to Christ, and I now know why. If I use a magnifying glass to examine a fine painting, the object in the center of the glass stays crisp and clear, while around the edges the view grows increasingly distorted. For me, Jesus has become the focal point. When I speculate about such imponderables as the problem of pain or providence versus free will, everything becomes fuzzy. But if I look at Jesus himself, at how he treated actual people in pain, at his calls to free and diligent action, clarity is restored. I can worry myself into a state of spiritual ennui over questions like "What good does it do to pray if God already knows everything?" Jesus silences such questions: he prayed, so should we.

During my work on *The Student Bible* I spent several years immersed in the Old Testament. With a steady diet of "the Old Covenant," I absorbed something like the attitude of an Orthodox Jew. The Old Testament underscores the vast gulf between God and humanity. God is supreme, omnipotent, transcendent, and any limited contact with him puts human beings at risk. The worship instructions in a book like Leviticus remind me of a manual on handling radioactive material. Bring only spotless lambs to the tabernacle. Do not touch the Ark. Always let smoke cover it; if you look at the ark, you'll die. Never enter the Most Holy Place, except for the high priest on the one permitted day of the year. On that day, Yom Kippur, fasten a rope around his ankle, and a bell, so that if he makes a mistake and dies inside, his corpse can be dragged out.

Jesus' disciples grew up in such an environment, never pronouncing God's name, complying with the intricate code of cleanliness, heeding the requirements of Mosaic law. They took for granted, as did most other religions of the time, that worship must include sacrifice: something had to die. Their God had forbidden human sacrifice, and so on a festival day Jerusalem was filled with the bleats and cries of a quarter million animals destined for the temple altar. The noise and smell of sacrifice were sharp sensory reminders of the great gulf between God and themselves.

I worked in the Old Testament for so long that, when one day I skipped over to the book of Acts, the contrast jolted me. Now God's followers, good Jews most of them, were meeting in private homes, singing hymns, and addressing God with the informal *Abba*. Where was the fear, and the solemn protocol required of anyone who dared approach *mysterium tremendum*? No one brought animals to sacrifice; death did not enter into worship except for the solemn moment when they broke bread and drank wine together, reflecting on the once-for-all sacrifice Jesus had made.

In these ways, Jesus introduced profound changes in how we view God. Mainly, he brought God near. To Jews who knew a distant, ineffable God, Jesus brought the message that God cares for the grass of the field, feeds the sparrows, numbers the hairs on a person's head. To Jews who dared not pronounce the Name, Jesus brought the shocking intimacy of the Aramaic word *Abba*. It was a familiar term of family affection, onomatopoeic like "Dada," the first word many children spoke. Before Jesus, no one would have thought of applying such a word to Yahweh, the Sovereign Lord of the universe. After him, it became a standard term of address even in Greek-speaking congregations; imitating Jesus, they borrowed the foreign word to express their own intimacy with the Father.

An event happened as Jesus hung on the cross that seemed to seal the new intimacy for the young church. Mark records that just as Jesus breathed his last, "The curtain of the temple was torn in two from top to bottom." This massive curtain had served to wall off the Most Holy

Place, where God's presence dwelled. As the author of Hebrews would later note, the tearing of this curtain showed beyond doubt exactly what was accomplished by Jesus' death. No more sacrifices would ever be required. No high priest need tremble to enter the sacred room.

Those of us in modern times have lived under the new intimacy for so long that we take it for granted. We sing choruses to God and converse in casual prayers. To us, the notion of sacrifice seems primitive. Too easily we forget what it cost Jesus to win for us all—ordinary people, not just priests—immediate access to God's presence. We know God as *Abba*, the loving Father, only because of Jesus.

The Lover. Left on my own, I would come up with a very different notion of God. My God would be static, unchanging; I would not conceive of God "coming" and "going." My God would control all things with power, stamping out opposition swiftly and decisively. As a Muslim boy told psychiatrist Robert Coles, "Allah would tell the world, everyone, 'God is great, very great' ... He would make everyone believe in Him, and if someone refused, he'd die—that's what would happen if Allah came here."

Because of Jesus, however, I must adjust my instinctive notions about God. (Perhaps that lay at the heart of his mission?) Jesus reveals a God who comes in search of us, a God who makes room for our freedom even when it costs the Son's life, a God who is vulnerable. Above all, Jesus reveals a God who is love.

On our own, would any of us come up with the notion of a God who loves and yearns to be loved? Those raised in a Christian tradition may miss the shock of Jesus' message, but in truth love has never been a normal way of describing what happens between human beings and their God. Not once does the Qur'an apply the word love to God. Aristotle stated bluntly, "It would be eccentric for anyone to claim that he loved Zeus"—or that Zeus loved a human being, for that matter. In dazzling contrast, the Christian Bible affirms, "God *is* love," and cites love as the main reason Jesus came to earth: "This is how God showed his love among us: He sent his one and only Son into the world that we might live through him."

As Søren Kierkegaard wrote, "The bird on the branch, the lily in the meadow, the stag in the forest, the fish in the sea, and countless joyful people sing: God is love! But under all these sopranos, as if it were a sustained bass part, sounds the *de profundis* of the sacrificed: God is love."

Jesus' own stories about God's love express a quality almost of desperation. In Luke 15 he tells of a woman who searches all night until she finds a valuable coin and of a shepherd who hunts in the darkness until he finds the one sheep who has wandered astray. Each parable concludes with a scene of rejoicing, a celestial party that erupts over the news of another sinner welcomed home. Finally, building to an emotional climax, Jesus tells the story of the lost son, a prodigal who spurns the love of his father and squanders his inheritance in a far country.

The priest Henri Nouwen sat in the Hermitage Museum in St. Petersburg, Russia, for many hours meditating on Rembrandt's great painting *Return of the Prodigal Son*. While staring at the painting, Nouwen gained a new insight into the parable: the mystery that Jesus himself became something of a prodigal son for our sakes. "He left the house of his heavenly Father, came to a foreign country, gave away all that he had, and returned through a cross to his Father's home. All of this he did, not as a rebellious son, but as the obedient son, sent out to bring home all the lost children of God ... Jesus is the prodigal son of the prodigal Father who gave away everything the Father had entrusted to him so that I could become like him and return with him to his Father's home."

In a nutshell, the Bible from Genesis 3 to Revelation 22 tells the story of a God reckless with desire to get his family back. God struck the decisive blow of reconciliation when he sent the Son on the long journey to planet earth. The Bible's last scene, like the parable of the lost son, ends in jubilation, the family united once again.

Elsewhere, the Gospels comment on the extent to which God went to accomplish that rescue plan of love.

> This is love: not that we loved God, but that he loved us and sent his Son as an atoning sacrifice for our sins.
> Greater love has no one than this, that he lay down his life for his friends.

For God so loved the world that he gave his one and only Son ...

I remember a long night sitting in uncomfortable Naugahyde chairs in O'Hare Airport, waiting impatiently for a flight that was delayed for five hours. I happened to be next to a wise woman who was traveling to the same conference. The long delay and the late hour combined to create a melancholy mood, and in five hours we had time to share all the dysfunctions of childhood, our disappointments with the church, our questions of faith. I was writing the book *Disappointment with God* at the time, and I felt burdened by other people's pains and sorrows, doubts and unanswered prayers.

My companion listened to me in silence for a very long time, and then out of nowhere she asked a question that has always stayed with me. "Philip, do you ever just let God love you?" she said. "It's pretty important, I think."

I realized with a start that she had brought to light a gaping hole in my spiritual life. For all my absorption in the Christian faith, I had missed the most important message of all. The story of Jesus is the story of a celebration, a story of love. It involves pain and disappointment, yes, for God as well as for us. But Jesus embodies the promise of a God who will go to any length to win us back. Not the least of Jesus' accomplishments is that he made us somehow lovable to God.

The novelist and literary critic Reynolds Price put it this way: "He says in the clearest voice we have the sentence that mankind craves from stories—*The Maker of all things loves and wants me* ... In no other book our culture owns can we see a clearer graph of that need, that tall enormous radiant arc—fragile creatures made by God's hand, hurled into space, then caught at last by a man in some ways like ourselves."

Portrait of Humanity. When a light is brought into a room, what was a window becomes also a mirror reflecting back the contents of that room. In Jesus not only do we have a window to God, we also have a mirror of ourselves, a reflection of what God had in mind when he created this "poor, bare, forked animal." Human beings were, after

271

all, created in the image of God; Jesus reveals what that image should look like.

"The Incarnation shows man the greatness of his misery by the greatness of the remedy which he required," said Pascal. In a most unsettling way Jesus exposed our failures as human beings. We tend to excuse our many faults by saying, "That's just human." A man gets drunk, a woman has an affair, a child tortures an animal, a nation goes to war: that's just human. Jesus put a stop to such talk. By enacting what we ought to be like, he showed who we were meant to be and how far we miss the mark.

"Behold the man!" Pilate cried. Behold the best example yet of humanity. Yet look at what it got him. Jesus unmasked for all time the jealousy, the lust for power, the violence that infects this planet like a virus. In a weird sort of way, that was the intent of the Incarnation. Jesus knew what he was getting into by coming to this planet; his death had been decreed from the beginning. He came to make an exchange of the most preposterous kind, as described in the Epistles:

> ... though he was rich, yet for your sakes he became poor, so that you through his poverty might become rich.
>
> Who, being in very nature God ... made himself nothing, taking the very nature of a servant, being made in human likeness.
>
> God made him who had no sin to be sin for us, so that in him we might become the righteousness of God.
>
> And he died for all, that those who live should no longer live for themselves but for him who died for them and was raised again.

Our riches for poverty, deity for servanthood, perfection for sin, his death for our life—the exchange seems entirely one-sided. But elsewhere in the Epistles can be found intriguing hints that the Incarnation had meaning for God as well as for human beings. Indeed, the suffering endured on earth served as a kind of "learning experience" for God. Such words sound faintly heretical, but I am merely following Hebrews: "Although he was a son, he learned obedience from what he suffered." Elsewhere, that book tells us that the author of our salvation was "made perfect" through suffering. Commentaries often avoid these phrases, for they are difficult to reconcile with traditional notions of an unchanging

God. To me, they demonstrate certain "changes" that had to take place within the Godhead before we could be reconciled.

During that wrinkle in time known as the Incarnation, God experienced what it is like to be a human being. In thirty-three years on earth God's Son learned about poverty and about family squabbles and social rejection and verbal abuse and betrayal. He learned, too, about pain. What it feels like to have an accuser leave the red imprint of his fingers on your face. What it feels like to have a whip studded with metal lashed across your back. What it feels like to have a crude iron spike pounded through muscle, tendon, and bone. On earth, God's Son "learned" all that.

God's character did not permit the option of simply declaring about this defective planet, "It doesn't matter." God's Son had to encounter evil personally in a way that perfect deity had never before encountered evil. He had to forgive sin by taking on our sin. He had to defeat death by dying. He had to learn sympathy for human beings by becoming one. The author of Hebrews reports that Jesus became a "sympathetic" advocate for us. There is only one way to learn sympathy, as signified by the Greek roots of the word, *syn pathos*, "to feel or suffer with." Because of the Incarnation, Hebrews implies, God hears our prayers in a new way, having lived here and having prayed as a weak and vulnerable human being.*

In one of his last statements before dying, Jesus prayed, "Father, forgive them"—all of them, the Roman soldiers, the religious leaders, his disciples who had fled in darkness, you, me, who have denied him in so many ways—"forgive them, for they do not know what they are doing." Only by becoming a human being could the Son of God truly say with understanding, "They do not know what they are doing." He had lived among us. Now, he understood.

---

*As a doctor who works in hospice told me, "When my patients pray, they are talking to someone who has actually died—something that's not true of any other adviser, counselor, or death expert."

The Wounded Healer. Goethe asked, "There the cross stands, thickly wreathed in roses. Who put the roses on the cross?"

In my travels to foreign countries, I have noticed the striking differences of the symbols used by the great religions. In India, where the four largest religions coexist, I took a brisk walk through the large city of Bombay in the course of which I came upon worship centers of all four.

Hindu temples were everywhere, even portable temples on mobile carts such as sidewalk vendors use, and each had an elaboration of carved, brightly painted images depicting some of the thousands of gods and goddesses in the Hindu pantheon. In stark contrast, a large Muslim mosque in the center of the city contained no images; a soaring spire or minaret pointed skyward, toward the one God, Allah, who could never be reduced to a graven image. Looking at Hindu and Muslim buildings, virtually side by side, I could better understand why each religion finds the other so incomprehensible.

I also visited a Buddhist center that afternoon. Compared to the crowded, noisy streets outside, it offered an atmosphere of serenity. Monks in saffron robes knelt in prayer in the dark, quiet room suffused with the smell of incense. A gilded statue of the Buddha dominated the room, his sly smile expressing the Buddhist belief that the key to contentment lies in developing inner strength that allows one to surmount any suffering in life.

And then I came across a Christian church, a Protestant church of a kind that discouraged images. It most closely resembled the Muslim mosque, with one exception: atop the spire above the church stood a large, ornate cross.

In a foreign country, uprooted from my own culture, I saw the cross with new eyes, and suddenly it struck me as bizarre. What possessed Christians to seize upon this execution device as a symbol for faith? Why not do everything within our power to squelch the memory of the scandalous injustice? We could stress the Resurrection, mentioning the cross only as an unfortunate footnote of history. Why make it the centerpiece of the faith? "Why, that picture might make some people lose their faith!" cried one of Dostoevsky's characters after viewing Holbein's painting of the crucified Christ.

There is, of course, the plain fact that Jesus commanded us to remember his death when we gather together in worship. He did not need to say, "This do in remembrance of me," about Palm Sunday or Easter, but clearly he did not want us to forget what happened on Calvary. Christians have not forgotten. In John Updike's words, the cross "profoundly offended the Greeks with their playful, beautiful, invulnerable pantheon and the Jews with their traditional expectations of a regal Messiah. Yet it answered, as it were, to the facts, to something deep within men. God crucified formed a bridge between our human perception of a cruelly imperfect and indifferent world and our human need for God, our human sense that God is present."

I realized, as I stood on a Bombay street corner with pedestrians, bicyclists, and farm animals swarming around me, why the cross had come to mean so much to Christians, why it had come to mean so much to me. The cross enacts for us deep truths that would make no sense apart from it. The cross gives hope when there is no hope.

The apostle Paul heard from God, "My [God's] power is made perfect in weakness," and then concluded about himself, "When I am weak, then I am strong." "That is why," he added, "I delight in weakness, in insults, in hardships, in persecutions, in difficulties." He was pointing to a mystery which goes several steps beyond the Buddhist way of coming to terms with suffering and hardship. Paul spoke not of resignation but of transformation. The very things that make us feel inadequate, the very things that plunder hope, these are what God uses to accomplish his work. For proof, look at the cross.

I wish someone with the talents of Milton or Dante would render the scene that must have transpired in hell on the day that Jesus died. No doubt an infernal celebration broke out. The snake of Genesis had struck at the heel of God; the dragon of Revelation had devoured the child at last. God's Son, sent to earth on a rescue mission, had ended up dangling from a cross like some ragged scarecrow. Oh, what a diabolical victory!

Oh, what a short-lived victory. In the most ironic twist of all history, what Satan meant for evil, God meant for good. Jesus' death on the cross bridged the gap between a perfect God and a fatally flawed humanity. On the day we call Good Friday, God defeated sin, routed death, triumphed over Satan, and got his family back. In that act of transformation, God took the worst deed of history and turned it into the greatest victory. No wonder the symbol never went away; no wonder Jesus commanded that we never forget.

Because of the cross, I have hope. It is through the Servant's wounds that we are healed, said Isaiah—not his miracles. If God can wrest such triumph out of the jaws of apparent defeat, can draw strength from a moment of ultimate weakness, what might God do with the apparent failures and hardships of my own life?

Nothing—not even the murder of God's own Son—can end the relationship between God and human beings. In the alchemy of redemption, that most villainous crime becomes our healing strength.

The fatally wounded healer came back on Easter, the day that gives a sneak preview of how all history will look from the vantage point of eternity, when every scar, every hurt, every disappointment will be seen in a different light. Our faith begins where it might have seemed to end. Between the cross and the empty tomb hovers the promise of history: hope for the world, and hope for each one of us who lives in it.

The German theologian Jürgen Moltmann expresses in a single sentence the great span from Good Friday to Easter. It is, in fact, a summary of human history, past, present, and future: "God weeps with us so that we may someday laugh with him."

The author and preacher Tony Campolo delivers a stirring sermon adapted from an elderly black pastor at his church in Philadelphia. "It's Friday, but Sunday's Comin'" is the title of the sermon, and once you know the title you know the whole sermon. In a cadence that increases in tempo and in volume, Campolo contrasts how the world looked on Friday—when the forces of evil won over the forces of good, when every friend and disciple fled in fear, when the Son of God died on a cross—with how it looked on Easter Sunday. The disciples who lived through both days, Friday and Sunday, never doubted God again. They had learned that when God seems most absent he may be closest of all, when God looks most powerless he may be most powerful, when God looks most dead he may be coming back to life. They had learned never to count God out.

Campolo skipped one day in his sermon, though. The other two days have earned names on the church calendar: Good Friday and Easter Sunday. Yet in a real sense we live on Saturday, the day with no name. What the disciples experienced in small scale—three days, in grief over one man who had died on a cross—we now live through on cosmic scale. Human history grinds on, between the time of promise and fulfillment. Can we trust that God can make something holy and beautiful and good out of a world that includes Bosnia and Rwanda, and inner-city ghettoes and jammed prisons in the richest nation on earth? It's Saturday on planet earth; will Sunday ever come?

That dark, Golgothan Friday can only be called Good because of what happened on Easter Sunday, a day which gives a tantalizing clue to the riddle of the universe. Easter opened up a crack in a universe winding down toward entropy and decay, sealing the promise that someday God will enlarge the miracle of Easter to cosmic scale.

It is a good thing to remember that in the cosmic drama, we live out our days on Saturday, the in-between day with no name. I know a woman whose grandmother lies buried under 150-year-old live oak trees in the cemetery of an Episcopal church in rural Louisiana. In accordance with the grandmother's instructions, only one word is carved on the tombstone: "Waiting."

SOURCES

Chapter 1

13: *Dickens*: Charles Dickens, *The Life of Our Lord*. London: Associated Newspapers Ltd., 1934.

15: *Pasolini*: Richard H. Campbell and Michael R. Pitts, *The Bible on Film*. Metuchen, N.J.: The Scarecrow Press, 1981, p. 54.

16: *Milliken*: Bill Milliken, *So Long, Sweet Jesus*. New York: Prometheus Press, n.d.

17: *H. G. Wells*: Quoted from *The Greatest Men in History* in Mark Link, S.J., *He Is the Still Point of the Turning World*. Chicago: Argus Communications, 1971, p. 111.

17: "*I tell you, whoever*": Luke 12:8.

17: "*Do you have eyes*": Job 10:4.

18: *Blake*: William Blake, "The Everlasting Gospel," *The Portable Blake*. New York: The Viking Press, 1968, p. 612.

18: *Barth*: Karl Barth, *The Word of God and the Word of Man*. New York: Harper & Row, Publishers, 1957, p. 62.

19: *Lakota*: Cullen Murphy, "Who Do Men Say That I Am?" *The Atlantic Monthly*, December 1986, p. 58.

19: *Norm Evans*: Quoted in "Making It Big," *The Reformed Journal*, December 1986, p. 4.

19: *Fritz Peterson*: Quoted in *The Chicago Tribune*, May 24, 1981.

20: "*scholar at the University of Chicago*": David Tracy, quoted in Murphy, "Who Do Men Say That I Am?" op cit., p. 38.

20: *Phillips*: J. B. Phillips, *Ring of Truth*. Wheaton, Ill.: Harold Shaw Publishers, 1977, p. 79.

20: "*With a loud cry*": Mark 15:37.

21: "*Blessed is he*": Matthew 11:6, RSV.

21: *McGrath*: Alister McGrath, *Understanding Jesus*. Grand Rapids: Zondervan Publishing House, 1987, p. 52.

22: *Kasper*: Walter Kasper, *Jesus the Christ*. New York: Paulist Press, 1977, p. 46.

23: "*Get behind me*": Matthew 16:23.

23: *Wink*: Walter Wink, *Engaging the Powers*. Minneapolis: Fortress Press, 1992, p. 129.

23: *Sayers*: Dorothy Sayers, *Christian Letters to a Post-Christian World*. Grand Rapids: William B. Eerdmans Publishing Company, 1969, p. 15.

24: *Tuchman*: Barbara Tuchman, *Practicing History*. New York: Alfred A. Knopf, 1981, p. 22.

24: *Pascal*: Blaise Pascal, *Pensées*. New York: E. P. Dutton, Inc., 1958, p. 228.

24: *Luther*: Quoted in Jürgen Moltmann, *The Way of Jesus Christ*. San Francisco: Harper-SanFrancisco, 1990, p. 84.

Chapter 2

30: *"salvation from"*: Luke 1:71.

30: *"sword will pierce"*: Luke 2:35.

31: *Lewis*: C. S. Lewis, "The Grand Miracle," in *God in the Dock: Essays on Theology and Ethics*. Grand Rapids: William B. Eerdmans Publishing Company, 1972, p. 84.

32: *Muggeridge*: Malcolm Muggeridge, *Jesus: the Man Who Lives*. New York: Harper & Row, 1975, p. 19.

32: *"I am the Lord's"*: Luke 1:38.

33: *Ricci*: Jonathan D. Spence, *The Memory Palace of Matteo Ricci*. New York: Penguin Books, 1984, p. 245.

33: *"This child is destined"*: Luke 2:34.

33: *Augustus*: John Dominic Crossan, *The Historical Jesus: The Life of a Mediterranean Jewish Peasant*. San Francisco: HarperCollins Publishers, 1991, p. 31.

34, see also p. 57: *Herod the Great*: Joseph Klausner, *Jesus of Nazareth: His Life, Times, and Teaching*. London: George Allen & Unwin, Ltd, 1925, p. 146.

34: *Auden*: *The Collected Poetry of W. H. Auden*. New York: Random House, 1945, p. 455.

36: *Donne*: John Donne, "Nativity," *The Complete English Poems*. New York: Penguin Books, 1971, p. 307.

36: *"made himself nothing"*: Philippians 2:7.

36: *"silver as common"*: 1 Kings 10:27.

36: *Figgis*: Neville Figgis, *The Gospel and Human Needs*. London: Longmans, Green, 1909, p. 11.

37: *"O here and now"*: W. H. Auden, *The Collected Poetry*, op cit., pp. 443–44.

39: *"brought down rulers"*: Luke 1:52.

39: *Tokes*: Laszlo Tokes, *The Fall of Tyrants*. Wheaton, Ill.: Crossway Books, 1990, p. 186.

41: *Lubavitcher*: David Remnick, "Waiting for the Apocalypse in Crown Heights," *The New Yorker*, December 21, 1992, p. 52ff.

42: *"Isn't his mother's name"*: Matthew 13:54–55.

42: *"Nazareth!"*: John 1:46.

42: *"demon-possessed"*: John 10:20.

42: *Chesterton*: G. K. Chesterton, *Orthodoxy*, Garden City, N.Y.: Doubleday/Image Books, 1959, p. 137.

43: *Phillips*: J. B. Phillips, *New Testament Christianity*. London: Hodder & Stoughton, 1958, pp. 27–33.

44: *Apollo astronauts*: Quoted in William M. Justice, *Our Visited Planet*. New York: Vantage Press, 1973, p. 167.

45: *"He is the image"*: Colossians 1:15, 17.

Chapter 3

50: *Buber*: Quoted in Geza Vermes, *Jesus the Jew: A Historian's Reading of the Gospels*. London: Collins, 1973, p. 9.

51: *Moltmann*: Jürgen Moltmann, *The Way of Jesus Christ*, op cit., p. 168.

52: *"My God, my God"*: Matthew 27:46.

52: *"I am not"*: John 3:28.

52: *"Are you the one"*: Matthew 11:3.

53: *"rend the heavens"*: Isaiah 64:1.

53: *"he hath practised sorcery"*: Joseph Klausner, *Jesus of Nazareth*, op cit., p. 27.

54: *"God did not beget"*: Jürgen Moltmann, *The Crucified God*. New York: Harper & Row, 1974, p. 235.

55: *Dodd*: C. H. Dodd, *The Founder of Christianity*. London: The Macmillan Company, 1970, p. 103.

55: *Pelikan*: Jaroslav Pelikan, *Jesus Through the Centuries*. New Haven, Conn.: Yale University Press, 1985, p. 20.

56: *Bonhoeffer*: Dietrich Bonhoeffer, *Christ the Center*. San Francisco: Harper & Row, Publishers, 1978, p. 61.

56: *Virgil*: Quoted in Jaroslav Pelikan, *Jesus Through the Centuries*, op cit., p. 35.

57: *Barclay*: Quoted in Malcolm Muggeridge, *Jesus: the Man Who Lives*, op cit., p. 74.

57: *Antiochus*: Donald B. Kraybill, *The Upside-Down Kingdom*. Scottsdale, Pa.: The Herald Press, 1990, p. 38.

57: *"Would the Romans"*: Joseph Klausner, *Jesus of Nazareth*, op cit., p. 144.

58: *Muggeridge*: Malcolm Muggeridge, *Jesus: the Man Who Lives*, op cit., p. 13.

60: *"How can the Christ"*: John 7:41.

60: *"Nazareth!"*: John 1:46.

60: *"Galilee, Galilee, you hate"*: Vermes, *Jesus the Jew*, op cit., p. 53.

60: *"Are you from Galilee"*: John 7:52.

60: *"You ought to leave"*: John 7:3.

61: *"His high priests"*: Joseph Klausner, *Jesus of Nazareth*, op cit., p. 151.

62: *Josephus*: A. N. Wilson, *Jesus*. New York: W. W. Norton & Company, 1992, p. xii.

62: *"It is better"*: John 11:50.

64: *"If anyone comes"*: Luke 14:26.

64: *"I am able"*: Matthew 26:61.

Chapter 4

70: *"Jesus, full of the Holy Spirit"*: Luke 4:1–2.

71: *Hopkins*: *The Sermons and Devotional Writings of Gerard Manley Hopkins*. London: Oxford University Press, 1959, pp. 180–83.

71: *Luther*: Quoted in F. Forrester Church, *Entertaining Angels*. San Francisco: Harper & Row, Publishers, 1987, p. 54.

72: *Muggeridge*: Malcolm Muggeridge, *Jesus: the Man Who Lives*, op cit., p. 52ff.

73: *"Out of my sight"*: Matthew 16:23.

73: *"Never, Lord"*: Matthew 16:22.

73: *"Aren't you"*: Luke 23:39.

73: *"Let him come down"*: Matthew 27:42–43.

74: *Milton*: "Paradise Regained," *The Complete Poems of John Milton*. New York: Washington Square Press, Inc., 1964, p. 393.

74: *Karamazov*: Fyodor Dostoevsky, *The Brothers Karamazov*. Garden City, N.Y.: Nelson Doubleday, Inc., n.d., pp. 229–39.

76n.: *Sayers*: Dorothy Sayers, *The Man Born to Be King*. Grand Rapids: William B. Eerdmans Publishing Company, n.d., p. 35.

76: *Kierkegaard*: Quoted in D. R. Davies, *On to Orthodoxy*. London: Hodder and Stoughton, 1939, p. 162.

77: *MacDonald*: George MacDonald, *Life Essential, The Hope of the Gospel*. Wheaton, Ill.: Harold Shaw Publishers, 1974, pp. 24–25.

77: *"O Jerusalem"*: Matthew 23:37.

78: *"I, when I am"*: John 12:32–33.

80: *"Jesus looked at him"*: Mark 10:21.

80: *"Because of the increase"*: Matthew 24:12.

80: *"held it more humane"*: Milton, "Paradise Regained," op cit., 368.

80: *"I have prayed"*: Luke 22:32.
80: *"You do not"*: John 6:67.
80: *"Take up your cross"*: Matthew 16:24.
81: *Thielicke*: Helmut Thielicke, *Our Heavenly Father*. Grand Rapids: Baker Book House, 1974, p. 123.
81: *"We do not have"*: Hebrews 4:15; 2:18.

Chapter 5
86: *Lentulus*: Sherwood Wirt, *Jesus, Man of Joy*. Nashville: Thomas Nelson, 1991, p. 28.
86: *"a gluttonous man"*: Luke 7:34, KJV.
87: *"How can the guests"*: Mark 2:19.
87: *"Just as there were many"*: Isaiah 52:14; 53:2–3.
87: *John the Baptist admitted*: John 1:33.
88: *"My soul is"*: Matthew 26:38.
88: *"Your faith"*: Matthew 9:22.
88: *"a true Israelite"*: John 1:47.
89: *Mary Gordon*: Alfred Corn, ed., *Incarnation: Contemporary Writers on the New Testament*. New York: Viking Penguin, 1990, p. 21.
90: *Lewis*: C. S. Lewis, *The Four Loves*. London: Geoffrey Bles, 1960, p. 67.
90: *"Son, why"*: Luke 2:48–49.
90: *"Quiet!"*: Mark 4:39.
91: *Maritain*: Quoted in John S. Dunne, *The Church of the Poor Devil*. New York: Macmillan Publishing Co., Inc., 1982, p.111.
91: *"If it is possible"*: Matthew 26:39.
91: *Crossan*: John Dominic Crossan, *The Historical Jesus*, op cit., p. xi.
91: *"Isn't he"*: Matthew 13:54–55, paraphrased.
92: *"wicked and adulterous"*: Matthew 12:39.
92: *"Believe me"*: John 14:11.
93: *Buechner*: Frederick Buechner, *Peculiar Treasures*. San Francisco: Harper & Row, Publishers, 1979, p. 70.
93: *"Foxes"*: Matthew 8:20.
94: *Berryman*: John Berryman, "Eleven Addresses to the Lord," in *Love & Fame*. New York: Farrar, Straus and Giroux, 1970, p. 92.
94: *Pelikan*: Jaroslav Pelikan, *Jesus Through the Centuries*, op cit., p. 13.
95: *"full of grace"*: John 1:14.
95: *"not impose"*: Joseph Klausner, *From Jesus to Paul*, quoted in Everett F. Harrison, *A Short Life of Christ*. Grand Rapids: Wm. B. Eerdmans Publishing Company, 1968, p. 98.
96: *"Be perfect"*: Matthew 5:48.
96: *Trueblood*: Elton Trueblood, *The Yoke of Christ and Other Sermons*. Waco, Tex.: Word Books, 1958, p. 113.
96: *"Count the cost"*: Luke 14:28, RSV.
96: *Neusner*: Jacob Neusner, *A Rabbi Talks with Jesus*. New York: Doubleday, 1993, pp. 24, 29, 31, 53.
96: *"he taught"*: Matthew 7:29.
96: *"You have heard"*: Matthew 5:21, et al.
97: *"This fellow"*: Matthew 9:3.
97: *"No one ever"*: John 7:46.
97: *"Be quiet"*: Mark 1:25.
97: *"You deaf"*: Mark 9:25.

97: "*We had hoped*": Luke 24:21.
97: "*the whole world*": John 12:19.
98: "*Whoever finds*": Matthew 10:39.
98: "*You don't know*": Matthew 20:22.
99: "*Are you so dull*": Mark 7:18.
99: "*How long*": Matthew 17:17.
99: "*that they might*": Mark 3:14.
100: "*At that time*": Luke 10:21.

Chapter 6

105: "*Blessed are . . .*": All Beatitudes taken from Matthew 5.
109: "*The spirit of self-sacrifice*": Quoted in Alister Hardy, *The Biology of God*. New York: Taplinger Publishing Company, 1975, p. 146.
111: *Lewis*: C. S. Lewis, *The Weight of Glory*. Grand Rapids: William B. Eerdmans Publishing Company, 1965, pp. 1–2.
113: *Phillips*: J. B. Phillips, *Good News*. London: Geoffrey Bles, 1964, pp. 33–4.
113n.: *Kasper*: Walter Kasper, *Jesus the Christ*, op cit., p. 84.
115: *Hellwig*: Monika Hellwig, "Good News to the Poor: Do They Understand It Better?" in *Tracing the Spirit*, James E. Hug, ed. Mahwah, N.J.: Paulist Press, 1983, p. 145.
118: *Mauriac*: François Mauriac, *What I Believe*. New York: Farrar, Straus and Company, 1963, pp. 47–56.
120: "*Adam is a 25-year-old*": Henri Nouwen, "Adam's Peace," in *World Vision Magazine*, August-September 1988, pp. 4–7.
122: "*Christianity has always insisted*": Martin Luther King Jr. Quoted in David J. Garrow, *Bearing the Cross*. New York: William Morrow and Company, Inc., 1986, p. 532.
122: "*to awaken a sense*": Ibid, p. 81.
125: "*Whoever wants*": Matthew 16:25, et al.
125: "*life to the full*": John 10:10.
125: "*in his joy*": Matthew 13:44.

Chapter 7

129: "*Be perfect*": Matthew 5:48.
129: "*I tell you, not seven*": Matthew 18:22.
129: "*In everything*": Matthew 7:12.
130: *Owens*: Virginia Stem Owens, "God and Man at Texas A&M," in *The Reformed Journal*, November 1987, pp. 3–4.
131: "*Do not think*": Matthew 5:17, 20.
132: "*You shall not misuse*": Exodus 20:7.
132: *bleeding Pharisees*: Mary Stewart Van Leeuwen, "Why Christians Should Take the Men's Movement Seriously," in *Radix*, Vol. 21, no. 3, p. 6.
133: "*I tell you . . .*": All such statements taken from Sermon on the Mount, Matthew 5–7.
133: *Updike*: John Updike, "Even the Bible Is Soft on Sex," in *The New York Times Book Review*, June 20, 1993, p. 3.
134: "*Give to Caesar*": Matthew 22:21.
136n.: *Muggeridge*: Malcolm Muggeridge, "Books," in *Esquire*, April 1972, p. 39.
137: *Tolstoy*: See William L. Shirer, *Love and Hatred: The Stormy Marriage of Lev and Sonya Tolstoy*. New York: Simon & Schuster, 1994.
138: "*There is so little genuine warmth*": From Sonya Tolstoy's diary, January 26, 1895.

139: *"What about you"*: Quoted in A. N. Wilson, *The Lion and the Honeycomb: The Religious Writings of Tolstoy*. San Francisco: Harper & Row, Publishers, pp. 147–8.

140: *Wilson*: Ibid, p. 17.

140: *Dostoevsky*: See Joseph Frank: *Dostoevsky, The Years of Ordeal, 1850–1859*. Princeton, N.J.: Princeton University Press, 1983.

141: *"We love because"*: 1 John 4:19.

142: *"Where sin increased"*: Romans 5:20.

142: *"There is now no"*: Romans 8:1.

143: *"Be perfect"*: Matthew 5:48.

143: *"Love the Lord"*: Matthew 22:37.

143: *"Father, forgive"*: Luke 23:34.

Chapter 8

150: *"Do you see"*: Luke 7:44–47.

151: *"the poor, the crippled"*: Luke 14:21.

151: *"For the Son"*: Luke 19:10.

151: *"It is not"*: Matthew 9:12.

152: *"If any one of you"*: John 8:7–11.

152: *Lewis*: C. S. Lewis, *The Problem of Pain*. New York: The Macmillan Company, 1962, p. 98.

152: *Kaminer*: Wendy Kaminer, from *By the Book: America's Self-Help Habit*, quoted in "Saving Therapy: Exploring the Religious Self-Help Literature," *Theology Today*, October 1991, p. 301.

153: *"No madman"*: Hans Küng, *On Being a Christian*. Garden City, N.Y.: Doubleday & Company, Inc., 1976, p. 235.

153: *"Blessed art thou"*: Marcus J. Borg, *Jesus, A New Vision*. San Francisco: Harper & Row, 1987, 133–34.

154: *Wink*: Wink, *Engaging the Powers*, op cit., p. 129.

154: *"There is neither"*: Galatians 3:28.

154n.: *Sayers*: Dorothy L. Sayers, *Are Women Human*. Downers Grove, Ill.: InterVarsity Press, 1971, p. 47.

154: *Wink*: Wink, *Engaging the Powers*, op cit., p. 130.

155: *"God, have mercy"*: Luke 18:13–14.

155: *Wilson*: A. N. Wilson, *Jesus*, op cit., p. 30.

156: *"Son, remember"*: Luke 16:25.

156n.: *Constantine, early Christians*: See Robin Lane Fox, *Pagans and Christians*. New York: Alfred A. Knopf, 1989.

157: *Third World base communities*: See Robert McAfee Brown, *Unexpected News: Reading the Bible with Third World Eyes*. Philadelphia: The Westminster Press, 1984.

157: *"he has anointed"*: Isaiah 61:1.

158: *Endo*: See Shusaku Endo, *A Life of Jesus*. New York: Paulist Press, 1973.

160: *"O Jerusalem"*: Matthew 23:37.

160: *"offered up loud"*: Hebrews 5:7.

161: *"My God"*: Matthew 27:46.

Chapter 9

167: *Miracle of water into wine*: John 2:1–11

168: *Lewis*: C. S. Lewis, "Miracles," in *God in the Dock*, op cit., p. 29.

169: *"There is no death"*: Footnote to John 9:2 in *The NIV Study Bible*. Grand Rapids: Zondervan Publishing House, 1985, p. 1614.

170: *Miracle of healed blindness*: John 9: 1–41.

171: *Koop*: From personal interview.

172: *Miracle of healed leprosy*: Matthew 8:1–4; Mark 1:40–44; Luke 5:12–14.

173n.: *"Holy Disease"*: Patrick Feeny, *The Fight Against Leprosy*. New York: American Leprosy Mission, 1964, pp. 25, 32.

173: *Teresa*: From television interview.

173: *Miracle of healed paralysis*: Matthew 9:1–8; Mark 2:1–12; Luke 5:17–26.

174n.: *"Any disabled person"*: Donald Senior, C. P., "With New Eyes," in *Stauros Notebook*, vol. 9, no. 2, p. 1.

176: *Miracle of feeding five thousand*: Matthew 14:13–21; Mark 6:30–44; Luke 9:10–17; John 6:5–71.

177: *Capon*: Robert Farrar Capon, *Parables of the Kingdom*. Grand Rapids: Zondervan Publishing House, 1985, p. 27.

177: *"A wicked and adulterous"*: Matthew 12:39.

178: *"he would not entrust"*: John 2:24.

178: *Miracle of raising Lazarus*: John 11:1–54.

181: *"If they do not listen"*: Luke 16:31.

181: *"not one [sparrow]"*: Matthew 10:29.

181: *Askew*: Eddie Askew, *Disguises of Love*. London: The Leprosy Mission International, 1983, p. 50.

181: *"I do believe"*: Mark 9:24.

182: *John the Baptist*: Matthew 11:1–7.

183: *Moltmann*: Jürgen Moltmann, *The Way of Jesus Christ*, op cit., p. 99.

Chapter 10

189: *"Blessed is the king"*: Luke 19:38.

189: *"I tell you"*: Luke 19:40.

189: *"Look how"*: John 12:19.

191: *"I confer on you"*: Luke 22:29.

191: *"I have overcome"*: John 16:33.

191: *"Jesus knew"*: John 13:3–4.

191: *Peck*: M. Scott Peck, *The Different Drum*. New York: Touchstone/Simon & Schuster, 1988, p. 293.

192: *"the greatest"*: Luke 22:26.

192: *"stared at one another"*: John 13:22.

192: *"Surely not I?"*: Mark 14:19.

193: *"I don't know"*: Matthew 26:74.

193: *"Satan entered"*: John 13:27.

194: *"Father, forgive"*: Luke 23:34.

194: *Gethsemane*: Matthew 26:36–56; Mark 14:32–52; Luke 22:39–53.

195: *Yoder*: John Howard Yoder, *The Politics of Jesus*. Grand Rapids: William B. Eerdmans Publishing Company, 1972, pp. 55–56, 61.

196: *"Did not the Christ"*: Luke 24:26.

197n.: *Klausner*: Joseph Klausner, *Jesus of Nazareth*, op cit., p. 348.

198: *"I charge you . . ."*: Matthew 26:63–65.

198: *"Are you the king"*: Luke 23:3.

199: *Barth*: Karl Barth, *The Word of God and the Word of Man*, op cit., p. 82.

200: *Cicero*: Quoted in Walter Kasper, *Jesus the Christ*, op cit., p. 113.

200: *"anyone who is hung"*: Deuteronomy 21:23.

201: *"I thirst"*: John 19:28, KJV.

201: *"Father, into"*: Luke 23:45.

201: *"It is finished"*: John 19:30.

201: *"My God, my God"*: Matthew 27:46; Mark 15:33.

201: *Lewis*: C. S. Lewis, *Letters to Malcolm: Chiefly on Prayer*. London: Geoffrey Bles, 1964, p. 65.

202: *"a curse for us"*: Galatians 3:13.

202: *"God made him"*: 2 Corinthians 5:21.

202: *Sayers*: Sayers, *The Man Born to Be King*, op cit., p. 5.

20n.: *Constantine*: Michael Grant, *Constantine the Great*. New York: Charles Scribner's Sons, 1994, pp. 149, 222.

203: *Lewis*: *Letters to Malcolm: Chiefly on Prayer*, op cit., p. 113.

203: *"Having disarmed"*: Colossians 2:15.

203: *"Surely this man"*: Mark 15:39.

203: *"remember me"*: Luke 23:42.

204: *Justin Martyr*: Hans Küng, *On Being a Christian*, op cit, p. 339.

204: *Peck*: M. Scott Peck, *People of the Lie*. New York: Simon and Schuster, 1983, p. 269.

205: *Sölle*: Dorothy Sölle, *Of War and Love*. Maryknoll, N.Y.: Orbis Books, 1984, p. 97.

Chapter 11

210: *May*: Rollo May, *My Quest for Beauty*. Dallas: Saybrook Publishing Company, 1985, p. 60.

211: *"And if Christ"*: 1 Corinthians 15:14.

212: *"nonsense"*: Luke 24:11.

212: *"some doubted"*: Matthew 28:17.

213: *"afraid yet"*: Matthew 28:8.

213: *"trembling and bewildered"*: Mark 16:8.

213: *Gospel of Peter*: Quoted in Frederick Buechner, *The Faces of Jesus*. San Francisco: Harper & Row Publishers, 1989, p. 218.

214: *"His disciples came"*: Matthew 28:13.

214: *"If they do not listen"*: Luke 16:31.

214: *"He is not here"*: Cited in Hans Küng, *On Being a Christian*, op cit, p. 365.

214: *Buechner*: Frederick Buechner, *Whistling in the Dark*. San Francisco: Harper & Row Publishers, 1988, p. 42.

214: *Emmaus story*: Luke 24:13–49

216: *"Because you have seen"*: John 20:29.

217: *Dodd*: C. H. Dodd, *The Founder of Christianity*, op cit., p. 163.

217: *Updike*: John Updike, "Seven Stanzas at Easter," in *Collected Poems 1953–1993*. New York: Alfred A. Knopf, 1993, p. 20. Used by permission.

218n. *Tolkien*: J. R. R. Tolkien, "On Fairy Tales," quoted in Robert McAfee Brown, *Persuade Us to Rejoice*. Louisville, Ky.: Westminster/John Knox Press, 1992, p. 145.

218: *Sayers*: Dorothy L. Sayers, *The Mind of the Maker*. London: Methuen & Co. Ltd., 1959, p. 67.

Chapter 12

226: *Buechner*: Frederick Buechner, *The Magnificent Defeat*. New York: The Seabury Press, 1979, p. 86.

226: *Wink*: Walter Wink, *Engaging the Powers*, op cit., p. 143.

226: *"I have brought you glory . . ."*: John 17:4–5.

227: *"Men of Galilee"*: Acts 1:11.
227: *"I am sending"*: Matthew 10:16.
227: *Endo*: Shusaku Endo, *Silence*. New York: Taplinger Publishing Company, 1979, p. 203.
227: *"Brother will betray"*: Matthew 10:21–22.
228: *"But I tell you"*: John 16:7.
228: *"As you sent"*: John 17:18.
228: *Hopkins*: "Inversnaid," in Gerard Manley Hopkins, *Poems and Prose*. Baltimore, Md.: Penguin Books, 1953, p. 51.
228: *"Unless a kernel"*: John 12:24.
229: *"Lord, are you at this time"*: Acts 1:6.
229: *Lewis*: C. S. Lewis, *The Weight of Glory*, op cit., p. 15.
230: *"He who listens"*: Luke 10:16.
231: *"When the Son"*: Matthew 25:31–46.
232: *"Men of Galilee"*: Acts 1:11.
232: *Edwards*: Gerald R. McDermott, "What Jonathan Edwards Can Teach Us About Politics," *Christianity Today*, July 18, 1994, p. 35.
234: *Küng*: Hans Küng, *On Being a Christian*, op cit., p. 132.
234: *Dillard*: Alfred Corn, *Incarnation*, op cit., p. 36.
234: *Buechner*: Ibid, p. 123.
234: *Augustine*: Quoted in Paul Johnson, *A History of Christianity*. New York: Atheneum, 1976, p. 115.
235: *"You did not choose"*: John 15:16.
235n.: *Williams*: Charles Williams, *He Came Down from Heaven*. London: William Heinemann Ltd., 1938, p. 108.
235: *"showed them the full"*: John 13:1.
236: *"We have this treasure"*: 2 Corinthians 4:7.
236: *O'Connor*: Flannery O'Connor, *The Habit of Being*. New York: Vintage Books, 1979, p. 307.

Chapter 13
241: *"The kingdom of God"*: Matthew 12:28.
241: *Barclay*: Quoted in Malcolm Muggeridge, *Jesus: the Man Who Lives*, op cit., p. 74.
241: *"The kingdom of heaven"*: Matthew 3:2.
241: *"For I tell you"*: Luke 10:24.
241: *"Now one greater"*: Matthew 12:42.
244: *"that fox"*: Luke 13:32.
244: *"so that we may not offend"*: Matthew 17:27.
244: *"Love your enemies"*: Matthew 5:44.
247: *"All men will know"*: John 13:35.
247: *"For God so loved"*: John 3:16.
247: *"My kingdom is not"*: John 18:36.
248: *"The kingdom of God does not come"*: Luke 17:20.
248: *"Give to Caesar"*: Matthew 22:21.
248: *Durant*: Will Durant, *The Story of Civilization Part III: Caesar and Christ*. New York: Simon & Schuster, 1944, p. 652.
249: *Legislative aide in China*: Karen M. Feaver, "Chinese Lessons," *Christianity Today*, May 16, 1994, p. 33.
249: *"If my people"*: 2 Chronicles 7:14.
250: *Barth*: Karl Barth, from *Church Dogmatics*, quoted in Stanley Hauerwas and William H. Willimon, *Resident Aliens*. Nashville: Abingdon Press, 1989, p. 83.

250: *Buber:* Quoted in Jürgen Moltmann, *The Way of Jesus Christ*, op cit., p. 28.
251: *"Your kingdom come":* Matthew 6:10.
251: *"In this world":* John 16:33.
251: *"You will hear of wars":* Matthew 24:6.
251: *Lewis:* C. S. Lewis, *Mere Christianity.* New York: The Macmillan Company, 1960, p. 65.
252: *"Lord, are you at this time":* Acts 1:6.
252: *"This same Jesus":* Acts 1:11.
252: *"every knee should bow":* Philippians 2:10–11.

Chapter 14
257: *Peck:* M. Scott Peck, *Further Along the Road Less Traveled.* New York: Simon & Schuster, 1993, p. 160.
259: *"Unless your righteousness":* Matthew 5:20.
261: *"I am the way":* John 14:6.
261: *"I am sending":* Matthew 23:34.
262: *"I and the Father":* John 10:30.
262: *"Before Abraham":* John 8:58.
262: *"Show us":* John 14:8.
262: *"Anyone who has seen":* John 14:9.
262: *"That which was":* 1 John 1:1.
262: *"was like the sun":* Revelation 1:16.
263: *"I am the way":* John 14:6.
263: *Lewis:* C. S. Lewis, *Miracles.* New York: The Macmillan Company, 1947, p. 113.
263: *Lewis: Mere Christianity*, op cit., p. 56.
264: *"I go to prepare":* John 14:2, KJV.
264: *Carter:* Quoted in Gordon Bridger, *A Day That Changed the World.* Downers Grove, Ill.: InterVarsity Press, 1975, p. 56.
264n.: *Buechner:* Frederick Buechner, *Wishful Thinking.* San Francisco: Harper & Row Publishers, p. 17.
265: *"image of the invisible":* Colossians 1:15.
265: *"For God was pleased":* Colossians 1:19.
266: *"The curtain":* Mark 15:38.
267: *Coles:* Robert Coles, *The Spiritual Life of Children.* Boston: Houghton Mifflin Company, 1990, p. 231.
267: *Aristotle:* Aristotle, *Magna Moralia,* Quoted in Diogenes Allen, *Love.* Cambridge, Mass.: Cowley Publications, 1987, p. 115.
267: *"God is love":* 1 John 4:8.
267: *"This is how God":* 1 John 4:9.
268: *Kierkegaard:* Quoted in Karl Barth, *The Word of God and the Word of Man,* p. 84.
268: *Nouwen:* Henri J. M. Nouwen, *The Return of the Prodigal Son.* New York: Image Books/Doubleday, 1994, p. 55.
268: *"This is love":* 1 John 4:10.
268: *"Greater love":* John 15:13.
269: *"For God so loved":* John 3:16.
269: *Price:* Quoted in Alfred Corn, *Incarnation,* op cit., p. 72.
270: *Pascal:* Blaise Pascal, *Pensées,* op cit., p. 143.
270: *"Behold the man":* John 19:5.
270: *"though he was rich":* 2 Corinthians 8:9, KJV.
270: *"Who, being in very nature":* Philippians 2:6–7.

270: "*God made him*": 2 Corinthians 5:21.
270: "*And he died for all*": 2 Corinthians 5:15.
270: "*Although he was a son*": Hebrews 5:8.
271: "*Father, forgive them*": Luke 23:34.
272: *Goethe*: Quoted in Walter Kasper, *Jesus the Christ*, op cit., p. 182.
272: *Dostoevsky*: Quoted in Hans Küng, *On Being a Christian*, op cit., p. 142.
273: *Updike*: Alfred Corn, *Incarnation*, op cit., p. 10.
273: "*my power is made perfect*": 2 Corinthians 12:9–10.
274: *Moltmann*: Jürgen Moltmann, *The Way of Jesus Christ*, op cit., p. 322.

Others

In addition to the specific citations above, I must express gratitude to the following authors for helping me understand Jesus better:

Anderson, Sir Norman. *Jesus Christ: the Witness of History*. Downers Grove, Ill.: InterVarsity Press, 1985.

Baillie, John. *The Place of Jesus Christ in Modern Christianity*. Edinburgh: T&T Clark, 1929.

Bainton, Roland H. *Behold the Christ*. New York: Harper & Row, 1974.

Baker, John Austin. *The Foolishness of God*. Atlanta: John Knox Press, 1970.

Barclay, William. *Jesus As They Saw Him*. Grand Rapids: William B. Eerdmans Publishing Company, 1962.

Barton, Bruce. *The Man Nobody Knows*. New York: Macmillan Publishing Company, 1987.

Batey, Richard. *Jesus and the Poor*. San Francisco: Harper & Row, Publishers, 1972.

Berkhof, Hendrik. *Christ and the Powers*. Scottsdale, Pa.: Herald Press, 1977.

Bright, John. *The Kingdom of God*. Nashville: Abingdon, 1980.

Brown, Colin. *Miracles and the Critical Mind*. Grand Rapids: William B. Eerdmans Publishing Company, 1984.

Bruce, F. F. *Jesus and Christian Origins Outside the New Testament*. Grand Rapids: William B. Eerdmans Publishing Company, 1974.

Bruce, F. F. *What the Bible Teaches About What Jesus Did*. Wheaton, Ill.: Tyndale House Publishers, 1979.

Capon, Robert Farrar. *Hunting the Divine Fox*. New York: The Seabury Press, 1974.

Cullman, Oscar. *Jesus and the Revolutionaries*. New York: Harper & Row, Publishers, 1970.

Ellul, Jacques. *The Subversion of Christianity*. Grand Rapids: William B. Eerdmans Publishing Company, 1986.

Falk, Harvey. *Jesus the Pharisee: A New Look at the Jewishness of Jesus*. New York: Paulist Press, 1985.

Fretheim, Terence E. *The Suffering of God*. Philadelphia: Fortress Press, 1984.

Guardini, Romano. *The Lord*. Chicago: Regnery Gateway, Inc., 1954.

Guthrie, Donald. *A Shorter Life of Christ*. Grand Rapids: Zondervan Publishing, 1970.

Hellwig, Monika. *Jesus, The Compassion of God*. Wilmington, Del.: Michael Glazier, Inc., 1983.

Hengel, Martin. *The Charismatic Leader and His Followers*. New York: Crossroad, 1981.

Kierkegaard, Søren, *Training in Christianity*. Princeton, N.J.: Princeton University Press, 1947.

Ladd, George Eldon. *The Gospel of the Kingdom*. Grand Rapids: William B. Eerdmans Publishing Company, 1959.

Macquarrie, John. *The Humility of God*. Philadelphia: The Westminster Press, 1978.

Macquarrie, John. *Jesus Christ in Modern Thought*. Philadelphia: Trinity Press International, 1990.

Mason, Steve. *Josephus and the New Testament*. Peabody, Mass.: Hendrickson Publishers, 1992.

McGrath, Alister. *Understanding Jesus*. Grand Rapids: Zondervan Publishing House, 1988.

Meier, John P. *A Marginal Jew*. New York: Doubleday, 1991.

Moltmann, Jurgen. *The Trinity and the Kingdom*. San Francisco: Harper & Row Publishers, 1981.

Morison, Frank. *Who Moved the Stone?* London: Faber and Faber Limited, 1944.

Niebuhr, H. Richard. *Christ and Culture*. New York: Harper & Brothers Publishers, 1956.

Oppenheimer, Helen. *Incarnation and Immanence*. London: Hodder and Stoughton, 1973.

Pfeiffer, Charles. *Between the Testaments*. Grand Rapids: Baker Book House, 1959.

Stott, John. *Christian Counter-Culture: The Message of the Sermon on the Mount*. Downers Grove, Ill.: InterVarsity Press, 1978.

van Buren, Paul M. *A Theology of the Jewish-Christian Reality: Part III, Christ in Context*. San Francisco: Harper & Row, 1988.

Willis, Wendell, ed. *The Kingdom of God in 20th-Century Interpretation*. Peabody, Mass.: Hendrickson Publishers, 1987.

Wright, N. T. *Who Was Jesus?* Grand Rapids: William B. Eerdmans Publishing Company, 1992.

Ziolkowski, Theodore. *Fictional Transfigurations of Jesus*. Princeton, N.J.: Princeton University Press, 1972.

DISAPPOINTMENT
WITH GOD

For my brother,
who is still disappointed

PREFACE

After I had begun work on this project, I received phone calls from a few people in my church who had heard about it. "Is it true you're writing a book about disappointment with God?" the callers would ask. "If so, I'd like to talk. I haven't told anyone before, but my life as a Christian has included times of great disappointment." I did interview some of those callers, and their stories helped set the direction of this book.

I found that for many people there is a large gap between what they *expect* from their Christian faith and what they actually experience. From a steady diet of books, sermons, and personal testimonies, all promising triumph and success, they learn to expect dramatic evidence of God working in their lives. If they do not see such evidence, they feel disappointment, betrayal, and often guilt. As one woman said, "I kept hearing the phrase, 'personal relationship with Jesus Christ.' But I found to my dismay that it is unlike any other personal relationship. I never saw God, or heard him, or felt him, or experienced the most basic ingredients of a relationship. Either there's something wrong with what I was told, or there's something wrong with me."

Disappointment occurs when the actual experience of something falls far short of what we anticipate. For that reason, the first half of this book explores the Bible to see what we can rightfully expect from God. I hesitated to start there since I know that some people, especially disappointed people, have little tolerance for the Bible. But what better place to begin than by letting God speak for himself? I tried to rid myself of preconceptions and read the Bible like a story, with a "plot." What I found there astonished me. It was very different from the story I had been told most of my life.

Actually, I set out to write two different books, and did so; but I ended up putting them both between the same covers. Book II moves to more practical, existential issues and applies the ideas I have developed to actual situations—the kinds of situations that foster disappointment with God. Ultimately, I concluded that the two approaches belonged in the same book; either would be incomplete on its own.

Once as I explained this project to a friend, he frowned and shook his head. "I guess I've never tried to psychoanalyze God before," he said. I hope that's not what I'm attempting! But I do wish to understand God better, to learn why he sometimes acts in such mysterious ways—or does not seem to act at all.

A few words of caution, however. This is not a book of apologetics, so I will not travel the path of pointing out evidences for God. Others have done that effectively, and, besides, I am dealing with doubts that are more emotional than intellectual. Disappointment implies a hoped-for relationship that somehow has not worked out.

Nor will I debate the question, "Does God ever perform miracles?" I take for granted that he has supernatural power and has used it. Yes, God can intervene; so why doesn't he do so more often? Why handicap himself among sincere skeptics who would like to believe, if only they had a sign? Why permit injustice and suffering to thrive on earth? Why aren't God's interventions "ordinaries" rather than "miracles"?

One last caution: by no means am I presenting a balanced view of the Christian faith. I am, after all, writing for people who have, at one time or another, heard the silence of God. Studying someone like Job as an example of faith is a little like studying the history of civilization by examining only the wars. On the other hand, there are many Christian books that leave out any mention of the wars and promise nothing but victory. This is a book about faith, but it looks at faith through the eyes of those who doubt.

And finally, I should explain the way I have chosen to handle Bible references. I resisted putting them in footnotes or parentheses within the text: that creates an awkwardness in reading not unlike listening to someone with a stutter. Instead, I have indicated the sources of direct citations at the end of each chapter. True sleuths should be able to track down the correct passage.

Awake, O Lord! Why do you sleep?
Rouse yourself! Do not reject us forever.
Why do you hide your face?

PSALM 44:23-24

BOOK I

GOD WITHIN
THE SHADOWS

You do not have to sit outside in the dark.
If, however, you want to look at the stars,
you will find that darkness is required.
The stars neither require it nor demand it.

ANNIE DILLARD

PART ONE

HEARING THE SILENCE

⎯⎯⎯⎯⎯∞∞∞⎯⎯⎯⎯⎯

CHAPTER 1

A FATAL ERROR

—⊷⊷⊷—

Ever since my book *Where Is God When It Hurts?* was published, I have received letters from people disappointed with God.

A young mother wrote that her joy had turned to bitterness and grief when she delivered a daughter with *spina bifida*, a birth defect that leaves the spinal cord exposed. In page after page of tiny, spidery script she recounted how medical bills had soaked up the family savings and how her marriage had cracked apart as her husband came to resent all the time she devoted to their sick child. As her life crumbled around her, she was beginning to doubt what she had once believed about a loving God. Did I have any advice?

A homosexual spilled out his story gradually, in a succession of letters. For more than a decade he had sought a "cure" for his sexual orientation, trying charismatic healing services, Christian support groups, and chemical treatment. He even underwent a form of aversion therapy in which psychologists applied electrical shocks to his genitals when he responded to erotic photos of men. Nothing worked. Finally he surrendered to a life of gay promiscuity. He still writes me occasionally. He insists that he wants to follow God but feels disqualified because of his peculiar curse.

A young woman wrote, with some embarrassment, about her ongoing depression. She has no reason to be depressed, she said. She is healthy, earns a good salary, and has a stable family background. Yet most days when she wakes up she cannot think of a single reason to go on living. She no longer cares about life or God, and when she prays, she wonders if anyone is really listening.

These and other letters I have received over the years all lead up to the same basic question, phrased in different ways. It goes something like this: "Your book is about physical pain. But what about pain like mine? Where is God when I hurt emotionally? What does the Bible say about that?" I answer the letters as best I can, sadly conscious of the inadequacy of words on paper. Can a word, any word, ever heal a wound? And I must confess that after reading these anguished accounts I ask the very same questions. Where is God in our emotional pain? Why does he so often disappoint us?

Disappointment with God does not come only in dramatic circumstances. For me, it also edges unexpectedly into the mundaneness of everyday life. I remember one night last winter, a cold, raw Chicago night. The wind was howling, and sleet slanted out of the skies, coating the streets with darkly shining ice. That night my car stalled in a rather ominous neighborhood. As I raised the hood and hunched over the engine, the sleet stinging my back like tiny pebbles, I prayed over and over, *Please help me get this car started.*

No amount of fiddling with wires and tubes and cables would start the car, and so I spent the next hour in a dilapidated diner waiting for a tow truck. Sitting on a plastic chair, my drenched clothes forming a widening pool of water around me, I wondered what God thought about my plight. I would miss a scheduled meeting that night and would probably waste many hours over the next few days trying to wring fair, honest work out of a service station set up to prey upon stranded motorists. Did God even care about my frustration or the waste of energy and money?

Like the woman embarrassed over her depression, I feel ashamed even to mention such an unanswered prayer. It seems petty and selfish, maybe even stupid, to pray for a car to start. But I have found that petty disappointments tend to accumulate over time, undermining my faith with a lava flow of doubt. I start to wonder whether God cares about everyday details—about me. I am tempted to pray less often, having concluded in advance that it won't matter. Or will it? My emotions and my faith waver. Once those doubts seep in, I am even less prepared for times of major crisis. A neighbor is dying of cancer; I pray diligently for her. But even as I pray, I wonder. Can God be trusted? If so many small prayers go unanswered, what about the big ones?

One morning in a motel room I switched on the television and the square, jowly face of a well-known evangelist filled the screen. "I'm mad at God!" he said, glowering. It was a remarkable confession from a man who had built his career around the notion of "seed faith" and absolute confidence in God's personal concern. But God had let him down, he said, and went on to explain. God had commanded him to build a large ministry complex; and yet the project proved to be a financial disaster, forcing him to sell off properties and cut back programs. He had kept his part of the bargain, but God had not.

A few weeks later I again saw the evangelist on television, this time exuding faith and optimism. He leaned toward the camera, his craggy face splitting into a big grin, and jabbed his finger toward a million viewers. "Something *good* is going to happen to you this week!" he said, coaxing three syllables out of the word "good." He was at his salesman best, utterly convincing. A few days later, however, I heard on the news that his son had committed suicide. I could not help wondering what the evangelist said to God in his prayers that fateful week.

Such struggles seem almost to mock the triumphant slogans about God's love and personal concern that I often hear in Christian churches. Yet no one is immune to the downward spiral of disappointment. It happens to people like the televangelist and to people like the letter writers, and it happens to ordinary Christians: first comes disappointment, then a seed of doubt, then a response of anger or betrayal. We begin to question whether God is trustworthy, whether we can really stake our lives on him.

I have been thinking about this topic of disappointment with God for a long time, but I hesitated to write about it for two reasons. First, I knew I would have to confront questions that have no easy answers—that may, in fact, have no answers. And second, I did not want to write a book that would, by focusing on failure, dampen anyone's faith.

Some Christians, I know, would reject the phrase "disappointment with God" out of hand. Such a notion is all wrong, they say. Jesus promised that faith the size of a grain of mustard seed can move mountains; that anything can happen if two or three gather together in prayer. The Christian life is a life of victory and triumph. God wants us happy, healthy, and prosperous, and *any* other state simply indicates a lack of faith.

During a visit among people who believe exactly this, I finally reached the decision to write this book. I was investigating the topic of physical healing for a magazine assignment, and the research led me to a rather infamous church headquartered in rural Indiana. I had learned of the church from a *Chicago Tribune* series and from a special report on ABC's *Nightline* program.

Members of this church believed that simple faith could heal any disease and that to look elsewhere for help—for example, to medical doctors—demonstrated a lack of faith in God. The *Tribune* articles told of parents who had looked on helplessly as their children fought losing battles with meningitis or pneumonia or a common flu virus—diseases that easily could have been treated. On a map of the United States, a *Tribune* artist had drawn tiny tombstone symbols to mark where people had died after refusing medical treatment in accordance with church teaching. There were fifty-two tombstones in all.

According to the reports, pregnant women in that church died in childbirth at a rate eight times the national average, and young children were three times more likely to die. Yet the church was growing and had established branches in nineteen states and five foreign countries.

I visited the mother church in Indiana on a sweltering August day. Heat waves shimmied off the asphalt roads, and parched brown cornstalks drooped in the fields. The building sat unmarked in the midst of one of those cornfields—huge, isolated, like a misplaced barn. In the parking lot I had to talk my way past two ushers with walkie-talkies; the church was nervous about publicity, especially since former members had recently filed lawsuits.

I suppose I expected a sign of fanaticism during the service: a swooning, hypnotic sermon delivered by a Jim Jones–type preacher. I saw nothing like that. For ninety minutes, seven hundred of us sitting in a large semicircle sang hymns and studied the Bible.

I was among simple people. The women wore dresses or skirts, no slacks, and used little makeup. The men, dressed in shirts and ties, sat with their families and helped keep the children in line.

Children were far more conspicuous here than in most churches; they were everywhere. Keeping quiet for ninety minutes stretches the limits of a small child's endurance, and I watched the parents try to cope. Coloring books abounded. Mothers played games with their children's fingers. Some had brought along a treasure trove of toys in oversized pocketbooks.

If I had come looking for sensationalism, I went away disappointed. I had seen a slice of old-fashioned Americana where the traditional family was still alive and well. Parents there loved their children as much as any parents on earth.

And yet—the map with the tiny tombstones leaped to mind—some of those same parents had sat by the bedsides of their dying youngsters and done nothing. One father told the *Tribune* of his prayer vigil as he watched his fifteen-month-old son battle a fever for two weeks. The illness first caused deafness, then blindness. The pastor of the church urged even more faith and persuaded the father not to call a doctor. The next day the boy was dead. An autopsy revealed that he had died from an easily treatable form of meningitis.

By and large, the members of the Indiana church do not blame God for their miseries, or at least they do not admit to doing so. Instead, they blame themselves for weak faith. Meanwhile, the tombstones multiply.

I went away from that Sunday service with a profound conviction that what we think about God and believe about God matters—*really* matters—as much as anything in life matters. Those people were not ogres or child-murderers, and yet several dozen of their children had died because of an error (I believe) in theology.

(Actually, the teaching of the Indiana church is not so different from what I hear in many evangelical churches and on religious television and radio; they simply apply the extravagant promises of faith more consistently.)

Because of those sincere people in Indiana, along with the questioning people who had written to me, I decided to confront issues I am sorely tempted to avoid. Thus, this book of theology. Not a technical book by any means, but a book about the nature of God and why he sometimes acts in puzzling ways and sometimes does not act.

We dare not confine theology to seminary coffee shops where professors and students play mental badminton. It affects all of us. Some people lose their faith because of a sharp sense of disappointment with God. They expect God to act a certain way, and God "lets them down." Others may not lose their faith, but they too experience a form of disappointment. They believe God will intervene, they pray for a miracle, and their prayers come back unanswered. Fifty-two times, at least, it happened that way in the Indiana church.

CHAPTER 2

UP IN SMOKE

⁓⚬⚬⚬⁓

One afternoon my phone rang and the caller identified himself as a theology student at Wheaton College Graduate School. "My name is Richard," he said. "We haven't met, but I feel a kinship with you because of some of your writings. Do you have a minute?"

Richard proceeded to tell me about his life. He had become a Christian as a university student when an InterVarsity worker befriended him and introduced him to the faith. Yet Richard hardly talked like a new Christian. Although he asked for my recommendations of Christian books, I found that he had already read each one I mentioned. We had a pleasant, wandering conversation, and not until the end of the call did I learn his real purpose in contacting me.

"I hate to bother you with this," he said nervously. "I know you're probably busy, but there is one favor I'd like to ask. You see, I wrote this paper on the Book of Job, and my professor told me I should make a book out of it. Is there a chance you could take a look and see what you think?"

I said yes, and the manuscript arrived within a few days. In truth, I did not expect much. Graduate school papers do not normally make compelling reading, and I doubted whether a relatively recent convert could come up with fresh insights on the daunting Book of Job. But I was wrong. The manuscript showed real promise, and over the next few months Richard and I discussed by phone and mail how the paper could be reshaped into book form.

A year later, with a finished manuscript and a signed contract in hand, Richard called to ask if I would write a foreword. I had still never met Richard, but I liked his enthusiasm, and he had written a book I could easily endorse.

Six months passed, during which the book went through final editing and revision. Then, shortly before its publication date, Richard called yet again. His voice sounded different: tense, edgy. To my surprise he fended off questions about his forthcoming book. "I need to see you, Philip," he said. "There's something I feel obligated to tell you, and it should be in person. Could I come over some afternoon this week?"

———✦———

Hot, hazy rays of sunlight streamed into my third-floor apartment. The open French doors had no screens, and flies buzzed in and out of the room. Richard, dressed in white tennis shorts and a T-shirt, sat on a couch across from me. Sweat glistened on his forehead. He had driven for an hour in heavy Chicago traffic for this meeting, and he first gulped down a glass of iced tea, trying to cool off.

Richard was lean and in good physical shape—"pure ecto-morph," as an aerobics instructor might say. A bony face and short-cropped hair gave him the severe, intense look of a God-haunted monk. If body language speaks, his was voluble: his fists clenched and unclenched, his tanned legs crossed and uncrossed, and his facial muscles often tightened with tension.

He skipped the small talk. "You've a right to be furious with me," he began. "I don't blame you a bit if you feel snookered."

I had no idea what he meant. "About what?"

"Well, it's like this. The book you helped me with—it's coming out next month, including your foreword. But the truth is, I don't believe what I wrote in that book anymore, and I feel I owe you an explanation."

He paused for a moment, and I watched the lines of tension working in his jaw. "I hate God!" he suddenly blurted out. "No, I don't mean that. I don't even believe in God."

I said nothing. In fact, I said very little for the next three hours as Richard told me his story, beginning with his parents' breakup. "I did everything I could to prevent the divorce," he said. "I'd just become a Christian at the university, and I was naive enough to believe that God cared. I prayed nonstop day and night that they'd get back together. I even dropped out of school for a while and went home to try to salvage my family. I thought I was doing God's will, but I think I made everything worse. It was my first bitter experience with unanswered prayer.

"I transferred to Wheaton College to learn more about the faith. I figured I must be doing something wrong. At Wheaton I met people who used phrases like 'I spoke with God,' and 'the Lord told me.' I sometimes talked like that too, but never without a twitch of guilt. Did the Lord really tell me anything? I never heard a voice or had any proof of God I could see or touch. Yet I longed for that kind of closeness.

"Each time I faced a crucial decision I would read the Bible and pray for guidance, like you're supposed to. Whenever I felt right about the decision, I would act on it. But, I swear, I ended up making the wrong choice every time. Just when I really thought I understood God's will, then it would backfire on me."

Street noises drifted in, and I could hear neighbors going up and down the stairs, but these sounds did not distract Richard. He kept talking, and I nodded occasionally, though I still did not understand the reason for his almost violent outburst against God. Lots of families break up; lots of prayers go unanswered. What was the true source of his molten rage?

He next told me about a job opportunity that had fallen through. The employer reneged on a promise to him and hired someone less deserving, leaving Richard with school debts and no source of income. About the same time, Richard's fiancée jilted him. With no warning she broke off contact, refusing to give any explanation for her abrupt change of heart. Sharon, the fiancée, had played a key role in Richard's spiritual growth, and as she left him, he felt some of his faith leach away as well. They had often prayed together about their future; now those prayers seemed like cruel jokes.

Richard also had a series of physical problems, which only added to his sense of helplessness and depression. Wounds of rejection, suffered when his parents had separated, seemed to reopen. Had God merely been stringing him along—like Sharon? He visited a pastor for advice. He felt like a drowning man, he said. He wanted to trust God, but whenever he reached out he grasped a fistful of air. Why should he keep believing in a God so apparently unconcerned about his well-being?

The pastor was barely sympathetic, and Richard got the clear impression that his own complaints did not measure up to the man's normal fare of broken marriages, cancer patients, alcoholics, and parents of wayward children. "When something straightens out with your girlfriend, you'll straighten out with God, too," the pastor said with a condescending smile.

To Richard, the problems were anything but minor. He could not understand why a loving heavenly Father would let him suffer such disappointment. No earthly father would treat his child like that. He continued going to church, but inside him a hard lump of cynicism began forming, a tumor of doubt. The theology he had learned in school and had written about in his book no longer worked for him.

"It was odd," Richard told me, "but the more anger I directed at God, the more energy I seemed to gain. I realized that for the last several years I had shrunken inside myself. Now, as I started doubting, and even hating the school and other Christians around me, I felt myself coming back to life."

One night something snapped. Richard attended a Sunday evening church service where he heard the usual testimonies and praise, but one report in particular rankled him. Earlier that week a plane carrying nine missionaries had crashed in the Alaskan outback, killing all aboard. The pastor solemnly related the details and then introduced a member of the church who had survived an unrelated plane crash that same week. When the church member finished describing his narrow escape, the congregation responded, "Praise the Lord!"

"Lord, we thank you for bringing our brother to safety and for having your guardian angels watch over him," the pastor prayed. "And please be with the families of those who died in Alaska." That prayer triggered revulsion, something like nausea, in Richard. You can't have it both ways, he thought. If God gets credit for the survivor, he should also get blamed for the casualties. Yet churches never hear testimonies from the grievers. What would the spouses of the dead missionaries say? Would they talk about a "loving Father"?

Richard returned to his apartment greatly agitated. Everything was coming to a head around one question: "Is God even there?" He had not seen convincing evidence.

———∞∞———

Richard interrupted his story at this point. The sun had strayed behind a large building to the west, gauzily softening the room's shadows and streaks of light. Richard closed his eyes and chewed on his lower lip. He pressed on his eyes with his thumbs, hard. He seemed to be setting a mental picture, as if to get it just right.

"What happened next?" I asked, after a few minutes of silence. "Was that the night you lost your faith?"

He nodded and resumed speaking, but in a subdued tone. "I stayed up late that night, long after my neighbors had gone to bed— I live on a quiet street in the suburbs—and it seemed like I was alone in the world. I sensed something important was about to happen. I was hurt. So many times God had let me down. I hated God, and yet I was afraid too. I was a theology student, right? Maybe God was there and I had it all wrong. How could I know? I went back over my whole Christian experience, from the very beginning.

"I remembered the first flush of faith at the university. I was young then, and vulnerable. Maybe I had just learned a few upbeat phrases and talked myself into believing in 'an abundant life.' Maybe I had been mimicking other people and living off their experiences. Had I deluded myself about God?

"Still, I hesitated to cast aside all that I believed. I felt I had to give God one last chance.

"I prayed that night as earnestly and sincerely as I knew how. I prayed on my knees, and I prayed stretched out flat on the oak floor.

'God! Do you care?' I prayed. 'I don't want to tell you how to run your world, but please give me some sign that you're really there! That's all I ask.'

"For four years I'd been straining for 'a personal relationship with God,' as the phrase goes, and yet God had treated me worse than any of my friends. Now everything narrowed down to one final question: How can you have a personal relationship if you're not sure the other person even exists? With God, I could never be sure.

"I prayed for at least four hours. At times I felt foolish, at times utterly sincere. I had the sensation of stepping off a ledge in the darkness with no idea where I might land. That was up to God.

"Finally, at four o'clock in the morning, I came to my senses. Nothing had happened. God had not responded. Why continue torturing myself? Why not just forget God and get on with life, like most of the rest of the world?

"Instantly I felt a sense of relief and freedom, like I had just passed a final exam or gotten my first driver's license. The struggle was over. My life was my own.

"It seems silly now, but this is what I did next. I picked up my Bible and a couple other Christian books and walked downstairs and out the back door. I shut the door softly behind me, so as not to wake anyone. In the backyard was a brick barbecue grill, and I piled the books on it, sprayed them with lighter fluid, and struck a match. It was a moonless night, and the flames danced high and bright. Bible verses and bits of theology curled, blackened, then broke off in tiny crumbs of ash and floated skyward. My faith was going up with them.

"I made another trip upstairs and brought down another armload of books. I did this maybe eight times over the next hour. Commentaries, seminary textbooks, the rough draft of my book on Job— all of them went up in smoke. I might have burned every book I owned if I hadn't been interrupted by an angry fireman in a yellow rain slicker who ran toward me, shouting, 'What do you think you're doing!' Someone had phoned in an alarm. I fumbled around for an excuse and finally told him I was just burning trash.

"After the fireman had squirted some chemicals on my bonfire and shoveled dirt over it, he let me go. I climbed the stairs and sank into bed, smelling of smoke. It was almost dawn by then, and at last I had peace. A great weight had lifted. I had been honest with myself. Any pretense was gone, and I no longer felt the pressure to believe what I could never be sure of. I felt converted—but converted *from* God."

———— ∞ ————

I'm glad I don't make my living as a professional counselor. When I sit across from someone spilling his guts like Richard did, I never know what to say. I said little that afternoon, and maybe that was best. It would not have helped for me to find fault with the "tests" Richard had devised for God.

He seemed especially concerned about the book on Job due out within the next few weeks. The publisher knew about his change of heart, he said, but the first edition was already on the presses. I assured him my endorsement of the book still held. It was the content of the book I was endorsing, more than his personal attachment. "Besides, I've certainly changed my mind about some things I've written in the last ten years," I told him.

Richard was exhausted after talking so long, but he seemed more relaxed as he stood to leave. "Maybe all my problems started with my study of Job," he said. "I used to love Job—he wasn't afraid to be honest with God. He took God on. I guess the difference between us is what happened at the end. God came through for Job, after all his pain. He didn't come through for me."

Dusk had fallen, and a photocell had already switched on the stairway lights. As Richard shook my hand and disappeared down the steps, I felt very sad. He was young and tanned and healthy. Some would say he had no real reason to despair. But listening to him, watching his hands clenching and the lines of tension in his face, I had recognized at last the source of his rage.

Richard was feeling a pain as great as any that a human being experiences: the pain of betrayal. The pain of a lover who wakes up and suddenly realizes *it's all over.* He had staked his life on God, and God had let him down.

CHAPTER 3

THE QUESTIONS
NO ONE ASKS ALOUD

——∞∞∞——

Sometimes the most important questions, those that float in vague suspension for much of our lives, can crystallize in a single moment. Richard's visit provided such a moment for me. In one respect his complaints—broken home, health problems, failed romance, lost job—hardly ranked as world-class disappointments. And yet that night by the barbecue grill he had, with theatrical finality, acted on the doubts that plague almost all of us. Does God really care? If so, why won't he reach down and fix the things that go wrong—at least some of them?

Absorbed in his anger and pain, Richard had not given voice to his doubts in a systematic way; he experienced them more as feelings of betrayal than as matters of faith. As I brooded over our conversation, however, I kept returning to three large questions about God that seemed to lurk just behind the thicket of his feelings. The longer I pondered them, the more I realized that these questions are lodged somewhere inside all of us. Yet few people ask them aloud, for they seem at best impolite, at worst heretical.

Is God unfair? Richard had tried to follow God, but his life fell apart anyway. He could not reconcile his miseries with the biblical promises of rewards and happiness. And what about the people who openly deny God yet prosper anyway? This is an old complaint, as old as Job and the Psalms, but it remains a stumbling block to faith.

Is God silent? Three times, as he faced crucial choices in his education, career, and romance, Richard begged God for clear direction. Each time he thought he had God's will figured out, only to have that choice lead to failure. "What kind of Father is he?" Richard asked. "Does he enjoy watching me fall on my face? I was told that God loves me and has a wonderful plan for my life. Fine. So why doesn't he tell me what that plan is?"

Is God hidden? This question, above all, obsessed Richard. It seemed to him an irreducible minimum, a theological bottom line, that God should somehow prove himself: "How can I have a relationship with a Person I'm not even sure exists?" Yet it seemed that God deliberately hid himself, even from people who sought him out. And when Richard's late-night vigil provoked no response, he simply gave up on God.

I thought about these three questions often on a subsequent writing assignment in South America. In Peru, a missionary pilot flew me to a small Shipibo Indian village. He landed the floatplane, taxied to the riverbank, and guided me along a jungle trail to the main "street" in town: a dirt path surrounded by a dozen huts built on stilts and covered with palm-frond roofs. He had brought me there to show me a thriving, forty-year-old church. But he also showed me a granite marker just off the main path and told me the story of the young missionary who had helped found that church.

When his six-month-old son died from a sudden onset of vomiting and diarrhea, the young missionary seemed to crack. He hewed a marker by hand from local stone—the marker we were looking at—buried the baby's body, and planted a tree beside the grave. At the hottest part of each day, when everyone else sought shade, the missionary walked to the river and hauled back a jug of water for the tree. Then he stood beside the grave, his shadow falling across it, as if to shield it from the blazing equatorial sun. Sometimes he would weep, sometimes pray, and sometimes just stand there with a vacant gaze. His wife, the Indian church members, and other missionaries all tried to comfort him, but to no avail.

Eventually, the missionary himself got sick. His mind wandered; he had constant diarrhea. He was flown to Lima, where doctors probed him for any sign of amoeba or other tropical organisms, but found nothing. None of the drugs they tried were effective. They diagnosed his problem as "hysterical diarrhea" and sent him and his wife back to the United States.

As I stood beside the crumbling granite marker, which the Indian women now used as a place to rest their water pots, I tried to put myself in that young missionary's place. I wondered what he had prayed as he stood there in the noonday sun, and Richard's three questions kept coming to mind. My guide had said the man was tormented by the question of unfairness. His baby had done nothing wrong. The missionary had brought his family to serve God in the jungle—was this their reward? He had also prayed for some sign of God's presence, or at least a word of comfort. But he felt none. As if distrustful of God's own sympathy, the missionary took on a form of sympathetic suffering in his own body.

True atheists do not, I presume, feel disappointed in God. They expect nothing and receive nothing. But those who commit their lives to God, no matter what, instinctively expect something in return. Are those expectations wrong?

I did not see my friend Richard for a long time. I prayed for him regularly, but all my efforts to contact him proved futile. His phone had been disconnected, and I heard he had moved out of the area. His publisher eventually sent me a copy of his book on Job, and it sat on my shelf as a potent warning against writing too hastily on matters of faith.

Then one day, about three years later, I bumped into Richard in downtown Chicago. He looked good: by putting on a little weight and letting his hair grow a few inches longer, he had lost the haunted, severe mien. He seemed glad to see me, and we scheduled a lunch.

"Last time I met with you, I guess I was in the pits," he said with a smile as he joined me in a Mexican restaurant a few days later. "Life is treating me much better now." He had a promising job and had long since put the failed romance behind him.

Soon our conversation turned to God, and it quickly became evident that Richard had not fully recovered. A thick scab of cynicism now covered the wounds, but he was as angry at God as ever.

The waitress poured a fresh cup of coffee, and Richard wrapped both hands around the cup and stared at the dark, steaming liquid. "I've gained some perspective on that crazy period," he said. "I think I've figured out what went wrong. I can tell you the exact hour and minute I began doubting God, and it wasn't at Wheaton or in my room that night I stayed up praying." He then related an incident that had occurred very early in his Christian life.

"One thing bugged me from the very beginning: the notion of faith. It seemed a black hole that could gobble up any honest question. I'd ask the InterVarsity leader about the problem of pain, and he would spout something about faith. 'Believe God whether you feel like it or not,' he'd say. 'The feelings will follow.' I faked it, but I can now see that the feelings never followed. I was just going through the motions.

"Even back then I was searching for hard evidence of God as an alternative to faith. And one day I found it—on television, of all places. While randomly flipping a dial, I came across a mass healing service being conducted by Kathryn Kuhlman. I watched for a few minutes as she brought various people up on the stage and interviewed them. Each one told an amazing story of supernatural healing. Cancer, heart conditions, paralysis—it was like a medical encyclopedia up there.

"As I watched Kuhlman's program, my doubts gradually melted away. At last I had found something real and tangible. Kuhlman asked a musician to sing her favorite song, 'He Touched Me.' That's what I needed, I thought: a touch, a personal touch from God. She held out that promise, and I lunged for it.

"Three weeks later when Kathryn Kuhlman came to a neighboring state, I skipped classes and traveled half a day to attend one of her meetings. The atmosphere was unbelievably charged—soft organ music in the background; the murmuring sound of people praying aloud, some in strange tongues; and every few minutes a happy interruption when someone would stand and claim, 'I'm healed!'

"One person especially made an impression, a man from Milwaukee who had been carried into the meeting on a stretcher. When he walked—yes, walked—onstage, we all cheered wildly. He told us he was a physician, and I was even more impressed. He had incurable lung cancer, he said, and was told he had six months to live. But now, tonight, he believed God had healed him. He was walking for the first time in months. He felt great. Praise God!

"I wrote down the man's name and practically floated out of that meeting. I had never known such certainty of faith before. My search was over; I had seen proof of a living God in those people on the stage. If he could work tangible miracles in them, then surely he had something wonderful in store for me.

"I wanted contact with the man of faith I had seen at the meeting, so much so that exactly one week later I phoned Directory Assistance in Milwaukee and got the physician's number. When I dialed it, a woman answered the phone. 'May I please speak to Dr. S_____,' I said.

"Long silence. 'Who are you?' she said at last. I figured she was just screening calls from patients or something. I gave my name and told her I admired Dr. S_____ and had wanted to talk to him ever since the Kathryn Kuhlman meeting. I had been very moved by his story, I said.

"Another long silence. Then she spoke in a flat voice, pronouncing each word slowly. 'My . . . husband . . . is . . . dead.' Just that one sentence, nothing more, and she hung up.

"I can't tell you how that devastated me. I was wasted. I half-staggered into the next room, where my sister was sitting. 'Richard, what's wrong?' she asked. 'Are you all right?'

"No, I was not all right. But I couldn't talk about it. I was crying. My mother and sister tried to pry some explanation out of me. But what could I tell them? For me, the certainty I had staked my life on had died with that phone call. A flame had flared bright for one fine, shining week and then gone dark, like a dying star."

Richard stared into his coffee cup. Marimba music playing in the background sounded tinny and jarringly loud. "I don't quite understand," I said. "That happened long before you went to Wheaton and got a theology degree and wrote a book—"

"Yeah, but it all started back then," he interrupted. "Everything that followed—Wheaton, the book on Job, the Bible study groups— was a grasping attempt to prove wrong what I should have learned from that one phone call. Nobody's out there, Philip. And if by some chance God does exist, then he's toying with us. Why doesn't he quit playing games and show himself?"

Richard soon changed the topic of conversation, and we spent the rest of the lunch catching up on the past three years. He kept insisting that he was happy. He may have been protesting too strongly, but he did indeed seem more content.

Toward the end, as we were digging into our ice cream desserts, he brought up our last meeting, three years before. "You must have thought I was half-crazy, charging in there and blurting out my whole life story when I'd never even met you."

"Not at all," I said. "In a strange sort of way, I've never been able to get that conversation out of my mind. Actually, your complaints against God helped me better understand my own."

I then told Richard about the three questions. After I had explained them, I asked if they summed up his complaints against God.

"Well, my doubt was more like a feeling—I felt jilted, like God had strung me along just to watch me fall. But you're right, as I think about it; those questions were behind my feelings. God was certainly unfair. And he always seemed hidden, and silent. Yeah, that's it. That's it exactly!" he said.

"Why on earth doesn't God answer those questions!" Richard had raised his voice and was waving his arms like a politician—like an evangelist. Fortunately, the restaurant had emptied. "If only God answered those questions—if only he answered *one* of them. If, say, he would just speak aloud one time so that everyone could hear, then I would believe. Probably the whole world would believe. Why doesn't he?"

CHAPTER 4

WHAT IF

———— ⚬⚬⚬ ————

I f only," Richard had said. If only God solved those three problems, then faith would flourish like flowers in springtime.
Wouldn't it?

The same year I met Richard in the Mexican restaurant, I happened to be studying the books of Exodus and Numbers. And even
though Richard's questions were still buzzing about in my mind, it
took a while for me to notice a curious parallel. Then one day it suddenly jumped out from the page: Exodus described the very world
Richard wanted! It showed God stepping into human history almost
daily. He acted with utter fairness and spoke so that everyone could
hear. Behold, he even made himself visible!

The contrast between the days of the Israelites and our days, the
twentieth century, got me thinking about how God runs the world,
and I went back to the three questions. If God has the power to act
fairly, speak audibly, and appear visibly, why, then, does he seem so
reluctant to intervene today? Perhaps the record of the Israelites in
the wilderness contained a clue.

331

Question: Is God unfair? Why doesn't he consistently punish evil people and reward good people? Why do awful things happen to people good and bad, with no discernible pattern?

Imagine a world designed so that we experience a mild jolt of pain with every sin and a tickle of pleasure with every act of virtue. Imagine a world in which every errant doctrine attracts a lightning bolt, while every repetition of the Apostles' Creed stimulates our brains to produce an endorphin of pleasure.

The Old Testament records a "behavior modification" experiment almost that blatant: God's covenant with the Israelites. In the Sinai Desert, God resolved to reward and punish his people with strict, legislated fairness. He signed the guarantee with his own hand, making it dependent on the one condition that the Israelites had to follow the laws he laid down. He then had Moses outline the terms of this guarantee to the people:

Results of Obedience	Results of Disobedience
Prosperous cities and rural areas	Violence, crime, and poverty everywhere
No sterility among men, women, or livestock	Infertility among people and livestock
Assured success in farming	Crop failure; locusts and worms
Dependable weather conditions	Scorching heat, drought, blight, and mildew
Guaranteed military victories	Domination by other nations
Total immunity to diseases	Fever and inflammation; madness, blindness, confusion of mind

If they were obedient, Moses said, God would set them "high above all the nations on earth"; they would "always be at the top, never at the bottom." In effect, the Israelites were promised protection from virtually every kind of human misery and disappointment. On the other hand, if they disobeyed they would become "a thing of horror and an object of scorn and ridicule to all the nations where the Lord will drive you. . . . Because you did not serve the Lord your God joyfully and gladly in the time of prosperity, therefore in hunger and thirst, in nakedness and dire poverty, you will serve the enemies the Lord sends against you."

I read on, scanning the books of Joshua and Judges to see the results of this covenant based on a "fair" system of rewards and punishment. Within fifty years the Israelites had disintegrated into a state of utter anarchy. Much of the rest of the Old Testament recounts the dreary history of the predicted curses—not blessings—coming true. Despite all the lavish benefits of the covenant, Israel failed to obey God and meet its terms.

Years later when New Testament authors looked back on that history, they did not hold up the covenant as an exemplary model of God relating to his people with absolute consistency and fairness. Rather, they said the old covenant served as an object lesson, demonstrating that human beings were incapable of fulfilling a contract with God. It seemed clear to them that a new covenant ("testament") with God was needed, one based on forgiveness and grace. And that is precisely why the "New Testament" exists.

Question: Is God silent? If he is so concerned about our doing his will, why doesn't he reveal that will more plainly?

Various people claim to hear the word of God today. Some of them are crazy, like the wild man who on "God's orders" attacked Michelangelo's *Pietà* with a hammer, or the political assassin who claimed God told him to shoot the president. Others seem sincere but misguided, like the six strangers who reported to author Joni Eareckson that God had instructed them to marry her. Still others seem to carry on the authentic tradition of the prophets and apostles, delivering the word of God to his people. So then, how can we know whether what we have heard is truly a word from God?

God simplified matters of guidance, I discovered, when the Israelites camped in the Sinai wilderness. *Should we pack up our tent and move today or stay put?* For the answer, an inquisitive Israelite need only glance at the cloud over the tabernacle. If the cloud moved, God wanted his people to move. If it stayed, that meant stay. (You could conveniently check God's will around the clock; at night the cloud glowed like a tower of fire.)

God set up other ways, like the casting of lots and the Urim and Thummim, to directly communicate his will, but most issues were pre-decided. He had spoken his will for the Israelites in a set of rules, codified into 613 laws that covered the complete range of behavior, from murder to boiling a young goat in its mother's milk. Few people complained about fuzzy guidance in those days.

But did a clear word from God increase the likelihood of obedience? Apparently not. "Do not go up and fight [the Amorites]," said God, "because I will not be with you. You will be defeated by your enemies." The Israelites promptly went up and fought the Amorites and were defeated by their enemies. They marched when told to sit tight, fled in fear when told to march, fought when told to declare peace, declared peace when told to fight. They made a national pastime out of inventing ways to break the 613 commands. Clear guidance became as much of an affront to that generation as unclear guidance is to ours.

I also noticed a telling pattern in the Old Testament accounts: the very clarity of God's will had a stunting effect on the Israelites' faith.

Why pursue God when he had already revealed himself so clearly? Why step out in faith when God had already guaranteed the results? Why wrestle with the dilemma of conflicting choices when God had already resolved the dilemma? In short, why should the Israelites act like adults when they could act like children? And act like children they did, grumbling against their leaders, cheating on the strict rules governing manna, whining about every food or water shortage.

As I studied the story of the Israelites, I had second thoughts about crystal-clear guidance. It may serve some purpose—it may, for example, get a mob of just-freed slaves across a hostile desert—but it does not seem to encourage spiritual development. In fact, for the Israelites it nearly eliminated the need for faith at all; clear guidance sucked away freedom, making every choice a matter of obedience rather than faith. And in forty years of wilderness wanderings, the Israelites flunked the obedience test so badly that God was forced to start over with a new generation.

Question: Is God hidden? Why doesn't he simply show up sometime, visibly, and dumbfound the skeptics once and for all?

What the Soviet cosmonaut wanted when he looked for God in the dark void outside his spacecraft window, what my friend Richard wanted, alone in his room at two in the morning, is the hungering desire of our age (for those who still hunger). We want proof, evidence, a personal appearance, so that the God we have heard about becomes the God we see.

What we hunger for happened once. For a time God did show up in person, and a man spoke to him face to face as he might speak with a friend. They met together, God and Moses, in a tent pitched just outside the Israelite camp. The rendezvous was no secret. Whenever Moses trudged over to the tent to talk with God, the whole camp turned out to watch. A pillar of cloud, God's visible presence, blocked the entrance to the tent. No one except Moses knew what transpired inside; no one wanted to know. The Israelites had learned to keep their distance. "Speak to us yourself and we will listen," they said to Moses. "But do not have God speak to us or we will die." After each meeting Moses would emerge glowing like a space alien, and the people turned their faces away until he covered himself with a veil.

There were few, if any, atheists in those days. No Israelites wrote plays about waiting for a God who never arrived. They could see clear evidence of God outside the tent of meeting or in the thick storm clouds hovering around Mount Sinai. A skeptic need only hike over to the trembling mountain and reach out a hand to touch it, and his doubts would vanish—one second before he did.

And yet what happened during those days almost defies belief. When Moses climbed the sacred mountain stormy with the signs of God's presence, those people who had lived through the ten plagues of Egypt, who had crossed the Red Sea on dry ground, who had drunk water from a rock, who were digesting the miracle of manna in their stomachs at that moment—those same people got bored or impatient or rebellious or jealous and apparently forgot all about their God. By the time Moses descended from the mountain, they were dancing like heathens around a golden calf.

God did not play hide-and-seek with the Israelites; they had every proof of his existence you could ask for. But astonishingly—and I could hardly believe this result, even as I read it—God's directness seemed to produce the very *opposite* of the desired effect. The Israelites responded not with worship and love, but with fear and open rebellion. God's visible presence did nothing to improve lasting faith.

I had distilled Richard's complaints about God into three questions. But Exodus and Numbers taught me that quick solutions to those three questions may not solve the underlying problems of disappointment with God. The Israelites, though exposed to the bright, unshaded light of God's presence, were as fickle a people as have ever lived. Ten different times on the melancholy pathless plains of the Sinai they rose up against God. Even at the very border of the Promised Land, with all its bounty stretching out before them, they were still keening for the "good old days" of slavery in Egypt.

These dismal results may provide insight into why God does not intervene more directly today. Some Christians long for a world well-stocked with miracles and spectacular signs of God's presence. I hear wistful sermons on the parting of the Red Sea and the ten plagues and the daily manna in the wilderness, as if the speakers yearn for God to unleash his power like that today. But the follow-the-dots journey of the Israelites should give us pause. Would a burst of miracles nourish faith? Not the kind of faith God seems interested in, evidently. The Israelites give ample proof that signs may only addict us to signs, not to God.

True, the Israelites were a primitive people emerging out of slavery. But the biblical accounts have a disturbingly familiar ring to them. The Israelites tended to behave, in Frederick Buechner's phrase, "just like everybody else, only more so."

I came away from my study of them both surprised and confused: surprised to learn how little difference it made in people's lives when three major reasons for disappointment with God—unfairness, silence, and hiddenness—were removed; confused by the questions stirred up about God's actions on earth. Has he changed? Has he pulled back, withdrawn?

As Richard sat in my living room telling me his story that first time, he had looked up suddenly and said in a fierce voice, "God doesn't know what the HELL he's doing with this world!" What is

God doing? What is the human experiment all about? What does he want from us, after all, and what can we expect from him?

———&&&———

Without somehow destroying me in the process, how could God reveal himself in a way that would leave no room for doubt? If there were no room for doubt, there would be no room for me.

Frederick Buechner

Bible references: Deuteronomy 9, 7, 28; Romans 3; Galatians 3; Exodus 28, 40; Deuteronomy 1–2; Exodus 19–20, 32–33; Deuteronomy 1.

CHAPTER 5

THE SOURCE

For two weeks I holed up in a Colorado cabin to ponder Richard's three questions in light of what I had seen in the Old Testament. I brought along a suitcase full of books to study, but during my entire time there I opened only a Bible.

I started at Genesis late the first afternoon, a day of heavy snowfall. It was a perfect setting for reading the story of creation. Clouds lifted in time for a spectacular alpenglow sunset, with puffs of snow pluming off the tops of the mountain peaks, like pink cotton candy. At night the clouds closed in again, and snow blew furiously.

I read straight through the Bible, slowly, cover to cover. By the time I reached Deuteronomy, snow covered the bottom step; when I hit the Prophets it had crept up the mailbox post; and when I finally made it to Revelation I had to call for a snowplow to unbury the driveway. Over seventy-two inches of fresh powder fell during the two weeks I spent in a loft reading the Bible and looking out the window at sugar-coated evergreens.

It struck me forcefully there that our common impressions of God may be very different from the God the Bible actually portrays.

What is he really like? In church and at a Christian college I had learned to think of God as an unchanging, invisible spirit who possesses such qualities as omnipotence, omniscience, and impassibility (incapable of emotion). These doctrines, which are supposed to help us understand God's point of view, can be found in the Bible, but they are well buried.

Simply reading the Bible, I encountered not a misty vapor but an actual Person. A Person as unique and distinctive and colorful as any person I know. God has deep emotions; he feels delight and frustration and anger. In the Prophets he weeps and moans with pain, even comparing himself to a woman giving birth: "I cry out, I gasp and pant." Again and again God is shocked by the behavior of human beings. When the Israelites commit infant sacrifice, he seems stunned by actions which—an omniscient God is speaking here—"I did not command or mention, nor did it enter my mind." He explains the need to punish by asking plaintively, "What else can I do?" I know, I know, the word "anthropomorphism" is supposed to explain all those humanlike characteristics. But surely the images God "borrows" from human experience point to an even stronger reality.

As I read through the Bible in my winter aerie, I marveled at how much God lets human beings affect him. I was unprepared for the joy and anguish—in short, the passion—of the God of the Universe. By studying "about" God, by taming him and reducing him to words and concepts that could be filed away in alphabetical order, I had lost the force of the passionate relationship God seeks above all else. The people who related to God best—Abraham, Moses, David, Isaiah, Jeremiah—treated him with startling familiarity. They talked to God as if he were sitting in a chair beside them, as one might talk to a counselor, a boss, a parent, or a lover. They treated him like a person.

That Colorado trip put my three questions about disappointment with God in a new light. They are not puzzles awaiting solution, such as you would encounter in the field of mathematics or computer programming or even philosophy. Rather, they are problems of relationship between human beings and a God who wants desperately to love and be loved by us.

I saw few people during my two-week retreat. Mostly I huddled indoors, behind the wall of snow, and read. Perhaps it was this aloneness, this isolation, that cleared the way for the conclusion that I reached: I had always considered just one point of view, the human point of view. I have shelves full of books presenting the dilemma of being human. Some are funny, some anguished, some sarcastic, some densely philosophical, but all express the same basic viewpoint: "Here's what it feels like to be a human being." People disappointed with God likewise focus on the human point of view. When we ask our questions—Why is God unfair? Silent? Hidden?—we're really asking, Why is God unfair *to me*? Why does he seem silent *with me*, and hidden *from me*?

I tried to set aside my existential questions, my personal disappointments, and consider instead *God's* point of view. Why does he seek contact with human beings in the first place? What is he pursuing in us, and what interferes with that pursuit? I turned to the Bible again, trying to hear God's words as if for the first time. He speaks for himself there, and I realized that I had not often paid attention. I had been too preoccupied with my feelings to listen attentively to *his* feelings.

I came away from Colorado with a very different mental image of God. After two weeks of studying the Bible, I had a strong sense that God doesn't care so much about being analyzed. Mainly, he wants to be loved. Nearly every page of his Word rustles with this message. And I returned home knowing I must somehow explore the relationship between a passionate God—hungry for the love of his people—and the people themselves. All feelings of disappointment with God trace back to a breakdown in that relationship. Thus, I determined to look for the answer to a question I had never before considered: "What does it feel like to be God?"

———∞∞∞———

The reason the mass of men fear God, and at bottom dislike Him, is because they rather distrust his heart, and fancy Him all brain like a watch.

HERMAN MELVILLE

Bible references: Isaiah 42; Jeremiah 19, 9.

PART TWO

MAKING CONTACT: THE FATHER

———∞∞∞———

CHAPTER 6

RISKY BUSINESS

⸙

To understand how it feels to be God, there is only one place to begin: the moment of creation. Often Genesis 1 gets read as a prelude, as our minds speed ahead to the major disruption in chapter 3 or to the modern debate over the process used in creation. But Genesis 1 says nothing of that process or of the tragedy to follow. It lays out the barest sketch of our world—sun and stars, oceans and plants, fish and beasts, man and woman—along with God's own comment on each new work.

"And God saw that it was good"—five times the understatement beats in cadence like a drum. And when he had finished, "God saw all that he had made, and it was very good." Other parts of the Bible recall the time with more exuberance. "The morning stars sang together and all the angels shouted for joy," God reported with pride to Job. Proverbs expands on the upbeat mood: "I was the craftsman at his side. I was filled with delight day after day, rejoicing always in his presence, rejoicing in his whole world and delighting in mankind."

Creation as it felt to God—since then every artist has felt an echo, a sympathetic vibration: a craftsman who squints at his finished product and reckons, "Very good"; a performer who cannot suppress a grin when the audience stands and cheers; even a child with her glued-together Popsicle sticks.

Anthropologist and essayist Loren Eiseley tells of a day when he felt the joy of original creation. An old man then, walking a deserted beach, he found shelter from damp fog under the prow of a wrecked boat and promptly fell asleep. When he opened his eyes, he was looking at the two small neat ears and inquisitive face of a young fox, so young that it had not learned to fear. There, under the boat's shadow, the distinguished naturalist and the fox pup stared at one another. And then the tiny fox, a vast and playful humor in his face, selected a chicken bone from a pile and shook it in his teeth. On impulse Eiseley bent over and grabbed the other end, and the frolic began.

Loren Eiseley: "It has been said repeatedly that one can never, try as he will, get around to the front of the universe. Man is destined to see only its far side, to realize nature only in retreat. Yet here was the thing in the midst of the bones, the wide-eyed innocent fox inviting me to play. The universe was swinging in some fantastic fashion around to present its face, and the face was so small that the universe itself was laughing. It was not a time for human dignity.

"For just a moment I had held the universe at bay by the simple expedient of sitting on my haunches before a fox den and tumbling about with a chicken bone." It was "the gravest, most meaningful act I shall ever accomplish," he later concluded, for in it he had caught at last a glimpse of the universe as it begins for all things. "It was, in reality, a child's universe, a tiny and laughing universe."[1]

Despite the awesome emptiness of our universe, despite the pain that haunts it, something lingers, like a scent of old perfume, from that moment of beginnings in Genesis 1. I too have sensed it. The first time I rounded a bend and saw Yosemite Valley spread out before me, its angel-hair waterfalls spilling over the snow-glazed granite. On a small peninsula of Ontario where five million migrating monarch butterflies stop to rest, their papery wings adorning every tree with shimmering, translucent orange. In the children's zoo in Chicago's Lincoln Park, where every beast born—gorilla, aardvark, or hippopotamus—begins life mischievous and full of play.

Eiseley is right: at the heart of the universe is a smile, a pulse of joy passed down from the moment of creation. A new parent who holds a baby, *my* baby, close against flesh for the first time knows it. And that is the feeling God had when he looked over what he had made and pronounced it good. In the beginning, the very beginning, there was no disappointment. Only joy.

Adam and Eve

Genesis 1 does not tell the whole story of creation, however. To understand what follows, you must create something for yourself.

Every creator, from a child with Play-Doh to Michelangelo, learns that creation involves a kind of self-limiting. You produce something that did not exist before, yes, but only by ruling out other options along the way. Stick the curved clay trunk on the front of the elephant; now it cannot go on the rear or on the side. Pick up a pencil and start drawing; now you limit yourself to black and white, not color.

No artist, no matter how great, escapes this limitation. Michelangelo knew that no *trompe l'oeil* would give the Sistine Chapel ceiling the three-dimensional reality he had achieved in his sculptures. When he decided on a medium, paint on plaster, he limited himself.

When God created, he invented the media as he went, calling into being what had existed only in his imagination, and along with every free choice came a limitation. He chose a world of time and space, a "medium" with peculiar restrictions: first A happens, then B happens, and then C. God, who sees future, past, and present all at once, selected sequential time as an artist selects a canvas and palette, and his choice imposed limits we have lived with ever since. (Hasidic scholars have a wonderful word for God's self-limitation: *zimsum,* they call it.)

"And God said, 'Let the water teem with living creatures.'" Behind that sentence lay a thousand decisions: fish with gills and not lungs, scales not fur, fins not feet, blood not sap. At every stage God the Creator made choices, eliminating alternatives.

Genesis tells of God's final set of choices, then pauses, backs up, and retells it in more detail. On the sixth day of creation, man and woman came into being, two creatures unlike all others. God designed them in his own image, desiring to recognize something of himself in them. They were like a mirror, reflecting back his own likeness.

But Adam and Eve had another distinction as well: alone of all God's creatures, they had a moral capacity to rebel against their creator. The sculptures could spit at the sculptor; the characters in the play could rewrite the lines. They were, in a word, free.

"Man is God's risk," said one theologian. Another, Søren Kierkegaard, put it this way: "God has, so to speak, imprisoned himself in his resolve." Nearly everything theologians say about human freedom sounds somehow right and somehow wrong. How can a sovereign God take risks or imprison himself? Yet God's creation of man and woman approached that kind of astonishing self-limitation.

Consider a rather fanciful rendition of creation by William Irwin Thompson:

> Imagine God in Heaven surrounded by the choirs of adoring angels singing hosannahs unendingly . . . "If I create a perfect world, I know how it will turn out. In its absolute perfection, it will revolve like a perfect machine, never devi-

ating from My absolute will." Since God's imagination is perfect, there is no need for Him to create such a universe: it is enough for Him to imagine it to see it in all its details. Such a universe would not be very interesting to man or God, so we can assume that the Divinity continued His meditations. "But what if I create a universe that is free, free even of me? What if I veil My Divinity so that the creatures are free to pursue their individual lives without being overwhelmed by My overpowering Presence? Will the creatures love Me? Can I be loved by creatures whom I have not programmed to adore me forever? Can love arise out of freedom? My angels love me unceasingly, but they can see Me at all times. What if I create beings in My own image as a Creator, beings who are free? But if I introduce freedom into this universe, I take the risk of introducing Evil into it as well, for if they are free, then they are free to deviate from My will. Hmmm. But what if I continue to interact with this dynamic universe, what if I and the creatures become the creators together of a great cosmic play? What if out of every occasion of evil, I respond with an unimaginable good, a good that overwhelms evil by springing out of the very attempts of evil to deny the Good? Will these new creatures of freedom then love Me, will they join with Me in creating Good out of Evil, novelty out of freedom? What if I join with them in the world of limitation and form, the world of suffering and evil? Ahh, in a truly free universe, even I do not know how it will turn out. Do even I dare to take that risk for love?"[2]

Why would Adam and Eve want to rebel? They lived in a garden paradise, and if they had a complaint they could talk it over with God as with a friend. But there was that one forbidden tree, the one with the enticing name, "the tree of the knowledge of good and evil." Apparently God was keeping something from them. What secret lay behind that name? And how would they ever know unless they tried? Adam and Eve made their own "creative" choice: they ate the fruit, and earth has never been the same.

Genesis 3 shows exactly what God felt when Adam and Eve disobeyed: sadness over the broken relationship; anger at their denials; and an emotion surprisingly like alarm. "The man has now become like one of us, knowing good and evil. He must not be allowed to reach out his hand and take also from the tree of life and eat, and live forever."

Creation, which seems like pure freedom, involves limitation. And as Adam and Eve soon learned, rebellion, which also seems like freedom, involves limitation as well. By their choice they put distance between themselves and God. Before, they had walked and talked with God. Now when they heard his approach, they hid in the shrubbery. An awkward separation had crept in to spoil the intimacy. And every quiver of disappointment in our own relationship with God is an aftershock from their initial act of rebellion.

Perhaps we do not realize the problem, so to call it, of enabling finite free wills to co-exist with Omnipotence. It seems to involve at every moment almost a sort of "divine abdication."

C. S. LEWIS

---

[1] Loren Eiseley, *The Star Thrower*, 64–65.
[2] William I. Thompson, *The Time Falling Bodies Take to Light*, 24–25.

Bible references: Job 38; Proverbs 8; Genesis 1–3.

CHAPTER 7

THE PARENT

A fter my return from Colorado, I read Genesis over and over, searching the book of beginnings for some clue into what God had in mind for this world. Even after that first landmark rebellion against him, God did not cast off his creation. Genesis tells amazing stories of his continuing personal encounters with humanity.

If I had to reduce the "plot" of Genesis to one sentence, it would be something like this: God learns how to be a parent.* The disruption in Eden changed the world forever, destroying the intimacy Adam and Eve had known with God. In a kind of warm-up to history, God and human beings had to get used to each other. The humans set the pace by breaking all the rules, and God responded with individualized punishments. What did it feel like to be God? What does it feel like to be the parent of a two-year-old?

---

*A phrase like "God learns" may seem strange because we normally think of learning as a mental process, moving in sequence from a state of not-knowing to a state of knowing. God, of course, is not bound by time or ignorance. He "learns" in the sense of taking on new experiences, such as the creation of free human beings. Using the word in a similar sense, Hebrews says that Jesus "learned obedience from what he suffered."

No one could accuse God of being shy to intervene in the early days. He seemed a close, even hovering parent. When Adam sinned, God met with him in person, explaining that all creation would have to adjust to the choice he, Adam, had made. Just one generation later a new kind of horror—murder—appeared on earth. "What have you done?" God demanded of Cain. "Listen! Your brother's blood cries out to me from the ground." Once again God met with the culprit and custom-designed a punishment.

The state of the earth and, indeed, the entire human race continued to deteriorate toward a point of crisis which the Bible sums up in the most poignant sentence ever written: "The Lord was grieved that he had made man on the earth, and his heart was filled with pain." Behind that one statement stands all the shock and grief God felt as a parent.

What human parent has not experienced at least a pang of such remorse? A teenage son tears away in a fit of rebellion. "I hate you!" he cries, fumbling for words that will cause the most pain. He seems bent on twisting a knife in the belly of his parents. That rejection is what God experienced not just from one child, but from the entire human race. As a result, what God had created, God destroyed. All the joy of Genesis 1 vanished under the churning waters of the Flood.

But there was Noah, that one man of faith who "walked with God." After the remorse expressed in Genesis 3 through 7, you can almost hear God sigh with relief as Noah, in his first act back on land, worships the God who had saved him. *At last, someone to build on.* (Years later, in a message to Ezekiel, God would mention Noah as one of his three most righteous followers.) With the whole planet freshly scrubbed and sprouting life anew, God agreed to a covenant or contract that bound him not just to Noah but to every living creature. It promised one thing only: that God would never again destroy all creation.

You could view the covenant with Noah as the barest minimum of a relationship: one party agrees not to obliterate the other. And yet even in that promise God limited himself. He, the sworn enemy of all evil in the universe, pledged to endure wickedness on this planet for a time—or, rather, to solve it through some means other than annihilation. Like the parent of a runaway teenager, he forced himself into the role of The Waiting Father (as Jesus' story of the Prodigal Son expresses so eloquently). Before long another mass rebellion, at a place called Babel, tested God's resolve, and he kept his promise not to destroy.

In earliest history, then, God acted so plainly that no one could grouse about his hiddenness or silence. Yet those early interventions shared one important feature: each was a punishment, a response to human rebellion. If it was God's intention to have a mature relationship with free human beings, he certainly met with a series of rude setbacks. How could he ever relate to his creation as adults when they kept behaving like children?

The Plan

Genesis 12 marks a momentous change. For the first time since the days of Adam, God stepped in not to punish, but to set into motion a new plan for human history.

There was no mystery about what he had in mind. He told Abraham forthrightly: "I will make you into a great nation, with many people bearing your name, and from that nation I will bless all peoples on earth." The plan appears in some form in Genesis 13, 15, 16, and 17 as well as dozens of other Old Testament passages. Rather than trying to restore the whole earth at once, God would begin with a pioneer settlement, a new race set apart from all others. Abraham, dazzled by God's promises, left home and migrated hundreds of miles to the land of Canaan.

Despite the honor accorded him as the father of this new race, however, Abraham emerges as the Bible's first example of a person severely disappointed in God. Miracles, he had. Abraham entertained angels in his home and dreamed mystical visions of smoking fire pots. But there was one nagging problem: after the promise, after the blaze of revelation, came silence—long years of bewildering silence.

"Go, claim the land I have for you," God said. But Abraham found Canaan dry as bone, its inhabitants dying of famine. To stay alive, he fled to Egypt.

"You'll have descendants as countless as the stars in the sky," God said. No promise could have made Abraham happier. At age seventy-five he still anticipated a tent filled with the sounds of children at play. At eighty-five he worked out a backup plan with a female servant. At ninety-nine the promise seemed downright ludicrous, and when God showed up to confirm it, Abraham laughed in his face. A father at ninety-nine? Sarah in maternity clothes at ninety? They both cackled at the thought.

A laugh of ridicule and also of pain. God had dangled a bright dream of fertility before a barren couple and then sat on his hands and watched as they advanced toward tottery old age. What kind of game was he playing? Whatever did he want?

God wanted faith, the Bible says, and that is the lesson Abraham finally learned. He learned to believe when there was no reason left to believe. And although he did not live to see the Hebrews fill the land as the stars fill the sky, Abraham did live to see Sarah bear one child—just one—a boy, who forever preserved the memory of absurd faith, for his name Isaac meant "laughter."

And the pattern continued: Isaac married a barren woman, as did his son Jacob. The esteemed matriarchs of the covenant—Sarah,

Rebekah, and Rachel—all spent their best childbearing years slender and in despair. They too experienced the blaze of revelation, followed by dark and lonely times of waiting that nothing but faith would fill.

A gambler would say God stacked the odds against himself. A cynic would say God taunted the creatures he was supposed to love. The Bible simply uses the cryptic phrase "by faith" to describe what they went through. Somehow, that "faith" was what God valued, and it soon became clear that faith was the best way for humans to express a love for God.

Joseph

If you read Genesis in one sitting, you cannot help noticing a change in how God related to his people. At first he stayed close by, walking in the garden with them, punishing their individual sins, speaking to them directly, intervening constantly. Even in Abraham's day he sent extraterrestrial messengers on house calls. By Jacob's time, however, the messages were far more ambiguous: a mysterious dream about a ladder, a late-night wrestling match. And toward the end of Genesis, a man named Joseph received guidance in the most unexpected ways.

Genesis slows down when it gets to Joseph, and it shows God working mostly behind the scenes. God spoke to Joseph not through angels, but through such means as the dreams of a despotic Egyptian pharaoh.

If anyone had a valid reason to be disappointed in God, it was Joseph, whose valiant stabs at goodness brought him nothing but trouble. He interpreted a dream to his brothers, and they threw him in a cistern. He resisted a sexual advance and landed in an Egyptian prison. There, he interpreted another dream to save a cell mate's life, and the cell mate promptly forgot about him. I wonder, as Joseph languished for his virtue in an Egyptian dungeon, did questions like Richard's—Is God unfair? Silent? Hidden?—occur to him?

But shift for a moment to the perspective of God the parent. Had he deliberately "pulled back" to allow Joseph's faith to reach a new level of maturity? And could this be why Genesis devotes more space to Joseph than to any other person? Through all his trials, Joseph learned to trust: not that God would prevent hardship, but that he would redeem even the hardship. Choking back tears, Joseph tried to explain his faith to his murderous brothers: "You intended to harm me, but God intended it for good. . . ."

——— ⌘ ———

The central idea of the great part of the Old Testament may be called the idea of the loneliness of God.

G. K. CHESTERTON

Bible references: Genesis 1–11; Hebrews 5; Ezekiel 14; Genesis 12–21, 25, 30; Hebrews 11; Genesis 37, 39–41, 45.

CHAPTER 8

UNFILTERED SUNLIGHT

———— ✦✦✦ ————

Genesis closes with a single family, small enough for the Bible to name all its sons, settling into the friendly haven of Egypt. The next book, Exodus, opens with a swarm of Israelites toiling as slaves under a hostile pharaoh. Nowhere in the Bible will you find an account of what happened during the intervening four hundred years.

I have heard many sermons on the life of Joseph, and many more on Moses and the miracle of the Exodus. But I have never heard a sermon on the four-hundred-year gap between Genesis and Exodus. (Could some of our feelings of disappointment stem from a habit of skipping over times of silence in favor of the Bible's stories of victory?) We tend to speed ahead to the exhilarating stories of liberation from slavery. But think of it! For an ellipsis of time twice as long as the U.S.A. has been in existence, heaven was silent. Surely the Hebrew slaves in Egypt felt profound disappointment with God.

You are a Hebrew, a descendant of Abraham. You grew up hearing about the wonderful promises God gave that great man. "Someday your race will become a mighty nation and will live at peace in their own land"—God swore that in person, first to Abraham, and then to Isaac and Jacob. As a child you obediently memorized those promises. But they now seem like fairy tales. Independent nation? You and your neighbors serve the most powerful empire on earth; daily, you suffer the insults and feel the whips of Egyptian taskmasters. Your own infant brother was slaughtered by the pharaoh's soldiers.

As for the vaunted Promised Land, it lies somewhere to the east, divided under the dominion of a dozen kings.

Four hundred years of silence, until Moses, when suddenly anything a skeptic might have wished for happened. First, God appeared in a burning bush, introducing himself to Moses by name. He spoke aloud. "My people have suffered enough," said God. "Now you will see what I will do." Next, he let loose with the most bravura display of divine power the world has ever seen. Ten times he intervened on a scale so massive that not a single person in Egypt could doubt the existence of the God of the Hebrews. Billions of frogs, gnats, flies, hailstones, and locusts gave empirical proof of the Lord of all creation.

For the next forty years, the years of wilderness wanderings, God carried his people "as a father carries his son." He fed the Israelites, clothed them, planned their daily itinerary, and fought their battles.

Is God unfair? Silent? Hidden? Such questions must have troubled the Hebrews until, in Moses' lifetime, God took off the wraps. He punished evil and rewarded good. He spoke audibly. And he made himself visible, first to Moses in a burning bush and then to the Israelites in a pillar of cloud and fire.

The response of the Israelites to such direct intervention offers an important insight into the inherent limits of all power. Power can do everything but the most important thing: it cannot control love. The ten plagues in Exodus show the power of God over a pharaoh. But the ten major rebellions recorded in Numbers show the impotence of power to bring about what God desired most, the love and faithfulness of his people. No pyrotechnic displays of omnipotence could make them trust and follow him.

We do not need the ancient Israelites to teach us this fact. We can see it today in societies where power runs wild. In a concentration camp, as so many witnesses have told us, the guards possess nearly unlimited power. By applying force, they can make you renounce your God, curse your family, work without pay, eat human excrement, kill and then bury your closest friend or even your own mother. All this is within their power. Only one thing is not: they cannot force you to love them.

The fact that love does not operate according to the rules of power may help explain why God sometimes seems shy to use his power. He created us to love him, but his most impressive displays of miracle—the kind we may secretly long for—do nothing to foster that love. As Douglas John Hall has put it, "God's problem is not that God *is not able* to do certain things. God's problem is that God loves. Love complicates the life of God as it complicates every life."[1]

And when his own love is spurned, even the Lord of the Universe feels in some way helpless, like a parent who has lost what he values most. The Bible records a kind of diary of God's tender relationship with the Israelites:

> On the day you were born your cord was not cut, nor were you washed with water to make you clean, nor were you rubbed with salt or wrapped in cloths. No one looked on you

with pity or had compassion enough to do any of these things for you. Rather, you were thrown out into the open field, for on the day you were born you were despised.

Then I passed by and saw you kicking about in your blood, and as you lay there in your blood I said to you, "Live!" I made you grow like a plant of the field. You grew up and developed and became the most beautiful of jewels. Your breasts were formed and your hair grew, you who were naked and bare.

Later I passed by, and when I looked at you and saw that you were old enough for love, I spread the corner of my garment over you and covered your nakedness. I gave you my solemn oath and entered into a covenant with you, declares the Sovereign Lord, and you became mine.

I bathed you with water and washed the blood from you and put ointments on you. I clothed you with an embroidered dress and put leather sandals on you. I dressed you in fine linen and covered you with costly garments. I adorned you with jewelry: I put bracelets on your arms and a necklace around your neck, and I put a ring on your nose, earrings on your ears and a beautiful crown on your head.

Yet God, all-seeing, knew the ultimate, tragic destiny of the Israelites: "I know what they are disposed to do, even before I bring them into the land," he said. As his people gathered beside the Jordan River, in an upbeat mood for a change, God allowed a remarkable glimpse into what it feels like to be God. He did not share the spirit of anticipation in the camp, and he visited Moses in the Tent of Meeting to explain why.

More than anything, God longed for the covenant to succeed: "Oh, that their hearts would be inclined to fear me and keep all my commands always, so that it might go well with them and their children forever!" But the repeated rebellions in the wilderness had taken a toll. God predicted a terrible disobedience to come and foretold his own response: "I will certainly hide my face on that day." He spoke with rueful resignation, like the parent of a drug addict, helpless to stop his own child from self-destructing; like the husband of an alcoholic who hears a blubbering promise to do better tomorrow or the next day, a promise his wife has already broken too many times to mention.

Then God gave Moses a very odd assignment. "Write down a song," he said, "and make the Israelites learn it as a witness to history." The song set God's point of view to music: the lament of a lover grieved to the point of desertion. Thus at the birth of their nation, euphoric over the crossing of the Jordan River, the Israelites premiered a kind of national anthem—the strangest that has ever been sung. It had virtually no words of hope, only doom.

They sang first of the favored times, when God found them in a howling wasteland and treasured them as the apple of his eye. They sang of the awful betrayal to come, when they would forget the God who gave them birth. They sang of the curses that would afflict them, the wasting famine, deadly plague, and arrows drunk with blood. With this bittersweet music ringing in their ears, the Israelites marched into the Promised Land.

Like a bloodhound on a trail, I keep zigzagging back to the wanderings in the wilderness to poke around for clues. The tabernacle luminous with God's presence, the miraculous breakfast food, the throng of unhappy Israelites shuffling along in the desert sand—somewhere between the bright promise and the blighted futility of those forty years lies the mystery of disappointment with God. What went wrong?

I have often longed for God to act in a direct, closeup manner. If only he would show himself! But in the Israelites' dreary stories of failure I can perceive certain "disadvantages" to God acting so directly. One problem they encountered immediately was the lack of personal freedom. For the Israelites to live in proximity to a holy God, nothing—not sex, menstruation, the content of clothing fabric, or dietary habits—could fall outside the purview of his laws. Being a "chosen people" had a cost. Just as God found it nearly impossible to live among sinful people, the Israelites found it nearly impossible to live with a holy God in their midst.

Petty things seemed to bother the Israelites most—witness their constant complaints about food. With a few exceptions, they ate the same thing every day for forty years: *manna* (meaning, literally, "What is it?") that appeared like dew on the ground each morning. A monotonous diet may seem a trivial exchange for liberation from slavery, but listen to the grumbling: "We remember the fish we ate in Egypt at no cost—also the cucumbers, melons, leeks, onions and garlic. But now we have lost our appetite; we never see anything but this manna!"

In addition to these mundane issues, a far more serious problem arose. The closer God drew toward his people, paradoxically, the more distant they felt from him. Moses laid down an amazing elaboration of rituals necessary to approach God, and no margin for error. The Israelites could see clear evidence of God's presence in the Most Holy Place—but no one dared enter. If you want to know what kind of "personal relationship with God" the Israelites enjoyed, listen to the words of the worshipers themselves: "We will die! We are lost, we are all lost! Anyone who even comes near the tabernacle of the Lord will die." And again, "Let us not hear the voice of the Lord our God nor see this great fire anymore, or we will die."

———— ∞∞∞ ————

Once, as an experiment, the great scientist Isaac Newton stared at the image of the sun reflected in a mirror. The brightness burned into his retina, and he suffered temporary blindness. Even after he hid for three days behind closed shutters, still the bright spot would not fade from his vision. "I used all means to divert my imagination from the sun," he writes, "but if I thought upon him I presently saw his picture though I was in the dark." If he had stared a few minutes longer, Newton might have permanently lost all vision. The chemical receptors that govern eyesight cannot withstand the full force of unfiltered sunlight.

There is a parable in Isaac Newton's experiment, and it helps illustrate what the Israelites ultimately learned from the wilderness wanderings. They had attempted to live with the Lord of the Universe visibly present in their midst; but, in the end, out of all the thousands who had so gladly fled Egypt, only two survived God's Presence. If you can barely endure candlelight, how can you gaze at the sun?

"Who of us can dwell with the consuming fire?" asked the prophet Isaiah. Is it possible that we should be grateful for God's hiddenness, rather than disappointed?

---

[1]Douglas John Hall, *God and Human Suffering,* 156.

Bible references: Exodus 1–12; Deuteronomy 1; Ezekiel 16; Deuteronomy 31, 5, 31–32; Numbers 11, 17; Deuteronomy 18; Isaiah 33.

CHAPTER 9

ONE SHINING MOMENT

———— ❈ ————

Nine-year-old Leo Tolstoy, convinced God would help him fly, dove headfirst out a third-floor window and had his first major crisis of disappointment with God. Fortunately, Tolstoy survived the crash landing and, years later, could laugh at his childish test of faith.

What child has not fantasized about supernatural powers? *Lord, help me walk across this lake. Help me beat up that bully. Make me smart without having to study.* And if God ever saw fit to answer some of those prayers, if, like a genie in a bottle, he granted us any wish we wanted, wouldn't we then try to please him out of gratitude? In my dark hours of disappointment, I instinctively think like that: *If God can get me out . . . if things calm down . . . if I get well . . . then I'll follow God.*

My friend Richard believed that anyone would, like a faithful puppy, follow a God who acted fairly, spoke clearly, and made himself obvious. The wilderness wanderings of the Israelites prove him wrong. But, some might argue, their faith faltered in a harsh land, a place remembered by Moses as a "vast and dreadful desert, that thirsty and waterless land, with its venomous snakes and scorpions." Who wouldn't lose heart in those circumstances. Were there happier times, when God seemed close *and* granted his people their desires?

The tone of the Old Testament brightens when the name David shows up. "Then the Lord awoke as from sleep, as a man wakes from the stupor of wine," Psalm 78 says about those days. God had at last found a man after his own heart, the kind of person he could build a nation around. Lusty King David broke every law on the books save one: he loved God with all his heart, all his mind, and all his soul. With David installed as king over Israel, dreams of the covenant came surging back.

And when David's son Solomon took the throne, God pulled out all the stops. What children only dream of, Solomon got. God offered him any wish—long life, riches, anything at all—and when Solomon chose wisdom God added bonus gifts of wealth, honor, and peace. He would rule over a Golden Age, a shining moment of tranquillity in the long, tormented history of the Hebrews.

Solomon

He took over the throne of Israel as a teenager and soon became the richest person of his time. The Bible says that silver was as common in Jerusalem as stones. A fleet of trading ships sought out exotica for the king's private collections—apes and baboons from Africa—and ivory and gold by the ton. Solomon had artistic talent as well: he wrote 1005 songs and 3000 proverbs.

Rulers traveled hundreds of miles to test Solomon's wisdom firsthand and to see the great city he had built. One such ruler, the queen of Sheba, said to him:

> The report I heard in my own country about your achievements and your wisdom is true. But I did not believe these things until I came and saw with my own eyes. Indeed, not

even half was told me; in wisdom and wealth you have far exceeded the report I heard. How happy your men must be! How happy your officials, who continually stand before you and hear your wisdom! Praise be to the Lord your God, who has delighted in you and placed you on the throne of Israel.

Impressive words from a queen who, as a farewell gift, gave Solomon four and a half tons of pure gold.

And what did God feel during these halcyon days? Relief, pleasure, delight—the Bible hints at all these. Israel's chronic grumblers had died off, and Solomon went out of his way to make God feel loved. He lavished the wealth of his kingdom on a tremendous temple, fashioned by 200,000 workmen, that ranked as one of the wonders of the world. From a distance, it shone like a snowcapped mountain.

Old Testament history reached a high-water mark on the day Solomon dedicated that temple to God. Think of a movie scene of the most blinding encounter with an extraterrestrial being. Something like that happened in Jerusalem, only this was no illusion staged by special-effects crews. Thousands of people were looking on in a huge public ceremony. When the glory of the Lord came down to fill the temple, even the priests were driven back by the blast.

God was making Solomon's temple the center of his activity on earth, and the crowd spontaneously decided to stay another two weeks to celebrate. Kneeling on a bronze platform, Solomon prayed aloud, "I have indeed built a magnificent temple for you, a place for you to dwell forever." Then he caught himself in astonishment. "But will God really dwell on earth? The heavens, even the highest heaven, cannot contain you. How much less this temple I have built!"

Later, God responded: "I have heard the prayer and plea you have made before me; I have consecrated this temple.... My eyes and my heart will always be there." God had done it! His promises to Abraham and Moses had finally come true. The Israelites now had land, a nation with secure boundaries, and a gleaming symbol of God's presence among them. No one present on the famous day of the temple dedication could doubt God; everyone saw the fire and the cloud of his presence. And all this came to pass not in a harsh desert full of snakes and scorpions, but in a land rich with silver and gold.

With everything imaginable working in his favor, at first it seemed Solomon would gratefully follow God. His prayer of dedication for the temple in 1 Kings 8 is one of the most majestic ever prayed. Yet by the end of his reign Solomon had squandered away nearly every advantage. The poetic man who had sung of romantic love broke all records for promiscuity: seven hundred wives in all, and three hundred concubines! The wise man who had composed so many commonsense proverbs flouted them with an extravagance that has never been equaled. And to please his foreign-born wives, the devout man who had built the temple of God took a final, terrible step: he introduced idol worship into God's holy city.

In one generation, Solomon took Israel from a fledgling kingdom dependent on God for bare survival to a self-sufficient political power. But along the way he lost sight of the original vision to which God had called them. Ironically, by the time of Solomon's death, Israel resembled the Egypt they had escaped: an imperial state held in place by a bloated bureaucracy and slave labor, with an official state religion under the ruler's command. Success in the kingdom of this world had crowded out interest in the kingdom of God. The brief, shining vision of a covenant nation faded away, and God withdrew his sanction. After Solomon's death, Israel split in two and slid toward ruin.

A quotation from Oscar Wilde might provide the best epitaph for Solomon: "In this world there are only two tragedies. One is not getting what one wants, and the other is getting it." Solomon got whatever he wanted, especially when it came to symbols of power and status. Gradually, he depended less on God and more on the props around him: the world's largest harem, a house twice the size of the temple, an army well-stocked with chariots, a strong economy. Success may have eliminated any crises of disappointment with God, but it also seemed to eliminate Solomon's desire for God at all. The more he enjoyed the world's good gifts, the less he thought about the Giver.

⸭

In the wilderness God dwelt in a pillar of fire and cloud, so nearby that his power sometimes "broke out" with destructive force. In Solomon's day God seemed to restrict that power, giving the king authority to represent him to the people. As for the Israelites, who had shrunk in fear from God in the wilderness, they simply took God for granted once his presence was centered in the temple. He became just another part of the royal landscape.

In response to this change, God quietly turned elsewhere. You can easily detect the shift by scanning the Old Testament, which gives lengthy accounts of the first three kings of Israel—Saul, David, and Solomon; but after Solomon, stories of the kings speed up into a forgettable blur. God turned instead to his prophets.

Bible references: Deuteronomy 8; 2 Samuel 7; 1 Kings 8–10.

CHAPTER 10

FIRE AND THE WORD

—❦—

It was an unholy coincidence that many took to be divine retribution. Two weeks ago, canon David Jenkins, 59, who had publicly asserted that neither the Virgin birth nor the Resurrection need be taken too literally, was formally consecrated as Bishop of Durham in York Minster amid cries of protest. Less than three days later, in the early hours of the morning, lightning forked down on the wooden roof of the minster's 13th century south transept. By 2:30 A.M., flames were leaping from the medieval masterpiece that is the largest Gothic cathedral in Northern Europe.... Jenkins' detractors lost no time in claiming that their views had been vindicated.... a vicar who had been evicted from the minster for voicing protests in the midst of the new bishop's consecration ceremony suggested that "divine intervention" might have caused the fire. Others ... cit[ed] the prophet Elijah, who brought down a fire from heaven, which destroyed an altar he had built in the presence of the prophets of Baal.

Time, July 23, 1984

The problem with the York Minster lightning bolt, of course, is that it stands as such an exception. So fire from the heavens hits a famous church—what about all the Unitarian churches that brashly deny orthodox Christian doctrines, not to mention the Muslim mosques and Hindu temples? Why should David Jenkins provoke divine wrath when the outright blasphemer Bertrand Russell lived unpunished into cranky old age? If God consistently sent lightning bolts in response to bad doctrine, our planet would sparkle nightly like a Christmas tree.

And yet fire did fall from heaven once, almost thirty centuries ago, and ministers ever since have harked back to that scene on Mount Carmel. The story has a mythic, Tolkienesque quality to it: like Frodo on his mission to Mordor, Elijah journeyed across Israel to a rugged desert mountain to wage war, single-combat style, against 850 false prophets.

Elijah, the wildest and woolliest prophet of Israel, worked the crowd like a master magician. He doused the site with twelve large jars of water—a most precious commodity after three years of drought. And just when it seemed Elijah was perpetrating a huge national joke, it happened. A ball of fire dropped like a meteor from a clear sky. The heat was so intense it melted the stones and soil, and flames lapped up water from the trenches like fuel. The crowd dropped to the ground in fear and awe. "The Lord—he is God! The Lord—he is God!" they cried.

In a dramatic public showdown, God clobbered the forces of evil. No wonder the scene looms large in the annals of faith. No wonder the people of Jesus' day mistook him for Elijah reincarnate. Even in modern times, when lightning strikes a cathedral, some wistfully recall Mount Carmel.

Yet when I sat in a Colorado cabin and read straight through the Bible, I saw the life of Elijah in a very different light. He and his miracle-working twin Elisha emerged not as prototypes of the Old Testament prophet, but as stellar exceptions: few successors had even a trace of their ability to work miracles. If we yearn for their power, we yearn for the wrong thing. The signs and wonders of Elijah's day were a blip in history, with no long-term effect on the Israelites. No wildfire revivals broke out, and after the briefest flurry of religious fervor, the nation settled back into its long, steady slide away from God. King Ahab, himself a spectator at Mount Carmel, left a legacy as Israel's wickedest king.

Apparently the fireball on Mount Carmel had no lasting impact on Elijah either. Terrified for his life, the prophet put forty days' distance between himself and Queen Jezebel, Ahab's vengeful consort. And when God next met with Elijah, he did not appear in a fire, or in a great and powerful wind, or in an earthquake. Rather, he came in a whisper, a thin, small voice almost like silence—a preview of a striking change to come.

The Prophets

It must have been hard to follow the prophet Elijah. Not long after the showdown on Mount Carmel another prophet, Micaiah, stood before the same king, Ahab, in very similar circumstances. Elijah-like, he faced down four hundred false prophets and delivered a stinging message from God. But instead of fire falling from heaven, Micaiah got a slap in the face and a stint in jail.

After Elijah and Elisha, God seemed to rein in his supernatural power, turning from spectacle to word. Most prophets—Isaiah, Hosea, Habakkuk, Jeremiah, Ezekiel—had no stunning displays of omnipotence to dangle before an audience; they had only the power of words. And as God seemed to draw farther and farther away, these prophets themselves began to ask questions: eloquent questions, haunting questions, questions wrapped in pain. They voiced aloud the cries of a people who felt abandoned by God.

I had always misread the prophets—when I bothered to read them at all. I had seen them as finger-wagging, fusty old men who, like Elijah, called down judgment on the pagans. I discovered to my surprise that the ancient prophets' writings actually sound the most "modern" of any part of the Bible. They deal with the very same themes that hang like a cloud over our century: the silence of God, the seeming sovereignty of evil, the unrelieved suffering in the world. The prophets' questions are, in fact, the questions of this book: God's unfairness, silence, hiddenness.

More passionately than anyone in history, the prophets of Israel gave voice to the feeling of disappointment with God. Why do godless nations flourish? they asked. Why is there such poverty and depravity in the world? Why so few miracles? Where are you, God? "Why do you always forget us? Why do you forsake us so long?" Show yourself; break your silence. For God's sake, literally, ACT!

There was the urbane voice of Isaiah, an aristocrat and adviser to kings, in personal style as far removed from Elijah as Winston Churchill was from Gandhi. "Truly you are a God who hides himself," Isaiah said. "Oh, that you would rend the heavens and come down, that the mountains would tremble before you!"

Jeremiah loudly protested the failure of "success theology." In his day, prophets were being tossed in dungeons and wells, and even sawed in half. Jeremiah compared God to a weakling, "a man taken by surprise . . . a warrior powerless to save." Voltaire himself could not have put it better: How can an all-powerful and all-loving God permit such a messed-up world?

Habakkuk challenged God to explain why, as he put it, "justice never prevails."

> How long, O Lord, must I call for help,
>   but you do not listen?
> Or cry out to you, "Violence!"
>   but you do not save?
> Why do you make me look at injustice?
>   Why do you tolerate wrong?

Like all Israelites, the prophets had been raised on victory stories. As children they had learned how God freed his people from slavery, descended to live among them, and carried them into the Promised Land. But now in visions of the future they saw, in slow-motion detail, all those victories being undone. In a stark reversal of the unforgettable scene from Solomon's day, the prophet Ezekiel watched God's glory rise, hover above the temple for a moment, and then vanish.

What Ezekiel saw in a vision, Jeremiah saw in stark reality. Babylonian soldiers entered the temple—pagans in the Most Holy Place!—looted it, then burned it to the ground. (Historians record that as they entered the temple the soldiers swept the empty air with their spears, seeking the unseen Hebrew God.) Jeremiah wandered the deserted streets of Jerusalem in a state of shock, like a survivor of Hiroshima staggering through the rubble. Israel's king was now shackled and blinded, the nation's princes slaughtered. In the final siege, Jerusalem's gentle women had cooked and eaten their own children.

How did it feel to be a prophet then? Jeremiah tells us:

Since my people are crushed, I am crushed;
  I mourn, and horror grips me. . . .
Oh, that my head were a spring of water
  and my eyes a fountain of tears!
I would weep day and night
  for the slain of my people. . . .
My heart is broken within me;
  all my bones tremble.
I am like a drunken man,
  like a man overcome by wine.

But the most amazing feature of the prophets is not their "modern" outlook or their passionate cry of disappointment. The reason these seventeen books merit a close look is that they include God's own reply to the prophets' bracing questions.

Bible references: 1 Kings 17–19, 22; Lamentations 5; Isaiah 45, 64; Jeremiah 14; Habakkuk 1; Jeremiah 8–9, 23.

CHAPTER 11

WOUNDED LOVER

⎯⎯◦◦◦⎯⎯

God talked back, defending the way he ran the world. He lashed out, stormed, and wept. And this is what he said:

I am not silent; I have been speaking through my prophets.

We tend to rank God's revelations by their dramatic effect, with spectacular personal appearances at the top, supernatural miracles just below, and the words of the prophets at the bottom. The fireball on Mount Carmel, for example, seems more convincing than one of Jeremiah's doleful sermons. But God acknowledged no such rating. In an ironic twist, he pointed to the prophets themselves—the very people who were questioning his silence—as proof of his concern. How can a nation complain about the silence of God when they have the likes of Ezekiel and Jeremiah and Daniel and Isaiah?

God did not consider "mere words" an inferior form of proof. Miracles, after all, had never had much lasting impact on the Israelites' faith; but the prophets would inscribe a permanent record, to be passed down over generations, of God's overtures toward his people. Sometimes God pointed to past miracles as proofs of his love, but more often he said something like this, in the familiar tone of an exasperated parent: "From the time your forefathers left Egypt until now, day after day, again and again I sent you my servants the prophets. But they did not listen to me or pay attention." God concluded that the people did not really want a word from the Lord, and they proved him right, warning Isaiah, "Tell us pleasant things, prophesy illusions . . . and stop confronting us with the Holy One of Israel."

I have indeed withdrawn my presence.

When the prophets complained loudly about God's hiddenness, God didn't argue. He agreed with them, and then explained why he was keeping his distance.

To Jeremiah, God expressed his disgust with what he saw in Israel: dishonest gain, the shedding of innocent blood, oppression, extortion. He covered his eyes, he said, refusing even to see hands spread out in a posture of prayer, for those hands were covered with blood.

To Ezekiel, God explained that once Israel's rebellions had passed a certain point, he simply "gave them over" to their sins. He withdrew, letting the people choose their own way and bear the consequences.

To Zechariah, he said, "When I called, they did not listen; so when they called, I would not listen."

My slowness to act is a sign of mercy, not of weakness.

When God did not punish quickly, the people of Israel presumed he had lost his power: "He will do nothing! No harm will come to us; we will never see sword or famine." They were wrong. God's restraint marked an interlude of mercy, a time of probation he was granting Israel. Reluctantly, like a parent out of options, God resorted to punishment.

For Israel, punishment took the form of foreign invasions. But the prophets also speak of a "day of the Lord" at the end of time.

Sandwiched between their shining accounts of a new heaven and new earth are some of the most dreadful apocalyptic visions ever set to words. Before we can hear the last word, said Dietrich Bonhoeffer, we must listen to the next-to-the-last word. And the more I study the prophets' accounts of the last days, the more content I become with God's apparent "shyness" to intervene in human affairs.

In my own times of disappointment with God, I have called on him to act with power. I have prayed against political tyranny and unfairness and injustice. I have prayed for miracle, for proof of God's existence. But as I read the prophets' descriptions of the day when God finally will take off all the wraps, one prayer overwhelms all others: "God, I hope I'm not around then." God freely admits he is holding back his power, but he restrains himself for our benefit. For all scoffers who call for direct action from the heavens, the prophets have ominous advice: Just wait.

Though my judgments appear stern, I am suffering with you.

God exposed his deepest feelings to the prophets. For example, here is how he felt about the destruction of Moab, one of Israel's enemies:

I wail over Moab,
for all Moab I cry out. . . .
My heart laments for Moab like a flute.

As for his chosen people of Israel, whatever shame and humiliation they endured, God also endured. The Israelites watched in horror as Babylonian axmen hacked apart the cedar beams of the temple—but it was God's own house they were invading, and he felt that invasion as a personal desecration. As the temple was razed, his dwelling place was razed. As the Jews were led captive, he was led captive. And when the conquerors divided the spoils of Israel, they joked not about

379

the Israelites but about their weakling God. "Wherever they went among the nations they profaned my holy name, for it was said of them, 'These are the Lord's people, and yet they had to leave his land.'"

A single, elegant sentence from Isaiah summarizes God's point of view: "In all their distress he too was distressed." God may have hidden his face, but that face was streaked with tears.

Despite everything, I am ready to forgive at any moment.

Often, in the midst of a stern reproof, God would stop—literally midsentence—and beg Israel to repent. Ahab, the most wicked king of Israel, got another chance after Mount Carmel, and then another, and another. "I take no pleasure in the death of the wicked," God explained to Ezekiel. "Turn! Turn from your evil ways! Why will you die, O house of Israel?" He told Jeremiah that if he could find just one honest person in Jerusalem, he would spare the whole city.

Nothing expresses God's yearning to forgive better than the Book of Jonah. It contains but one line of prophecy: "Forty more days and Nineveh will be overturned." But, to Jonah's disgust, that simple announcement of doom sparked a spiritual revival in hated Nineveh and changed God's plans for punishment. Jonah, sulking under a shriveled vine, admitted he had suspected God's soft heart all along. "I knew that you are a gracious and compassionate God, slow to anger and abounding in love, a God who relents from sending calamity." Thus the whole madcap scenario of balky prophet, ocean storm, and whale detour came about because Jonah could not trust God—could not, that is, trust him to be harsh and unrelenting toward Nineveh. As Robert Frost summed up the story, "After Jonah, you could never trust God not to be merciful again."

Passion

Although God answered the prophets' questions directly, his explanations did not satisfy Israel. Knowing the reason behind a disaster does not lessen the sense of pain and betrayal. And in truth God's rational "defense" seems tossed in almost as an aside. The prophets are not as concerned about intellectual questions as they are about God's *passion*. How does it feel to be God? To understand, consider the human images stressed again and again by the prophets: God as parent, and as lover.

Follow around some first-time parents. Their conversation seems limited to one topic: The Child. They crow that their wrinkled, ruddy baby is the most beautiful child ever born. They spend hundreds of dollars on equipment to videotape the first babbling words and the first lurching steps—ordinary skills mastered by almost all five billion people on earth. Such strange behavior expresses a new parent's pride and joy in a human relationship like no other.

In choosing Israel, God was seeking such a relationship. He wanted what any parent wants: a happy household of children who return their parent's love. His voice sings with pride as he reminisces about the early days: "Is not Ephraim my dear son, the child in whom I delight?" But the joy fades away as God abruptly shifts from the perspective of a parent to that of a lover, a wounded lover. *What have I done wrong?* he demands in a tone of sadness, and horror, and rage.

> I supplied all their needs,
>   yet they committed adultery
>   and thronged to the houses of prostitutes.
> They are well-fed, lusty stallions,
>   each neighing for another man's wife.
> Should I not punish them for this?

In reading the prophets I cannot help envisioning a counselor with God as a client. The counselor gets out one stock sentence, "Tell me how you really feel," and then God takes over.

"I'll tell you how I feel! I feel like a rejected parent. I find a baby girl lying in a ditch, near death. I take her home and make her my daughter. I clean her, pay for her schooling, feed her. I dote on her, clothe her, hang jewelry on her. Then one day she runs away. I hear reports of her debased life. When my name comes up, she curses me.

"I'll tell you how I feel! I feel like a jilted lover. I found my lover thin and wasted, abused, but I brought her home and made her beauty shine. She is my precious one, the most beautiful woman in the world to me, and I lavish on her gifts and love. And yet she forsakes me. She pants after my best friends, my enemies—anyone. She stands by a highway and under every spreading tree and, worse than a prostitute, she *pays* people to have sex with her. I feel betrayed, abandoned, cuckolded."

God does not hide his hurt. He employs shocking language, comparing Israel to "a swift she-camel running here and there, a wild donkey accustomed to the desert, sniffing the wind in her craving—in her heat who can restrain her?"

As if words alone were too weak to convey his passion, God asked one brave prophet, Hosea, to act out a living parable. On God's orders, Hosea married Gomer, a woman with a most unsavory reputation. From then on, the poor man lived a soap-opera existence. Time after time Gomer wandered off, fell for another man, and moved out. And each time, incredibly, God instructed Hosea to welcome Gomer back and forgive her.

God used Hosea's unhappy story to illustrate his own whipsaw emotions. That first blush of love when he found Israel, God said, was like finding grapes in the desert. But as Israel broke his trust again and again, he was forced to endure the awful shame of a wounded lover. His words carry a tone not far from self-pity: "I am like a moth to Ephraim, like rot to the people of Judah."

The powerful image of a jilted lover explains why, in his speeches to the prophets, God seems to "change his mind" every few seconds. He is preparing to obliterate Israel—wait, now he is weeping, holding out open arms—no, he is sternly pronouncing judgment again. Those shifting moods seem hopelessly irrational, except to anyone who has been jilted by a lover.

The words of the prophets sound like the words of a lovers' quarrel drifting through thin apartment walls. A neighbor of mine endured two years of such conflict. In November she was ready to kill her unfaithful husband. In February she forgave him and invited him back in. In April she filed for divorce. In August she stopped the proceedings and asked her husband to return again. It took two years for her to face the ugly truth that her love had been rejected forever.

And that is the precise cycle of anger, grief, forgiveness, jealousy, love, pain that God himself went through. The prophets show God struggling for a language, any language, that might break through to his people. Just as my neighbor would hang up the phone on her estranged husband, God would tell the prophets that he would no longer listen to the prayers of Israel. And just as my friend would soften, God would soften and beg his people to try again. Sometimes his love and anger seemed to collide. But at last, all alternatives exhausted, God concluded that he must give up: "What else can I do because of the sin of my people?"

***

My friend Richard described to me his deep sense of betrayal when God "let him down." He felt exactly as he had when his fiancée abruptly cut him off. But the prophets, and especially Hosea, communicate one message above all others: God is the betrayed one. It was Israel, not God, who had gone a-whoring. The prophets of Israel had expressed a profound disappointment in God, accusing him of acting aloof, unconcerned, silent. But when God spoke, he poured out emotions pent up for centuries. And he, not Israel, was the truly disappointed party.

"What else can I do?" God's poignant question to Jeremiah points up the dilemma of an omnipotent God who has made room for freedom. The stork in the sky knows her seasons, the ocean tide rolls in on schedule, snow always covers the high mountains, but human beings are like nothing else in nature. God cannot control them. Yet he cannot simply thrust them aside either. He cannot get humanity out of his mind.

Bible references: Jeremiah 7; Isaiah 30; Jeremiah 5; Ezekiel 20; Zechariah 7; Jeremiah 5, 48; Ezekiel 36; Isaiah 63; Ezekiel 33; Jonah 3–4; Jeremiah 31, 5, 2; Hosea 9, 5; Jeremiah 9.

CHAPTER 12

TOO GOOD TO BE TRUE

Grief melts away
Like snow in May
As if there were no such cold thing.
GEORGE HERBERT, "THE FLOWER"

One day when George MacDonald, the great Scottish preacher and writer, was talking with his son, the conversation turned to heaven and the prophets' version of the end of all things. "It seems too good to be true," the son said at one point. A smile crossed MacDonald's whiskered face. "Nay," he replied, "it is just so good it must be true!"[1]

Does any human emotion run as deep as hope? Fairy tales pass on through the centuries a stubborn hope in a happy ending, a belief that in the end the wicked witch will die and the brave and innocent children will somehow find a way of escape. A dozen cartoons in a row on Saturday morning television crank out a similar message to children who sit enthralled, too young to sneer at impossibly cheery endings. In real life, a mother caught in a war zone holds her infant son tight against her breast, pats his head, and whispers, illogically, "It'll be all right," even as the percussive blasts grow closer.

385

Where does such hope come from? Searching for words to explain the ageless attraction of fairy tales, Tolkien said:

> [Fairy tale] does not deny the existence of . . . sorrow and failure: the possibility of these is necessary to the joy of the deliverance; it denies (in the face of much evidence, if you will) universal final defeat . . . giving a fleeting glimpse of Joy, Joy beyond the walls of the world, poignant as grief.[2]

No summary of the prophets would be complete apart from one last message: their loud insistence that the world will not end in "universal final defeat," but in Joy. They spoke in foreboding times to audiences filled with fear, and often their dire predictions of droughts and locust plagues and enemy sieges fueled that fear. But always, in every one of their seventeen books, the prophets of the Old Testament got around to a word of hope. The wounded lover will recover from his pain, Isaiah promises: "For a brief moment I abandoned you, but with deep compassion I will bring you back."

Their voices soar like songbirds' when the prophets turn at last to describe the Joy beyond the walls of the world. In that final day, God will roll up the earth like a carpet and weave it anew. Wolves and lambs will feed together in the same field, and a lion graze in peace beside an ox.

One day, says Malachi, we will leap like calves released from the stall. There will be no fear then, and no pain. No infants will die; no tears will fall. Among the nations, peace will flow like a river, and armies will melt their weapons into farm tools. No one will complain about the hiddenness of God in that day. His glory will fill the earth, and the sun will seem dim by contrast.

For the prophets, human history is not an end in itself but a transition time, a parenthesis between Eden and the new heaven and new earth still to be formed by God. Even when everything seems out of control, God is firmly in control, and someday will assert himself.*

The Meantime

But what about right now? Must we wait past death for all meaningful answers to the problem of disappointment with God? After the prophets had died off, the Jewish people began to raise such questions, for once again the heavens went silent: "We are given no miraculous signs; no prophets are left, and none of us knows how long this will be. How long will the enemy mock you, O God?"

Torn from their homeland and sold once more into bondage, the Jews hung onto the prophets' promises of a deliverer and a peaceful future. As the decades, even centuries passed, empires—Babylon, Persia, Egypt, Greece, Syria, Rome—rose and fell, their armies chasing each other across the plains of Palestine. Each new empire subjugated the Jews with ease, as if scraping their feet on a doormat. Sometimes the entire race verged on extinction.

No Moses figure appeared to lead the Jews out of bondage. No Elijahs called down fireballs from heaven. No luminous glow radiated from the temple in Jerusalem. Until King Herod came along with his penchant for ostentatious buildings, the temple site remained half-finished, a pile of rubble recalling more shame than glory.

---

*Some people find no comfort in the prophets' vision of a future world. "Mere pie in the sky," they say. "The church has used that line for centuries to justify slavery, oppression, and all manner of injustice. They force-feed the hope of heaven to the poor in order to keep them from demanding too much on earth." The criticism sticks because the church has abused the prophets' vision. But you will never find that "pie in the sky" rationale in the prophets themselves. Amos, Hosea, Isaiah, and Jeremiah have scathing words about the need to care for widows and orphans and aliens, and to clean up corrupt courts and religious systems. The people of God are not merely to mark time, waiting for God to step in and set right all that is wrong. Rather, they are to model the new heaven and new earth, and by so doing awaken longings for what God will someday bring to pass.

At the end of the Old Testament, God was in hiding. He had threatened to hide his face, and when he finally did a dark shadow fell across the planet. Our disappointment with God twenty-five centuries later is a faint aftershock of what the Jews felt when God turned his back. Today, we may find some comfort in looking back on lessons from the past. We may see the "disadvantages" to God's closeup interventions: his Presence, too bright for us, leaves scorch marks; it creates distance; and worse, it doesn't even seem to foster faith. We may also find comfort in looking ahead to eternal life free of tears and pain, in a new dimension somewhere, after we're transformed into beings who can endure God's Presence. But what of the meantime? The mean times? Like the Jews, we feel God's hiddenness as a disappointment, an aching in the heart, a doubt never fully set to rest.

Four centuries separate the last words of Malachi in the Old Testament from the first words of Matthew in the New Testament. "The four hundred silent years," they are called, and that phrase marks an era bordered by disappointment with God. Did God care? Was he even alive? He seemed deaf to the Jews' prayers. Still, despite everything, they waited for a Messiah—they had no other hope.

"What else can I do?" God had asked. There was something else. What could not be won through power, he would win through suffering.

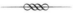

God weeps with us so that we may one day laugh with him.

JÜRGEN MOLTMANN

[1]Greville MacDonald, *George MacDonald and His Wife,* 172.
[2]J. R. R. Tolkien, *The Tolkien Reader,* 68–69.

Bible references: Isaiah 54; Malachi 4; Psalm 74.

PART THREE

DRAWING CLOSER:
THE SON

CHAPTER 13

THE DESCENT

———— ∞∞ ————

S uppose there was a king who loved a humble maiden," begins a
story by Kierkegaard.

*The king was like no other king. Every statesman trembled before
his power. No one dared breathe a word against him, for he had the
strength to crush all opponents. And yet this mighty king was melted by
love for a humble maiden.*

*How could he declare his love for her? In an odd sort of way, his
very kingliness tied his hands. If he brought her to the palace and crowned
her head with jewels and clothed her body in royal robes, she would surely
not resist—no one dared resist him. But would she love him?*

*She would say she loved him, of course, but would she truly? Or
would she live with him in fear, nursing a private grief for the life she had
left behind. Would she be happy at his side? How could he know?*

*If he rode to her forest cottage in his royal carriage, with an armed
escort waving bright banners, that too would overwhelm her. He did not
want a cringing subject. He wanted a lover, an equal. He wanted her to
forget that he was a king and she a humble maiden and to let shared love
cross over the gulf between them.*

"For it is only in love that the unequal can be made equal," concluded Kierkegaard. The king, convinced he could not elevate the maiden without crushing her freedom, resolved to *descend.* He clothed himself as a beggar and approached her cottage incognito, with a worn cloak fluttering loosely about him. It was no mere disguise, but a new identity he took on. He renounced the throne to win her hand.[1]

What Kierkegaard expressed in parable form, the apostle Paul expressed in these words about Jesus the Christ:

> Who, being in very nature God,
>   did not consider equality with God
>   something to be grasped,
> but made himself nothing,
>   taking the very nature of a servant,
>   being made in human likeness.
> And being found in appearance as a man,
>   he humbled himself
>   and became obedient to death—
>   even death on a cross!

In his dealings with human beings, God had often humbled himself. I see the Old Testament as one long record of his "condescensions" ("to descend to be with"). God condescended in various ways to speak to Abraham, and to Moses, and to the nation of Israel and the prophets. But no condescension could match what came next, after the four hundred years of silence. God, like the king in Kierkegaard's parable, took on a new form: he became a man. It was the most shocking descent imaginable.

Fear Not

We hear the words every Christmas season at church pageants when children dress up in bathrobes and act out the story of Jesus' birth. "Fear not!" lisps the six-year-old angel, his bedsheet costume dragging the ground, his coat-hanger-frame wings flapping ever so slightly from the trembling of his body. He sneaks a glance at the script hidden in the folds of his sleeve. "Fear not, for I bring you good tidings of great joy." Already he has appeared to Zechariah (his older brother with a taped-on cotton beard) and to Mary (a freckled blonde from the second grade). He used the same greeting for both, "Fear not!..."

These were also God's first words to Abraham, and to Hagar, and to Isaac. "Fear not!" the angel said in greeting Gideon and the prophet Daniel. For supernatural beings, that phrase served almost as the equivalent of "Hello, how are you?" Little wonder. By the time the supernatural being spoke, the human being was usually lying face down in a cataleptic state. When God made contact with planet Earth, sometimes the supernatural encounter sounded like thunder, sometimes it stirred the air like a whirlwind, and sometimes it lit up the scene like a flash of phosphorous. Nearly always it caused fear. But the angel who visited Zechariah and Mary and Joseph heralded that God was about to appear in a form that would not frighten.

What could be less scary than a newborn baby with jerky limbs and eyes that do not quite focus? In Jesus, born in a barn or cave and laid in a feeding trough, God found at last a mode of approach that humanity need not fear. The king had cast off his robes.

Think of the condescension involved: the Incarnation, which sliced history into two parts (a fact even our calendars grudgingly acknowledge), had more animal than human witnesses. Think, too, of the risk. In the Incarnation, God spanned the vast chasm of fear that had distanced him from his human creation. But removing that barrier made Jesus vulnerable, terribly vulnerable.

The child born in the night among beasts. The sweet breath and steaming dung of beasts. And nothing is ever the same again.

Those who believe in God can never in a way be sure of him again. Once they have seen him in a stable, they can never be sure where he will appear or to what lengths he will go or to what ludicrous depths of self-humiliation he will descend in his wild pursuit of man. . . .

For those who believe in God, it means, this birth, that God himself is never safe from us, and maybe that is the dark side of Christmas, the terror of the silence. He comes in such a way that we can always turn him down, as we could crack the baby's skull like an eggshell or nail him up when he gets too big for that.[2]

How did Christmas day feel to God? Imagine for a moment becoming a baby again: giving up language and muscle coordination, and the ability to eat solid food and control your bladder. God as a fetus! Or imagine yourself becoming a sea slug—that analogy is probably closer. On that day in Bethlehem, the Maker of All That Is took form as a helpless, dependent newborn.

"Kenosis" is the technical word theologians use to describe Christ emptying himself of the advantages of deity. Ironically, while the emptying involved much humiliation, it also involved a kind of freedom. I have spoken of the "disadvantages" of infinity. A physical body freed Christ to act on a human scale, without those "disadvantages." He could say what he wanted without his voice blasting the treetops. He could express anger by calling King Herod a fox or by reaching for a bullwhip in the temple, rather than shaking the earth with his stormy presence. And he could talk to anyone—

a prostitute, a blind man, a widow, a leper—without first having to announce, "Fear not!"

———∞∞∞———

'Twas much, that man was made like God before,
But that God should be made like man, much more.

JOHN DONNE, "HOLY SONNET 15"

---

[1] Paraphrase of Søren Kierkegaard, *Philosophical Fragments*, 31–43.
[2] Frederick Buechner, *The Hungering Dark*, 13–14.

Bible reference: Philippians 2.

CHAPTER 14

GREAT EXPECTATIONS

———⚬⚬⚬———

Every year around Christmastime the air vibrates with lyrical promises of the Messiah. From high school choristers to distinguished professionals, musicians trek to practices as if on a pilgrimage, clutching sheet music tattered from overuse. Nowadays you don't even have to belong to a choir to sing the famous prophecies that Handel set to music; most major cities offer a "Do-It-Yourself *Messiah*" (amazing phrase!) open to all.

And what is it that we celebrate in grand concert style? These are the words Handel lifted from the biblical prophets:

> Every valley shall be exalted, and every mountain and hill made low; the crooked straight, and the rough places plain.
>
> The people that walked in darkness have seen a great light: and they that dwell in the land of the shadow of death, upon them hath the light shined.
>
> For unto us a Child is born, unto us a Son is given, and the government shall be upon His shoulder: and His name shall be called Wonderful, Counsellor, the Mighty God, the Everlasting Father, the Prince of Peace.

Those same words were on the lips of faithful Jews during the years of God's silence. Disappointment, even despair, metastasized throughout Israel as history, ever crueler, destroyed all hopes but one: the prophets' promise of a King of Kings. When the Messiah comes, then at last justice will roll down like a river—the Jews clung to that promise fiercely, like capsized sailors clinging to a life raft.

Four centuries after the last biblical prophet, strange rumors started circulating: first about a desert prophet named John, and then about Jesus, a carpenter's son from Nazareth. As word of Jesus' miraculous powers began to leak out, speculation spread. Could he be the One? Some insisted the Messiah truly had come. With their own eyes they had seen Jesus heal the blind and make the lame walk. "God has come to help his people!" they declared when he raised a young man from death. Others remained skeptical. Jesus fulfilled the messianic promises, but—an important but—not in the way anyone expected.

⸎

When I went through the Bible searching for signs of disappointment with God, I expected to find a decisive change when I reached the Gospels. The prophets' Messiah—as a quick scan of Handel's libretto easily shows—would seem to dispel such feelings. To the contrary, disappointment did not vanish from the earth in Jesus' day, and has not vanished yet, two thousand years later. What went wrong? Or, ask the question another way: What did Jesus' life contribute to the three questions that stalk this book?

Is God silent? "Follow me!" "This, then, is how you should pray." "We are going up to Jerusalem." In certain respects, Jesus made God's will clearer than it had ever been before. Incredibly, he opened himself to the scientific method of investigation, which is exactly what he got from Pharisees, Sadducees, and other skeptics. Anyone could walk right up to the Son of God and ask a question or debate with him. As the Gospels tell it, God broke his silence loudly and convincingly while Jesus lived on earth: the *Word* was made flesh.

Is God hidden? With Jesus, God actually took on a shape in the world, acquiring a face, a name, and an address. He was a God you could touch and smell and hear and see. "Anyone who has seen me has seen the Father," Jesus said bluntly.

And yet Jesus' visibility, his very ordinariness, introduced a new problem for Jews raised on stories of Mount Sinai and Mount Carmel. Where was the smoke, the fire, the burst of light? Jesus did not match their image of what God should look like. He was a man, for goodness' sake, one who hailed from the jerkwater town of Nazareth at that—Mary's boy, a common carpenter. Jesus' neighbors, who had watched him play in the streets with their own children, never could accept him as the Messiah. And Mark notes in a remarkable aside that even Jesus' own family once concluded, "He is out of his mind." His mother and brothers! Mary, who on seeing the angel Gabriel had spontaneously let loose with the annunciation hymn; his brothers, who had spent more time with him than anyone else— these, too, could not reconcile the strange combination of wondrous and ordinary. Jesus' skin got in the way.

Is God unfair? Perhaps this lingering question produced the most doubt about Jesus, for Jews believed the Messiah would set right all that was wrong with the world. Had not the prophets promised the Lord would swallow up death forever and wipe the tears from all faces? Indeed, Jesus did heal some people; but many more went unhealed. He raised Lazarus from the dead, but many others died during his time on earth. He did not wipe away tears from all faces.

The problem of unfairness bothers many people who are otherwise attracted to Jesus' life. The great theologian Augustine, for example, puzzled over the arbitrariness of the healings in the Gospels. If Jesus had the power, why didn't he heal everyone? One story especially, from the Gospel of John, caught Augustine's attention.

The disabled of Jerusalem—the blind, the lame, the paralyzed—used to flock around a certain pool in the city, the Lourdes shrine of its day. Sometimes the water in the pool would ripple, and they would run, limp, or crawl to enter the water while it was astir. One day Jesus struck up a conversation with a pathetic man who lay there. He had been crippled for thirty-eight years, he told Jesus, but he had never made it to the pool. Whenever the waters stirred, someone would always push in ahead. Without batting an eye, Jesus ordered the invalid to get up and walk. "At once the man was cured; he picked up his mat and walked." After thirty-eight years of lying flat, he walked! He was the happiest man in Jerusalem.

But the storyteller, John, adds one significant detail: Jesus then slipped away, into the crowd. He ignored the rest of that great throng of disabled people, leaving all but the one unhealed. Why? Augustine wondered: "There lay so many there, and yet only one was healed, whilst He could by a word have raised them all up."[1]

Jesus' cousin was another person troubled by unfairness. John the Baptist, a true believer if there ever was one, had excited the nation's hopes about Jesus. In the early days, when people used to ask if John himself was the Messiah, he would set them straight: "After me will come one more powerful than I, the thongs of whose sandals I am not worthy to stoop down and untie." That promised one—Jesus of Nazareth—came to John for baptism, and he watched in amazement as the Spirit of God descended from the sky in the form of a dove. As if to eliminate all doubts about Jesus, a voice spoke from heaven, loud as thunder.

Two years later, however, John the Baptist had his own doubts, his own crisis of disappointment. Although he had served God faithfully, he had ended up in Herod's prison. While languishing on death row, he smuggled out a message to Jesus: "Are you the one who was to come, or should we expect someone else?" That single question—from John!—captures the ambivalence, the hope-yet-uncertainty, that swirled around Jesus.

The Kingdom Within

If Jesus had just avoided one emotionally charged word, *kingdom,* everything might have been different. As soon as he said it, images sprang to life in the minds of his audience: bright banners, glittering armies, the gold and ivory of Solomon's day, a nation restored to grandeur. But then something would happen to dash those expectations and all the feelings of disappointment would wash in again. As it turned out, the word *kingdom* meant one thing to the crowd and quite another to Jesus.

The masses wanted more than a sprinkling of miracles here and there; they wanted a visible kingdom of power and glory. But Jesus talked instead about "the kingdom of heaven," an invisible kingdom. Yes, he solved some problems in the world around him, but mainly he used his energy to battle unseen forces. He once encountered a paralytic so desperate for healing that the man had persuaded four friends to dig up a roof and lower him through the hole to Jesus. Jesus' response: "Which is easier, to say to the paralytic, 'Your sins are forgiven,' or to say, 'Get up, take your mat and walk'?" He made plain which was easier. No physical deformity could withstand his healing touch. The real battle was against invisible, spiritual powers.

Faith, the forgiveness of sins, the power of the Evil One— these were the concerns that drove Jesus to his Father in prayer each day. Such an emphasis confused the crowds, who primarily sought solutions to their problems in the physical world: poverty, illness, political oppression. In the end, Jesus failed to measure up to their expectations of a king. (Has anything changed? I know of many ministries that emphasize physical healing and prosperity, but few that direct their focus to such persistent human problems as pride, hypocrisy, and legalism—the problems that so troubled Jesus.)

Whatever notions Jesus' followers had of a new and mighty Solomon recapturing Israel evaporated as they watched what took place in Jerusalem. A few days after a "triumphal procession"—a slapstick comedy affair compared to the lavish parades of the Romans—Jesus was arrested and put on trial. He told the Roman governor that he was in fact a king, but added, "My kingdom is not of this world. If it were, my servants would fight to prevent my arrest by the Jews. But now my kingdom is from another place."

Jesus a king? A mock king if ever there was one, with his purple robe clotted with blood from the beatings and a crown of thorns jammed onto his head. The disciples ran away, their loyalty overwhelmed by their fear of immediate danger. If Jesus would not protect himself, why should he protect them? The visible world of Roman might met the invisible world of the kingdom of heaven and seemed for a time to snuff it out.

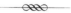

In Cat's Cradle *the contemporary novelist Kurt Vonnegut shows a physicist who helped father the atomic bomb visiting his laboratory during the Christmas season. Office employees are all standing around a crèche singing Christmas carols. "The hopes and fears of all the years are met in thee tonight," they sing. It is a scene of biting irony, a modern counterpart to Jewish disillusionment in Jesus' day.*

Do the carolers really believe that the hopes and fears of all the years—which will vanish in a moment if someone presses the wrong button—rest on faith in a Bethlehem newborn destined to live only thirty-three years?

---

[1]Colin Brown, *Miracles and the Critical Mind*, 10.

Bible references: Luke 7; John 14; Mark 3; John 5; John 1; Matthew 11; John 18.

CHAPTER 15

DIVINE SHYNESS

———————— ∞∞∞ ————————

My project is the first scientific experiment in history to settle once and for all the question of God's existence. As things presently stand, there may be signs of his existence but they point both ways and are therefore ambiguous and so prove nothing. For example, the wonders of the universe do not convince those most conversant with the wonders, the scientists themselves. Whether or not this testifies to the stupidity of scientists or to God's success at concealing himself doesn't matter.

WALKER PERCY, *THE SECOND COMING*

I f ever the time was ripe to settle the question of God's existence, it was while Jesus walked on earth. Jesus had one splendid opportunity to silence the critics forever.

If, for example, my friend Richard had lived in Jesus' day, he could have demanded proof to Jesus' face. "You say you're the Son of God? Okay, show me!" We need not speculate about what would have happened, for Jesus often faced a similar challenge. When religious experts begged him for a miraculous sign, he turned on them in anger, calling them a "wicked and adulterous generation." When a curious king asked to see a miracle, Jesus refused to cooperate though it might have saved his life.

Why the divine restraint? Perhaps a clue can be found in the first "event" in Jesus' ministry, the Temptation, a kind of final exam to prepare him for public life.

You couldn't ask for a more dramatic confrontation: Jesus versus the ultimate skeptic, Satan himself, with the cracked and wrinkled hills of Palestine serving as a backdrop. Satan wanted some proof: "If you are the Son of God . . ." He challenged Jesus to make bread from a stone, asked to see a sample of Jesus' powers of self-protection, and offered him authority over all the kingdoms of the world.

I believe that Satan's challenge was a true temptation for Jesus, not a staged, predetermined contest. A loaf of bread would tempt anyone who had fasted for forty days. A guarantee of physical safety surely held appeal for someone facing torture and execution. And the splendor of all the kingdoms of earth—had not the prophets predicted as much for the Messiah? All three of the "temptations" lay within Jesus' grasp; all three were, in fact, his prerogatives. In effect, Satan was offering him a shortcut to achieve his messianic goals.

Russian novelist Fyodor Dostoyevsky made the Temptation scene a centerpiece in his masterwork *The Brothers Karamazov.* Ivan Karamazov calls the Temptation the most stupendous miracle on earth: the miracle of restraint. If he had yielded to the Temptation, Jesus would have earned his credentials, not just with Satan but with all Israel, establishing himself beyond dispute. According to Dostoyevsky's view, Satan offered three easy means of inciting belief— miracle, mystery, and authority—and Christ refused all three. In Ivan Karamazov's words, "You would not enslave man by a miracle, and craved faith given freely, not based on miracle."[1]

As I studied Matthew's concise account of the Temptation and then Dostoyevsky's long, embellished reconstruction, a question arose, abruptly, disturbingly. How does the Temptation in the desert differ from what took place in Richard's suburban apartment? He too pleaded for a supernatural display: a light, a voice, *something* that would demonstrate God's power beyond dispute. Or, getting more personal, how does the Temptation differ from times when I beg, almost demand, that God intervene and save me from a predicament?

There are differences, of course, and my self-defense quickly fills them in. Richard was, presumably, sincere; I was needy; we were both asking God for help, not taunting him or demanding worship. And yet I cannot easily dismiss the haunting similarity between Satan's "Throw yourself down!" and Richard's "Show yourself!" In each case the challenge is the same: a demand for God to take off the wraps and prove himself. In each case, God demurred.

One more instance of divine restraint comes to mind. It occurred in Jerusalem very near the site of Satan's third challenge. Jesus looked down from a high hill and cried out, "O Jerusalem, Jerusalem, you who kill the prophets and stone those sent to you, how often I have longed to gather your children together, as a hen gathers her chicks under her wings, but you were not willing!" That wail of grief over Jerusalem has about it a quality almost like shyness. Jesus, who could destroy Jerusalem with a word, who could call down legions of angels to force subjection, instead looks over the city and weeps.

God holds back; he hides himself; he weeps. Why? Because he desires what power can never win. He is a king who wants not subservience, but love. Thus, rather than mowing down Jerusalem, Rome, and every other worldly power, he chose the slow, hard way of Incarnation, love, and death. A conquest from within.

George MacDonald summed up Christ's approach: "Instead of crushing the power of evil by divine force; instead of compelling justice and destroying the wicked; instead of making peace on the earth by the rule of a perfect prince; instead of gathering the children of Jerusalem under His wings whether they would or not, and saving them from the horrors that anguished His prophetic soul—He let evil work its will while it lived; He contented Himself with the slow unencouraging ways of help essential; making men good; casting out, not merely controlling Satan.... To love righteousness is to make it grow, not to avenge it.... Throughout His life on earth, He resisted every impulse to work more rapidly for a lower good—strong, perhaps, when He saw old age and innocence and righteousness trodden under foot."[2]

The Miracles

I have not told the whole story about Jesus, of course. Yes, his humanity represented a kind of disguise, at least in contrast to God's glory in the Old Testament. Yes, Jesus showed restraint, refusing to overwhelm people with a brash display of power. But what about the miracles he did perform, three dozen of which are recounted in the Gospels? No one who saw him provide lunch for five thousand, or order Lazarus from his tomb, or shout down a summer squall could easily speak of a quality like "divine shyness."

Yet Jesus, who presumably could work a wonder any day of his life if he wanted, seemed curiously ambivalent about miracles. With his disciples, he used them as proof of who he was ("Believe me when I say that I am in the Father and the Father is in me; or at least believe on the evidence of the miracles themselves"). But even as he performed them, he often seemed to downplay them. When he resurrected the daughter of a Jewish VIP, he gave strict orders to keep it quiet. Mark records seven separate occasions when Jesus told a person he had healed, "Tell no one!"

Jesus knew well the shallow effect of miracles in Moses' day, and in Elijah's: they attracted crowds, yes, but rarely encouraged long-term faithfulness. He was bringing a hard message of obedience and sacrifice, not a sideshow for gawkers and sensation-seekers. (Sure enough, the true skeptics of his day—much like people today—explained away his powers. If God's voice spoke from heaven, some dismissed it as thunder. Others credited his gifts to Satan. And Jesus' staunchest enemies refused to trust him even when faced with solid evidence. Once, they assembled a formal tribunal to study a reported healing. Ignoring firsthand testimony—"One thing I do know. I was blind but now I see!"—they hurled insults at the healed man and threw him out of court. Likewise, when Lazarus showed up alive after four days in a tomb, those enemies conspired to kill him off again.)

With remarkable consistency, the Bible's accounts show that miracles—dramatic, showstopping miracles like many of us still long for—simply do not foster deep faith. For proof, we need look no further than the Transfiguration, when Jesus' face shone like the sun and his clothes became dazzling, "whiter than anyone in the world could bleach them." To the disciples' astonishment, two long-dead giants of Jewish history—Moses and Elijah—appeared in a cloud with them. God spoke audibly. It was too much to take; the disciples fell down, terrified.

Yet what effect did this stupendous event have on Jesus' three closest friends, Peter, James, and John? Did it permanently silence their questions and fill them with faith? A few weeks later, when Jesus needed them the most, they all forsook him.

I have read books on signs and wonders that presume to silence doubters, as if Jesus' miracles prove he is the answer to the world's problems. But I must confess that most of these arguments strike me as irrelevant to people disappointed in God. They are more interested in the miracles Jesus did *not* perform. Why does a God who possesses the power to right what is wrong sometimes choose not to? Or, why did Jesus bother with miracles at all? Why heal one paralyzed man at Bethesda—but only one?

A hint may be found in a fanciful depiction of Jesus' life that never made it into the Bible, for good reason. The spurious *Gospel of the Infancy of Jesus Christ* purports to reveal unknown stories about Jesus' childhood. It shows Jesus as a person might *want* him to be. According to this ancient book, he would perform "tricks" on demand to impress his friends—something the real Jesus always refused to do. The apocryphal Jesus had the allure of a pet genie or a neighborhood magician. Whenever his father Joseph messed up an important carpentry assignment, Jesus would step in and magically repair the flaw.

This mythical Jesus was not afraid to use his power for revenge, either. When a neighbor woman hurt one of Jesus' playmates, she mysteriously fell into a well and died of a crushed skull. When Jesus approached a town, its idols disintegrated into mounds of sand.

These hotheaded actions are uncharacteristic of Jesus as depicted in the Gospels, who used his powers compassionately to meet human needs, not for showy tricks. Every time someone asked directly, he healed. When his audience got hungry he fed them, and when wedding guests grew thirsty he made wine. The real Jesus rebuked his disciples for suggesting that he avenge a resistant city. And when soldiers came to arrest him, he used his supernatural power only once—to restore the slashed ear of one of the arresters. In short, the miracles in the authentic Gospels are about love, not power.

Although Jesus' miracles were far too selective to solve every human disappointment, they served as *signs* of his mission, previews of what God would someday do for all creation. In Helmut Thielicke's words, the miracles were "signal fires which announce the coming kingdom of God." For people who experienced them—the paralytic lowered like a chandelier for cleaning—the healings offered convincing proof that God himself was visiting earth. For everyone else, they awakened longings that will not be fulfilled until a final restoration ends all pain and death.

The miracles did just what Jesus had predicted. To those who chose to believe him, they gave even more reason to believe. But for those determined to deny him, the miracles made little difference. Some things just have to be believed to be seen.

---

[1]Fyodor Dostoyevsky, *The Brothers Karamazov*, 235.
[2]George MacDonald, *Life Essential: The Hope of the Gospel*, 24.

Bible references: Matthew 12, 16; Luke 4; Matthew 23 and Luke 13; John 14, 9; Mark 9.

CHAPTER 16

THE POSTPONED MIRACLE

—⸺∞∞∞⸺—

When Charlemagne, king of the Franks, first heard the story of Jesus' arrest and execution, he exploded in rage. Grabbing his sword and rattling it in the scabbard, he shouted, "Oh, if only I had been there; I would have slain them all with my legions!" We smile at the simple warrior loyalty of Charlemagne, or of Simon Peter, who actually drew a sword in Jesus' defense. Yet behind their outrage lies a dark, dark question. Charlemagne, after all, was not present in Gethsemane and could not have helped. But God the Father, who *could* have helped, did not lift a finger on behalf of his condemned Son.

Why didn't God act? Anyone who thinks about disappointment with God must pause at Gethsemane, and at Pilate's palace, and at Calvary—the scenes of Jesus' arrest, trial, and execution. For in those three places Jesus himself experienced a state very much like disappointment with God.

The ordeal began as Jesus prayed in a quiet, cool grove of olive trees, with three of his disciples waiting sleepily outside. Inside the garden all seemed peaceful; but outside, the forces of hell itself were loose. A disciple had turned traitor, Satan was on the prowl, and a large mob with swords and clubs was heading toward Gethsemane.

"My soul is overwhelmed with sorrow to the point of death," Jesus said to his three disciples. Although he claimed the authority to dispatch an army of angels in his own defense, Jesus did not. He had come to live in a world of skin and blood and tissue, and he would die by its rules as well. At one point he fell facedown on the ground and prayed for some way, *any* way, out. His sweat fell to the ground in large drops, like blood.

And God stayed silent.

At Pilate's palace, the restraint continued. In the most literal way, God—in Jesus—had his hands tied. "Prophesy!" some cried, taunting him with a challenge toward miracle. "Who hit you?" The Son of God did not resist as their fists fell on his blindfolded face and their spit ran down his beard.

The next scene, at Calvary, has been imagined for us so many times in passion plays and sermons and paintings that, benumbed, we can hardly imagine it for ourselves. Start by remembering your time of most acute disappointment. You staked everything on what seemed within God's power—a recovery from cancer, perhaps, or the birth of a healthy baby, or God's help in stitching a marriage together. But everything turned out wrong. The cancer killed, despite your prayers; the baby was born with brain damage; you got divorce papers in the mail. Think of Calvary as that time. Or as a time like the night Richard spent in his apartment, kneeling on the floor, pleading with God. Think of it as a time of No Miracle.

Everybody craved a miracle then: Pilate and Herod, who had heard the sensational rumors; the women who had trailed Jesus all the way from Galilee; the disciples who cowered in the shadows. One dying thief begged for a miracle; the other mocked, and spectators took up the cry, "Let him come down from the cross, and we will believe in him.... Let God rescue him now if he wants him."

But there was no rescue, no miracle. There was only silence. Charles Williams looks back on the scene and says, "The taunt flung at Christ, at the moment of his most spectacular impotency, was: 'He saved others; himself he cannot save.' It was a definition as precise as any in the works of the medieval schoolmen."[1]

"My God, my God, why have you forsaken me?" Jesus cried out at last. It was a quotation from the Psalms, the ultimate wail of disappointment. The Father had turned his back, or so it surely seemed, letting history take its course, letting all that was wrong with the world triumph over all that was right. Nature itself convulsed: the ground shook as in an earthquake, tombs cracked open. The solar system shuddered in the chill: the sun hid, and the sky went black.

Sunday Morning

Two days later came the Resurrection, with a sound like an earthquake and a flash like lightning. Shouldn't that have vindicated God and solved the problem of disappointment once and for all?

What a missed opportunity! If only the risen Jesus had reappeared on Pilate's porch to deliver a withering blast against his enemies—that would have showed them! But his dozen or so appearances after resurrection show a clear pattern: Christ presented himself only to people who already believed in him. So far as we know, not a single unbeliever saw Jesus after his death.

Consider two men who could have seen the risen Christ, if they had tarried long enough. These coarse Roman guards were standing outside the tomb when the Miracle of Miracles occurred. They trembled and became like dead men. Then, showing an incurably human reflex, they ran to the authorities; and later that afternoon these two, the only witnesses to the actual event of resurrection, agreed to a cover-up. Stacks of freshly minted silver seemed far more significant than the resurrection of the Son of God. And so the two eyewitnesses of that great day, the forgotten men of Easter, died apparent unbelievers.

Today, the major events of Jesus' life are marked on calendars around the world—Christmas, Good Friday, and Easter. Of the three, however, only the middle one, the Crucifixion, took place in the open for all the world to see. At the moment when God seemed downright helpless, the cameras of history were rolling, recording it all. Large crowds watched every excruciating detail. And when four men wrote up accounts of Jesus' life, they collectively devoted one-third of their Gospels to that time of apparent failure.

The spectacle of the Cross, the most public event of Jesus' life, reveals the vast difference between a god who proves himself through power and One who proves himself through love. Other gods, Roman gods, for example, enforced worship: in Jesus' own lifetime, some Jews were slaughtered for not bowing down to Caesar. But Jesus Christ never forced anyone to believe in him. He preferred to act by appeal, drawing people out of themselves and toward him.

Paradoxically, that scene of weakness inspired new hope. "If God is for us, who can be against us?" concluded the apostle Paul, resting his faith in the boundless love of a God "who did not spare his own Son, but gave him up for us all." Love is most persuasive when it involves sacrifice, and the Gospels make clear that Jesus came to die. In his own words, "Greater love has no one than this, that one lay down his life for his friends." Somehow, the possibility of eternal happiness required this time of silence and profound disappointment.

[1]Charles Williams, *He Came Down from Heaven*, 115.

Bible references: Matthew 26–27; Romans 8; John 15.

CHAPTER 17

PROGRESS

———— ⟨∞∞⟩ ————

"Madame," I said, "if our God were a pagan god or the god of intellectuals—and for me it comes to much the same—He might fly to His remotest heaven and our grief would force Him down to earth again. But you know that our God came to be among us. Shake your fist at Him, spit in His face, scourge Him, and finally crucify Him: what does it matter? My daughter, it's already been done to Him."

GEORGE BERNANOS, *DIARY OF A COUNTRY PRIEST*

Let me be blunt: What difference does Jesus make to our feelings of disappointment with God? How does it help us to learn that he too tasted disappointment?

Theologians, following the apostle Paul, usually explain Christ's contribution in legal terms: justification, reconciliation, propitiation. But these words merely hint at what took place. To understand the difference Jesus makes to the problem of disappointment, we must look past such words to the underlying story of God's passionate pursuit of human beings.

Think back to one of the main images in the Prophets: an anxious father grieving over his runaway child. Jesus' story of the Prodigal Son provides a happy ending at last. The Waiting Father has waited long enough; he flings open the front door and *races* to welcome home the runaway, no questions asked.

The Torn Curtain

What difference did Jesus make? Both for God and for us, he made possible an *intimacy* that had never before existed. In the Old Testament, Israelites who touched the sacred Ark of the Covenant fell down dead; but people who touched Jesus, the Son of God in flesh, came away healed. To Jews who would not pronounce or even spell out the letters in God's name, Jesus taught a new way of addressing God: *Abba,* or "Daddy." In Jesus, God came close.

Augustine's *Confessions* describes how this closeness affected him. From Greek philosophy he had learned about a perfect, timeless, incorruptible God, but he could not fathom how an oversexed, undisciplined person like himself could relate to such a God. He tried various heresies of the day and found them all unsatisfying, until he met at last the Jesus of the Gospels, a bridge between ordinary human beings and a perfect God.

The Book of Hebrews explores this startling new advance in intimacy. First the author elaborates on what was required just to approach God in Old Testament times. Only once a year, on the Day of Atonement—Yom Kippur—could one person, the high priest, enter the Most Holy Place. The ceremony involved ritual baths, special clothing, and five separate animal sacrifices; and still the priest entered the Most Holy Place in fear. He wore bells on his robe and a rope around his ankle so that if he died and the bells stopped ringing, other priests could pull out his body.

Hebrews draws the vivid contrast: we can now "approach the throne of grace with confidence," without fear. Charging boldly into the Most Holy Place—no image could hold more shock value for Jewish readers. Yet at the moment of Jesus' death, a thick curtain inside the temple literally ripped in two from top to bottom, breaking open the Most Holy Place. Therefore, concludes Hebrews, "Let us draw near to God."

Jesus contributes at least this to the problem of disappointment with God: because of him, we can come to God directly. We need no human mediator, for God himself became one.

A Face

No one in the Old Testament could claim to know the face of God. No one, in fact, could survive a direct gaze. The few who caught a glimpse of God's glory came away glowing like extraterrestrials, and all who saw them hid in fear. But Jesus offered a long, slow look at the face of God. "Anyone who has seen me has seen the Father," he said. Whatever Jesus is, God is. As Michael Ramsey put it, "In God is no unChristlikeness at all."

People grow up with all sorts of notions of what God is like. They may see God as an Enemy, or a Policeman, or even an Abusive Parent. Or perhaps they do not see God at all, and only hear his silence. Because of Jesus, however, we no longer have to wonder how God feels or what he is like. When in doubt, we can look at Jesus to correct our blurry vision.

If I wonder how God views deformed or disabled people, I can watch Jesus among the crippled, the blind, and those with leprosy. If I wonder about the poor, and whether God has destined them to lives of misery, I can read Jesus' words in the Sermon on the Mount. And if I ever wonder about the appropriate "spiritual" response to pain and suffering, I can note how Jesus responded to his own: with fear and trembling, with loud cries and tears.

Not Yet

I could not help noticing an abrupt mood shift in the Bible around the Book of Acts. If you scour the rest of the New Testament, you will find none of the outrage of Job nor the despair of Ecclesiastes nor the anguish of Lamentations. Clearly, the writers of the New Testament were convinced that Jesus had changed the universe forever. The apostle Paul, for example, spraying sentence fragments across the page, spared no superlative: "In Christ all things hold together ... through him he reconciled all things to himself, whether things on earth or things in heaven.... Christ is seated far above all rule and authority, power and dominion, and every title that can be given, not only in the present age but also in the one to come."

Yet as he was writing those very words, the Roman Empire was grinding on with its grim succession of wars and tyrants; people everywhere were still lying and stealing and killing each other; diseases continued to spread; and Christians themselves were being lashed with whips and thrown in jail. Such common reasons for doubt and disappointment did not seem to shake the apostles' confidence that Jesus would come again as he had promised, in power and great glory. It was simply a matter of time. They had doubted him once, but after the Resurrection they would not doubt him again.

The sure, settled tone of the New Testament writers creates a problem, though: the problem of why, some twenty centuries after the apostle Paul, I am devoting an entire book to the topic of disappointment with God. And the people who told me their wrenching stories—why do they lack the bold assurance of the New Testament writers? Why hasn't all our disappointment melted away?

As I think about these things, I keep coming back to the single question of unfairness. *Is God unfair?* In a remarkable way, Jesus gave a direct response to the problems of God's hiddenness and silence. But the problem of unfairness only seemed to worsen. Jesus' own life ended in the greatest unfairness of history: the best man who ever lived suffering the worst of punishments. One more victim of a cruel planet. Conditions hardly improved after his death, when Jesus' disciples received the "rewards" of prison, torture, and martyrdom. The problem of unfairness did not disappear.

Amazingly, the author of Hebrews seemed to anticipate that very situation, almost as a backhanded acknowledgment that people would continue to feel disappointed in God. Chapter 2 begins with a lofty quotation from the Psalms about God putting everything under Jesus' feet. Then follows this single, pregnant sentence: "Yet at present we do not see everything subject to him."

As an author, I know what it's like to write what I believe to be true and then wonder, as soon as I've written it, *Do I really mean that?* The author of Hebrews, after recording the gust of grand theology from the Psalms, likewise seems to pause and reconsider. Yes, it's true that Jesus is in control—but it sure doesn't look like it: "at present we do not see everything subject to him." That one sentence encompasses all unfairness: all war and violence, all hatred and lust, all triumph of evil over good, all illness and death, all tears and groans, all the disappointment and despair of this chaotic world. It may be the "truest" sentence in the Bible.

The paragraph continues, "But we see Jesus ... who suffered death, so that by the grace of God he might taste death for everyone." Pointedly, Hebrews does not summon up a triumphant image of Jesus on the Mount of Transfiguration or in his resurrected body; it shows Jesus on the cross. Then the author goes on to use some of the most mysterious language of the New Testament. He tells of Christ "being made perfect" and "learning obedience" through the things that he suffered. Commentators often skirt these phrases, for they are not easy to reconcile with traditional notions of an unchanging, passionless God. But I must not skirt them, for they are presented in Hebrews as Jesus' direct contribution to the continuing problem of disappointment with God.

From Hebrews, it seems clear that the Incarnation had meaning for God as well as for us. It was the ultimate way for him to identify with us. He, a spirit, had never before been confined in the world of matter, had never experienced the soft vulnerability of human flesh, had never sensed the clamorous warnings from pain cells. Jesus changed all that. He went through the entire human experience, from the blood and pain of birth to the blood and pain of death.

From the Old Testament we can gain much insight into what it "feels like" to be God. But the New Testament records what happened when God learned what it feels like to be a human being. Whatever we feel, God felt. Instinctively, we want a God who not only knows about pain but shares in it; we want a God who is affected by our own pain. As the young theologian Dietrich Bonhoeffer scribbled on a note in a Nazi prison camp, "Only the Suffering God can help." Because of Jesus, we have such a God. Hebrews reports that God can now sympathize with our weaknesses. The very word expresses how it was done: "sympathy" comes from two Greek words, *sym pathos,* meaning "suffer with."

Would it be too much to say that, because of Jesus, God understands our feelings of disappointment with him? How else can we interpret Jesus' tears, or his cry from the cross? One could almost pour the three questions of this book into that dreadful cry, "My God, my God, why have you forsaken me?" God's Son "learned obedience" from his suffering, says Hebrews. A person can only learn obedience when tempted to disobey, can only learn courage when tempted to flee.

Why didn't Jesus brandish a sword in Gethsemane, or call on his legions of angels? Why did he decline Satan's challenge to dazzle the world? For this reason: if he had done so, he would have failed in his most important mission—to become one of us, to live and die as one of us. It was the only way God could work "within the rules" he had set up at Creation.

All through the Bible, especially in the Prophets, we see a conflict raging within God. On the one hand he passionately loved the people he had made; on the other hand, he had a terrible urge to destroy the Evil that enslaved them. On the cross, God resolved that inner conflict, for there his Son absorbed the destructive force and transformed it into love.

The only ultimate way to conquer evil is to let it be smothered within a willing, living, human being. When it is absorbed there, like blood in a sponge or a spear thrown into one's heart, it loses its power and goes no further.

GALE D. WEBBE, *THE NIGHT AND NOTHING*

Bible references: Hebrews 4, 10; John 14; Colossians 1; Ephesians 1; Hebrews 2–5.

PART FOUR

TURNING IT OVER: THE SPIRIT

CHAPTER 18

THE TRANSFER

———⌘———

Your stomach is churning with that first-day-on-the-job tension. *Will I make it? What if I do the wrong thing? Will the boss like me?* You glance around at the others who are squinting against the bright sun, shifting from one leg to the other, nervously carving designs in the sand with the edges of their sandals. Seventy of you received the summons to appear for a special assignment.

Jesus is giving a full-fledged speech. He looks worried, and his words convey alarm: "I am sending you out like lambs among wolves. Do not take a purse or bag or sandals; and do not greet anyone on the road." By the time he gets to the closing line, his voice has risen in timbre, commanding attention: "He who listens to you listens to me; he who rejects you rejects me; but he who rejects me rejects him who sent me." What is that supposed to mean? The group begins to disperse, and, swallowing your uncertainties, you head out with your designated partner on the assigned mission.

The next time you see Jesus, a few days later, it looks as if he has changed faces. All severity and alarm have drained away. He's grinning at your stories, urging you to elaborate. He can't seem to get enough details about the healings and the exorcisms and the trans-formed lives. It really did work, this perilous mission into the hill country, and Jesus is jubilant. It's a victory party. Listen to him long enough and you'll believe you can do anything: trample on snakes, scorpions, whatever.

Right in the middle of your report he holds up his hand to inter-rupt. He can't wait. You've never seen him so excited. "I saw Satan fall like lightning from heaven!" he announces, and though you have no clue to what he means, you are swept up in the sudden rush of enthusiasm. Some enormous breakthrough must have just occurred. Then he bends closer and says in a hushed voice, "Many prophets and kings wanted to see what you see but did not see it, and to hear what you hear but did not hear it."

Final Exam

Another scene, about six months later. This time you are din-ing with the rest of the Twelve in a small room in Jerusalem. A stuffy, cloistered feeling pervades the place, and you are a bit light-headed after the meal and the wine. Everything's happening too fast. Earlier this week Jesus, permitting a rare display of public acclaim, rode into the city in a triumphant procession. It seemed all your dreams would come true after all. But tonight's mood is foreboding.

First came the incident of the foot-washing, when Jesus embar-rassed Peter. And even now as he talks, Jesus' mood wavers. One minute he seems nostalgic and comforting, and the next minute he suddenly rebukes you for dullness and lack of faith. He keeps allud-ing to a betrayal. Some of it you do not grasp. But one thing he insists on, over all protests: he is leaving. Someone else will come to take his place; someone he calls the Counselor.

There is a sudden stirring in the room, like wind over grass. For months you have waited for Jesus to take command of his kingdom.

But now he says he is turning the whole thing over—to you, the Twelve! He looks around the table and says with finality, "I confer on you a kingdom, just as my Father conferred one on me."

Departure

Okay, you failed—all of you, even Peter, who had bragged about his loyalty just a few hours before the great denial. "I have overcome the world!" Jesus had said in the small room that night. But you simply could not reconcile his words with what happened next. Less than twenty-four hours later you saw him hanging naked on a cross, his frail body glimmering in the torchlight. This one, the Savior of your nation, the King of Kings? It was too much to ask anyone to believe.

That was Friday.

On Sunday, wild, crazy rumors shot through the close-knit community of mourners. And then later in the week you saw him. It was true! You touched him with your own hands. Jesus! He had done what no one had done before: he had walked voluntarily into death, and walked back out. You would never, never doubt him again.

For forty days Jesus appeared and disappeared seemingly at will. When he showed up, you listened eagerly to his explanations of what had happened. When he left, you and the others plotted the new kingdom. Think of it: Jerusalem free at last from Roman rule!

Friends had long mocked your stubborn obsession with this peasant preacher. Now you'd show them. No one would push you around anymore; no one would push Israel around. Peter, James, and John would naturally have the inside track on the top positions, but a kingdom would need many leaders—and, after all, you had followed Jesus for three years. The Messiah, the true Messiah, had counted you among his most intimate disciples.

During those forty days, none of the glow wore off. How could it? Every reappearance of Jesus was a new miracle. At last someone broke the question to him, the burning question you had all been debating. "Lord, are you at this time going to restore the kingdom to Israel?" You waited breathless for some sign—a call to arms perhaps, a battle plan. The Romans wouldn't walk away without a fight.

No one was prepared for Jesus' reaction. At first it seemed he hadn't heard the question well. He brushed it aside and began talking not about Israel, but about neighboring countries and other faraway places. He said you were to go there eventually as his witnesses. But for now, you should simply return to Jerusalem and wait for the Holy Spirit.

Then the most amazing thing happened. You were standing there, listening to him, when suddenly his body began to lift off the ground. He hung in midair for a moment; then a cloud hid him from sight. And you never saw Jesus again.

Three Scenes

These scenes—the Sending of the Seventy, the Last Supper, and the Ascension—all reveal something about why Jesus came to earth, and why he left. True, he came to settle divine justice and to show us what God is like. But he also came to establish a Church, a new dwelling place for the Spirit of God.

And that is why, when the seventy reported back to him, Jesus nearly erupted with joy. "He who listens to you listens to me," he had told them, and indeed the plan was working. His own mission—more, his own life—was being lived out through seventy commonplace human beings.

At the last supper with the disciples, Jesus conveyed a greater sense of urgency. They were his closest friends in all the world, and it was time to turn the entire mission over to them—these well-meaning friends so quick with their protestations of loyalty now, so quick with their denials later. "As the Father has sent me, I am sending you," he said, knowing they did not comprehend. This little band would take his message to Jerusalem, and to all Judea and Samaria, and then to places he himself had never visited—all the way to the ends of the earth.

At the Ascension, Jesus' body left the earth before his astonished disciples' eyes. But soon, very soon, at Pentecost, the Spirit of God would take up residence in other bodies. Their bodies.

Bible references: Luke 10; John 13–17; Acts 1.

CHAPTER 19

CHANGES IN THE WIND

———∞∞∞———

A documentary film series about religion for PBS. Great. One more yawner of an assignment. "Explore images of the deity through the ages," or some such abstraction, they say. Just fine. Who comes up with these schemes? For starters, the central character is invisible.

Well, until someone finds a way to arrange an interview with God himself, they'll have to settle for vignettes *about* God.

14th Century B.C. *Begin with helicopter shot of the Sinai peaks. Uninhabited area, so no TV antennae to dismantle, etc. Zoom to a clump of Bedouin extras impersonating ancient Hebrews. Voice-over on how they eat, what they wear. In tight on a Jewish boy about twelve years old. Interrupt him from play and call him over.*

"Tell me about your God. What's he like?" narrator asks.

Boy's eyes widen. "You mean ... you mean ..." Can't bring himself to say the word.

"That's right, Yahweh, the God you worship."

"What's he like? Him? See that mountain over there? [*Cut to volcano. Lots of steam, smoke. Close-up of magma.*] That's where he lives. Don't go near it or you'll die! He's ... he's ... well, most of all he's scary. *Real* scary."

A.D. 1st Century. Pan across a broad, flat horizon of Palestine. Same Bedouins, now milling around the desert in a group. Oasis in the background. Tighten in on a clump of bystanders, then on a woman along the edge, sitting down, leaning against a desert shrub. Prompt her.

"God? I'm still trying to figure him out. I thought I knew, but when I started following this teacher around, I got confused. He claims he's the Messiah. My friends laugh. But I was in the crowd the day he fed five thousand people—who else could do that? I ate a piece of the fish. And with my own eyes I saw him heal a blind man.

"Somehow God is like that man named Jesus, over there."

A.D. 20th Century. Move film crew to picturesque church in small town, U.S.A. Pan across the faces of people in the pews. Voice-over from narrator, "And what is God like now?"

The New Testament asks us to believe that the answer lies in that ordinary church, among those ordinary people in the pews. God in Christ is one thing, but in *us*? The only way to sense the shock of it is to read the Bible straight through, from Genesis to Revelation, as I did during those snowy days in Colorado.

The mighty, awesome Lord of the Universe, full of passion and fire and holiness, dominates the first nine hundred pages. Four Gospels follow, about one hundred pages long, recounting Jesus' life on earth. But after Acts, the Bible shifts to a series of personal letters. Grecians, Romans, Jews, slaves, slave owners, women, men, children—the letters address all these diverse groups, and yet each letter assumes its readers belong to an overarching new identity. They are all "in Christ."

"The Church is nothing but a section of humanity in which Christ has really taken form," said Dietrich Bonhoeffer. The apostle

Paul expressed much the same thought with his phrase "the body of Christ." The way he saw it, a new species of humanity was emerging on earth, in whom God himself—the Holy Spirit—was living. They extended the arms and legs and eyes of God on earth. What's more, Paul acted as if that had been God's goal all along.

"Don't you know that you yourself are God's temple and that God's Spirit lives in you?" Paul wrote to the unruly bunch at Corinth. To the Jews, of course, the temple was an actual building, the central place on earth where the Presence of God dwelt. Was Paul claiming, to put it plainly, that God had "moved?"

Three temples appear in the Bible, and, taken together, they illustrate a progression: God revealed himself first as Father, then as Son, and finally as Holy Spirit.* The first temple was a magnificent structure built by Solomon and rebuilt by Herod. The second was the "temple" of Jesus' body ("Destroy it," he said, "and I will raise it again in three days"). And now a third temple has taken shape, fashioned out of individual human beings.

Delegation

He seems to do nothing of Himself which He can possibly delegate to His creatures. He commands us to do slowly and blunderingly what He could do perfectly and in the twinkling of an eye.

Creation seems to be delegation through and through. I suppose this is because He is a giver.[1]

The progression—Father, Son, Spirit—represents a profound advance in intimacy. At Sinai the people shrank from God, and begged Moses to approach him on their behalf. But in Jesus' day

---

*I realize the Trinity is by no means a simple doctrine, and activities of the Son and the Spirit can be traced throughout the Old Testament. But we would probably not speak of a Trinity at all apart from the Incarnation and Pentecost. Each event revealed something about God that had not been known before, and each caused an upheaval in the way people thought about God.

people could hold a conversation with the Son of God; they could touch him, and even hurt him. And after Pentecost the same flawed disciples who had fled from Jesus' trial became carriers of the Living God. In an act of delegation beyond fathom, Jesus turned over the kingdom of God to the likes of his disciples—and to us.

But enough. All these misty ideas about the Spirit must somehow accord with the glaring reality of the actual church. Look at the people in the pews of any church. Is this what God had in mind?

Delegation always entails risk, as any employer soon learns. When you turn over a job, you let go. And when God "makes his appeal through us" (Paul's phrase), he takes an awful risk: the risk that we will badly misrepresent him. Slavery, the Crusades, pogroms against the Jews, colonialism, wars, the Ku Klux Klan—all these movements have claimed the sanction of Christ for their cause. The world God wants to love, the world God is appealing to, may never see him; our own faces may get in the way.

Yet God took that risk, and because he did so the world will know him primarily through Christians. The doctrine of the Holy Spirit is the doctrine of "the church": God living in us. Such a plan is the "foolishness of God," as Paul says in one place, and writer Frederick Buechner marvels at the folly: "to choose for his holy work in the world . . . lamebrains and misfits and nitpickers and holier-than-thous and stuffed shirts and odd ducks and egomaniacs and milquetoasts and closet sensualists."[2]

"And yet," Paul continues, "the foolishness of God is wiser than men."

We who live among the flawed, ordinary people of the church, we who *are* the lamebrains and misfits and odd ducks of the church, may want to water down the Bible's extravagant statements about the body of Christ, for we know how poorly we embody him. But the Bible is unequivocal. Consider just two examples.

1. We represent God's holiness on earth. Holiness, above all else, constitutes the great distance between God and human beings. It's what made the Most Holy Place forbidden ground. But the New Testament insists that a seismic change has taken place. A perfect God now lives inside very imperfect human beings. And because he respects our freedom, the Spirit in effect "subjects himself" to our behavior. The New Testament tells of a Spirit we can lie to, or grieve, or quench. And when we choose wrongly, we quite literally subject God to that wrong choice.

No passage illustrates this strange truth more forcefully than 1 Corinthians 6, a passage in which Paul scolds the randy members of the church at Corinth for hiring prostitutes. One by one, he smashes all their rationalizations. Then, finally, he settles on the most sobering warning of all: "Do you not know that your bodies are members of Christ himself?" Paul seems to mean this in the most literal sense, and he does not shrink from the next, astounding conclusion: "Shall I then take the members of Christ and unite them with a prostitute? Never!"

You don't have to be a biblical scholar to see the contrast. In the Old Testament, adulterers were stoned to death for disobeying God's law. But in the age of the Spirit, God delegates his reputation, even his essence, to us. We incarnate God in the world; what happens to us happens to him.

2. Human beings do the work of God on earth. Or, to be strictly accurate, God does his work through us—the tension comes into play as soon as you try to phrase it. "Without God, we cannot. Without us, God will not," said Augustine. In a similar vein, Paul wrote, "Continue to work out your salvation with fear and trembling," in one clause, and "for it is God who works in you" in the next. Whatever else they mean, such conundrums surely contradict a "Leave it up to God" attitude.

439

God miraculously provided food for the Israelites wandering through the Sinai desert, and even made sure their shoes would not wear out. Jesus, too, fed hungry people and ministered directly to their needs. Many Christians who read those thrilling stories look back with a sense of nostalgia, or even disappointment. "Why doesn't God act like that now?" they wonder. "Why doesn't he miraculously provide for my needs?"

But the New Testament letters seem to show a different pattern at work. Locked in a cold dungeon, Paul turned to his long-time friend Timothy to meet his physical needs. "Bring my cloak and my scrolls," he wrote, "and also bring Mark, who has always been so helpful." In other straits, Paul received "God's comfort" in the form of a visit from Titus. And when a famine broke out in Jerusalem, Paul himself led a fund-raising effort among all the churches he had founded. God was meeting the needs of the young church as surely as he had met the needs of the Israelites, but he was doing so indirectly, through fellow members of his body. Paul made no such distinction as "the church did this, but God did that." Such a division would miss the point he had made so often. The church is Christ's body; therefore if the church did it, God did it.

Paul's insistence on this truth may trace back to his first, dramatic personal encounter with God. At the time, he was a fierce persecutor of Christians, a notorious bounty hunter. But on the road to Damascus he saw a light bright enough to blind him for three days, and heard a voice from heaven: "Saul, Saul, why do you persecute me?"

Persecute you? Persecute who? I'm only after those heretics the Christians.

"Who are you, Lord?" asked Saul at last, knocked flat on the ground.

"I am Jesus, whom you are persecuting," came the reply.

That sentence summarizes as well as anything the change brought about by the Holy Spirit. Jesus had been executed months before. It was the Christians Saul was after, not Jesus. But Jesus, alive again, informed Saul that those people were in fact his own body. What hurt them, hurt him. It was a lesson the apostle Paul would never forget.

—⌘—

I must not leave this thought without applying its meaning in a most personal way. The doctrine of the Holy Spirit has great significance for the underlying questions of this book. My friend Richard had asked, "Where is God? Show me. I want to see him." Surely at least part of the answer to his question is this: *If you want to see God, then look at the people who belong to him—they are his "bodies." They are the body of Christ.*

"His disciples will have to look more saved if I am to believe in their Savior," said Nietzsche to such a challenge. But maybe if Richard could find a saint, someone like Mother Teresa, to embody the qualities of love and grace, maybe then he would believe. *There— see her? That is what God is like. She is doing the work of God.*

Richard does not know Mother Teresa, but he does know me. And that is the most humbling aspect of the doctrine of the Holy Spirit. Richard probably will never hear a voice from a whirlwind that drowns out all questions. He will likely never get a personal glimpse of God in this life. He will only see me.

---

[1]C. S. Lewis, *The World's Last Night,* 9.
[2]Frederick Buechner, *A Room Called Remember,* 142.

Bible references: 1 Corinthians 3; John 2; 2 Corinthians 5; Philippians 2; 2 Timothy 4; 2 Corinthians 7; Romans 15; Acts 9.

CHAPTER 20

THE CULMINATION

If we could, for a moment, set aside preconceptions about the Bible and simply read that huge book as an unfolding story, the plot line might emerge as something like this:

> In the beginning God, a Spirit, created the vast world of matter. Of all God's remarkable works, only human beings possessed a likeness to him that could be called "the image of God." It was at once a great gift and a great burden, this image of God. Man and woman, spirit-ual beings, could commune directly with God. But of all species they alone had the free-dom to rebel against him.
>
> Rebel they did, and something died inside Adam and Eve that fateful day. Their bodies lived on for many years, but their spirits lost the free and open communion with God.
>
> The Bible tells of God's efforts to restore that fallen spirit. He worked with individual families: first Adam's fam-ily, later Noah's, and finally Abraham's family, the central focus of most of the Old Testament. Sometimes the Bible portrays God as a parent raising a child, sometimes as a lover

in passionate pursuit, but always it shows him seeking to "break through" to human beings in order to restore what had been lost.

With a few glowing exceptions, the Old Testament recounts failures. But the New Testament opens with a radical move by God: an "invasion," the birth of Jesus. Jesus represented a whole new beginning. "The second Adam" he was called, the leader of a new species. He at last tore down the barriers and made possible a truce between God and humanity.

After Jesus had left, at Pentecost the Spirit of God descended and filled individual human beings. Thus their fallen spirit was finally restored. More than walking in a garden with human beings, God was now living inside them.

You don't have to read far in the New Testament letters to catch the excitement. The apostle Paul could not have expressed it more strongly: "The creation waits in eager expectation for the sons of God to be revealed." He pictured the entire universe pausing to watch the events on earth: "[God's] intent was that now, *through the church,* the manifold wisdom of God should be made known to the rulers and authorities in the heavenly realms." Peter added breathlessly that "even angels long to look into these things."

Meanwhile, the little band of Christians spread out toward Samaria, Greece, Ethiopia, Rome, and Spain. According to the New Testament, they were engaged in the great reversal of history, helping to reclaim all of creation for God.

Why Better?

I determined from the outset of this book to be honest; I am writing, after all, for victims of overwrought promises and dashed expectations. So I must state frankly that it is difficult for disappointed people to share the enthusiasm of the New Testament writers. My friend Richard, for example, claims he lost his faith because God acts all too subtly. He longs for something more convincing, something along the lines of a burning bush, perhaps, or the parting of the Red Sea. The "manifold wisdom of God" being made known through the church? Have you been to a church lately? Jesus would have been impressive; the shekinah glory cloud would have stopped you flat; but the church?

How can we reconcile the exalted words of the New Testament with the everyday reality around us? Some people have a quick reply: "Oh, but Paul was talking about the New Testament church; we've strayed far from that ideal." I cannot agree. The Epistles were written to a motley crew of converted angel worshipers, thieves, idolaters, backbiters, and prostitutes—those were the people in whom God took up residence. Read Paul's descriptions of the supposed "ideal church" in a city like Corinth: a raucous, ornery bunch that rivals any church in history for their *un*holiness. And yet Paul's most stirring depiction of the church as Christ's body appears in a letter to them.

There is no way to pose the question elegantly, so I will simply ask it: What, exactly, does God's plan for the ages accomplish? If one could submit that plan to something like a "cost-benefit analysis" used by corporations, what would be the "gains" and "costs" of such a plan—for God and for us?

The church's obvious defects would seem to be the greatest cost to God. Just as he committed his name to the nation Israel and had it dragged through mud, he now commits his Spirit to flawed human beings. You don't have to look far—the church in Corinth, racism in South Africa, bloodshed in Northern Ireland, scandals among U.S. Christians—for proof that the church does not measure up to God's ideal. And the watching world judges God by those who carry his name. A large measure of disappointment with God stems from disillusionment with other Christians.

Dorothy Sayers has said that God underwent three great humiliations in his efforts to rescue the human race. The first was the Incarnation, when he took on the confines of a physical body. The second was the Cross, when he suffered the ignominy of public execution. The third humiliation, Sayers suggested, is the church. In an awesome act of self-denial, God entrusted his reputation to ordinary people.

Yet in some way invisible to us, those ordinary people filled with the Spirit are helping to restore the universe to its place under the reign of God. At our repentance, angels rejoice. By our prayers, mountains are moved. The gain to God can be seen in a passage already mentioned: Luke 10. "I saw Satan fall like lightning from heaven," Jesus exclaimed exuberantly when the seventy returned with success stories. He responded like a proud father who had just seen his children perform far above what he had ever thought possible.

We must not press the point so far as to think God "needs" our cooperation. Rather, he has chosen us as the preferred way to reclaim his creation here on earth. He uses human instruments just as my brain uses the instruments of fingers and hand and wrist to write this sentence. That is the metaphor Paul used most frequently to describe Christ's role in the world today: the Head of the body, directing its members to carry out his will.

To understand the gain to God, think back to the images from the Prophets: God as Parent and as Lover. Both those human relationships contain elements of what God has always been seeking from human beings. One word, *dependence,* holds the key—the key to what they have in common and the key to how they differ.

For a baby, dependence is everything; someone else must meet its every need or the child will die. Parents stay up all night, clean up vomit, teach toilet training, and perform other unpleasant chores out of love because they sense the child's dependence. But such a pattern cannot continue forever. An eagle stirs the nest to force its eaglets to fly; a mother covers her breast to wean her child.

No healthy parent wants a permanently dependent child on his hands. And so a father does not push his daughter around in a large carriage for life, but teaches her to walk, knowing that she may one day walk away. Good parents nudge their children from dependence toward freedom.

Lovers, however, reverse the pattern. A lover possesses complete freedom, yet chooses to give it away and become dependent. "Submit to one another," says the Bible, and any couple can tell you that's an apt description of the day-to-day process of getting along. In a healthy marriage, one submits to the other's wishes voluntarily, out of love. In an unhealthy marriage, submission becomes part of a power struggle, a tug-of-war between competing egos.

The difference between those two relationships shows, I believe, what God has been seeking in his long history with the human race. He desires not the clinging, helpless love of a child who has no choice, but the mature, freely given love of a lover. He has been "romancing" us all along.

God never got such mature love from the nation Israel. The record shows God nudging the young nation toward maturity: on the day Israel advanced into the Promised Land, the manna ceased. God had provided a new land; now it was up to the Israelites to grow their own food. In a typically childish response, Israel promptly started worshiping fertility gods. God wanted a lover; he got a permanently stunted child.

What about now, in the age of the Spirit? Does God now have a lover rather than a child? Amazingly, the New Testament seems to answer yes. This sampling of phrases from the New Testament expresses how God views us: "Christ loved the church . . . a radiant church, without stain or wrinkle or any other blemish, but holy and blameless"; "without fault in a crooked and depraved generation, in which you shine like stars in the universe"; "you who once were far away have been brought near"; "you are no longer foreigners and aliens, but . . . members of God's household . . . a dwelling in which God lives by his Spirit."

The Bible, in fact, presents the union of ordinary people with God's Spirit as the supreme achievement of creation. God's goal all along was to equip *us* to accomplish his will in the world. That slow, difficult process will one day result in the total restoration of the earth.

Our Gain

Such grand thoughts, however—agents of God, supreme achievement of creation—represent God's point of view, a vantage unavailable to us. What are the costs and gains of God's plan for us who live on earth? We still inhabit a world cursed with pain, tragedy, and disappointment. And what I have presented as a great advance in *closeness*—from the smoke of Sinai to the person of Jesus to the indwelling Holy Spirit—may, ironically, seem like God's *withdrawal* from direct involvement.

Some people pine for the "good old days" of the Old Testament when God used a more obvious, hands-on approach. The Old Testament tells of an actual contract signed by God guaranteeing physical safety and prosperity, under certain terms; the New Testament offers no such contract. The change from the visible presence of God in the wilderness to the invisible presence of the Holy Spirit involves a certain kind of loss as well. We lose the clear, sure proof that God exists. Nowadays, God does not hover over us in a cloud that we can gaze at for reassurance. For some, like Richard, this seems a great loss indeed.

In fact, God's reliance on the church almost guarantees that disappointment with God will be permanent and epidemic. In the old days, if the Hebrews wanted to know God's will about a military maneuver, or what kind of wood to use in the sanctuary, the high priests had ways of discerning the answer. But 1,275 denominations in the U.S. alone attest to the difficulty of the church agreeing on God's will about anything nowadays. The confused voice of the modern church is part of the cost, the disadvantage to living today rather than with the Hebrews in the desert or among the disciples who followed Jesus.

What, then, is the gain? The New Testament takes great pains to spell it out, especially in Hebrews, Romans, and Galatians. I can almost picture the apostle Paul, an excitable sort, responding to a question like "What is the gain?"

> What, are you crazy?! The gain? Go back and read Leviticus, Numbers, and Deuteronomy at one sitting, and then we can talk. You call those "good old days"? Who wants to live like that? Do you want to spend every day of your life worrying about your eternal destiny? Do you want to scramble all day to make sure you keep all those rules? Do you want to go through long rituals and animal sacrifices and a fancy-dressed high priest just to approach God? Hey, I spent half my life trying to measure up to those demands, and you can have them. The difference between the Law and Spirit is the difference between death and life, between slavery and freedom, between perpetual childhood and growing up. Why would anyone want to go back to that?

To use Paul's own words, the Old Testament way was "the ministry that brought death, which was engraved in letters of stone." It was a mere "*schoolmaster*" to lead us to Christ." Who wants to stay in kindergarten forever? As Paul said, "We are not like Moses, who would put a veil over his face to keep the Israelites from gazing at it while the radiance was fading away. . . . Now the Lord is the Spirit, and where the Spirit of the Lord is, there is freedom."

God's plan includes risk on both sides. For us, it means risking our independence by committing to follow an invisible God who requires of us faith and obedience. For God, it means risking that we, like the Israelites, may never grow up; it means risking that we may never love him. Evidently, he thought it a gamble worth taking.

A Trinity of Voices

Think of God's plan as a series of Voices. The first Voice, thunderingly loud, had certain advantages. When the Voice spoke from the trembling mountain at Sinai, or when fire licked up the altar on Mount Carmel, no one could deny it. Yet, amazingly, even those who heard the Voice and feared it—the Israelites at Sinai and at Carmel, for example—soon learned to ignore it. Its very volume got in the way. Few of them sought out that Voice; fewer still persevered when the Voice fell silent.

The Voice modulated with Jesus, the *Word* made flesh. For a few decades the Voice of God took on the timbre and volume and rural accent of a country Jew in Palestine. It was a normal human voice, and though it spoke with authority, it did not cause people to flee. Jesus' voice was soft enough to debate against, soft enough to kill.

After Jesus departed, the Voice took on new forms. On the day of Pentecost, tongues—*tongues*—of fire fell on the faithful, and the church, God's body, began to take shape. That last Voice is as close as breath, as gentle as a whisper. It is the most vulnerable Voice of all, and the easiest to ignore. The Bible says the Spirit can be "quenched" or "grieved"—try quenching Moses' burning bush or the molten rocks of Sinai! Yet the Spirit is also the most intimate Voice. In our moments of weakness, when we do not know what to pray, the Spirit within intercedes for us with groans that words cannot express. Those groans are the early pangs of birth, the labor pains of the new creation.

The Spirit will not remove all disappointment with God. The very titles given to the Spirit—Intercessor, Helper, Counselor, Comforter—imply there will be problems. But the Spirit is also "a deposit, guaranteeing what is to come," Paul said, drawing on an earthy metaphor from the financial world. The Spirit reminds us that such disappointments are temporary, a prelude to an eternal life with God. God deemed it necessary to restore the spiritual link *before* re-creating heaven and earth.

In two places the New Testament compares being Spirit-filled with the state of drunkenness. Both states change the way you view life's trials, but there is a profound difference between them. Many people turn to drink to drown out the sadness of unemployment, illness, and personal tragedy. Inevitably, however, a drunk must awake from the fantasy world of inebriation and return to an unchanged reality. But the Spirit whispers of a new reality, a fantasy that is actually true, one into which we will awake for eternity.

Bible references: Romans 8; Ephesians 3; 1 Peter 1; 1 Corinthians 12; Ephesians 5; Philippians 2; Ephesians 2; 2 Corinthians 3; Galatians 3 (KJV); 2 Corinthians 3, 5.

BOOK II

SEEING IN THE DARK

*I said to my soul, be still, and let the dark
come upon you
Which shall be the darkness of God....
I said to my soul, be still, and wait without hope
For hope would be hope for the wrong thing;
wait without love
For love would be love of the wrong thing;
there is yet faith
But the faith and the love and the hope are all
in the waiting.*

T. S. ELIOT, "EAST COKER"

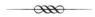

CHAPTER 21

INTERRUPTED

—◦◦◦—

R ather late one night I sat in my basement office and began to
outline the next part of this book, which I intended to be a
review and summation. Over the years I had filled several file folders
with miscellaneous notes on the subject of disappointment with God,
and I started to sift through these scraps of paper, reviewing them in
light of what I had learned from the Bible.

As I worked, I thought about the original meeting with Richard
in my living room, when his three large questions had first emerged.
These questions about God's fairness and silence and hiddenness had
become my own and had launched my search through the Bible.
When I began that search, I wanted a more active God, one who
would on occasion roll up his sleeves and step into my life with visible power. At the least, I thought, I wanted a God who did not stay
quite so hidden and silent, one who worked in slightly *less* mysterious ways. Surely that wasn't asking too much.

But the Bible contained some surprises: notably that such times
of frequent miracles usually did not foster long-term belief. Just the
opposite—most of them stand out as examples of faith*less*ness. The

more I studied the Bible, the less I longed for the "good old days" of daily manna and fireballs from heaven.

Most important, in the Bible I caught a glimpse of God's point of view. God's "goal," if one can speak in such terms, is not to overpower all skeptics with a flashy miracle; he could do that in an instant if he wished. Rather, he seeks to reconcile: to love, and to be loved. And the Bible shows a clear progression in God's efforts to break through to human beings without overwhelming them: from God the Father who hovered parentally over the Hebrews; to God the Son who taught the will of God "from the bottom up," rather than by fiat, from above; and finally, to the Holy Spirit who fills us with the literal presence of God. We who live now are not disadvantaged but wonderfully privileged, for God has chosen to rely primarily on *us* to carry out his will on earth.

I reviewed these thoughts with growing enthusiasm as I worked on my outline that night. Then, shuffling through another stack of papers, I found a letter from Meg Woodson.

I have known Meg for more than a decade. She is a devout Christian, a pastor's wife, and a very fine writer. Yet I cannot think of Meg without feeling a stab of grief.

The Woodsons had two children—Peggie and Joey—both born with cystic fibrosis. Peggie and Joey stayed skinny no matter how much food they ate. They coughed constantly and labored to breathe—twice a day Meg had to pound on their chests to clear out mucus. They spent several weeks each year in a local hospital, and both grew up knowing they would probably die before reaching adulthood.*

---

*Meg has written strong, moving books about both her children: *Following Joey Home; I'll Get to Heaven Before You Do!* and *The Time of Her Life.*

Joey, a bright, happy, all-American boy, died at the age of twelve. Peggie defied the odds by living much longer. I joined Meg in desperate prayers for Peggie. Although we knew of no recorded miraculous healings of cystic fibrosis, we prayed for healing anyway. Peggie survived several health crises in high school and went away to college. She seemed to grow stronger, not weaker, and our hopes rose that she would find healing after all.

But there was no miracle: Peggie died at the age of twenty-three. And that night in my basement office I came across the letter Meg had written to me after Peggie's death.

> I find myself wanting to tell you something of how Peggie died. I don't know why except that the need to talk about it is so compelling and, since I refuse to put my friends here through it more than once, I have run out of people to tell.
>
> The weekend before she went into the hospital for the last time, Peggie came home all excited about a quotation from William Barclay her minister had used. She was so taken with it that she had copied it down on a 3 x 5 card for me: "Endurance is not just the ability to bear a hard thing, but to turn it into glory." She said her minister must have had a hard week, because after he read it he banged the pulpit and then turned his back to them and cried.
>
> After Peggie had been in the hospital for a while and things were not going well, she looked around at all the paraphernalia of death to which she was attached. Then she said, "Hey, Ma, remember that quotation?" And she looked around again at all the tubes, stuck the tip of her tongue out of the corner of her mouth, nodded her head, and raised her eyes in excitement at the experiment to which she was committing herself.
>
> Her commitment held as long as her awareness of anything in the real world held. Once, the president of her college came

457

to see her and asked if there was anything specific he could pray for. She was too weak to talk, but nodded to me to explain the Barclay quote and ask him to pray that her hard time would be turned into glory.

I was sitting beside her bed a few days before her death when suddenly she began screaming. I will never forget those shrill, piercing, primal screams. Nurses raced into the room from every direction and surrounded her with their love. "It's okay, Peggie," one said. "Jeannie's here."

The nurses stroked her body. Eventually with their words and their touches they soothed her (though as time went on and the screaming continued, they could not). I've rarely seen such compassion. Wendy, Peggie's special nurse-friend, tells me there isn't a nurse on the floor who does not have at least one patient she would give one of her lungs to save if she could.

So, it's against this background of human beings falling apart—nurses can only stay on that floor so long—because they could not do more to help, that God, who could have helped, looked down on a young woman devoted to Him, quite willing to die for Him to give Him glory, and decided to sit on His hands and let her death top the horror charts for cystic fibrosis deaths.

I tell you, Philip, it does not help to talk of the good that results from pain. Nor does it help to talk of God almost always letting the physical process of disease run its course. Because if He ever intervenes, then at every point of human suffering He makes a decision to intervene or not, and in Peggie's case His choice was to let C.F. rip. There are moments when my only responses are grief and an anger as violent as any I have ever known. Nor does expressing it dissipate it.

Peggie never complained against God. It was no pious restraint: I don't think it ever occurred to her to complain.

And none of us who lived through her death with her complained at the time either. We were upheld. God's love was so real, one could not doubt it or rail against its ways.

If I've been telling you all this in an effort to come to some kind of resolution to the problem of Peggie's and my pain, perhaps I've been brought once again to the only thing that helps me experience God's love: His stroking, His "I'm here, Meg." But, again I wonder, how could He be in a situation like that and sit on His hands?

As I think of it, I've never expressed all this to anyone before, for fear of disturbing someone's faith. Don't think you must say anything to "make me feel better." But thanks for listening. Most people have no idea how much that helps.

After reading Meg's letter, I could not work anymore that evening.

The View from Here

Old questions churned up again, my own questions about social injustices, unanswered prayers, unhealed bodies, and countless other instances of unfairness. And Richard's questions came surging back with new emotional force, a fraction of the force Meg herself must have felt as she sat helpless by her daughter's hospital bed.

I had searched the Bible for insights into what God is up to in this world and how it must feel to be God—knowing, of course, that we can never come close to comprehending such an exalted viewpoint. Meg's letter, however, pushed me in another direction and changed my whole approach to the last part of this book.

It's fine to consider God's viewing level, but what about *our* point of view? I had been exploring what it feels like to be God; Meg's letter jarred me back to what it feels like to be human. Her questions are questions of the heart, not the head. As a mother, she watched her children die slow, horrible deaths. Yet as a Christian she believes in God the loving Father. How can she fit the two together?

That night, I realized this book was not over. Theological concepts don't amount to very much unless they can speak to someone like Meg Woodson, who gropes for God's love in a world bordered by grief. I recalled a floundering minister in a John Updike novel who said, "Something's gone wrong. I have no faith. Or, rather, I have faith, but it doesn't seem to apply." How does it apply? What do we have a right to expect from God?

Then the Lord said to Satan, "Have you considered my servant Job? There is no one on earth like him; he is blameless and upright, a man who fears God and shuns evil."

JOB 1:8

CHAPTER 22

THE ONLY PROBLEM

There is one church here, so I go to it. On Sunday mornings I quit the house and wander down the hill to the white frame church in the firs. On a big Sunday there might be twenty of us there; often I am the only person under sixty, and feel as though I'm on an archaeological tour of Soviet Russia. The members are of mixed denominations; the minister is a Congregationalist, and wears a white shirt. The man knows God. Once, in the middle of the long pastoral prayer of intercession for the whole world—for the gift of wisdom to its leaders, for hope and mercy to the grieving and pained, succor to the oppressed, and God's grace to all—in the middle of this he stopped, and burst out, "Lord, we bring you these same petitions every week." After a shocked pause, he continued reading the prayer. Because of this, I like him very much.

ANNIE DILLARD, *HOLY THE FIRM*

So far, I have avoided one book in the Bible, a book that confronts the very issues raised by the Congregationalist minister, and by Richard and Meg, and almost everyone who thinks about God. Not surprisingly, then, after reading Meg's letter I found myself turning to the Book of Job.

Possibly the oldest book in the Bible, Job reads like the most modern. Its extreme portrayal—one man confronting the abyss in a universe that makes no sense—foreshadows the predicament of modern humanity. People who reject nearly everything else in the Bible keep coming back to Job for inspiration. Its recurring theme—How can a good God allow suffering?—is "the only problem worth discussing," said contemporary British novelist Muriel Spark in her book *The Only Problem*. The problem of pain is a modern obsession, the theological kryptonite of our time, and the ancient man Job expressed it as well as it has ever been expressed.

Richard complained about the loss of a fiancée and a job and a stable home life. Meg cried out in pain over the loss of a son and a daughter. Yet by any standard Job lost far more: 7000 sheep, 3000 camels, 5000 oxen, 500 donkeys, and numerous servants. Then all Job's children—seven sons and three daughters—died in one mighty gust of wind. Finally Job's health, his last consolation, failed him, as sores broke out from the soles of his feet to the top of his head. Overnight, the greatest man in all the East was reduced to the most pitiable.

Job is the Bible's prime case study of disappointment with God, and as such it seems to anticipate whatever disappointment Richard or Meg or any of us might feel. An American rabbi wrote a popular book called *When Bad Things Happen to Good People*. The Book of Job raises the ante: it portrays the very worst things happening to the very best person.

A Misreading

If you had asked me when I began my study what the Book of Job was about, I would have been quick to respond. *Job? Everybody knows what Job is about. It's the Bible's most complete treatment of the problem of suffering. It's about terrible grief and bewildering pain.* Without doubt the bulk of the book does center on the theme of suffering. Chapters 3–37 contain no action to speak of, just the opinionated dialogues of five prickly men—Job, his three friends, and the enigmatic Elihu—concerning the problem of pain. They are all trying to account for the slings and arrows of outrageous fortune that have fallen upon poor Job, who sits forlorn in the ashes of what used to be his mansion.

I now believe I misread the book—or, more accurately, didn't take into account the entire book. Despite the fact that all but a few pages of Job deal with the problem of pain, I am coming to the conclusion that Job is not really about the problem of pain. Suffering contributes the ingredients of the story, not its central theme. Just as a cake is not about eggs, flour, milk, and shortening, but uses those ingredients in the process of creating a cake, Job is not "about" suffering; it merely uses such ingredients in its larger story, which concerns even more important questions, cosmic questions. Seen as a whole, Job is primarily about *faith* in its starkest form.

I am drawn to this conclusion mainly because of the introductory "plot" in chapters 1 and 2, which reveals that Job's personal drama on earth had its origin in a cosmic drama in heaven. I once regarded Job as a profound expression of human disappointment—something on the order of Meg Woodson's letter, only longer and more detailed, and with direct biblical sanction. As I studied the book further, however, I discovered that it does not really present the human viewpoint. God is the central character in the Bible, and nowhere does this come through more clearly than in the Book of Job. I realized that I had always read it from the perspective of chapter 3 on—in other words, from Job's perspective.

Let me explain.

It helps to think of the Book of Job as a mystery play, a "who-dunit" detective story. Before the play itself begins, we in the audience get a sneak preview, as if we have showed up early for a press conference in which the director explains his work (chapters 1–2). He relates the plot and describes the main characters, then tells us in advance who did what in the play, and why. In fact, he solves every mystery in the play except one: how will the main character respond? Will Job trust God or deny him?

Later, when the curtain rises, we see only the actors on stage. Confined within the play, they have no knowledge of what the director has told us in the sneak preview. We know the answer to the "who-dunit" questions, but the star detective, Job, does not. He spends all his time on stage trying to discover what we already know. He scratches himself with shards of pottery and asks, "Why me? What did I do wrong? What is God trying to tell me?"

To the audience, Job's questions should be mere intellectual exercises, for we learned the answers in the prologue, the first two chapters. What did Job do wrong? Nothing. He represents the very best of the species. Didn't God himself call Job "blameless and upright, a man who fears God and shuns evil"? Why, then, is Job suffering? Not for punishment. Far from it—he has been selected as the principal player in a great contest of the heavens.

The Wager

In retrospect, I sometimes wonder how I could have misread the Book of Job so badly. Part of the reason, I think, lies in the eloquence of chapters 3–37, which express the human dilemma with such power that we can get trapped in their force field, forgetting that the questions they raise have already been answered in chapters 1 and 2.

But there is yet another reason: no one knows quite what to make of the first two chapters. Even biblical scholars tend to view the prologue with embarrassment, or discount it as the addition of a later editor. The prologue shows God and Satan involved in—and you can almost see blush marks on the commentary pages—something resembling a wager. All Job's trauma traces back to, well, a kind of bet, placed by the two cosmic powers.

The trouble starts with Satan's claim that Job is a spoiled favorite, loyal only because God has "put a hedge around him." Satan scoffs that God, unworthy of love in himself, only attracts people like Job because they're "bribed" to follow him. If times ever get tough, Satan charges, such people will quickly abandon God. When God accepts the challenge to test Satan's theory, thus consenting to let Job's response settle the issue, the calamities begin to rain down on poor, unsuspecting Job.

I would certainly not deny the strangeness of this heavenly contest. On the other hand, I cannot sidestep the account of The Wager in Job, for it offers a rare peek through the keyhole of eternity. When people experience pain, questions spill out—the very questions that tormented Job. Why me? What's going on? Does God care? Is there a God? This one time, in the raw recounting of Job's travail, we the onlookers—not Job—are granted a view behind the curtain. What we long for, the prologue to Job provides: a glimpse into how the world is run. As nowhere else in the Bible, the Book of Job shows us God's point of view, including the supernatural activity normally hidden from us.

Job has put God on trial, accusing him of unfair acts against an innocent party. Angry, satirical, betrayed, Job wanders as close to blasphemy as he can get—just to the edge. His words have a startlingly familiar ring because they are so modern. He gives voice to our most deeply felt complaints against God. But chapters 1 and 2 prove that, regardless of what Job thinks, God is not on trial in this book. Job is on trial. The point of the book is not suffering: Where is God when it hurts? The prologue dealt with that issue. The point is faith: Where is Job when it hurts? How is he responding? To understand the Book of Job, I must begin there.

To believe in the supernatural is not simply to believe that after living a successful, material, and fairly virtuous life here one will continue to exist in the best-possible substitute for this world, or that after living a starved and stunted life here one will be compensated with all the good things one has gone without: it is to believe that the supernatural is the greatest reality here and now

T. S. ELIOT

Bible references: Job 1–2.

What is man that you make so much of him,

that you give him so much attention,

that you examine him every morning

and test him every moment?

Will you never look away from me,

or let me alone even for an instant?

Job 7:17–18

CHAPTER 23

A ROLE IN THE COSMOS

———— ⚬⚬⚬ ————

*Some say that to the gods we are like flies that boys idly swat on a
summer day. Others say that not a feather from a sparrow falls to the
ground without the will of the Heavenly Father.*

THORNTON WILDER, *THE BRIDGE OF SAN LUIS REY*

To my friend Richard, who wrote a book about Job, that ancient
man seemed a larger-than-life hero who had dared arm wrestle
with God Almighty. Once, after listening to Richard expound on the
valor of Job, I brought up the account of The Wager. Anger rose in
his face. "All I can say," he snapped, "is that Job paid one *hell* of a
price just to make God feel good!"

I, too, found it hard to avoid such sentiments at first. There is
no easy way around the difficulty, for the heavenly contest played
itself out in Job's life in the form of marauders, firestorms, wind-
storms, and boils. How can God's winning a contest, *any* contest, be
worth such a price? As C. G. Jung asked in his caustic book on Job,
"Is it worth the lion's while to terrify the mouse?"

As I studied Job further, however, I saw that I had been harboring the wrong image of what took place. Yes, there was an arm wrestling match, but not between Job and God. Rather, *Satan* and God were the chief combatants, although—most significantly—God had designated the man Job as his stand-in. The first and last chapters make clear that Job was unknowingly performing in a cosmic showdown before spectators in the unseen world.

Disturbing the Universe

The strange scene of The Wager reminded me of a few other places where the Bible affords a brief glimpse behind the curtain. Consider, for example, Revelation 12, which depicts an even more bizarre contest: a pregnant woman, wearing the sun for a dress and twelve stars for a crown, opposes a red dragon so enormous he can dislodge a third of the stars from the sky with one sweep of his tail. The dragon lies in wait, seeking to devour the pregnant woman's child at birth. And there's more: a flight into the desert, a serpent who tries to drown the woman, and a fierce war in heaven.

Biblical commentators propose as many interpretations of the details in Revelation 12 as there are commentaries, but almost all agree that the weird images point to the great disruption in the universe caused by Jesus' birth in Bethlehem. In a sense, Revelation 12 presents another side of Christmas, adding a new set of holographic images to the familiar scenes of manger and shepherds and the slaughter of the innocents. Which is the "true" story of Christmas: Luke's pastoral version or Revelation's account of the cosmos at war? They are the same story, of course; only the level of viewing differs. Luke gives the view from earth and Revelation shades in details from the unseen world.

The two worlds come together vividly in three of Jesus' most famous stories, the parables of the lost sheep, the lost coin, and the lost son. All three make the same point: great joy breaks out in heaven when a sinner repents. Today, anyone can watch a sinner repenting, for televised Billy Graham crusades portray the scene live and in color. The camera follows a young woman as she makes her way through the stands to an area set aside for repentance and conversion. But Jesus' stories imply that far more may be going on out there: beyond that stadium scene, in a place concealed from all camera lenses, a great party has erupted, a gigantic celebration in the unseen world.

Belief in an unseen world forms a crucial dividing line of faith today. Many people get up, eat, drive their cars, work, make phone calls, tend to their children, and go to bed without giving a single thought to the existence of an unseen world. But according to the Bible, human history is far more than the rising and falling of people and nations; it is a staging ground for the battle of the universe. Hence what seems like an "ordinary" action in the seen world may have an extraordinary effect on the unseen world: a short-term mission assignment causes Satan to fall like lightning from heaven (Luke 10); a sinner's repentance sets off celestial celebration (Luke 15); a baby's birth disturbs the entire universe (Revelation 12). Much of that effect, however, remains hidden from our view—except for the occasional glimpses granted us in places like Revelation, and in Job.

An ordinary person in the seen world, Job was called upon to endure a trial with cosmic consequences. He had no glimmer of light to guide him, no hint that the unseen world cared about him, or even existed. Yet like a laboratory test animal, he was handpicked to settle one of the most urgent issues of humanity and to determine a small piece of the history of the universe.

Is it absurd to believe that one human being, a tiny dot on a tiny planet, can make a difference in the history of the universe? It certainly seemed so to Job's friends. Listen to Elihu, the last of Job's comforters:

> If you sin, how does that affect him [God]?
> If your sins are many, what does that do to him?
> If you are righteous, what do you give to him,
> or what does he receive from your hand?
> Your wickedness affects only a man like yourself,
> and your righteousness only the sons of men.

Elihu, however, was flat wrong. The opening and closing chapters of Job prove that God was greatly affected by the response of one man and that cosmic issues were at stake. (Later, in a message to the prophet Ezekiel, God would point with pride to Job—along with Daniel and Noah—as one of his three favorites.)

Job's example, drawn in sharp relief, shows how life on earth affects the universe. When I began my study, I tended to avoid the "embarrassing" scene in chapter 1, but I have since come to believe that, whether drama or history, The Wager offers a message of great hope to all of us—perhaps the most powerful and enduring lesson from Job. In the end, The Wager resolved decisively that the faith of a single human being counts for very much indeed. Job affirms that our response to testing *matters*. The history of mankind—and, in fact, my own individual history of faith–is enclosed within the great drama of the history of the universe.

God has granted us "the dignity of causation," said Pascal. We may doubt, with Elihu, whether one person can make any appreciable difference. But the Bible rustles with hints that something like The Wager is played out in other believers as well. We are God's Exhibit A, his demonstration piece to the powers in the unseen world. The apostle Paul, borrowing an image from the processional of gladiators into the Colosseum, pictured himself on public display: "We have been made a spectacle to the whole universe, to angels as well as to men." And in the same letter he commented, in an astonishing aside, "Do you not know that we will judge angels?"

We humans inhabit a mere speck of a planet in the outer suburbs of a spiral galaxy that is only one of about a million million such galaxies in the observable universe, but the New Testament insists that what happens among us here will, in fact, help determine the future of that universe. Paul is emphatic: "The whole creation is on tiptoe to see the wonderful sight of the sons of God coming into their own." Natural creation, "groaning" in travail and decay, can only be set free by the transformation of human beings.

The Great Reversal

In the Christian view, all of human history takes place somewhere between the first part of Genesis and the last part of Revelation, which paint the same scene, with the same brush strokes: Paradise, a river, the luminous glory of God, and the Tree of Life. History begins and ends at the same place, and everything in between comprises the struggle to regain what was lost.*

After the fall from Paradise, history entered a new phase. Creation God had done by himself, starting with nothing and ending up with the universe in all its splendor. The new work is Re-creation, and for this God employs the very human beings who had originally spoiled his work. Creation progressed through stages: first stars, then the sky and sea, and on through plants and animals, and finally man and woman. Re-creation reverses the sequence, starting with man and woman and culminating in the restoration of all the rest.

*John MacQuarrie discusses our ultimate destiny in this passage from *The Humility of God:* "If the doctrine of original sin is not to have the last word, it must be confronted with a doctrine of original righteousness. After all, in the Old Testament story righteousness is more original than sin."

In many ways the act of Re-creation is "harder" than creation, for it relies on flawed human beings. Surely, it has cost God more: the death of his Son. Still, God insists on healing the world from the bottom up, rather than from the top down.

As I studied Job, it struck me that The Wager was, at its heart, a stark reenactment of God's original question in creation: Will the humans choose for or against me? From God's point of view that has been the central question of history, beginning with Adam and continuing on through Job and every man and woman who has ever lived. The Wager in the Book of Job called into question the whole human experiment.

Satan denied that human beings are truly free. We have freedom to descend, of course—Adam and all his descendants proved that. But freedom to ascend, to believe God for no other reason than, well . . . for no reason at all? Can a person believe even when God appears to him as an enemy? Or is faith one more product of environment and circumstance? The opening chapters of Job expose Satan as the first great behaviorist: Job was *conditioned* to love God, he implied. Take away the rewards, and watch his faith crumble. The Wager put Satan's theory to the test.

I have come to see Job's trials as a crucial test of human freedom, an important issue in modern times as well. In our century, it takes faith to believe that a human being amounts to more than a combination of DNA programming, instincts of the gene pool, cultural conditioning, and the impersonal forces of history. Yet even in this behaviorist century, we want to believe differently. We want to believe that the thousand hard and easy choices we make each day somehow count. And the Book of Job insists that they do; one person's faith can make a difference. There is a role for human beings, after all, and by fulfilling that role Job set a pattern for anyone who ever faces doubt or hardship.

Very often, disappointment with God begins in Job-like circumstances. The death of a child, a tragic accident, or a loss of job may bring on the same questions Job asked. Why me? What does God have against me? Why does he seem so distant? As readers of Job's story, we can see behind the curtain to a contest being waged in the invisible world. But in our own trials, we will not have such insight. When tragedy strikes, we will live in shadow, unaware of what is transpiring in the unseen world. The drama that Job lived through will then replicate itself in our individual lives. Once again, God will let his reputation ride on the response of unpredictable human beings.

For Job, the battleground of faith involved lost possessions, lost family members, lost health. We may face a different struggle: a career failure, a floundering marriage, sexual orientation, a body shape that turns people off, not on. At such times the outer circumstances—the illness, the bank account, the run of bad luck—will seem the real struggle. We may beg God to change those circumstances. *If only I were beautiful or handsome, then everything would work out. If only I had more money—or at least a job—then I could easily believe God.*

But the more important battle, as shown in Job, takes place inside us. Will we trust God? Job teaches that at the moment when faith is hardest and *least* likely, then faith is most needed. His struggle presents a glimpse of what the Bible elsewhere spells out in detail: the remarkable truth that our choices matter, not just to us and our own destiny but, amazingly, to God himself and the universe he rules.

In short, God has granted to ordinary men and women the dignity of participating in the Great Reversal which will restore the cosmos to its pristine state. All the reasons for disappointment with God that I have mentioned in this book, as well as all cancers, all deaths, all broken relationships, all the collected groanings of our savage planet—

all these imperfections will be wiped away. We may at times question God's wisdom and lose patience with his timetable. (The disciples, after all, felt bitter disappointment when Jesus rejected their dream of a physical kingdom in favor of an invisible, spiritual kingdom.) But all the prophets' lavish promises will someday come true, and we, you and I, are the ones selected to help bring that about.

No one has expressed the pain and unfairness of this world more poignantly than Job; no one has voiced disappointment with God more passionately. We must still attend to Job's complaints and to God's fierce response. But the Book of Job begins not with the complaints—the human viewpoint—but with God's point of view. In the prologue, the scene of The Wager establishes a darkly shining truth: Job—and you and I—can join the struggle to reverse all that is wrong with the universe. We can make a difference.

The Book of Job gives no satisfying answers to the question "Why?" Instead, it substitutes another question, "To what end?" By remaining faithful to God through his trials Job, crotchety, sardonic old Job, helped abolish the very pain and unfairness of this world that he had protested so vigorously. And Meg Woodson, who stubbornly clings to God's love in the shadows, even after watching two children die . . . she too is helping to reverse those wrongs.

Why the delay? Why does God let evil and pain so flagrantly exist, even thrive, on this planet? Why does he let us do slowly and blunderingly what he could do in an eyeblink?

He holds back for our sakes. Re-creation involves us; we are, in fact, at the center of his plan. The Wager, the motive behind all human history, is to develop us, not God. Our very existence announces to the powers in the universe that restoration is under way. Every act of faith by every one of the people of God is like the tolling of a bell, and a faith like Job's reverberates throughout the universe.

Our present life feels like a real fight—as if there were something really wild in the universe which we, with all our idealities and faithfulnesses, are needed to redeem.

WILLIAM JAMES, *THE WILL TO BELIEVE*

I had far rather walk, as I do, in daily terror of eternity, than feel that this was only a children's game in which all the contestants would get equally worthless prizes in the end.

T. S. ELIOT

Bible references: Job 35; 1 Corinthians 4, 6; Romans 8 PHILLIPS.

Yet when I hoped for good, evil came;
when I looked for light, then came darkness.
The churning inside me never stops.

JOB 30:26–27

CHAPTER 24

IS GOD UNFAIR?

—⊶⊷—

T*he Road Less Traveled*, by M. Scott Peck, opens with a blunt
three-word sentence: "Life is difficult." If reduced to a single
sentence, the Book of Job would express something similar, for the
loud cry, "Life is unfair!" resounds from almost every page.

Unfairness is no easier for us to swallow today than it was for Job
thousands of years ago. Consider the most common curse word in the
English language: "God" followed by the word "damn." People say it
not only in the face of great tragedy, but also when their cars won't
start, when a favored sports team loses, when it rains on their picnic.
That oath renders an instinctive judgment that life *ought* to be fair
and that God should somehow "do a better job" of running his world.

The world as it is versus the world as it ought to be—the constant tension between those two states bursts into the open in the
Book of Job. For three long, windy rounds, Job and his friends spar
in a verbal boxing match. On the ground rules, they all agree: God
should reward those who do good and punish those who do evil.

Why, then, is Job, a supposedly good man, suffering so much
apparent punishment? Job's friends, confident of God's fairness,

defend the world as it is. "Use your common sense," they tell Job. "God would not afflict you without a cause. You must have committed some secret sin." But Job, who knows beyond doubt he has done nothing to deserve such punishment, cannot agree. He pleads innocent.

Gradually, however, the suffering wears down Job's most cherished beliefs. How can God be on his side? Job wonders. He is, after all, squatting in a heap of ashes, the ruins of his life. He is a broken, despairing man, "betrayed" by God. "Look at me and be astonished; clap your hand over your mouth," Job cries.

A crisis of faith brews inside him. Is God unfair? Such a notion calls into question everything Job believes, but how else can he explain what has happened? He looks around for other examples of unfairness and sees that evil people sometimes do prosper—they don't get punished, as he'd like to believe—while some godly people suffer. And many other people live happy, fruitful lives without ever giving a thought to God. For Job, the facts simply do not add up. "When I think about this, I am terrified; trembling seizes my body."

The reason the Book of Job seems so modern is that for us, too, the facts do not add up. Job's strident message of life's unfairness seems peculiarly suited to our own pain-racked century. Simply plug contemporary illustrations into his arguments: "innocent" but starving children in the Third World; faithful pastors imprisoned in South Africa; Christian leaders who die in their prime; Mafia dons and spoiled entertainers who profit obscenely from flouting God's rules; the millions in Western Europe who live quiet, happy lives and never give God a thought. Far from fading away, Job's questions about this world's unfairness have only grown louder and shriller. We still expect a God of love and power to follow certain rules on earth. Why doesn't he?

Coming to Terms with Unfairness

At some point, every human being confronts the mysteries that caused Job to tremble in terror. Is God unfair?

One option seemed obvious to Job's wife: "Curse God and die!" she advised. Why hold on to a sentimental belief in a loving God when so much in life conspires against it? And in this Job-like century, more people than ever before have come to agree with her. Some Jewish writers, such as Jerzy Kosinski and Elie Wiesel, began with a strong faith in God, but saw it vaporize in the gas furnaces of the Holocaust. Face to face with history's grossest unfairness, they concluded that God must not exist. (Still, the human instinct asserts itself. Kosinski and Wiesel cannot avoid a tone of outrage, as if they too feel betrayed. They overlook the underlying issue of where our primal sense of fairness comes from. Why ought we even *expect* the world to be fair?)

Others, equally mindful of the world's unfairness, cannot bring themselves to deny God's existence. Instead, they propose another possibility: perhaps God agrees that life is unfair, but cannot do anything about it. Rabbi Harold Kushner took this approach in his best-selling book *When Bad Things Happen to Good People*. After watching his son die of the disease progeria, Kushner concluded that "even God has a hard time keeping chaos in check," and that God is "a God of justice and not of power."

According to Rabbi Kushner, God is as frustrated, even outraged, by the unfairness on this planet as anyone else, but he lacks the power to change it. Millions of readers found comfort in Kushner's portrayal of a God who seemed compassionate, albeit weak. I wonder, however, what those people make of the last five chapters of Job, which contain God's "self-defense." No other part of the Bible conveys God's power so impressively. If God is less-than-powerful, why did he choose the worst possible situation, when his power was most called into question, to insist on his omnipotence? (Elie Wiesel said of the God described by Kushner, "If that's who God is, why doesn't he resign and let someone more competent take his place?")

A third group of people evades the problem of unfairness by looking to the future, when an exacting justice will work itself out in the universe. Unfairness is a temporary condition, they say. The Hindu doctrine of Karma, which applies a mathematical precision to this belief, calculates it may take a soul 6,800,000 incarnations to realize perfect justice. At the end of all those incarnations, a person will have experienced exactly the amount of pain and pleasure that he or she deserves.

A fourth approach is to flatly deny the problem and insist the world is fair. Echoing Job's friends, these people insist the world does run according to fixed, regular laws: good people will prosper and evil ones will fail. I encountered this point of view at the faith-healing church in Indiana, and I hear it virtually every time I watch religious television, where some evangelist promises perfect health and financial prosperity to anyone who asks for it in true faith.

Such lavish promises have obvious appeal, but they fail to account for all the facts. The babies who contract AIDS *in utero*, for example, or the roll call of persecuted saints in *Foxe's Book of Martyrs*—how do these fit into a doctrine of life's fairness?* There is nothing I would rather have said to Meg Woodson than, "The world is fair, and therefore if you pray hard enough, your daughter will not

---

*One of the "apocryphal" books circulating among early Christians told the story of a woman named Thecla, a convert of the apostle Paul. Her faith supposedly warded off all attacks: wild beasts refused to eat her, and men suddenly stopped in the act of ravishing her. When her tormentors tried to burn her at the stake, a cloud of rain and hail appeared overhead and doused the flames. The book circulated widely, but one needs only to read other books of church history, like *Foxe's Book of Martyrs*, to see why Thecla's story was ultimately dismissed as apocryphal.

die." But I could not say that, any more than I can now say, "God took Peggie away because of something you did wrong." Both points of view are represented in the Book of Job; both are dismissed by God in the end.

It takes an Olympian leap of faith to argue that life is completely fair. More commonly, Christians respond to life's unfairness not by denying it outright, but by watering it down. They, like Job's friends, search for some hidden reason behind suffering:

"God is trying to teach you something. You should feel privileged, not bitter, about your opportunity to lean on him in faith."

"Meditate on the blessings you still enjoy—at least you are alive. Are you a fair-weather believer?"

"You are undergoing a training regimen, a chance to exercise new muscles of faith. Don't worry—God will not test you beyond your endurance."

"Don't complain so loudly! You will forfeit this opportunity to demonstrate your faithfulness to non-believers."

"Someone is always worse off than you. Give thanks despite your circumstances."

Job's friends offered a version of each of these words of wisdom, and each contains an element of truth. But the Book of Job plainly shows that such "helpful advice" does nothing to answer the questions of the person in pain. It was the wrong medicine, dispensed at the wrong time.

And finally, there is one more way to explain the world's unfairness. After hearing all the alternatives, Job was driven to the conclusion I have suggested as the one-sentence summary of the entire book: *Life is unfair!* It came to Job more as a reflex reaction than a philosophy of life, and that is how it strikes anyone who suffers. "Why me?" we ask. "What have I done?"

A Modern Job

While working on this book, I made it a point to meet regularly with people who felt betrayed by God. I wanted to keep before me the actual look, the facial expressions, of disappointment and doubt. When it came time to write about the Book of Job, I decided to interview the one person I know whose life most resembles Job's, a man I will call Douglas.

To me, Douglas seems "righteous" in the same sense as Job: not perfect, of course, but a model of faithfulness. After years of training in psychotherapy, he had declined a lucrative career in favor of starting an urban ministry. Douglas's troubles began some years ago when his wife discovered a lump in her breast. Surgeons removed that breast, but two years later the cancer had spread to her lungs. Douglas took over many household and parental duties as his wife battled the debilitating effects of chemotherapy. Sometimes she couldn't hold down any food. She lost her hair. And always she felt tired and vulnerable to fear and depression.

One night, in the midst of this crisis, as Douglas was driving down a city street with his wife and twelve-year-old daughter, a drunk driver swerved across the center line and smashed head-on into their car. Douglas's wife was badly shaken, but unhurt. His daughter suffered a broken arm and severe facial cuts from windshield glass. Douglas himself received the worst injury, a massive blow to the head.

After the accident, Douglas never knew when a headache might strike. He could not work a full day, and sometimes he would become disoriented and forgetful. Worse, the accident permanently affected his vision. One eye wandered at will, refusing to focus. He developed double vision and could hardly walk down a flight of stairs without assistance. Douglas learned to cope with all his disabilities but one: he could not read more than a page or two at a time. All his life, he had loved books. Now he was restricted to the limited selections and the sluggish pace of recorded books.

When I called Douglas to ask for an interview, he suggested meeting over breakfast; and when the scheduled time came, I braced myself for a difficult morning. By then I had interviewed a dozen people and had heard the full range of disappointment with God. If anyone had a right to be angry at God, Douglas did. Just that week, his wife had gotten a dismaying report from the hospital: there was another spot on her lung.

As our meal was being served, we caught up on the details of our lives. Douglas ate with great concentration and care. Thick glasses corrected some of his vision problems, but he had to work hard at focusing just to guide his fork to his mouth. I forced myself to look directly at him as he talked, trying to ignore the distraction of his wandering eye. At last, as we finished breakfast and motioned to the waitress for more coffee, I described my book on disappointment with God. "Could you tell me about your own disappointment?" I asked. "What have you learned that might help someone else going through a difficult time?"

Douglas was silent for what seemed like a long time. He stroked his peppery gray beard and gazed off beyond my right shoulder. I fleetingly wondered if he was having a mental "gap." Finally he said, "To tell you the truth, Philip, I didn't feel any disappointment with God."

I was startled. Douglas, searingly honest, had always rejected easy formulas like the "Turn your scars into stars!" testimonials of religious television. I waited for him to explain.

"The reason is this. I learned, first through my wife's illness and then especially through the accident, not to confuse God with life. I'm no stoic. I am as upset about what happened to me as anyone could be. I feel free to curse the unfairness of life and to vent all my grief and anger. But I believe God feels the same way about that accident—grieved and angry. I don't blame him for what happened."

Douglas continued, "I have learned to see beyond the physical reality in this world to the spiritual reality. We tend to think, 'Life should be fair because God is fair.' But God is not life. And if I confuse God with the physical reality of life—by expecting constant good health, for example—then I set myself up for a crashing disappointment.

"God's existence, even his love for me, does not depend on my good health. Frankly, I've had more time and opportunity to work on my relationship with God during my impairment than before."*

There was a deep irony in that scene. For months I had been absorbed in the failures of faith, having sought out stories of people disappointed in God. I had chosen Douglas as my modern Job, and had expected from him a bitter blast of protest. The last thing I anticipated was a graduate-school course in faith.

"If we develop a relationship with God *apart* from our life circumstances," said Douglas, "then we may be able to hang on when the physical reality breaks down. We can learn to trust God despite all the unfairness of life. Isn't that really the main point of Job?"

Although Douglas's strict separation of "physical reality" and "spiritual reality" bothered me, I found his notion intriguing. For the next hour, we worked through the Bible together, testing out his ideas. In the Sinai wilderness, God's guarantees of *physical* success—health, prosperity, and military victory—did nothing to help the Israelites' *spiritual* performance. And most heroes of the Old Testament (Abraham, Joseph, David, Elijah, Jeremiah, Daniel) went

---

*Douglas's answer reminded me of a statement by Dr. Paul Brand. To the question "Where is God when it hurts?" Dr. Brand replied, "He is in you, the one hurting, not in it, the thing that hurts."

through trials much like Job's. For each of them, at times, the physical reality surely seemed to present God as the enemy. But each managed to hold on to a trust in him despite the hardships. In doing so, their faith moved from a "contract faith"—I'll follow God if he treats me well—to a relationship that could transcend any hardship.

Suddenly, Douglas glanced at his watch and realized he was already late for another appointment. He put his coat on hurriedly and stood up to leave, and then leaned forward with one final thought. "I challenge you to go home and read again the story of Jesus. Was life 'fair' to him? For me, the cross demolished for all time the basic assumption that life will be fair."

Douglas and I had started out discussing Job and ended up discussing Jesus, and that pattern stayed with me: in the Old Testament one of God's favorites suffered terrible unfairness, and in the New Testament God's own Son suffered even more.

When I returned home, I took Douglas's advice and went through the Gospels again, wondering how Jesus would have answered the direct question, "Is life unfair?" Nowhere did I find him denying unfairness. When Jesus encountered a sick person, he never delivered a lecture about "accepting your lot in life"; he healed whoever approached him. And his scathing words about the rich and powerful of his day show clearly what he thought about social inequities. The Son of God reacted to life's unfairness much like anybody else. When he met a person in pain, he was deeply moved with compassion. When his friend Lazarus died, he wept. When Jesus himself faced suffering, he recoiled from it, asking three times if there was any other way.

God responded to the question of unfairness not with words, but with a visit, an Incarnation. And Jesus offers flesh-and-blood proof of how God feels about unfairness, for he took on the "stuff" of life, the physical reality at its unfairest. He gave, in summary, a final answer to all lurking questions about the goodness of God. (It occurred to me as I read the Gospels that if all of us in his Body would spend our lives as he did—ministering to the sick, feeding the hungry, resisting the powers of evil, comforting those who mourn, and bringing the Good News of love and forgiveness—then perhaps the question "Is God unfair?" would not be asked with such urgency today.)

The Great Unfairness

Is God unfair? The answer depends on how closely we identify God and life. Surely life on earth is unfair. Douglas was correct in saying that the Cross settled that issue forever.

Author Henri Nouwen tells the story of a family he knew in Paraguay. The father, a doctor, spoke out against the military regime there and its human rights abuses. Local police took their revenge on him by arresting his teenage son and torturing him to death. Enraged townsfolk wanted to turn the boy's funeral into a huge protest march, but the doctor chose another means of protest. At the funeral, the father displayed his son's body as he had found it in the jail—naked, scarred from the electric shocks and cigarette burns and beatings. All the villagers filed past the corpse, which lay not in a coffin but on the blood-soaked mattress from the prison. It was the strongest protest imaginable, for it put injustice on grotesque display.

Isn't that what God did at Calvary? "It's God who ought to suffer, not you and me," say those who bear a grudge against God for the unfairness of life. The curse word expresses it well: God be damned. And on that day, God was damned. The cross that held Jesus' body, naked and marked with scars, exposed all the violence and injustice of this world. At once, the Cross revealed what kind of world we have and what kind of God we have: a world of gross unfairness, a God of sacrificial love.

No one is exempt from tragedy or disappointment—God himself was not exempt. Jesus offered no immunity, no way *out* of the unfairness, but rather a way *through* it to the other side. Just as Good Friday demolished the instinctive belief that this life is supposed to be fair, Easter Sunday followed with its startling clue to the riddle of the universe. Out of the darkness, a bright light shone.

The primal desire for fairness dies hard, and it should. Who among us does not sometimes yearn for more justice in this world here and now? Secretly, I admit, I yearn for a world "fault-proof" against disappointment, a world where my magazine articles will always find acceptance and my body does not grow old and weak, a world where my sister-in-law does not deliver a brain-damaged child, and where Peggie Woodson lives into ripe old age. But if I stake my faith on such a fault-proof earth, my faith will let me down. Even the greatest of miracles do not resolve the problems of this earth: all people who find physical healing eventually die.

We need more than miracle. We need a new heaven and a new earth, and until we have those, unfairness will not disappear.

A friend of mine, struggling to believe in a loving God amid much pain and sorrow, blurted out this statement: "God's only excuse is Easter!" The language is non-theological and harsh, but within that phrase lies a haunting truth. The Cross of Christ may have overcome evil, but it did not overcome unfairness. For that, Easter is required. Someday, God will restore all physical reality to its proper place under his reign. Until then, it is a good thing to remember that we live out our days on Easter Saturday.

491

To be commanded to love God at all, let alone in the wilderness, is like being commanded to be well when we are sick, to sing for joy when we are dying of thirst, to run when our legs are broken. But this is the first and great commandment nonetheless. Even in the wilderness— especially in the wilderness—you shall love him.

FREDERICK BUECHNER

Bible references: Job 21, 2.

Surely I spoke of things I did not understand,
things too wonderful for me to know.

JOB 42:3

———◦∞∞∞◦———

CHAPTER 25

WHY GOD DOESN'T EXPLAIN

———∞∞∞———

Toward the end of the Book of Job, brash young Elihu delivers a stinging address in which he ridicules Job's desire for a visit from God. "Do you think God cares about a puny creature like you? Do you imagine that Almighty God, the Maker of the Universe, will deign to visit earth and meet with you in person? Does he owe you some kind of explanation? Get serious, Job!"

As Elihu drones on, a tiny cloud appears on the horizon, just over his shoulder. And as the cloud draws closer, roiling into a full-fledged storm, a Voice like no other voice booms out. Elihu's fine speech abruptly ends, and Job begins to tremble. God himself has arrived on the scene. He has come to reply in person to Job's accusations of unfairness.

If Job serves as the Bible's main case study of disappointment with God, then surely this dramatic speech out of the whirlwind should yield important insights into all other times of confusion and doubt. What, then, does God say in his own defense?

I can think of several helpful things God could have said: "Job, I'm truly sorry about what's happened. You've endured many unfair trials on my behalf, and I'm proud of you. You don't know what this means to me and even to the universe." A few compliments, a dose of compassion, or at the least a brief explanation of what transpired "behind the curtain" in the unseen world—any of these would have given Job some solace.

God says nothing of the kind. His "reply," in fact, consists of more questions than answers. Sidestepping thirty-five chapters' worth of debates on the problem of pain, he plunges instead into a magnificent verbal tour of the natural world. He seems to guide Job through a private gallery of his favorite works, lingering with pride over dioramas of mountain goats, wild donkeys, ostriches, and eagles, speaking as if astonished by his own creations. The beauty of the poetry at the end of Job rivals anything in world literature. Even as I marvel at God's dazzling portrayal of the natural world, however, a sense of bewilderment steals in. Of all moments, why did God choose this one to give Job a course in wilderness appreciation? Are these words relevant?

In his book *Wishful Thinking*, Frederick Buechner sums up God's speech. "God doesn't explain. He explodes. He asks Job who he thinks he is anyway. He says that to try to explain the kind of things Job wants explained would be like trying to explain Einstein to a little-neck clam. . . . God doesn't reveal his grand design. He reveals himself."[1] The message behind the splendid poetry boils down to this: *Until you know a little more about running the physical universe, Job, don't tell me how to run the moral universe.*

"Why are you treating me so unfairly, God?" Job has whined throughout the book. "Put yourself in my place."

"NO!!!" God thunders in reply. "You put yourself in *my* place! Until you can offer lessons on how to make the sun come up each day, or where to scatter lightning bolts, or how to design a hippopotamus, don't judge how I run the world. Just shut up and listen."

The impact of God's speech on Job is almost as amazing as the speech itself. Although God never answers question one about Job's predicament, the blast from the storm flattens Job. He repents in dust and ashes, and every trace of disappointment with God is swept away.

What We Cannot Know

The rest of us, however, who may never hear a voice speaking out of the whirlwind, must try to figure out what God actually said to Job. Quite frankly, for me God's evasive reply creates as many problems as it solves. I cannot simply wish the "Why?" questions away. They come up every time I talk to someone like Meg Woodson, every time my own life starts to unravel.

God's refusal to answer Job's questions does not sit well with modern minds. We don't like—*I* don't like—being told something is beyond our grasp. I own a book titled *The Encyclopedia of Ignorance* which outlines many areas of science we cannot yet explain; but scientists all over the world are doing their best to explore those areas and fill in the gaps of knowledge. Has God perhaps fenced off an area of knowledge, *The Encyclopedia of Theological Ignorance,* that no human being will ever understand?

Much as I resist, I am pushed toward such a conclusion by the Book of Job. Why is life so unfair? When does God cause suffering and when merely permit it—and what is the difference? Why does God sometimes seem silent and sometimes close and intimate? When God had the perfect opportunity to settle those issues for good, he scowled and shook his head. Why bother to explain? Not Job nor any other human being could possibly understand.

I cannot offer answers to Job's specific questions, because God offered none. I can only ask why God gives no answers, why there must be an *Encyclopedia of Theological Ignorance.* Because I am entering an area on which the Bible stays silent, what follows is pure speculation. I include it for people who are never satisfied with a non-answer, for those who cannot stop asking questions even God has declined to answer.

1. Perhaps God keeps us ignorant because enlightenment might not help us.

The same urgent questions torment almost every suffering person: Why? Why me? What is God trying to tell me? In the Book of Job, God deflects those questions of *cause,* and focuses instead on our *response* of faith. But think what might happen if God did answer our questions forthrightly. We assume that we would bear suffering better if we only knew the reason behind it. But would we?

I find striking similarities in two biblical books: Job and Lamentations. Job stared in disbelief at the ruins of his house and possessions; the author of Lamentations stared in disbelief at the ruins of his city, Jerusalem. Both books express anger and bitterness and deep disappointment with God. In fact, many passages from Lamentations sound like paraphrases of the much older Book of Job. Yet the prophet who wrote Lamentations (probably Jeremiah) was not in the dark. He knew exactly why Jerusalem had been destroyed: the Hebrews had broken their covenant with God. Nevertheless, knowing the cause did nothing to alleviate the suffering or the feelings of despair and abandonment. "The Lord is like an enemy," he pronounced, Job-like. "Why do you always forget us? Why do you forsake us so long?" he asked of God, though he knew full well the answers—other parts of the book spell them out in exhaustive detail.

What possible explanation could comfort a Job, a Jeremiah, or a Meg Woodson? Knowledge is passive, intellectual; suffering is active, personal. No intellectual answer will solve suffering. Perhaps this is why God sent his own Son as one response to human pain, to experience it and absorb it into himself. The Incarnation did not "solve" human suffering, but at least it was an active and personal response. In the truest sense, no words can speak more loudly than the Word.

If you look to the Book of Job for an answer to the "Why?" questions, you will come away disappointed. God declined to answer, Job withdrew his questions, and the three friends repented of all their mistaken assumptions. Jesus likewise avoided the issue of the direct cause of suffering. When his disciples drew certain conclusions about a man born blind (John 9) and about two local catastrophes (Luke 13), Jesus rebuked them. From the biblical evidence, I must conclude that any hard-and-fast answers to the "Why?" questions are, quite simply, out of reach.

Whenever we take on one of God's prerogatives, we tread on dangerous ground. Even a well-meaning attempt to comfort a child, "God took your Dad home because he liked him so much," crosses over into an area that the Bible seems to rule out of bounds. Though catastrophes—an airplane crash, a plague, a sniper's random killings, the deliberate poisoning of medicines, a famine in Africa—cry out for some authoritative interpretation, the Book of Job offers an important reminder: God himself did not attempt an explanation.

2. Perhaps God keeps us ignorant because we are incapable of comprehending the answer.

Maybe God's majestic non-answer to Job was no ploy, no clever way of dodging questions; maybe it was God's recognition of a plain fact of life. A tiny creature on a tiny planet in a remote galaxy simply could not fathom the grand design of the universe. You might as well try to describe colors to a person born blind, or a Mozart symphony to a person born deaf, or expound the theory of relativity to a person who doesn't even know about atoms.

To appreciate the problem, imagine yourself trying to communicate with a creature on a microscope slide. The "universe" to such a creature consists of only two dimensions, the flat plane of the glass slide; its senses cannot perceive anything beyond the edges. How could you convey a concept of space or height or depth to such a creature? Looking "from above," you can understand the creature's two-dimensional world as well as the three-dimensional world surrounding it. The creature, however, "from below," can only comprehend a world of two dimensions.* In a similar way, the unseen world exists outside our range of perception—except for rare interventions into our "plane," which we call miracles. Job, or you and I, cannot comprehend the total picture with our present faculties.

Filmmaker Woody Allen playfully explored this "two worlds" level of viewing in his movie *Purple Rose of Cairo*. We first see the hero through Mia Farrow's eyes as she watches him play a role in a movie. Then, incredibly, that hero steps out—literally—from the two-dimensional movie screen and lands in the New Jersey theater; suddenly he is in the "real" world with the flabbergasted character played by Miss Farrow.

The outside world holds many surprises for the movie actor. When someone hits him with a fist, he dutifully falls down, as he was taught to do on-screen, but rubs his jaw with amazement—those blows aren't supposed to hurt! When he and Mia kiss, he pauses, waiting for the fadeout. And when someone tries to explain the concept of God—"He's the one in control of everything. He's what the whole world is about"—the actor nods, "Oh, you mean Mr. Mayer, the owner of the movie company." His perceptions are confined to the world of the movie.

---

*Anthropologists report a very similar "perception gap" among remote cultures. If a rural Indian in Papua New Guinea is shown a photograph of a forest, he sees only marks and splotches of colors on a flat paper. He must, through experience, learn to "see" that the two-dimensional photograph actually contains three-dimensional images: birds, trees, waterfalls.

Eventually, the actor climbs back onto the two-dimensional movie screen and tries to explain the real world to the rest of the cast. They stare at him as if he belongs in a mental asylum. He's talking nonsense. There is no "other" world out there; only the world of the movie is real for them.

Woody Allen makes the same point as the analogy of the two-dimensional creature. If one world (the world of two-dimensions, or the world of the movie) exists inside another, it will only make sense from the "higher" world's point of view. And, to carry the analogy a long way, all the way back to the Book of Job, most of Job's questions concerned activity in the "higher" world, a world beyond his comprehension.

God lives on a "higher" level, in another dimension. The universe does not contain him; he created the universe. In a way we cannot fathom, he is not bound by space and time. He can step into the material world—if he did not, in fact, our senses would never perceive him—but it is for him a "stepping into," like an author who introduces himself as a character in his own play, like a person in the real world who makes a brief appearance in a movie.

A Matter of Time

There was a young lady named Bright
Whose speed was much greater than light
    So she set off one day
    In a relative way
And returned on the previous night.

The perception of time, especially, points up the huge difference between God's perspective (the view from above) and ours, and I have come to believe that this difference accounts for many of our unanswered questions on disappointment with God. For that reason, it merits what may seem like a diversion.

St. Augustine devoted Book 11 of *The Confessions* to a discussion of time. "What, then, is time?" he begins. "If no one asks me, I know; if I want to explain it to someone who does ask me, I do not know." When asked, "What was God doing *before* creation?" Augustine responded that since God invented time along with the created world, such a question is nonsense, and merely betrays the time-bound perspective of the questioner.* "Before" time there is only eternity, and eternity for God is a never-ending present. For God, one day is like a thousand years, and a thousand years are like a day.[2]

What would Augustine make of all that has happened since Einstein connected time and space? Now we understand time as relative, not as absolute. Perception of time, we are told, depends on the relative position of the observer. Take a recent example: on the night of February 23, 1987, an astronomer in Chile observed with his naked eye the explosion of a distant supernova, a blast so powerful that it released as much energy in one second as our sun will release in ten billion years. But did that event truly occur on February 23, 1987? Only from the perspective of our planet. Actually, the supernova exploded 170,000 years prior to our 1987, but the light generated by that faraway event, traveling almost 6 trillion miles a year, took 170,000 years to reach our galaxy.

And here is where the "higher" view of eternity defies our normal understanding of time. Imagine, if you will, a very large Being, larger than the entire universe—so large that the Being exists simultaneously on earth and in the space occupied by Supernova 1987A.

---

*Martin Luther was not nearly so polite. "When one asked, where God was before heaven was created? St. Augustine answered: He was in himself. When another asked me the same question, I said: He was building hell for such idle, presumptuous, fluttering and inquisitive spirits as you."

In 1987, *what time was it* for that Being? It depends on the perspective. From the perspective of earth, the Being would have "observed" 1987 history, which included the discovery of Supernova 1987A. But from the perspective of Supernova 1987A, the Being would have experienced what the earth will not know about for another 170,000 years! The Being thus observed both past (from earth, he saw the supernova explosion of 170,000 years before), present (the events of 1987 on earth), and future (what was happening on Supernova 1987A "now" that earthlings will not learn about for 170,000 years) simultaneously.

Such a Being, big as the universe, could, from some lookout post, see what is happening anywhere in the universe at any given time. For example, if he wants to know what is taking place on our sun right now, he can "watch" from the perspective of the sun. If he wants to see what took place on the sun eight minutes ago, he can "watch" from earth—that's what we see, after light has traveled the 93 million miles from the sun to earth.

The analogy is inexact, for it traps such a Being in space even as it frees him from time. But it may illustrate how our "first A happens, then B happens" conception of time expresses the very limited perspective of our planet. God, outside both time and space, can view what happens on earth in a way we can only guess at, and never fully comprehend.

Such notions are not mere flights of fancy. High school physics students learn about theoretical astronauts of the future who will travel into space faster than the speed of light and thus return even younger than when they left. Theories that seemed wildly speculative just a decade ago are being proved by modern researchers who bounce laser beams off the moon and send atomic clocks into space. Science is fulfilling fantasy: "It is a poor memory indeed that only works backwards!" said the White Queen to Alice in Wonderland.

God and Time

One more analogy: as a writer, I live in two different "time zones." First, there is the time zone of the real world that encompasses my daily ritual of waking, getting dressed, eating breakfast, and then moving to my office to plan out chapters, pages, and words. Meanwhile, the book itself is creating another, artificial world with its own self-contained time zone.

If I were writing a book of fiction, I might write these two sentences: "The phone rang. Immediately she got up from the couch and ran to answer it." Within the book, the time sequence goes like this: phone rings, immediate response. But outside the book, in the author's world, minutes, hours, even days may separate those two sentences. Perhaps I end one day's work with the sentence "The phone rang," and then go on vacation for two weeks. Regardless of when I return to the book, I am bound by the laws of its time zone. I could never write, "The phone rang. Two weeks later she got up and answered it." Mixing the two time zones would create an absurdity.

After I finish the book, in a way peculiar to me as its author, I carry around the entire book inside my mind. "From above," I can see the whole plot at once: beginning, middle, and end. No one else can do that—not unless they too experience it within time by plodding through it sentence by sentence.

I keep reaching for analogies because analogies are the only means we have to imagine human history as God sees it. We see history like a sequence of still frames, one after the other, as in a motion picture reel; but God sees the entire movie at once, in a flash. He sees it simultaneously from the viewpoint of a faraway star and from the viewpoint of my living room where I sit praying. He sees it in entirety, like a whole book, rather than sentence by sentence and page by page.

We can imagine such a perspective dimly, as if through a fog. But merely recognizing our incurable time-boundedness may help us understand why God did not answer Job's "Why?" Instead, God replied by reeling off a few fundamental facts of the universe that Job could barely comprehend, and warning, "Leave the rest to me." Perhaps God keeps us ignorant because neither Job, nor Einstein, nor you or I could possibly understand the view "from above."

We cannot understand what "rules" apply to a God who lives outside of time, as we perceive it, and yet sometimes steps into time. Consider all the confusion that surrounds the word "foreknowledge." Did God know in advance whether Job would stay faithful to him and thus win The Wager? If he did, how was it a real wager? Or what about natural disasters on earth? If God knows about them in advance, isn't he to blame? In our world, if a person knows in advance that a bomb will explode in a parked car and fails to warn authorities, he or she is legally responsible. Is God therefore "responsible" for everything that happens, even tragedies, because he knows about them in advance?

But—and this may be the main message underlying God's vigorous speech to Job—we cannot apply our simplistic rules to God. The very word *fore* knowledge betrays the problem, for it expresses the B-follows-A viewpoint of someone trapped inside time. Strictly speaking, God does not "foresee" us doing things. He simply *sees* us doing them, in an eternal present. And whenever we try to figure out God's role in any given event, we necessarily see things "from below," judging his behavior by the frail standards of a time-contingent morality. One day we may see such problems as "Did God cause that airplane to crash?" in a very different light.

505

The church's long arguments over *fore*knowledge and *predesti-nation* illustrate our awkward attempts to comprehend what, to us, only makes sense as it enters time. In another dimension, we will undoubtedly view such matters very differently. The Bible hints at the viewpoint "from above" in some of its most mysterious passages. It says that Christ "was chosen before the creation of the world," which means before Adam and before the Fall and thus before the need for redemption at all. It says grace and eternal life were "given us in Christ Jesus before the beginning of time." How could anything be said to occur "*before* the beginning of time"? Such wording suggests the viewpoint of a God who lives outside time. Before creating time, he made provision to redeem a fallen planet that did not yet even exist! But when he "stepped into" time (as I, an author, might write myself into my own book), God had to live, and die, by the rules of our world, trapped within time.*

The Eternal Present

There is a sense in which we humans also perceive time in something like a never-ending present. True, we experience it in sequence—

---

*This difference in perception may also help clarify one of the most confusing aspects of the Prophets. Often they did not bother telling whether the predicted events—invasions, earthquakes, a coming Leader, a re-created earth—would occur the next day, or a thousand years later, or three thousand years later. In fact, near and distant predictions often appear in the same paragraph, blurring together. Isaiah's famous prophecy, "Therefore the Lord himself will give you a sign: The virgin will be with child and will give birth to a son, and will call him Immanuel," fits this category. The next two verses make clear that the sign had a fulfillment in Isaiah's own day (many scholars assume the child to be Isaiah's own), and yet Matthew applies the prophecy's final fulfillment to the Virgin Mary. Biblical scholars have names for this common characteristic of the prophets: double or triple fulfillment, part-for-the-whole, creative bisociation.

For a God who encompasses all time, sequence is the least important issue. Should we be surprised, then, that incursions into time by a timeless Being would have overtones that resound in Isaiah's day, and Mary's, and also our own?

506

morning happens, then afternoon, then evening—but we do all our thinking in the present. If I think about the breakfast I ate earlier this morning, I think *in the present* about what happened in the past. If I contemplate dinner this evening, I think *in the present* about what will happen in the future. Because I only exist in the present, I can only perceive the past and the future from the perspective of the present.

That insight gives a slight glimpse into the eternal present from which God "sees" the world. And it may explain the Bible's consistent pattern for people who doubt God. To such people, trapped in the present, disappointed with God, the Bible offers two cures: remember the past and consider the future. In the Psalms, in the Prophets, in the Gospels and Epistles, the Bible constantly urges us to look back and remember the great things God has done. He is the God of Abraham, Isaac, and Jacob, the One who delivered the Hebrews from slavery in Egypt. He is the God who, out of love, sent his Son to die, and who then resurrected him from death. By focusing too myopically on what we want God to do on our behalf, we may miss the significance of what he has already done.

Likewise, the Bible points us toward the future. For disappointed people everywhere—the Jews held captive in Babylon, the Christians persecuted by Rome, or by Iran or South Africa or Albania—the prophets envision a future state of peace and justice and happiness; and they call us to live in light of the future they image up. Can we live now "as if" God is loving, gracious, merciful, and all-powerful, even while the blinders of time are obscuring our vision? The prophets proclaim that history will be determined not by the past or present, but by the future.

I have taken such a long diversion into the mysteries of time because I believe there is no other answer to the question of unfairness. No matter how we rationalize, God will sometimes *seem* unfair from the perspective of a person trapped in time. Only at the end of time, after we have attained God's level of viewing, after every evil has been punished or forgiven, every illness healed, and the entire universe restored—only then will fairness reign. Then we will understand what role is played by evil, and by the Fall, and by natural law, in an "unfair" event like the death of a child. Until then, we will not know, and can only trust in a God who does know.

We remain ignorant of many details, not because God enjoys keeping us in the dark, but because we have not the faculties to absorb so much light. At a single glance God knows what the world is about and how history will end. But we time-bound creatures have only the most primitive manner of understanding: we can let time pass. Not until history has run its course will we understand how "all things work together for good." Faith means believing in advance what will only make sense in reverse.

I have a friend who bristles at such a definition of faith: "You never blame God for the bad things and yet you give him credit for the good things!" In a curious sort of way, my friend is right. That, I believe, is also what faith sometimes requires: trusting God when there is no apparent evidence of him—as Job did. Trusting in his ultimate goodness, a goodness that exists outside of time, a goodness that time has not yet caught up with.

The Eternal may meet us in what is, by our present measurements, a day, or (more likely) a minute or a second; but we have touched what is not in any way commensurable with lengths of time, whether long or short. Hence our hope finally to emerge, if not altogether from time (that might not suit our humanity) at any rate from the tyranny, the unilinear poverty, of time, to ride it, not to be ridden by it, and so to cure that always aching wound which mere succession and mutability inflict on us, almost equally when we are happy and when we are unhappy. For we are so little reconciled to time that we are even astonished at it. "How he's grown!" we exclaim, "How time flies!" as though the universal form of our experience were again and again a novelty. It is as strange as if a fish were repeatedly surprised at the wetness of water. And that would be strange indeed; unless of course the fish were destined to become, one day, a land animal.

C. S. LEWIS, *REFLECTIONS ON THE PSALMS*

[1]Frederick Buechner, *Wishful Thinking,* 46.
[2]Saint Augustine, *The Confessions of Saint Augustine,* 286–287.

Bible references: Job 36–38; Lamentations 2, 5; 1 Peter 1; 2 Timothy 1; Isaiah 7:14; Romans 8.

Why is life given to a man
whose way is hidden,
whom God has hedged in?
For sighing comes to me instead of food;
my groans pour out like water.

JOB 3:23–24

———⊛⊛⊛———

CHAPTER 26

IS GOD SILENT?

Once a friend of mine went swimming in a large lake at dusk. As he was paddling at a leisurely pace about a hundred yards offshore, a freak evening fog rolled in across the water. Suddenly he could see nothing: no horizon, no landmarks, no objects or lights on shore. Because the fog diffused all light, he could not even make out the direction of the setting sun.

For thirty minutes he splashed around in panic. He would start off in one direction, lose confidence, and turn ninety degrees to the right. Or left—it made no difference which way he turned. He could feel his heart racing uncontrollably. He would stop and float, trying to conserve energy, and force himself to breathe slower. Then he would blindly strike out again. At last he heard a faint voice calling from shore. He pointed his body toward the sounds and followed them to safety.

Something like that sensation of utter lostness must have settled in on Job as he sat in the rubble and tried to comprehend what had happened. He too had lost all landmarks, all points of orientation. Where should he turn? God, the One who could guide him through the fog, stayed silent.

The whole point of The Wager was to keep Job in the dark. If God had delivered an inspiring pep talk—"Do this for me, Job, as a Knight of Faith, as a martyr"—then Job, ennobled, would have suffered gladly. But Satan had challenged whether Job's faith could survive with no outside help or explanation. When God accepted those terms, the fog rolled in around Job.

God ultimately "won" The Wager, of course. Though Job lashed out with a stream of bitter complaints, and though he despaired of life and longed for death, still he defiantly refused to give up on God: "Though he slay me, yet will I hope in him." Job believed when there was no reason to believe. He believed in the midst of the fog.

You could read Job's story, puzzle over The Wager, then breathe a deep sigh of relief: *Phew! God settled that problem. After proving his point so decisively, surely he will return to his preferred style of communicating clearly with his followers.* You could think so—unless, that is, you read the rest of the Bible. I hesitate to say this, because it is a hard truth and one I do not want to acknowledge, but Job stands as merely the most extreme example of what appears to be a universal law of faith. The kind of faith God values seems to develop best when everything fuzzes over, when God stays silent, when the fog rolls in.

Survivors of the Fog

A flash of light from a beacon on shore and then a long, dreadful time of silence and darkness—that is the pattern I find not only in the Book of Job, but throughout the Bible. Recall tottery old Abraham as he neared the century mark, holding feebly to the lustrous vision that he would father a great nation. For twenty-five years that vision had seemed a desert mirage until one son, just one, was born. And when God spoke again, he called Abraham to a test of faith every bit as severe as Job's. "Take your son, your only son, Isaac, whom you love," said God, in words that stabbed deep into Abraham's heart, "and sacrifice him as a burnt offering."

Then there was Joseph, who heard from God in his dreams but landed at the bottom of a well and later in an Egyptian dungeon for trying to follow that guidance. And Moses, handpicked liberator of the Hebrew people, who hid in a desert for forty years, hunted by a pharaoh's security guards. And the fugitive David, anointed king on God's command, who spent the next decade dodging spears and sleeping in caves.

The baffling, Morse-code pattern of divine guidance—a clear message followed by a long, silent gap—is spelled out bluntly in 2 Chronicles. There we read of a rare good king, Hezekiah, who so pleased God that he was granted an unprecedented fifteen-year extension to his life. What happened next? "*God left him* to test him and to know everything that was in his heart."

Most of these Old Testament characters show up in the honor roll of Hebrews 11, a chapter some have labeled "The Faith Hall of Fame." I prefer to call that chapter, "Survivors of the Fog," for many of the heroes listed have one common experience: a dread time of testing like Job's, a time when the fog descends and everything goes blank. Torture, jeers, floggings, chains, stonings, sawings in two—Hebrews records in grim detail the trials that may befall faith-full people.

Saints become saints by somehow hanging on to the stubborn conviction that things are not as they appear, and that the unseen world is as solid and trustworthy as the visible world around them. God deserves trust, even when it looks like the world is caving in. "The world was not worthy of them," Hebrews 11 concludes about its amazing assemblage, adding this intriguing comment: "Therefore God is not ashamed to be called their God." For me, that phrase puts a reverse spin on Dorothy Sayers's remark about the three great humiliations of God—the church, in particular, has borne God shame, but it has also brought him moments of pride, and the gaunt saints of Hebrews 11 demonstrate how.

God's favorites, *especially* God's favorites, are not immune from the bewildering times when God seems silent. As Paul Tournier said, "Where there is no longer any opportunity for doubt, there is no longer any opportunity for faith either." Faith demands uncertainty, confusion. The Bible includes many proofs of God's concern—some quite spectacular—but no guarantees. A guarantee would, after all, preclude faith.

Two Kinds of Faith

My friend Richard found the word "faith" a central obstacle to belief: "Just have faith," other Christians would counsel when he doubted. What did they mean? "Faith" seemed to him a method of avoiding questions, not of answering them.

Some of the difficulty comes, I think, from the elastic way in which we use the word. First, we use it to describe great, childlike gulps of faith, when a person swallows the impossible. David exercised this kind of extravagant faith when he strode out to meet Goliath, as did the Roman centurion whom Jesus commended (he was "astonished" by the man's unflinching confidence). In our day, "faith missionaries" write stirring accounts of miracles that may result from childlike trust. This is the "seed faith" that can feed a houseful of orphans or move a mountain, and the Bible contains many proddings toward such.

But Job, along with the saints in Hebrews 11, points to a different kind of faith, the kind I have circled around in this book on disappointment with God. Childlike trust may not survive when the miracle does not come, when the urgent prayer gets no answer, when a dense gray mist obscures any sign of God's concern. Such times call for something more, and I will use the musty word "fidelity" for that hang-on-at-any-cost faith.

I interviewed a young nurse whose disappointment with God stemmed directly from confusing these two kinds of faith. Reared in a Christian home, she seldom doubted God, even through her college years. On her wall hung a painting of Jesus with a child in his arms, illustrating the poem "Footprints." That plaque portrayed faith at its most childlike: simply trust God and you will not even feel the burden. As you look back on hard times, you'll see only one set of footprints in the sand, for Jesus has carried you through.

At the age of twenty-four, this nurse was assigned to work in a cancer ward. She told me, one by one, the case histories of people she had nursed there. Some of her patients had prayed with childlike faith, crying out to God for healing and comfort, for relief from pain. Yet they died cruel, ugly deaths. And each night this nurse would come home, weighed down by the scenes of unsolvable suffering, and face the footprints plaque with its bright, alluring promise.

To get the picture vividly, simply read two psalms back-to-back. Start with Psalm 23: "The Lord is my Shepherd, I shall not be in want . . . he guides me . . . I will fear no evil . . . goodness and love will follow me all the days of my life." Then turn back one page to Psalm 22. "My God, my God, why have you forsaken me? Why are you so far from saving me? . . . I cry out by day, but you do not answer . . . I can count all my bones; people stare and gloat over me."

Psalm 23 models childlike faith; Psalm 22 models fidelity, a deeper, more mysterious kind of faith. Life with God may include both. We may experience times of unusual closeness, when every prayer is answered in an obvious way and God seems intimate and caring. And we may also experience "fog times," when God stays silent, when nothing works according to formula and all the Bible's promises seem glaringly false. Fidelity involves learning to trust that, out beyond the perimeter of fog, God still reigns and has not abandoned us, no matter how it may appear.

Paradoxically, the most perplexing, Job-like times may help "fertilize" faith and nurture intimacy with God.* The deepest faith, what I have called fidelity, sprouts at a point of contradiction, like a blade of grass between stones. Human beings grow by striving, working, stretching; and in a sense, human nature needs problems more than solutions. Why are not all prayers answered magically and instantly? Why must every convert travel the same tedious path of spiritual discipline? Because persistent prayer, and fasting, and study, and meditation are designed primarily for our sakes, not for God's.

Kierkegaard said that Christians reminded him of schoolboys who want to look up the answers to their math problems in the back of the book rather than work them through. I confess to such schoolboy sentiments, and I doubt that I am alone. We yearn for shortcuts. But shortcuts usually lead away from growth, not toward it. Apply the principle directly to Job: what was the final result of the testing he went through? As Rabbi Abraham Heschel observed, "Faith like Job's cannot be shaken because it is the result of having been shaken."

In an essay on prayer, C. S. Lewis suggested that God treats new Christians with a special kind of tenderness, much as a parent dotes on a newborn.[1] He quotes an experienced Christian: "I have seen many striking answers to prayer and more than one that I thought miraculous. But they usually come at the beginning before conversion, or soon after it. As the Christian life proceeds, they tend to be

*American Christians who have visited churches in places like Ethiopia and China can attest to this fact.

rarer. The refusals, too, are not only more frequent; they become more unmistakable, more emphatic."[1]

At first glance, such a suggestion seems to have it all backward. Shouldn't faith become easier, not harder, as a Christian progresses? But, as Lewis points out, the New Testament gives two strong examples of unanswered prayers: Jesus pled three times for God to "Take this cup from me" and Paul begged God to cure the "thorn in my flesh."

Lewis asks, "Does God then forsake just those who serve Him best? Well, He who served Him best of all said, near His tortured death, 'Why hast thou forsaken me?' When God becomes man, that Man, of all others, is least comforted by God, at His greatest need. There is a mystery here which, even if I had the power, I might not have the courage to explore. Meanwhile, little people like you and me, if our prayers are sometimes granted, beyond all hope and probability, had better not draw hasty conclusions to our own advantage. If we were stronger, we might be less tenderly treated. If we were braver, we might be sent, with far less help, to defend far more desperate posts in the great battle."

The Unavoidable Question

C. S. Lewis's words sound impressive. Yet I cannot simply reduce the pattern of fidelity—faith toughened through testing—to a cheery formula. This book began with the story of Richard, who was secure and well-grounded until his faith was tested. And then he felt betrayed. Why would God submit him or, for that matter, *anyone* he loves, to such a test? Richard could no longer trust such a God. I have spoken with many others whose exuberant, childlike faith likewise foundered in the time of testing.

An unavoidable question lurks just under the surface of the Book of Job. If, for the sake of a "test" of love, a husband subjected his wife to the trauma that Job had to endure, we would call him pathological and lock him away. If a mother hid herself from her children, refusing to call out directions from the shore in the fog, we would judge her an unfit mother. How, then, can we understand such behavior, such a wager, by God himself?

I offer no neat formula, only two observations.

1. We have little comprehension of what our faith means to God. In some mysterious way, Job's terrible ordeal was "worth" it to God because it went to the core of the entire human experiment. More than Job's faith, the motive behind all creation was at stake. Ever since God took the "risk" of making room for free human beings, faith— true, unbribed, freely offered faith—has had an intrinsic value to God that we can barely imagine. There is no better way for us to express love to God than by exercising fidelity to him.

It is wrong to speak of God's need of love from his creation, but remember how God himself expressed his longing for that love: like a father starved for some response, *any* response, from his rebellious children; like a jilted lover who, against all reason, gives his faithless beloved one more chance. Those are the images God summoned up again and again throughout the time of the prophets. The deepest longings we feel on earth, as parents, as lovers, are mere flickers of the hungering desire God feels for us. It is a desire that cost him the Incarnation and the Crucifixion.

All human metaphors fail to contain these matters, but they fail from understatement, not exaggeration. As Jesus said, at the end of history (when the fog lifts for good) only one question will matter: "When the Son of Man comes, will he find faith on the earth?" And the apostle Paul, after sketching out the scheme of the world from creation up to Jesus, concluded, "God did this so that men would seek him and perhaps reach out for him and find him, though he is not far from each one of us." Sending his Son was the "cost" to God; a faithful response from someone like Job—or you or me—represents the "reward."

I admit, it is hard for any of us with our limited vision to perceive the "reward" gained by Job's trials. C. S. Lewis may have come close in his comment about God sending us to "far more desperate posts in the great battle." According to the Bible, human beings serve as the principal foot soldiers in the warfare between unseen forces of good and evil; and faith is our most powerful weapon. Perhaps God sends us to dangerous posts with the same mixture of pride, love, anguish, and remorse that any parent feels when sending a son or daughter off to war.

Was Job's trial "worth it" to God? Only God can answer that. I have had to conclude that divine sovereignty means at least this: only God can determine what is of value to God. "Blessed are those who have not seen and yet have believed," Jesus said in a mild rebuke to doubting Thomas. Job saw the darkest side of life, heard the deepest silence of God, and still believed.

2. God did not exempt himself from the same demands of faith. Job's trials cannot stand apart from their louder echo in the life of Jesus. He too was tempted. He too lost everything of value, including his friends and his health. As Hebrews says, he "offered up prayers and petitions with loud cries and tears to the one who could save him from death." Finally, he lost his life.

We can never fully plumb the mystery of what took place on the cross, but it does offer the consolation that God is unwilling to put his creatures through any test that he himself has not endured. I have spoken with many suffering people over the years, and I cannot emphasize too strongly how important this fact seems to them. From famous people like Joni Eareckson Tada, from unknowns in county hospitals, from inmates in hellish Third World prisons, I have heard something like this: "At least, because of Jesus, God understands how I feel."

I think again of Richard's comment, "All I can say is that Job paid one *hell* of a price just to make God feel good!" He was thinking of Job, sitting in the ashes, scratching his sores. But as Richard said those words I was thinking of Jesus, hanging on a cross, unable to reach his wounds. I had to agree—it was a hell of a price to pay. In one sense, God tied his own hands in the wager over Job; in the most literal sense, he let his hands be tied the night of the Crucifixion. (Jesus, speaking of his death: "Now my heart is troubled, and what shall I say? 'Father, save me from this hour'? No, it was for this very reason I came to this hour. Father, glorify your name!")

In my study of the Bible, I was struck by a radical shift in its authors' attitudes about suffering, a shift that traces directly back to the Cross. When New Testament writers speak of hard times, they express none of the indignation that characterized Job, the prophets, and many of the psalmists. They offer no real explanation for suffering, but keep pointing to two events—the death and resurrection of Jesus—as if they form some kind of pictographic answer.

The apostles' faith, as they freely confessed, rested entirely on what happened on Easter Sunday, when God transformed the greatest tragedy in all history, the execution of his Son, into a day we now celebrate as Good Friday. Those disciples, who gazed at the cross from the shadows, soon learned what they had failed to learn in three years with their leader: When God seems absent, he may be closest of all. When God seems dead, he may be coming back to life.

The three-day pattern—tragedy, darkness, triumph—became for New Testament writers a template that can be applied to all our times of testing. We can look back on Jesus, the proof of God's love, even though we may never get an answer to our "Why?" questions.

Good Friday demonstrates that God has not abandoned us to our pain. The evils and sufferings that afflict our lives are so real and so significant to God that he willed to share them and endure them himself. He too is "acquainted with grief." On that day, Jesus himself experienced the silence of God—it was Psalm 22, not Psalm 23, that he quoted from the cross.

And Easter Sunday shows that, in the end, suffering will not triumph. Therefore, "Consider it pure joy . . . whenever you face trials of many kinds," writes James; and "In this you greatly rejoice, though now for a little while you may have had to suffer grief in all kinds of trials," writes Peter; and "we also rejoice in our sufferings," writes Paul. The apostles go on to explain what good can result from such "redeemed suffering": maturity, wisdom, genuine faith, perseverance, character, and many rewards to come.

Why rejoice? Not for the masochistic thrill of the trial itself, but because what God did Easter Sunday on large scale he can do on small scale for each of us. The afflictions addressed by James, Peter, and Paul would likely have ignited a major crisis of faith in the Old Testament. But New Testament writers came to believe that, as Paul expressed it, "All things work together for good."

That well-known passage is often distorted. Some people interpret its meaning as "Only good things will happen to those who love God." Paul meant just the opposite, and in the very next paragraph he defines what "things" we might expect: trouble, hardship, persecution, famine, nakedness, danger, sword. Paul endured all those. Yet, he insists, "in all these things we are more than conquerors"; no amount of hardship can separate us from the love of God.

It's a matter of time, Paul says. Just wait: God's miracle of transforming a dark, silent Friday into Easter Sunday will someday be enlarged to cosmic scale.

Though thou with clouds of anger do disguise
Thy face; yet through that mask I know those eyes,
Which, though they turn away sometimes,
They never will despise.

JOHN DONNE, "A HYMN TO CHRIST"

Everything difficult indicates something more than our theory of life yet embraces.

GEORGE MACDONALD

---

[1] C. S. Lewis, *The World's Last Night,* 10.

Bible references: Job 13; Genesis 22; 2 Chronicles 32; Matthew 8; Mark 14; 2 Corinthians 12; Luke 18; Acts 17; John 20; Hebrews 5; John 12; Isaiah 53 (KJV); James 1; 1 Peter 1; Philippians 3; Romans 8.

But if I go to the east, he is not there;
if I go to the west, I do not find him.
When he is at work in the north, I do not see him;
when he turns to the south, I catch no
glimpse of him.

Job 23:8–9

CHAPTER 27

WHY GOD DOESN'T INTERVENE

———⚬⚬⚬———

I know what my friend Richard would think about the ideas in the last few chapters. In fact, I know what he does think, because I discussed them with him at length. Richard, you may remember, had written a book on Job, so I had no need to review the story with him. I concentrated instead on the ending, speculating aloud on why God declined to answer Job. I went over my thoughts about timelessness, and Job's inability to comprehend God's perspective, and the inherent value of faith to God.

Richard listened carefully, and when I had finished meandering through my ideas, he nodded approvingly. "That's good, Philip. You may well be right. I have no problem with what you say. But there's one big difference between Job's story and mine. For all his troubles, Job finally did receive a word from God. Supposedly, he heard an actual voice out of the whirlwind. But for me, God stayed silent. And I guess that's why Job chose to believe, and I chose not to."

As we talked further, it became clear that Richard simply could not accept the notion of two worlds. Living in a seen world of trees and buildings and cars and people, he could not believe in another, unseen world existing alongside it. "I want proof," he said. "How can I be certain that God even exists if he won't enter into my world?"

The conversation took me back to a time when I too was a skeptic. Richard, ironically, lost his faith at a Christian college, surrounded by believers who professed an intimate knowledge of God; and it was in a similar environment—a Bible college no less—that I found faith most difficult.

A Skeptic's View

I ran into the same stumbling block as Richard: actions regarded as "spiritual" by the believers on campus seemed utterly ordinary to me. If the unseen world really was making contact with the seen world, where were the scorch marks, the sure signs of a supernatural Presence?

Take the matter of prayer: the believers seemed to distort events to make everything look like an answer to prayer. If an uncle sent an extra fifty dollars to help with school bills, they would grin and shout and call a prayer meeting to thank God. They accepted these "answers to prayer" as final proof that God was out there listening to them. But I could always find another explanation. Perhaps the uncle had sent *all* his nephews fifty dollars that month, and the prayers were merely coincidental. After all, I had an uncle who occasionally sent me gifts, though I never prayed for them. And what of these students' many requests that went unanswered? Prayer, it seemed to me, involved nothing more than talking to the walls and an occasional self-fulfilling prophecy.

As an experiment, I began mimicking "spiritual" behavior on campus. I prayed devoutly in prayer meetings, gave phony testimonies about my conversion, and filled my vocabulary with pious jargon. And it worked, confirming my doubts. I the skeptic soon passed for a veritable saint, just by following the prescribed formula. Could Christian experience be genuine if most of it was reproducible by a skeptic?

I conducted this experiment as a result of my reading in the psychology of religion. Books like *The Varieties of Religious Experience*, by William James, had persuaded me that religion was just a complex psychological reaction to the stresses of life. James examined the claims that the sincere Christian is a new creature formed out of new fabric. But, concluded James, "Converted men as a class are indistinguishable from natural men; some natural men even excel some converted men in their fruits; and no one ignorant of doctrinal theology could guess by mere every-day inspection of the 'accidents' of the two groups of persons before him that their substance differed as much as divine differs from human substance."[1] I too could see no unusual radiance, no distinguishing mark in the believers around me.

For reasons I will explain later, I did not remain a skeptic. But in honesty I must admit that even now, after two decades of rich and rewarding faith, I am vulnerable to Richard's kind of doubt. Spiritual experience does not bear introspection easily; shine a spotlight on it, and it vaporizes. If I probe my times of communion with God, I can usually uncover another, more natural explanation for what has taken place. There is no blinding difference between the natural and supernatural worlds, no gulf fixed with barbed wire separating the two.

I do not stop being a "natural" person when I pray: I get sleepy, lose concentration, and suffer the same frustrations and miscommunications while conversing with God that I do with other people. When I write on "spiritual" topics, I am not suddenly lifted heavenward by the muses; I still must sharpen pencils, cross out words, consult the dictionary, wad up and throw away countless false starts. Instances of "knowing God's will" in my life have never been as straightforward as the examples I see in the life of a Moses or Gideon. I have never heard the booming Voice from the whirlwind. I could, if I wished, do what Richard does now: explain away spiritual behavior through some combination of psychological theories.

Why, then, do I believe in an unseen world? I have received great help in this struggle from the writings of C. S. Lewis. The theme of two worlds runs like a thread through most of his work—in the early writings, in letters to his friends, and in all his fiction, until it finally develops into a full-blown theory in an essay called "Transposition."[2] Lewis defined the problem as being "that of the obvious continuity between things which are admittedly natural and things which, it is claimed, are spiritual; the reappearance in what professes to be our supernatural life of all the same old elements which make up our natural life." Most of what follows in this chapter will simply expand on his ideas.

Looking Along the Beam

Lewis began his essay by referring to the curious phenomenon of *glossolalia* or speaking in tongues. How odd, he commented, that an undeniably "spiritual" event, the descent of the Holy Spirit at Pentecost, would express itself in the strange human phenomenon of speaking in another language. To the bystanders at Pentecost it resembled drunkenness; to many "scientific" observers today glossolalia resembles hysteria or a nervous disorder. How can such natural actions as the movement of vocal cords express the supernatural indwelling of the Holy Spirit of God?

Lewis suggested the analogy of a beam of light in a dark toolshed. When he first entered a shed, he saw a beam and looked *at* the luminous band of brightness filled with floating specks of dust. But when he moved over to the beam and looked *along* it, he gained a very different perspective. Suddenly he saw not the beam, but, framed in the window of the shed, green leaves moving on the branches of a tree outside and beyond that, 93 million miles away, the sun. Looking at the beam and looking along the beam are quite different.

Our century excels in techniques of looking *at* the beam, and "reductionism" is the word most commonly used to describe this process. We can "reduce" human behavior down to neurotransmitters and enzymes, reduce butterflies to molecules of DNA, and reduce sunsets to particle waves of light and energy. In its most extreme forms, reductionism sees religion as psychological projection, world history as evolutionary struggle, and thought itself as only the opening and shutting of billions of I/O computer gates in the brain.

This modern world, so skilled in looking at the beam from every angle, is a world hostile to "faith." Throughout most of history, all societies took for granted the existence of an unseen, supernatural world. How else could they explain such marvels as a sunrise, an eclipse, a thunderstorm? But now we can explain them, and much more. We can reduce most natural phenomena, and even most spiritual phenomena, to their component parts. As Lewis observed about glossolalia, even the most "supernatural" acts express themselves on this earth in "natural" ways.

From the theory of transposition, I draw these conclusions about living in such a world.

1. First, we must simply acknowledge the powerful force of reductionism. That force offers both a blessing and a curse. It blesses us with the ability to analyze earthquakes and thunderstorms and tornadoes and thus defend ourselves against them. By looking *at* the beam, we have learned to fly—all the way to the moon and back—

and to tour the world while staring at a box in our living rooms, and to bring the sounds of orchestras to our ears as we jog along country lanes. By looking at the beam of human behavior, we can recognize chemical components and thus, through drugs, rescue people from severe depression and schizophrenia.

But reductionism has also brought a curse. Looking at the beam rather than along it, we risk reducing life to nothing more than its constituent parts. We will never again view the sunrise or moonrise with the same sense of awe and near-worship that our "primitive" ancestors—or even the sixteenth-century poets—felt. And if we reduce behavior to *merely* hormones and chemistry, we lose all human mystery and free will and romance. The ideals of romantic love that have inspired artists and lovers through the centuries suddenly reduce to a matter of hormonal secretions.

Reductionism may exert undue influence over us unless we recognize it for what it is: a way of looking. It is not a True or False concept; it is a point of view that informs us about the parts of a thing, but not the whole.

Spiritual acts, for example, can be viewed from both a lower and higher level. One does not supplant the other; each merely sees the same behavior differently (just as looking *at* a beam of light differs from looking *along* it). From the "lower" perspective, prayer is a person talking to himself (and glossolalia the same, only gibberish). The "higher" perspective presumes that a spiritual reality is at work, with human prayer serving as a contact point between the seen and unseen worlds.

I can attend a Billy Graham rally as a curious spectator and, selecting one person in the vast audience, theorize on all the sociological and psychological factors that might entice this one woman to be receptive to Graham's message. Her marriage is falling apart; she's looking for stability; she remembers the strength of a pious grand-mother; the music takes her back to childhood church experiences. But those "natural" factors do not rule out the supernatural; to the contrary, they may be the means God chooses to prompt that person toward him. Perhaps the continuity between natural and supernatural is a continuity of design from the same Creator. That, at least, is the "higher" view of faith. The one level of viewing does not exclude the other; they are two ways of looking at the same event.

2. *Oddly, the lower viewpoint may even seem superior to the higher.* C. S. Lewis recalled that as a child he had first learned to appreciate orchestral music by listening to the single, undifferentiated sound produced by a primitive gramophone. He could hear the melody, but not much else. Later, when he went to live concerts, he was disillu-sioned. A multitude of sounds came from many instruments playing different notes! He longed for "the real thing," which to his untrained ear was the mongrel sound of the gramophone. To Lewis, at that moment, the substitute seemed superior to the reality.[3]

Similarly, a person raised on a steady diet of television might find real mountain hiking, complete with mosquitoes, shortness of breath, and annoying weather changes, inferior to the vicarious expe-rience afforded by a *National Geographic* special.

More to the point, the lower viewpoint may seem superior in moral issues as well. The ideal of romantic love has inspired our great-est sonnets and novels and operas. But reductionists like Hugh Hefner now argue quite articulately that sex is superior when freed from the constraints of love and relationship. (Certainly, *Playboy* has more visceral appeal than the works of Elizabeth Barrett Browning.) And secularists, dismissing religion as a crutch, extol the "braver" challenge of surviving in this world without an appeal to a higher Being.

3. *The reality of the higher world is carried by the faculties of the lower world.* The word "transposition" belongs to the vocabulary of music. A song can be transposed from one musical key into another. Or a symphony score written for 110 orchestral instruments can be transposed into a version for the piano. Naturally, something will get lost in the process: ten fingers striking piano keys cannot possibly reproduce all the aural nuances of an orchestra. Yet the transposer, limited to the range of sounds made by those keys, must somehow convey the essence of the symphony through them.

C. S. Lewis cited a diary entry from Samuel Pepys regarding a rapturous musical concert. Pepys said the sound of the wind instruments was so sweet that it ravished him "and, indeed, in a word, did wrap up my soul so that it made me really sick, just as I have formerly been when in love with my wife." Try to analyze the physiology of any emotional response, said Lewis. What happens in our bodies when we experience beauty, or pride, or love? To Pepys it felt at once ravishing, yet not unlike nausea. A kick in the stomach, a flutter, a muscular contraction—he experienced the very same bodily reactions that he might at a moment of illness![4]

Looked at from the lower viewing level, our physical responses to joy and fear are almost identical. In each case the adrenal gland secretes the same hormone, and neurons in the digestive system fire off the same chemicals; but the brain interprets one message as joy and one as fear. At its lower levels, the human body has a limited vocabulary, just as a transposer has a limited number of piano keys to express the sounds of a full orchestra.

And this is where reductionism reveals its greatest weakness: if you look only "at the beam," reducing human emotions to their most basic components (neurons and hormones), you might logically deduce that joy and fear are the same, when they are in fact near-opposites. The human body has no nerve cells specially assigned to convey a sensation of pleasure—nature is never so lavish. All our experiences of pleasure come from "borrowed" nerve cells that also carry sensations of pain and touch and heat and cold.

A Way of Life

The human brain offers a nearly perfect model of transposition. Although the brain represents the "higher" point of view within the body, there is no more isolated or helpless organ. It sits in a box of thick bone, utterly dependent on lower faculties for information about the world. The brain has never seen anything, or tasted anything, or felt anything. All messages to it arrive in the same coded form, our many sensory experiences reduced down to an electrical sequence of dots and dashes (−.−−..−...−−). The brain relies totally on these Morse code messages from the extremities, which it then assembles into meaning.

As I write, I am listening to Beethoven's magnificent Ninth Symphony. What is that symphony but a series of codes transposed across time and technology. It began as a musical idea which Beethoven "heard" in his mind (an extraordinary mental feat, for the composer, by then totally deaf, had only memory to guide him and could not test his idea on musical instruments). Beethoven then transposed the symphony onto paper, using a series of codes known as musical notation.

More than a century later, an orchestra read those codes, interpreted them, and reassembled them into a glorious sound approximating what Beethoven must have "heard" in his mind. Recording engineers captured that orchestra's sound as a series of magnetic impulses on a streaming tape, and a studio transposed that code into a more mechanical form, eventuating in the tiny ripples on my record album.

My turntable is now "reading" those ripples and amplifying the variations through loudspeakers. Molecular vibrations caused by those speakers reach my ears, setting into motion another series of mechanical acts: tiny bones beat against my eardrums, transferring the vibrations through a viscous fluid on into the Organ of Corti, where 25,000 sound receptor cells lie in wait. Once stimulated, the appropriate cells fire off their electrical message. Finally, those impulses, mere dots and dashes of code, reach my brain, where the cortical screen assembles them into a sound I recognize as Beethoven's Ninth Symphony. I experience pleasure, even joy, as I pause and listen to that great work of music—the joy being once again carried to me by "lower" faculties of my body.

Transposition is a way of life. All knowledge comes to us through a process of translating downward into code and then upward into meaning. I have just written three paragraphs on Beethoven's Ninth Symphony. These were thoughts originating in my mind that I then transposed into words and typed into a computer, which recorded them in code on a magnetic disk. Eventually, my computer will transpose that magnetic code into a binary code, and a device called a modem will transpose the binary code into digital sounds that it will send over telephone wires to a publisher. If I listen in as my modem transmits the three paragraphs on Beethoven, I will hear nothing but a cloud of static, yet that static will somehow contain my thoughts and words.

The publisher's computer, receiving the digital sounds, will translate them back into magnetic codes stored on a disk. The publisher will retranslate those codes into words visible on a screen, edit them, and then transpose the words into patterned ink marks on paper—the very ink marks you are reading right now. To your trained eye, these blobs of ink on a page form letters and words that are conveyed to your eye cells and transposed into electrical impulses that your brain is assembling into some kind of meaning.

All communication, all knowledge, all sensory experience—all of life on this planet—relies on the process of transposition: meaning travels "downward" into codes which can later be reassembled. We instinctively trust that process, believing that the lower codes really do carry something of the original meaning. I trust that the words I choose, and even the staticky transmissions of my modem, will carry my original thoughts about Beethoven's Ninth Symphony. I look at a photograph, an image of the Rocky Mountains transposed on a small, flat, glossy sheet, and mentally relive a visit there. I scratch a magazine ad to smell a perfume sample, and the image of my wife, who wears that perfume, suddenly comes to mind. The lower carries something of the higher.

Transposition of the Spirit

Should it surprise us, then, to find the same universal principle operating in the realm of the spirit?

Think back to Richard's questions posed early in this book and restated at the beginning of this chapter. Why doesn't God intervene and make himself obvious? Why doesn't he speak aloud so we can hear him? We yearn for miracle, for the supernatural in its pure, unadulterated form.

I chose the word "unadulterated" deliberately because it betrays a sentiment that is central to this issue. We moderns strive to separate natural from supernatural. The natural world that we can touch and smell and see and hear seems self-evident; the supernatural world, however, is another matter. There is nothing certain about it, no skin on it, and that bothers us. We want proof. We want the supernatural to enter the natural world in a way that retains the glow, that leaves scorch marks, that rattles the ear drums.

The God revealed in the Bible does not seem to share our desire. Whereas we cleave natural from supernatural, and seen from unseen, God seeks to bring the two together. His goal, one might say, is to rescue the "lower" world, to restore the natural realm of fallen creation to its original state, where spirit and matter dwelt together in harmony.

When we become Christians and thus establish contact with the unseen world, we are not mysteriously transported upward; we do not suddenly put on space-suit bodies that remove us from the natural world (ever since the Gnostics and Manichaeans, the church has consistently judged such notions heretical). Rather, our physical bodies reconnect with spiritual reality and we begin to listen to the code through which the unseen world transposes itself into this one. One might say our task is the very opposite of reductionism. We look for ways to re-enchant or "hallow" the world: to see in nature an engine of praise, to see in bread and wine a sacrament of grace, to see in human love a shadow of ideal Love.

Granted, we have a limited vocabulary for this higher realm. We speak to God as we would speak to another person; could anything be more commonplace, more "natural"? Praying, proclaiming the gospel, meditating, fasting, offering a cup of cold water, visiting prisoners, observing the sacraments—these everyday acts, we are told, carry the "higher" meaning. They somehow express the unseen world.

Looked at from the lower, reductionist perspective, all spiritual acts have natural "explanations." Prayer is mumbling in the void; a sinner repenting, contrived emotionalism; the Day of Pentecost, an outbreak of drunkenness. A skeptic might say that the natural faculties are an impoverished lot if that's all we have to express the exalted world beyond.

But faith, looking *along* the beam, sees such natural acts as hallowed carriers of the supernatural. From that perspective, the natural world is not impoverished, but graced with miracle. And the miracle of a natural world reclaimed reached a point of climax in the Grand Miracle, when the actual Presence of God took up residence in a "natural" body exactly like ours: the Word transposed into flesh.

In one body, Christ brought the two worlds together, joining spirit and matter at long last, unifying creation in a way that had not been seen since Eden. The theologian Jürgen Moltmann puts it this way, in a sentence that merits much reflection: "Embodiment is the end of all God's works."[5] And this is how the apostle Paul puts it: "And he is the head of the body, the church. . . . For God was pleased to have all his fullness dwell in him, and through him to reconcile to himself all things, whether things on earth or things in heaven, by making peace through his blood, shed on the cross."

When that Word-become-flesh ascended, he left behind his actual Presence in the form of his body, the church. Our goodness becomes, literally, God's goodness ("Whatever you did for one of the least of these brothers of mine, you did for me"). Our suffering becomes, in Paul's words, "the fellowship of sharing in his sufferings." Our actions become his actions ("He who receives you receives me"). What happens to us, happens to him ("Saul, Saul, why do you persecute me?"). The two worlds, seen and unseen, merge in Christ; and we, as Paul kept insisting, are quite literally "in Christ." Embodiment is the end of all God's work, the goal of all creation.

From below, we tend to think of miracle as an invasion, a breaking into the natural world with spectacular force, and we long for such signs. But from above, from God's point of view, the real miracle is one of transposition: that human bodies can become vessels filled with Spirit, that ordinary human acts of charity and goodness can become nothing less than the incarnations of God on earth.

To complete the analogy, I need search no further than the words of Paul, for the image he gives to describe Christ's role in the world today is the same image I have used to illustrate transposition. Jesus Christ, said Paul, now serves as the head of the body. We know how a human head accomplishes its will: by translating orders downward in a code that the hands and eyes and mouth can understand. A healthy body is one that follows the will of the head. In that same way, the risen Christ accomplishes his will through us, members of his body.

Is God silent? I answer that question with another question: Is the church silent? We are his mouthpiece, his designated vocal chords on this planet. A plan of such awesome transposition guarantees that God's message will sometimes seem garbled or incoherent; it guarantees that God will sometimes seem silent. But embodiment was his goal, and in that light the Day of Pentecost becomes a perfect metaphor: God's voice on earth, speaking through human beings in a manner even they could not comprehend.

The Hope

I have a bright, talented, and very funny friend in Seattle named Carolyn Martin. But Carolyn has cerebral palsy, and it is the peculiar tragedy of her condition that its outward signs—drooling, floppy arm movements, inarticulate speech, a bobbing head—cause people who meet her to wonder if she is retarded. Actually, her mind is the one part of her that works perfectly; it is muscular control that she lacks.

Carolyn lived for fifteen years in a home for the mentally retarded, because the state had no other place for her. Her closest friends were people like Larry, who tore all his clothes off and ate the institution's houseplants, and Arelene, who only knew three sentences and called everyone "Mama." Carolyn determined to escape from that home and to find a meaningful place for herself in the outside world.

Eventually, she did manage to move out and establish a home of her own. There, the simplest chores posed an overwhelming challenge. It took her three months to learn to brew a pot of tea and pour it into cups without scalding herself. But Carolyn mastered that feat and many others. She enrolled in high school, graduated, then signed up for community college.

Everyone on campus knew Carolyn as "the disabled person." They would see her sitting in a wheelchair, hunched over, painstakingly typing out notes on a device called a Canon Communicator. Few felt comfortable talking with her; they could not follow her jumbled sounds. But Carolyn persevered, stretching out a two-year Associate of Arts degree program over seven years. Next, she enrolled in a Lutheran college to study the Bible. After two years there, she was asked to speak to her fellow students in chapel.

Carolyn worked many hours on her address. She typed out the final draft—at her average speed of forty-five minutes a page—and asked her friend Josee to read it for her. Josee had a strong, clear voice.

On the day of the chapel service, Carolyn sat slumped in her wheelchair on the left side of the platform. At times her arms jerked uncontrollably, her head lolled to one side so that it almost touched her shoulder, and a stream of saliva sometimes ran down her blouse. Beside her stood Josee, who read the mature and graceful prose Carolyn had composed, centered around this Bible text: "But we have this treasure in jars of clay to show that this all-surpassing power is from God but not from us."

For the first time, some students saw Carolyn as a complete human being, like themselves. Before then her mind, a very good mind, had always been inhibited by a "disobedient" body, and difficulties with speech had masked her intelligence. But hearing her address read aloud as they looked at her onstage, the students could see past the body in a wheelchair and imagine a whole person.

Carolyn told me about that day in her halting speech, and I could only understand about half the words. But the scene she described became for me a parable of transposition: a perfect mind locked inside a spastic, uncontrolled body, and vocal cords that fail at every second syllable. The New Testament image of Christ as head of the body took on new meaning as I gained a sense of both the humiliation that Christ undergoes in his role as head, and also the exaltation that he allows us, the members of his body.

We, the church, are an example of transposition taken to extreme. Sadly, we do not give off indisputable proof of God's love and glory. Sometimes, like Carolyn's body, we obscure rather than convey the message. But the church is the reason behind the entire human experiment, the reason there are human beings in the first place: to let creatures other than God bear the image of God. He deemed it well worth the risk, and the humiliation.

He who descended is the very one who ascended higher than all the heavens, in order to fill the whole universe. It was he who gave some to be apostles, some to be prophets, some to be evangelists, and some to be pastors and teachers, to prepare God's people for works of service, so that the body of Christ may be built up until we all reach unity in the faith and in the knowledge of the Son of God and become mature, attaining to the whole measure of the fullness of Christ.

Then we will no longer be infants. . . . Instead . . . we will in all things grow up into him who is the Head, that is, Christ. From him the whole body, joined and held together by every supporting ligament, grows and builds itself up in love, as each part does its work.

---

[1] William James, *The Varieties of Religious Experience,* 233.
[2] C. S. Lewis, *The Weight of Glory,* 18, 19.
[3] C. S. Lewis, *God in the Dock,* 212.
[4] C. S. Lewis, *Christian Reflections* 37.
[5] Jürgen Moltmann, *God in Creation,* 244.

Bible references: Colossians 1; Matthew 25; Philippians 3; Matthew 10; Acts 9; 2 Corinthians 4; Ephesians 4.

Why do you hide your face
and consider me your enemy?
Will you torment a windblown leaf?
Will you chase after dry chaff?

JOB 13:24–25

CHAPTER 28

IS GOD HIDDEN?

————∞∞————

To get the full emotional impact of Job's plight, I winnowed the book's speeches for Job's own words. I expected to find him complaining about his miserable health and lamenting the loss of his children and fortune; but to my surprise Job had relatively little to say about those matters. He focused instead on the single theme of God's absence. What hurt Job most was the sense of crying out in desperation and getting no response. I had heard that same feeling described by many suffering people, perhaps best by C. S. Lewis, who wrote these words in the midst of deep grief after his wife's death from cancer:

> Meanwhile, where is God? This is one of the most disquieting symptoms. When you are happy, so happy that you have no sense of needing Him . . . you will be—or so it feels—welcomed with open arms. But go to Him when your need is desperate, when all other help is vain, and what do you find? A door slammed in your face, and a sound of bolting and double bolting on the inside. After that, silence. You may as well turn away. The longer you wait, the more emphatic the silence will become.[1]

Above all else, Job demanded a chance to plead his case before God. His friends' pieties he shook off like a dog shaking off fleas. He wanted the real thing, a personal appointment with God Almighty. Despite what had happened, Job could not bring himself to believe in a God of cruelty and injustice. Perhaps if they met together, at least he could hear God's side of things. But God was nowhere to be found. Job heard only the whining cant of his friends and then a dreadful, vacuous sound. The door slammed in his face.

A Fact of Faith

Oh sweet Lord,
I really want to see you,
I really want to be with you. . . .
GEORGE HARRISON SONG

I know God is alive: I talked with him this morning!
BUMPER STICKER

God loves you and has a wonderful plan for your life.
EVANGELISM BOOKLET

And he walks with me and he talks with me, and he tells me I am his own.
CHRISTIAN HYMN

Human longing for the actual presence of God may crop up almost anywhere. But we dare not make sweeping claims about the promise of God's intimate presence unless we take into account those times when God seems absent. C. S. Lewis encountered it, Job encountered it, Richard encountered it: at some point nearly everyone must face the fact of God's hiddenness.

The cloud of unknowing can descend without warning, sometimes at the very moment we most urgently desire a sense of God's presence. A South African minister, the Reverend Allan Boesak, was thrown in jail for speaking against the government. He spent three weeks in solitary confinement, almost constantly on his knees, praying for God to set him free. "I do not mind telling you," he later related to his congregation, "that this was the most difficult moment of my life. As I knelt there, the words couldn't come anymore and there were no more tears to cry."[2] His experience was one common to blacks in South Africa: they pray, they weep, they wait, and still they provoke no answer from God.

Some would argue that God does not hide. One religious bumper sticker reads, "If you feel far from God, guess who moved?" But the guilt implicit in the slogan may be false guilt: the Book of Job details a time when, apparently, it was God who moved. Even though Job had done nothing wrong and pled desperately for help, God still chose to stay hidden. (If you ever doubt that an encounter with God's hiddenness is a normal part of the pilgrimage of faith, simply browse in a theological library among the works of the Christian mystics, men and women who have spent their lives in personal communion with God. Search for one, just one, who does not describe a time of severe testing, "the dark night of the soul.")

For those who suffer, and those who stand beside them, Job offers up an important lesson. The doubts and complaints of Meg Woodson and of Allan Boesak, and of Job, are valid responses, not symptoms of weak faith—so valid, in fact, that God made sure the Bible included them all. One does not expect to find the arguments of God's adversaries—say, Mark Twain's *Letters from the Earth* or Bertrand Russell's *Why I Am Not a Christian*—bound into the Bible, but nearly all of them make an appearance, if not in Job, then in the Psalms or Prophets. The Bible seems to anticipate our disappointments, as if God grants us in advance the weapons to use against him, as if God himself understands the cost of sustaining faith.

And, because of Jesus, perhaps he does understand. At Gethsemane and Calvary in some inexpressible way God himself was forced to confront the hiddenness of God. "God striving with God" is how Martin Luther summarized the cosmic struggle played out on two crossbeams of wood. On that dark night, God learned for himself the full extent of what it means to feel God-forsaken.

Job's friends insisted that God was not hidden. They brought up reminders—dreams, visions, past blessings, the splendors of nature—of how God had proved himself to Job in the past. "Don't forget in the darkness what you learned in the light," they chided. And those of us who live after Job have even more light: the record of fulfilled prophecy, and the life of Jesus. But sometimes all insights or "proofs" will fail. Mere memory, no matter how pleasant, will not deaden pain or loneliness. Perhaps, for a time, all verses of Scripture and all inspirational slogans will likewise fail.

Three Responses

I know too well my own instinctive response to the hiddenness of God: I retaliate by ignoring him. Like a child who thinks he can hide from adults by holding a chubby hand over his eyes, I try to shut God out of my life. If he won't reveal himself to me, why should I acknowledge him?

The Book of Job gives two other responses to such disappointment with God. The first was shown by Job's friends, who were scandalized by his assaults on the most basic tenets of their faith. Job's profound disappointment with God did not match their theology. They saw a clear-cut choice between a man who claimed to be just and a God they knew to be just. The very idea of Job demanding an audience with God! Suppress your feelings, they told him. We know for a fact that God is not unjust. So stop thinking that! Shame on you for the outrageous things you're saying!

The second response, Job's, was a rambling mess, a jarring counterpoint to his friend's relentless logic. "Why then did you bring me out of the womb?" he demanded of God. "I wish I had died before any eye ever saw me." Job lashed out in a protest he knew to be futile, like a bird repeatedly hurling itself against a windowpane. He had few sound arguments, and even admitted that his friends' logic sounded right. He wavered, contradicted himself, backtracked, and sometimes collapsed in despair. This man renowned for his righteousness railed against God: "Turn away from me so I can have a moment's joy before I go to the place of no return, to the land of gloom and deep shadow."

And which of the two responses does the book endorse? Both parties needed some correction, but after all the windy words had been uttered, God ordered the pious friends to crawl repentantly to Job and ask him to pray on their behalf.

One bold message in the Book of Job is that you can say anything to God. Throw at him your grief, your anger, your doubt, your bitterness, your betrayal, your disappointment—he can absorb them all. As often as not, spiritual giants of the Bible are shown *contending* with God. They prefer to go away limping, like Jacob, rather than to shut God out. In this respect, the Bible prefigures a tenet of modern psychology: you can't really deny your feelings or make them disappear, so you might as well express them. God can deal with every human response save one. He cannot abide the response I fall back on instinctively: an attempt to ignore him or treat him as though he does not exist. That response never once occurred to Job.

The Big Picture

Freedom to express feelings is not the only lesson from Job, however. The "behind the curtain" view of proceedings in the unseen world shows that an encounter with the hiddenness of God may badly mislead. It may tempt us to see God as the enemy and to interpret his hiddenness as a lack of concern.

Job concluded just that: "God assails me and tears me in his anger." Those of us in the audience know that Job was mistaken. For one thing, the prologue makes the subtle but important distinction that God did not personally cause Job's problems. He permitted them, yes, but the account of The Wager presents Satan, not God, as the instigator of Job's suffering. In any event, God was surely not Job's enemy. Far from being abandoned by God, Job was getting direct, almost microscopic scrutiny from him. At the very moment Job was pleading for a courtroom trial to present his case, he was actually participating in a trial of cosmic significance—not as the prosecuting attorney jabbing his finger at God, but as the main witness in a test of faith.

By no means can we infer that our own trials are, like Job's, specially arranged by God to settle some decisive issue in the universe. But we can safely assume that our limited range of vision will in similar fashion distort reality. Pain narrows vision. The most private of sensations, it forces us to think of ourselves and little else.

From Job, we can learn that much more is going on out there than we may suspect. Job felt the weight of God's absence; but a look behind the curtain reveals that in one sense God had never been more present. In the natural world, human beings only receive about 30 percent of the light spectrum. (Honeybees and homing pigeons can, for example, detect ultraviolet light waves invisible to us.) In the supernatural realm, our vision is even more limited, and we get only occasional glimpses of that unseen world.

An incident in the life of another famous Bible character makes this same point in a very different way. The prophet Daniel had a mild—mild in comparison with Job's—encounter with the hiddenness of God. Daniel puzzled over an everyday problem of unanswered prayer: why was God ignoring his repeated requests? For twenty-one days Daniel devoted himself to prayer. He mourned. He gave up choice foods. He swore off meat and wine, and used no lotions on his body. All the while he called out to God, but received no answer.

Then one day Daniel got far more than he bargained for. A supernatural being, with eyes like flaming torches and a face like lightning, suddenly showed up on a riverbank beside him. Daniel's companions all fled in terror. As for Daniel, "I had no strength left. My face turned deathly pale and I was helpless." When he tried talking to the dazzling being, he could hardly breathe.

The visitor proceeded to explain the reason for the long delay. He had been dispatched to answer Daniel's very first prayer, but had run into strong resistance from "the prince of the Persian kingdom." Finally, after a three-week standoff, reinforcements arrived and Michael, one of the chief angels, helped him break through the opposition.

I will not attempt to interpret this amazing scene of the universe at war, except to point out a parallel to Job. Like Job, Daniel played a decisive role in the warfare between cosmic forces of good and evil, though much of the action took place beyond his range of vision. To him, prayer may have seemed futile, and God indifferent; but a glimpse "behind the curtain" reveals exactly the opposite. Daniel's limited perspective, like Job's, distorted reality.

What are we to make of Daniel's angelic being who needed reinforcements, not to mention the cosmic wager in Job? Simply this: the big picture, with the whole universe as a backdrop, includes much activity that we never see. When we stubbornly cling to God in a time of hardship, or when we simply pray, more—much more—may be involved than we ever dream. It requires faith to believe that, and faith to trust that we are never abandoned, no matter how distant God seems.

At the end, when he heard the Voice from the whirlwind, Job finally attained that faith. God reeled off natural phenomena—the solar system, constellations, thunderstorms, wild animals—that Job could not begin to explain. *If you can't comprehend the visible world you live in, how dare you expect to comprehend a world you cannot even see!* Conscious of the big picture at last, Job repented in dust and ashes.

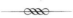

God is like a person who clears his throat while hiding and so gives himself away.

MEISTER ECKHARDT

[1]C.S. Lewis, *A Grief Observed*, 9.

[2]Allan Boesak, "If You Believe," *Reformed Journal*, (November 1985), 11.

Bible references: Job 10, 16; Daniel 10.

I know that my Redeemer lives,
and that in the end he will stand upon the earth.
And after my skin has been destroyed,
yet in my flesh I will see God;
I myself will see him
with my own eyes—I, and not another.
How my heart yearns within me!

JOB 19:25–27

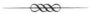

CHAPTER 29

WHY JOB DIED HAPPY

A fter its account of tragedy and woe, of breast-beating and fierce debate, of a cosmic wager lost and won—after all that, the story of Job ends almost cozily, with Job entertaining his great-great-great-grandchildren in perfect serenity. The book gives a meticulous accounting of Job's restored fortunes: 14,000 sheep, 6000 camels, 1000 donkeys, and 10 new children.

That halcyon ending frustrates some readers, such as Elie Wiesel (Nobel Prize-winning author).[1] For him, Job had been a hero, a champion of dissent against God's injustices. Yet, says Wiesel, Job caved in. He shouldn't have let God off the hook. No amount of new prosperity could make up for the suffering Job had undergone. What of the ten children who died? No parent could believe for a moment that a bustling new brood of children would erase the sorrow of the ones Job lost.

But let Job speak for himself. This is what he said after God's majestic speech from the whirlwind:

> Surely I spoke of things I did not understand,
>   things too wonderful for me to know. . . .

My ears had heard of you
  but now my eyes have seen you.
Therefore I despise myself
  and repent in dust and ashes.

Evidently, what I have called God's "non-answer" satisfied Job completely.

On the other hand, some readers point to the happy ending as the final answer to disappointment with God. See, they say, God delivers his people from adversity. He restored Job's health and riches, and he will do the same for all of us if we learn to trust him as Job did. These readers, however, overlook one important detail: Job spoke his contrite words before any of his losses had been restored. He was still sitting in a pile of rubble, naked, covered with sores, and it was in *those* circumstances that he learned to praise God. Only one thing had changed: God had given Job a glimpse of the big picture.

I have a hunch that God could have said anything—could, in fact, have read from the Yellow Pages—and produced the same stunning effect on Job. What he said was not nearly so important as the mere fact of his appearance. God spectacularly answered Job's biggest question: Is anybody out there? Once Job caught sight of the unseen world, all his urgent questions faded away.

From God's viewpoint, Job's comfort was—however harsh it may sound—insignificant *in comparison with* the cosmic issues at stake. The real battle ended when Job refused to give up on God, thus causing Satan to lose The Wager. After that tough victory, God hastened to shower good gifts on Job. *Pain? I can fix that easily. More children? Camels and oxen? No problem. Of course I want you happy and wealthy and full of life! But, Job, you must understand that something far more important than happiness was at stake here.*

Of Two Worlds

My friend Richard, who still looks to Job as the most honest part of the Bible, has yet another response to its conclusion. He finds it almost irrelevant. "Job got a personal appearance by God, and I'm happy for him. That's what I've been asking for all these years. But since God hasn't visited me, how does Job help with my struggles?"

I believe that Richard has put his finger on an important dividing line of faith. In a sense, our days on earth resemble Job's *before* God came to him in a whirlwind. We too live among clues and rumors, some of which argue against a powerful, loving God. We too must exercise faith, with no certainty.

Richard lay prone on the wooden floor of his apartment, pleading for God to "reveal" himself, gambling all his faith on God's willingness to step into the seen world as he had done for Job. And Richard lost that gamble. Frankly, I doubt whether God feels any "obligation" to prove himself in such a manner. He did so many times in the Old Testament, and with finality in the person of Jesus. What further incarnations do we require of him?

I say this with great care, but I wonder if a fierce, insistent desire for miracle—even a physical healing—sometimes betrays a *lack* of faith rather than an abundance of it. Such prayers may, like Richard's, set conditions for God. When yearning for a miraculous resolution to a problem, do we make our loyalty to God contingent on whether he reveals himself yet again in the seen world?*

If we insist on visible proofs from God, we may well prepare the way for a permanent state of disappointment. True faith does not so much attempt to manipulate God to do our will as it does to position us to do his will. As I searched through the Bible for models of great faith, I was struck by how few saints experienced anything like

---

*In his mercy, God may answer a prayer of mixed motives—witness all the "Lord, if you only get me out of here..." foxhole conversions. But that is for him to decide, not us.

Job's dramatic encounter with God. The rest responded to God's hiddenness not by demanding that he show himself, but by going ahead and believing him though he stayed hidden. Hebrews 11 pointedly notes that the giants of faith "did not receive the things promised; they only saw them and welcomed them from a distance."

We human beings instinctively regard the seen world as the "real" world and the unseen world as the "unreal" world, but the Bible calls for almost the opposite. Through faith, the unseen world increasingly takes shape as the real world and sets the course for how we live in the seen world. Live for God, who is invisible, and not for other people, said Jesus in his words about the unseen world, or "the kingdom of heaven."

Once the apostle Paul directly addressed the question of disappointment with God. He told the Corinthians that, in spite of incredible hardships, he did not "lose heart": "Though outwardly we are wasting away, yet inwardly we are being renewed day by day. For our light and momentary [!] troubles are achieving for us an eternal glory that far outweighs them all. So we fix our eyes not on what is seen, but on what is unseen. For what is seen is temporary, but what is unseen is eternal."

A Taste of the Future

Paul endured trials and died a martyr, still anticipating his reward. Job endured trials, but received a fine reward in this life. So what, exactly, can we expect from God? Perhaps the best way to view the ending in Job is to see it not as a blueprint for what will happen to us in this life, but rather as a *sign* of what is to come. It stands as a sweet, satisfying symbol, a solution to one man's disappointment that offers us all a foretaste of the future.

In one respect, Elie Wiesel is right: the pleasures of Job's old age did not make up for the losses that had gone before. Even Job, happy and full of days, died, passing on the cycle of grief and pain to his survivors. The worst mistake of all would be to conclude that God is somehow content to make a few minor adjustments to this tragic, unfair world.

Some people stake all their faith on a miracle, as if a miracle would eliminate all disappointment with God. It wouldn't. If I had filled this book with case studies of physical healings, rather than the stories of Richard and Meg Woodson and Douglas and Job, that would not solve the problem of disappointment with God. Something is still badly wrong with this planet. For one thing, all of us die; the ultimate mortality rate is the same for atheists and saints alike.

Miracles serve as signs pointing on to the future. They are appetizers that awaken a longing for something more, something permanent. And the happiness of Job's old age was a mere sampling of what he would enjoy after death. The good news at the end of Job and the good news of Easter at the end of the Gospels are previews of the good news described at the end of Revelation. We dare not lose sight of the world God wants.

The promise of Job 42, then, is that God will finally right the wrongs that mark our days. Some sorrows—the deaths of Job's children, for example, or the deaths of Meg Woodson's children—never heal in this life. No words of solace can assuage the grief in Meg Woodson's heart, for that grief has a precise shape, the shape of her daughter Peggie and her son Joey. But at the end of time, that grief too will vanish. Meg will get her daughter back, and her son, remade. And if I did not believe that, did not believe that Peggie and Joey Woodson are right now breathing in great gulps, and dancing, and exploring new worlds, then I would not believe anything and would have abandoned the Christian faith long ago. "If only for this life we have hope in Christ, we are to be pitied more than all men."

The Bible stakes God's reputation on his ability to conquer evil and restore heaven and earth to their original perfection. Apart from that future state, God could be judged less-than-powerful, or less-than-loving.* So far the prophets' visions of peace and justice have not come true. Swords aren't being melted into plowshares. Death, with ugly new mutations of AIDS and environmental cancers, is still swallowing people up, not being swallowed. Evil, not good, appears to be winning. But the Bible calls us to see beyond the grim reality of history to the view of all eternity, when God's reign will fill the earth with light and truth.

In any discussion of disappointment with God, heaven is the last word, the most important word of all. Only heaven will finally solve the problem of God's hiddenness. For the first time ever, human beings will be able to look upon God face to face. In the midst of his agony, Job somehow came up with the faith to believe that "in my flesh I will see God; I myself will see him with my own eyes." That prophecy will come true not just for Job but for all of us.

Homesick

Many people have trouble even imagining such a future state. As Charles Williams said, "Our experience on earth makes it difficult for us to apprehend a good without a catch in it somewhere."[2] Rather than try to project ourselves into a future we can never quite grasp, perhaps we would do better to look at the unfulfilled dreams—the disappointments—of the present.

To a refugee or peasant, heaven represents a dream of a new country, a place of safety, a family reunited, a home abundant with simple things like food and fresh drinking water. (Many of the

*Once the Spanish mystic Unamuno, conversing with a peasant, suggested that perhaps there was a God but no heaven. The peasant thought a minute and then replied, "So what is this God for?"

prophets spoke to refugees, which may explain why they used such earthly images.)

At some level, we all share such longings. This world may be full of pollution, war, crime, and greed, but inside us—all of us— linger remnants that remind us of what the world could be like, of what *we* could be like. You can sense such longings in the environmental movement, whose leaders yearn for a world preserved in its pristine state; and in the peace movement that dreams of a world without war; and in therapy groups that try to reconnect broken strands of love and friendship. All the beauty and joy we meet on earth represent "only the scent of a flower we have not found, the echo of a tune we have not heard, news from a country we have never yet visited."[3]

The prophets proclaim that such sensations are not illusions or mere dreams, but advance echoes of what will come true. We are given few details about that future world, only a promise that God will prove himself trustworthy. When we awake in the new heaven and new earth, we will possess at last whatever we longed for. Somehow, from all the bad news, incredible Good News emerges—a good without a catch in it somewhere. Heaven and earth will again work the way God intended. There is a happy ending after all.

Fantasy writer J. R. R. Tolkien invented a new word for this good news: it will be a "eucatastrophe," he said. A scene from his trilogy, *The Lord of the Rings,* expresses it well:

> "Is everything sad going to come untrue? What's happened to the world?" [asked Sam].
>
> "A great Shadow has departed," said Gandalf, and then he laughed, and the sound was like music, or like water in a parched land; and as he listened the thought came to him that he had not heard laughter, the pure sound of merriment, for

days upon days without count. It fell upon his ears like the echo of all the joys he had ever known. But he himself burst into tears. Then, as a sweet rain will pass down a wind of spring and the sun will shine out the clearer, his tears ceased, and his laughter welled up, and laughing he sprang from his bed.

"How do I feel?" he cried. "Well, I don't know how to say it. I feel, I feel"—he waved his arms in the air—"I feel like spring after winter, and sun on the leaves; and like trumpets and harps and all the songs I have ever heard!"[3]

For people who are trapped in pain, or in a broken home, or in economic misery, or in fear—for all those people, for all of us, heaven promises a time, far longer and more substantial than the time we spent on earth, of health and wholeness and pleasure and peace. If we do not believe that, then, as Paul plainly stated, there's little reason to believe at all. Without that hope, there is no hope.

The Bible never belittles human disappointment (remember the proportion in Job—one chapter of restoration follows forty-one chapters of anguish), but it does add one key word: temporary. What we feel now, we will not always feel. Our disappointment is itself a sign, an aching, a hunger for something better. And faith is, in the end, a kind of homesickness—for a home we have never visited but have never once stopped longing for.

And the end of all our exploring
Will be to arrive where we started
And know the place for the first time.
T. S. ELIOT

Then I saw a new heaven and a new earth, for the first heaven and the first earth had passed away, and there was no longer any sea. I saw the Holy City, the new Jerusalem, coming down out of heaven from God, prepared as a bride beautifully dressed for her husband. And I heard a loud voice from the throne saying, "Now the dwelling of God is with men, and he will live with them. They will be his people, and God himself will be with them and be their God. He will wipe every tear from their eyes. There will be no more death or mourning or crying or pain, for the old order of things has passed away.

---

[1]Elie Wiesel, *Messengers of God,* 233.
[2]Charles Williams, *The Image of the City,* 136.
[3]C. S. Lewis, *The Weight of Glory,* 5.
[4]J. R. R. Tolkien, *The Return of the King,* 283.

Bible references: Job 42; Hebrews 10; 2 Corinthians 4; 1 Corinthians 15; Job 19; Revelation 21.

CHAPTER 30

TWO WAGERS, TWO PARABLES

———— ✦✦✦ ————

Is there then any terrestrial paradise where amidst the whispering of the
olive leaves people can be with whom they like and have what they like
and take their ease in shadows and in coolness, or are all men's lives
. . . broken, tumultuous, agonized and unromantic lives, periods punc-
tuated by screams, by imbecilities, by deaths, by agonies?

FORD MADOX FORD, *THE GOOD SOLDIER*

Italian author Umberto Eco tells of a day when, at the age of thir-
teen, he accompanied his father to a soccer match. Umberto did
not really enjoy sports, and as he sat in the stadium observing the
game his mind began to wander. "As I was observing with detachment the senseless movements down there on the field, I felt how the
high noonday sun seemed to enfold men and things in a chilling
light, and how before my eyes a cosmic, meaningless performance
was proceeding. . . . For the first time I doubted the existence of God
and decided that the world was a pointless fiction."[1]

Perched high in the stadium, the adolescent Eco had imagined a viewpoint from above, like God's. But from that vantage the frantic scramblings of the human race seemed as senseless as the frantic scramblings of grown men chasing a leather ball across grass. It occurred to Eco that there must be no one "up there" watching what takes place on this planet. And if someone was there after all, he must care as little about life on earth as Umberto Eco cared about soccer.

Eco's image of the stadium raises the most basic question of faith, the question on which all else hinges: *Is anyone watching?* Are we dashing about in meaningless chaos, engulfed in "the benign indifference of the universe," or are we *performing* for Someone who cares? Job received his answer in a blinding revelation, but what about the rest of us? There is no more important question, and five years after the conversation that spawned this book I found myself discussing this question at length with my skeptical friend Richard.

When I had first met Richard, he was like an estranged lover in the early stages of separation and divorce—from God. Anger smoldered in his eyes. But when I saw him five years later, it was clear that the passage of time had mellowed him. His passion would still break out as we talked, but mingled with wistfulness, or nostalgia. He could not put God completely out of mind, and God's absence made itself felt, hauntingly, like pain from a phantom limb. Even if I didn't bring up matters of faith, Richard, still hurt, betrayed, would circle back to them.

Once he turned to me with a puzzled look. "I don't get it, Philip," he said. "We read many of the same books, and share many of the same values. You seem to understand my doubt and disappointment. And yet somehow you find it possible to believe, but I don't. What's the difference? Where did you get your faith?"

My mind sped through possible answers. I could have suggested all the evidences for God: design in creation, the story of Jesus, proofs of the Resurrection, examples of Christian saints. But Richard knew those answers as well as I, and still did not believe. Besides, I did not get my faith from them. I got it in a dorm room in a Bible college, on a particular night in February, and so I proceeded to tell Richard about that night.

A Night of Faith

I have already mentioned that Bible college was for me, initially, a breeding ground of doubt and skepticism. I survived by learning to mimic "spiritual" behavior—a student had to, in fact, just to get good grades. There was the odious matter of "Christian service," for instance. The college required each student to participate in a regular service activity, such as street evangelism, prison ministry, or nursing home visitation. I signed up for "university work."

Every Saturday night I would visit a student center at the University of South Carolina and watch television. I was supposed to be "witnessing," of course, and the next week I would dutifully report on all the people I had approached about personal faith. My embellished stories must have sounded authentic, because no one ever questioned them.

I was also required to attend a weekly prayer meeting with four other students involved in university work. Those meetings followed a consistent pattern: Joe would pray, and then Craig, and Chris, and the other Joe, and then all four would pause politely for about ten seconds. I never prayed; and after the brief silence, we would open our eyes and return to our rooms.

But one February night to everyone's surprise, including my own, I did pray. I have no idea why. I had not planned to. But after Joe and Craig and Chris and Joe had finished, I found myself praying aloud. "God," I said, and I could sense the tension level in the room rise.

As I recall it, I said something like this: "God, here we are, supposed to be concerned about those ten thousand students at the University of South Carolina who are going to hell. Well, you know that I don't care if they all go to hell, if there is one. I don't even care if I go to there."

You would have to attend a Bible college to appreciate how these words must have sounded to the others in the room. I may as well have been invoking witchcraft or offering child sacrifices. But no one stirred or tried to stop me, and I continued praying.

For some reason, I started talking about the parable of the Good Samaritan. We Bible college types were supposed to feel the same concern for university students as the Samaritan felt for the bloodied Jew lying in the ditch. But I felt no such concern, I said. I felt nothing for them.

And then it happened. In the middle of my prayer, just as I was describing how little I cared for our assigned targets of compassion, I saw that story in a new light. I had been visualizing the scene as I spoke: an old-fashioned-looking Samaritan, dressed in robes and a turban, bending over a dirty, blood-crusted form in a ditch. But suddenly, in the internal screen of my brain, those two figures changed. The kindly Samaritan took on the face of Jesus. The Jew, pitiable victim of a highway robbery, took on another face too—a face I recognized with a start as my own.

In a flash I saw Jesus reaching down with a moistened rag to clean my wounds and stanch the flow of blood. And as he bent over, I saw myself, the wounded robbery victim, open my eyes and purse my lips. Then, as if watching in slow motion, I saw myself spit at him, full in the face. I saw all that—I, who did not believe in visions, or in biblical parables, or even in Jesus. It stunned me. Abruptly, I stopped praying, got up, and left the room.

All that evening I thought about what had happened. It wasn't exactly a vision—more like a daydreamed parable with a moral twist. Still, I couldn't put it behind me. What did it mean? Was it genuine? I wasn't sure, but I knew that my cockiness had been shattered. On that campus I had always found security in my agnosticism. No longer. I had caught a new glimpse of myself. Perhaps in all my self-assured and mocking skepticism I was the neediest one of all.

I wrote a brief note to my fiancée that night, saying guardedly, "I want to wait a few days before talking about it, but I may have just had the first authentic religious experience of my life."

Two Wagers

I told that story to Richard, who listened with genuine interest. Everything in my life had changed from that moment on, I said. Before then, if anyone had suggested I would spend my life writing about the Christian faith, I would have thought him insane. But since that February night I have been on a slow, steady pilgrimage to reclaim what I had once rejected as religious nonsense. I received eyes of faith that opened up belief in the unseen world.

Richard was kind, but unconvinced. He pointed out gently that there were, after all, alternative explanations for what had happened. For several years I had been resisting a fundamentalist upbringing, and undoubtedly that repression had caused a deep "cognitive dissonance" within me. Since I had not prayed for so long, should it surprise me that my first prayer, no matter how tentative, would release a flood of emotions that might find an outlet in such form as the "revelation" of the Good Samaritan parable?

I had to smile as Richard talked, because I recognized myself in his words. I had used that same language to explain away the personal testimonies of scores of my fellow students. But ever since that night in February I have seen things differently.

Richard and I were describing the same phenomenon two different ways: he was looking "at the beam," while I was looking along it. He had certain evidence on his side. I had certain evidence on mine—mainly the profound and unexpected change in my outlook on life. But conversions only make sense from the inside out, to the fellow-converted. We were back where we had started in our conversation five years before: we had arrived at the mystery of *faith*, a word Richard detested.

I found myself wishing I could make faith crystal clear for him, but I felt powerless to do so. I sensed in Richard the same restlessness and alienation that I had lived with, and that God had gradually healed. But I could not transplant faith into Richard; he must exercise it for himself.

It was during this conversation that I realized there are actually two cosmic wagers transpiring. I have focused on The Wager from God's point of view, The Wager as pictured in the Book of Job, in which God "risks" the future of the human experiment on a person's response. I doubt anyone fully understands that wager, but Jesus taught that the end of human history will boil down to the one issue: "When the Son of Man comes, will he find faith on the earth?"

The second wager, reflecting the human viewpoint, is the one that Job himself engaged in: should he choose for God or against him? Job weighed the evidence, most of which did not suggest a trustworthy God. But he decided, kicking and screaming all the way, to place his faith in God.

Each one of us must choose whether to live as if God exists, or as if he does not exist. When Umberto Eco sat high in the stadium under a noonday sun and looked down on a field of soccer players, he seized upon the most important question of his life—of any life. Is anyone watching? And the answer to that question rests squarely upon faith—by that and only that the just shall live.

Two Parables

I end this book with two stories, both of them true, which for me stand as parables for the alternatives: the way of faith and the way of non-faith.

The first comes from a sermon by Frederick Buechner:

> It is a peculiarly twentieth-century story, and it is almost too awful to tell: about a boy of twelve or thirteen who, in a fit of crazy anger and depression, got hold of a gun somewhere and fired it at his father, who died not right away but soon afterward. When the authorities asked the boy why he had done it, he said that it was because he could not stand his father, because his father demanded too much of him, because he was always after him, because he hated his father. And then later on, after he had been placed in a house of detention somewhere, a guard was walking down the corridor late one night when he heard sounds from the boy's room, and he stopped to listen. The words that he heard the boy sobbing out in the dark were, "I want my father, I want my father."[1]

Buechner says that this story is "a kind of parable of the lives of all of us." Modern society is like that boy in the house of detention. We have killed off our Father. Few thinkers or writers or moviemakers or television producers take God seriously anymore. He's an anachronism, something we've outgrown. The modern world has accepted The Wager and bet against God. There are too many unanswered questions. He has disappointed us once too often.*

---

*"Have you not heard of the man who lit a lamp on a bright morning and went to the marketplace crying ceaselessly, 'I seek God. I seek God'. . . . They laughed, and . . . the man sprang into their midst and looked daggers at them. 'Where is God?' he cried. 'I will tell you. We have killed Him, you and I.' We are all His killers, but how can we have done that? How could we swallow up the sea? Who gave us the sponge to wipe away the horizon? What will we do as the earth is set loose from its sun?"—Friedrich Nietzsche, *The Gay Science*

It is a hard thing to live, uncertain of anything. And yet, sobs can still be heard, muffled cries of loss, such as those expressed in literature and film and almost all modern art. The alternative to disappointment with God seems to be disappointment without God. ("The center of me," said Bertrand Russell, "is always and eternally a terrible pain—a curious wild pain—a searching for something beyond what the world contains.")

I see that sense of loss in the eyes of my friend Richard, even now. He says he does not believe in God, but he keeps bringing up the subject, protesting too loudly. From where comes this wounded sense of betrayal if no one is there to do the betraying?

———— ⟨⟨⟨⟩⟩⟩ ————

Frederick Buechner's parable concerns the loss of a father; the second concerns the discovery of a father. It too is a true story, my own story.

One holiday I was visiting my mother, who lives seven hundred miles away. We reminisced about times long past, as mothers and sons tend to do. Inevitably, the large box of old photos came down from the closet shelf, spilling out a jumbled pile of thin rectangles that mark my progression through childhood and adolescence: the cowboy-and-Indian getups, the Peter Cottontail suit in the first grade play, my childhood pets, endless piano recitals, the graduations from grade school and high school and finally college.

Among those photos I found one of an infant, with my name written on the back. The portrait itself was not unusual. I looked like any baby: fat-cheeked, half-bald, with a wild, unfocused look to my eyes. But the photo was crumpled and mangled, as if one of those childhood pets had got hold of it. I asked my mother why she had hung onto such an abused photo when she had so many other undamaged ones.

There is something you should know about my family: when I was ten months old, my father contracted spinal lumbar polio. He died three months later, just after my first birthday. My father was totally paralyzed at age twenty-four, his muscles so weakened that he had to live inside a large steel cylinder that did his breathing for him. He had few visitors—people had as much hysteria about polio in 1950 as they do about AIDS today. The one visitor who came faithfully, my mother, would sit in a certain place so that he could see her in a mirror bolted to the side of the iron lung.

My mother explained to me that she had kept the photo as a memento, because during my father's illness it had been fastened to his iron lung. He had asked for pictures of her and of his two sons, and my mother had had to jam the pictures in between some metal knobs. Thus, the crumpled condition of my baby photo.

I rarely saw my father after he entered the hospital, since children were not allowed in polio wards. Besides, I was so young that, even if I had been allowed in, I would not now retain those memories.

When my mother told me the story of the crumpled photo, I had a strange and powerful reaction. It seemed odd to imagine someone caring about me whom, in a sense, I had never met. During the last months of his life, my father had spent his waking hours staring at those three images of his family, my family. There was nothing else in his field of view. What did he do all day? Did he pray for us? Yes, surely. Did he love us? Yes. But how can a paralyzed person express his love, especially when his own children are banned from the room?

I have often thought of that crumpled photo, for it is one of the few links connecting me to the stranger who was my father, a stranger who died a decade younger than I am now. Someone I have no memory of, no sensory knowledge of, spent all day every day thinking of me, devoting himself to me, loving me as well as he could. Perhaps, in some mysterious way, he is doing so now in another dimension. Perhaps I will have time, much time, to renew a relationship that was cruelly ended just as it had begun.

I mention this story because the emotions I felt when my mother showed me the crumpled photo were the very same emotions I felt that February night in a college dorm room when I first believed in a God of love. *Someone is there,* I realized. Someone is watching life as it unfolds on this planet. More, Someone is there who loves me. It was a startling feeling of wild hope, a feeling so new and overwhelming that it seemed fully worth risking my life on.

---

[1]Umberto Eco, *Travels in Hyper Reality,* 167-168.
[2]Frederick Buechner, *The Magnificent Defeat,* 65.

*Bible reference: Luke 18.

THANKS

Someday I may have to write a book on my own, but I hope that time doesn't come soon because I now rely very heavily on the editorial suggestions of other readers. I am hopelessly and gratefully dependent on my friend Tim Stafford, who read this manuscript in three successive drafts. That was a labor of love: before Tim's expert suggestions on needed cuts, the manuscript was fifty percent longer.

I also had the good fortune of participating in a manuscript evaluation session with four other writers—Steve Lawhead, Karen Mains, Luci Shaw, and Walter Wangerin, Jr.—who helped me set the tone for the final draft. Then in separate sessions Walter unveiled to me some of the mysteries of storytelling. And these others also read and critiqued the manuscript, giving me valuable advice: Elsie Baker, Dr. John Boyle, Dr. Paul Brand, Harold Fickett, Hal Knight, Lee Phillips, and Dr. Cornelius Plantinga.

After I had acted on all these folks' advice, Judith Markham, my editor on three previous books, edited the final result. Judith offers a rare combination of diplomacy, literary wisdom, kindness, and, above all, a pursuit of excellence. She is a good friend, and a fine editor.

Some names—Augustine, Buechner, Chesterton, Eliot, Lewis, Moltmann, MacDonald, Pascal, Sayers, Thielicke, and Williams— you have already met, for they appear throughout the book. In the truest sense, they are my "pastors." Because of them, in no small measure, I continue to believe.

A class I taught at LaSalle Street Church assured that for at least five years I would study the Old Testament in detail, and its members contributed many fine insights and daunting questions.

I referred several times to an inspiring visit to the Colorado mountains: I'm grateful to the Konemans and the Braytons, who made that time possible.

And I want to thank Richard. He has the courage to be honest; I have learned much from him. I hope that he never stops asking questions, that he never abandons his search.

BIBLIOGRAPHY

Augustine, Saint. *The Confessions of Saint Augustine.* Translated by John K. Ryan. Garden City: Doubleday, 1960.

Brown, Colin. *Miracles and the Critical Mind.* Grand Rapids: Eerdmans, 1984.

Buechner, Frederick. *The Hungering Dark.* New York: Seabury, 1981.

_____. *The Magnificent Defeat.* New York: Seabury, 1979.

_____. *A Room Called Remember: Uncollected Pieces.* New York: Harper & Row, 1984.

_____. *Wishful Thinking: A Theological ABC.* Harper & Row, 1973.

Dostoyevsky, Fyodor. *The Brothers Karamazov.* Garden City: Nelson Doubleday (no date).

Eco, Umberto. *Travels in Hyper Reality: Essays.* Edited by Helen & Kurt Wolff. Translated from the Italian by William Weaver. New York: Harcourt Brace Jovanovich, 1983.

Eiseley, Loren. *The Star Thrower.* Harcourt Brace Jovanovich, 1979.

Hall, Douglas John. *God and Human Suffering.* Minneapolis: Augsburg, 1986.

James, William. *The Varieties of Religious Experience.* New York: Modern Library, 1936.

Kierkegaard, Søren. *Philosophical Fragments.* Translated by David Swenson. Princeton: Princeton University Press, 1962.

Lewis, C. S. *Christian Reflections.* Grand Rapids: Eerdmans, 1974.

_____. *God in the Dock.* Edited by Walter Hooper. Grand Rapids: Eerdmans, 1970.

_____. *A Grief Observed*. New York: Seabury, 1961.

_____. *The Weight of Glory and Other Addresses*. Grand Rapids: Eerdmans, 1975.

_____. *The World's Last Night and Other Essays*. New York: Harcourt Brace Jovanovich, Inc., 1959.

MacDonald, George. *Life Essential: The Hope of the Gospel*. Edited by Rolland Hein. Wheaton, Ill.: Harold Shaw, 1978.

MacDonald, Greville. *George MacDonald and His Wife*. London: George Allen and Unwin, Ltd., 1924.

Moltmann, Jürgen. *God in Creation: A New Theology of Creation and the Spirit of God*. New York: Harper & Row, 1985.

Spark, Muriel. *The Only Problem*. New York: Putnam, 1984.

Thompson, William I. *The Time Falling Bodies Take to Light*. New York: St. Martin's Press, 1982.

Tolkien, J. R. R. *The Return of the King*. New York: Ballantine, 1976.

_____. *The Tolkien Reader*. New York: Ballantine Books, 1966.

Wiesel, Elie. *Messengers of God: Biblical Portraits and Legends*. New York: Summit Books, 1985.

Williams, Charles. *He Came Down from Heaven*. London: William Heinemann, Ltd., 1938.

_____. *The Image of the City*. London: Oxford University Press, 1958.

READ AN EXCERPT FROM PHILIP YANCEY'S

PRAYER

When a doctoral student at Princeton asked,
"What is there left in the world
for original dissertation research?"
visiting lecturer Albert Einstein replied,
"Find out about prayer.
Somebody must find out about prayer."

CHAPTER 1
OUR DEEPEST LONGING

I chose the wrong time to visit St. Petersburg, Russia. I went in November of 2002, just as the city was reconstructing itself to prepare for its three hundredth birthday the following year. Rubble marred every quaint cobblestone street, and scaffolding covered every building of note. As a result, my normal morning jogging routine turned into an adventure. I ran in complete darkness (the sun rose midmorning at that latitude) with my head down, dodging the workmen's piles of brick and sand while looking ahead for the dull gloss that betrayed the presence of ice.

I must have lost concentration one morning for suddenly I found myself facedown on the street, dazed and shivering. I sat up. I could remember jerking my head sideways as I fell, to avoid a piece of steel rebar protruding from the curb at a wicked angle. I removed my gloves, reached for my right eye, and felt blood. The entire right side of my face was wet with blood. I got up, dusted dirt and flecks of snow from my running suit, and felt for more damage. I walked slowly, testing my throbbing knees and elbows. I tasted blood, and a couple of blocks away I realized a front tooth was missing. I returned to search for it in the dark, in vain.

When I reached Nevsky Prospekt, a busy boulevard, I noticed that Russians were staring at me. They rarely look strangers in the eye, I knew. I must be a sight. I limped to the hotel and had to talk my way past the security guards to get back to my room. I knocked on the door and said, "Janet, let me in—I'm hurt."

We had heard horror stories about the medical system in Russia. You can go in with a surface wound and come out with AIDS or hepatitis. We decided on self-treatment. After raiding the mini-bar for a couple of bottles of vodka, we started cleaning the scrapes on my face. My upper lip was split in two. I gritted my teeth, poured the alcohol over the cut, and scrubbed it with a packaged refresher-cloth left over from the Lufthansa flight. We taped the lip together with a tight Bandaid, hoping it would heal straight. By now the area around my eye had swollen and turned a spectacular purple, but fortunately my sight seemed unimpaired.

I took a few aspirin and rested a few hours. Then I went back out to Nevsky Prospekt and looked for an Internet café. I climbed three flights of stairs, used sign language to negotiate the price in rubles, and settled in at a computer terminal. I stared for awhile at the strange keyboard and Cyrillic alphabet onscreen. After ten minutes of false starts, I finally found my way to an AOL screen in English. Ah, connections. I typed a message to a prayer support team at my home church in

Colorado, and to a few friends and family members. The wireless network kept cutting on and off, and each time I had to find AOL again, and retype the message.

The message was simple: a few background details, then "We need help. Please pray." I didn't know the extent of my injuries. The next few days I was supposed to speak at a booksellers' convention in St. Petersburg, then go on to Moscow for more speaking assignments. The news banner on AOL was telling me that Chechen rebels had seized a theater full of patrons and Moscow was under military lockdown. I finished my message and pressed "Send" just as a warning screen came up informing me my time was running out.

Is this how prayer works? I wondered as I walked back to the hotel. We send signals out from a visible world into an invisible one, in hope that Someone receives them. And how will we know? Still, for the first time that day I felt the lump of fear and anxiety in my stomach begin to loosen. In a few hours my friends and family, people who cared, would turn on their computers, read my message, and pray on my behalf. I was not alone.[1]

A UNIVERSAL CRY, FRUSTRATED

Every faith has some form of prayer. Remote tribes present offerings and then pray for everyday things such as health, food, rain, children, and victory in battles. Inca and Aztec civilizations went so far as to sacrifice humans in order to attract the gods' attention. Five times a day modern Muslims stop whatever they are doing—driving, having a coffee break, playing soccer—when the summons comes to pray.

Even atheists find ways to pray. During the heady days of Communism in Russia, true believers kept a "red corner," placing a portrait of Lenin where Christians used to keep their icons. Caught up in the fervor, *Pravda* ran this advice to its readers in 1950:

> If you meet with difficulties in your work, or suddenly doubt your abilities, think of him—of Stalin—and you will find the confidence you need. If you feel tired in an hour when you should not, think of him—of Stalin— and your work will go well. If you are seeking a correct decision, think of him—of Stalin—and you will find that decision.

We pray because we want to thank someone or something for the beauties and glories of life, and also because we feel small and helpless, and sometimes afraid. We pray for forgiveness, for strength, for contact with the One who is, for assurance that we are not alone. We pray because we can't help it. According to the dictionary, the very word prayer comes from the Latin root *precarius*—a linguistic cousin to *precarious*. In St. Petersburg, Russia, I prayed out of desperation. I had nowhere else to turn.

Prayer is universal because it speaks to some basic human need. As Thomas Merton put it, "Prayer is an expression of who we are. . . . We are a living incompleteness. We are a gap, an emptiness that calls for fulfillment." In prayer we break silence, and sometimes those words flow out of the deepest parts. I remember after September 11, 2001, saying over and over the prayer, "God, bless America." "Save America," is what I meant. Save us. Let us live. Give us another chance.

According to Gallup polls, more Americans will pray this week than will exercise, drive a car, have sex, or go to work. Nine in ten of us pray regularly, and three out of four claim to pray every day. To get some idea of the universal interest in prayer, type "prayer" or "pray" in an Internet search engine like Google and see how many millions of links pop up. Yet behind those impressive numbers lies a dark mystery.

When I started investigating the subject of Christian prayer, I first went to libraries and read accounts of some of the great pray-ers in history. George Müller began each day with several hours of prayer, imploring God to meet the practical needs of his orphanage. Bishop Andrews allotted five hours per day to prayer, and Charles Simeon rose at 4:00 a.m. to begin his four-hour regimen. Susannah Wesley, a busy mother with no privacy, would sit in a rocking chair with an apron over her head praying for John and Charles and the rest of her brood. Martin Luther, who devoted two to three hours daily to prayer, said we should do it as naturally as a shoemaker makes a shoe and a tailor makes a coat. Jonathan Edwards wrote of the "sweet hours" on the banks of the Hudson River, "rapt and swallowed up in God."

As a next step, I started interviewing ordinary people about prayer. Typically, the results went like this. Is prayer important to you? *Oh, yes.* How often do you pray? *Every day.* Approximately how long? *Five minutes—well, maybe seven.* Do you find prayer satisfying? *Not really.* Do you sense the presence of God when you pray? *Occasionally, not often.* Many of those I talked to experienced prayer more as a burden than as a pleasure. They regarded it as important, even paramount, and felt guilty about their failure, blaming themselves.

Everywhere, I encountered the discrepancy between prayer in theory and prayer in practice. In theory (and the great prayers of history color that theory) prayer is the essential human act, a priceless point of contact between us and the God of the universe. In practice, prayer is often frustrating, confusing, and fraught with mystery. My publisher conducted a website poll, and of the 678 respondents only 23 felt satisfied with the time they were spending in prayer. That very discrepancy made me want to write this book.

Why does prayer rank so high on surveys of importance and so low on surveys of satisfaction? What causes the disjunction between Luther and Simeon on their knees for several hours and the modern pray-er fidgeting in a chair after ten minutes?

Advances in science and technology no doubt contribute to our confusion about prayer. In former days farmers lifted their heads and appealed to brazen heavens for an end to drought. Now we study low-pressure fronts, dig irrigation canals, and seed clouds with metallic crystals. In former days when a child fell ill the parents cried out to God; now they call for an ambulance or phone the doctor.

In much of the world, modern skepticism taints prayer. We breathe in the atmosphere of doubt. Why does God let the world go on as it does, and not intervene? Prayer seems to some, wrote the pastor George Buttrick, "a spasm of words lost in a cosmic indifference"—and he wrote those words in 1942. What good will it do against a nuclear threat, against terrorism and hurricanes and global climate change?

Perhaps prosperity helps dilute prayer as well. In my travels in different countries, I have noticed that Christians in developing countries spend less time pondering the effectiveness of prayer and more time actually praying. The wealthy rely on talent and resources to solve immediate problems and insurance policies and retirement plans to secure the future. We can hardly pray with sincerity, "Give us this day our daily bread" when the pantry is stocked with a month's supply of provisions.

Increasingly, time pressures crowd out the leisurely time that prayer seems to require. Communication with other people keeps getting shorter and more cryptic: text messages, email, instant messaging. We seem to have less and less time for conversation, much less solitude or contemplation. We have the constant sensation of *not enough*: not enough time, not enough rest, not enough exercise, not enough leisure. Where does God fit into a life that already seems inadequate and behind schedule?

If we do choose to bare our souls, therapists and support groups now offer outlets that used to be reserved for God alone. Those who pray to an invisible God do not get the immediate feedback they get from a counselor or from friends who nod their heads in sympathy. Is anyone really listening to our prayers? As Ernestine, the telephone operator with the nasal voice played by comedian Lily Tomlin, used to ask, "Have I reached the party to whom I am speaking?"

Prayer is to the skeptic a delusion, a waste of time. To the believer it represents perhaps the most important way to spend time. As a Christian, I believe the latter. Why, then must prayer be so problematic? The British pastor Martyn Lloyd-Jones summed up the confusion: "Of all the activities in which the Christian engages, and which are part of the Christian life, there is surely none which causes so much perplexity, and raises so many problems, as the activity which we call prayer."

PILGRIM QUEST

I write about prayer as a pilgrim, not an expert. I have the same questions that plague most everyone at some point. Is God listening? Why should God care about me? If God knows everything, what's the point of prayer? Why do answers to prayer seem so inconsistent, capricious? Does a person with many praying friends have a better chance at physical healing than my friend who also has cancer but has only a handful of people praying for her? Why does God sometimes seem close and sometimes faraway? Does prayer change God or change me?

Until I began this book I mostly avoided the topic of prayer out of guilt and a sense of inferiority. Deep down, I believed that contact with God should be fulfilling and even transforming, yet I rarely found it so. I concluded that I must be doing something wrong. Furthermore, I'm embarrassed to admit, I do not keep a journal, do not see a spiritual director, and do not belong to a regular prayer group. And I readily confess that I tend to view prayer through a skeptic's lens, obsessing more over the problems of prayer than seeking advice on healthy prayers. In short, my main qualification for writing about prayer is that I feel unqualified—and desperately want to learn.

More than anything else in life, I want to know God. The psychiatrist Gerald C. May, who died in 2005, observed, "After twenty years of listening to the yearnings of people's hearts, I am convinced that human beings have an inborn desire for God. Whether we are consciously religious or not, this desire is our deepest longing and most precious treasure." Surely, if God made us in his own image, God will find a way of responding to that deepest longing. Prayer is that way.

As I pass the midpoint of my life, I ask myself if I am loving God more and growing closer to God. If prayer stands as the place where God and human beings meet, then I must learn about prayer. Most of my struggles with the Christian life circle around the same two themes: why God doesn't act the way we want God to, and why I don't act the way God wants me to. Prayer is the precise point where those themes converge.

By journalistic instinct, I asked many other people about prayer: my neighbors, fellow church members, spiritual mentors, ordinary people. I have included some of their reflections in drop-in boxes scattered throughout the book, as examples of actual down-to-earth experiences with prayer and also as a reminder to myself not to stray far from their questions.

I have not attempted a guide book that details such techniques as fasting, prayer retreats, and spiritual direction. I investigate the topic of prayer as a pilgrim, walking around, staring at the monuments, asking questions, mulling things over, testing the waters. I have little to offer but a promise to err on the side of honesty and not pretense. I admit to an imbalance, an overreaction to time spent among Christians who promised too much and pondered too little. By nature, I worry more over unanswered prayers than rejoice over answered prayers, and I consider this a personal flaw.

In the process of writing, however, I have come to see prayer as a privilege, not a duty. I hope that my musings about prayer open an invitation to a practice that is both healthy and beneficial. Like all good things, prayer requires some discipline. Yet I believe that life with God should seem more like friendship than duty. Prayer includes moments of ecstasy and also dullness, mindless distraction and acute concentration, flashes of joy and bouts of irritation. In other words, prayer has features in common with all relationships that matter.

ENDNOTE

1. Everything healed fine. And the request for prayer had one very practical benefit. The wife of my dentist, who was on the prayer team and received the message, immediately reserved an appointment for me so that the day after my return from Russia I had a root canal procedure!

About the Author

Philip Yancey serves as editor-at-large for *Christianity Today* magazine. He has written eleven Gold Medallion Award-winning books, including *Where Is God When It Hurts? Disappointment with God, The Bible Jesus Read,* and *The Gift of Pain.* His books *The Jesus I Never Knew* and *What's So Amazing About Grace?* were also awarded the Christian Book of the Year. He is also the author of *Reaching for the Invisible God, Rumors of Another World,* and *Prayer.*

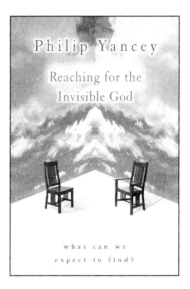

Philip Yancey

Reaching for the
Invisible God

what can we
expect to find?

Reaching for the Invisible God
What Can We Expect to find?

Philip Yancey

Life with God doesn't always work like we thought. High expectations slam against the reality of personal weaknesses and unwelcome surprises. And the God who we've been told longs for our company may seem remote, emotionally unavailable.

Is God playing games? What can we count on this God for?
How can we know? *How can we know God?*
This relationship with a God we can't see, hear, or touch—how does it really work?

Reaching for the Invisible God offers deep, satisfying insights that affirm and dignify the questions we're sometimes afraid to ask. Award-winning author Philip Yancey explores six foundational areas: our thirst for God, faith during times when God seems unavailable, the nature of God himself, our personal relationship with God, stages along the way, and the end goal of spiritual transformation. Honest and deeply personal, here is straight talk on Christian living for the man or woman who wants more than pat answers to life's imponderables. Ultimately, Yancey shifts the focus from our questions to the One who offers himself in answer. The God who invites us to reach for him—and find.

"I love Philip Yancey's work. He is a brilliant, graceful writer."
—Anne Lamott, Author, *Traveling Mercies*

"This passionate book, unflinching in its honesty, will build your faith by helping you wrestle authentically with your doubts. Join Philip Yancey in this quest and you'll come closer still to our invisible but very real God."
—Lee Strobel, Author, *The Case for Faith*

Softcover 0-310-24730-6
Study Guide 0-310-24057-3
Audio CD, Unabridged 0-310-24168-5
Audio Download,
   Unabridged 0-310-26172-4

Audio Download,
   Abridged 0-310-26092-2
Ebook, Microsoft 0-310-23933-8
Ebook, Palm 0-310-24919-8
Ebook, Mobipocket 0-310-26247-X

What's So Amazing About Grace?
Philip Yancey

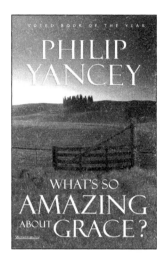

We speak of grace often. But do we understand it? More important, do we truly believe in it . . . and do our lives proclaim it as powerfully as our words?

In *What's So Amazing About Grace?* award-winning author Philip Yancey explores grace at street level. If grace is God's love for the undeserving, he asks, then what does it look like in action? And if Christians are its sole dispensers, then how are we doing at lavishing grace on a world that knows far more of cruelty and unforgiveness than it does of mercy?

Yancey sets grace in the midst of life's stark images, tests its mettle against horrific "ungrace". Can grace survive in the midst of such atrocities as the Nazi holocaust? Can it triumph over the brutality of the Ku Klux Klan? Grace does not excuse sin, says Yancey, but it treasures the sinner.

In his most personal and provocative book ever, Yancey offers compelling, true portraits of grace's life-changing power. He searches for its presence in his own life and in the church. He asks, How can Christians contend graciously with moral issues that threaten all they hold dear? And he challenges us to become living answers to a world that desperately wants to know, *What's So Amazing About Grace?*

Hardcover 0-310-21327-4
Softcover 0-310-24565-6
Study Guide 0-310-21904-3
Leader's Guide 0-310-23326-7
Participant's Guide 0-310-23325-9

ZondervanGroupware™ 0-310-23323-2
Ebook, Microsoft 0-310-26438-3
Ebook, Palm 0-310-26439-1
Ebook, Mobipocket 0-310-26440-5
Ebook, Adobe 0-310-26437-5

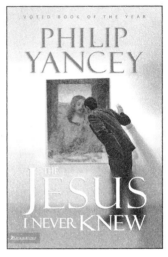

The Jesus I Never Knew
Philip Yancey

What happens when a respected Christian journalist decides to put his preconceptions aside and take a long look at the Jesus described in the Gospels? How does the Jesus of the New Testament compare to the "new, rediscovered" Jesus— or even the Jesus we think we know so well? Best-selling author Philip Yancey says, "The Jesus I got to know in writing this book is very different from the Jesus I learned about in Sunday school. In some ways he is more comforting; in some ways more terrifying."

Yancey offers a new and different perspective on the life of Christ and his work—his teaching, his miracle, his death and resurrection—and ultimately, who he was and why he came. Relating the gospel events to the world we live in today, *The Jesus I Never Knew* gives a moving and refreshing portrait of the central figure of history. With a willingness to tackle difficult questions, Yancey looks at the radical words of this itinerant Jewish carpenter and asks whether we are taking him seriously enough in our own day and age.

From the manger in Bethlehem to the cross in Jerusalem, Yancey presents a complex character who generates questions as well as answers; a disturbing and exhilarating Jesus who wants to radically transform your life and stretch your faith.

Hardcover 0-310-38570-9   ZondervanGroupware™ 0-310-22358-X
Softcover 0-310-21923-X   Leader's Guide 0-310-22432-2
Study Guide 0-310-21805-5   Participant's Guide 0-310-22433-0

Pick up a copy today at your favorite bookstore!

ZONDERVAN®
.com

The Bible Jesus Read
Philip Yancey

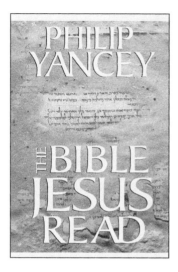

With his candid, signature style, Yancey interacts with the Old Testament from the perspective of his own deeply personal journey. From Moses, the amazing prince of Egypt, to the psalmists' turbulent emotions and the prophets' oddball rantings, Yancey paints a picture of Israel's God—and ours—that fills in the blanks of a solely New Testament vision of the Almighty.

Probing some carefully selected Old Testament books—Job, Deuteronomy, Psalms, Ecclesiastes, and the Prophets—Yancey reveals how the Old Testament deals in astonishing depths and detail with the issues that trouble us most. The Old Testament, in fact, tackles what the New Testament often only skirts. But that shouldn't surprise us. It is, after all, the Bible Jesus read.

Join Philip Yancey as he explores these sometimes shocking, often cryptic, divine writings. You will come to know God more intimately, anticipate Jesus more fervently, and find a wonderful, wise companion for your faith journey.

Softcover 0-310-24566-4   Leader's Guide 0-310-24184-7
Zondervan *Groupware*™ 0-310-24182-0   Participant's Guide 0-310-24185-5

Pick up a copy today at your favorite bookstore!

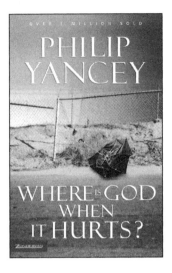

Where Is God When It Hurts?
Philip Yancey

"If there is a loving God, then why is it that . . ." You've heard that question, perhaps asked it yourself. No matter how you complete it, at its root lies the issue of pain. Does God order our suffering? Does he decree an abusive childhood, orchestrate a jet crash, steer a tornado through a community? Or did he simply wind up the world's mainspring and now is watching from a distance?

In this Gold Medallion Award-winning book, Philip Yancey reveals a God who is neither capricious nor unconcerned. Using examples from the Bible and from his own experiences, Yancey looks at pain—physical, emotional, and spiritual—and helps us understand why we suffer. This most current edition of what is perhaps Yancey's best-known book will speak to those for whom life sometimes just doesn't make sense. And it will help equip anyone who wants to reach out to someone in pain but just doesn't know what to say.

Softcover 0-310-24572-9
Mass Market 0-310-21437-8

Pick up a copy today at your favorite bookstore!

Church: Why Bother?

My Personal Pilgrimage
Philip Yancey

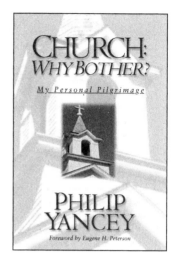

Philip Yancey asks the question that haunts many believers: Why should I bother with the church? From growing up in rural Georgia in a fundamentalist church to his experience at LaSalle Street Church in inner city Chicago, he reflects on the church, his own perceptions of it, and the various metaphors the Bible uses to describe it. Yancey's own early church experience set his faith back by many years. In *Church: Why Bother?* he offers us a glimpse of his pilgrimage back to faith and to the church as a place of real community and spiritual vitality.

In this candid, thought-provoking account, he reveals the reasons behind his own journey back from skepticism to wholehearted participation in the church, and weighs the church's human failings against its compelling excellencies as the body of Christ.

Softcover 0-310-24313-0

Pick up a copy today at your favorite bookstore!

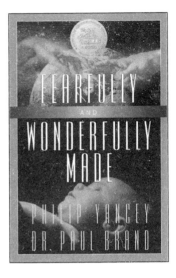

Fearfully and Wonderfully Made
Philip Yancey
Dr. Paul Brand

Mysterious, intricate, pulsing with energy . . . the human body is an endlessly fascinating repository of secrets. The miracle of the skin, the strength and structure of the bones, the dynamic balance of the muscles . . . your physical being is knit according to a pattern of incredible purpose. In *Fearfully and Wonderfully Made,* renowned surgeon Dr. Paul Brand and best-selling writer Philip Yancey explore the human body. Join them in a remarkable journey through inner space—a spellbinding world of cells, systems, and chemistry that bears the impress of a still deeper, unseen reality. This Gold Medallion Award-winning book uncovers eternal statements that God has made in the very structure of our bodies, presenting captivating insights into the Body of Christ.

Softcover 0-310-35451-X

Pick up a copy today at your favorite bookstore!

In His Image
Philip Yancey
Dr. Paul Brand

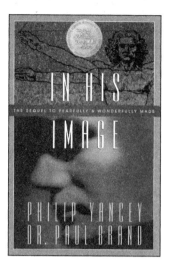

The voice of God is a heartbeat away...

This companion book to *Fearfully and Wonderfully Made,* skillfully coauthored by award-winning writer Philip Yancey, unfolds spiritual truths through a physician's knowledge of the blood, the head, the spirit, and pain.

In *Fearfully and Wonderfully Made,* Philip Yancey and Dr. Paul Brand revealed how God's voice is encoded in the very structure of our bodies. *In His Image* takes up where its predecessor left off, beckoning us once again inward and onward to fresh exploration and discovery.

Yancey and Brand show how accurately and intricately the human body portrays the Body of Christ. In five sections—Image, Blood, Head, Spirit, and Pain—the acclaimed surgeon and the award-winning writer unlock the remarkable, living lessons contained in our physical makeup. This Gold Medallion Award-winning book will open your eyes to the complex miracle of the human body, and the even more compelling spiritual truths that it reflects.

Softcover 0-310-35501-X

Rumors of Another World
What on Earth Are We Missing?

Philip Yancey

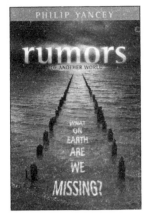

What on earth are we missing? Philip Yancey believes we are missing the supernatural hidden in everyday life.

In *Rumors of Another World*, Yancey investigates the natural world and discovers the supernatural hiding in plain view. He grapples with why God made the world and what our role truly is and seeks to answer the question, "How do I live in the natural world while expressing the values of the supernatural?"

Philip writes, "I have come to understand faith as the highest form of integrated encounter. Faith puts together, assembles, reorders, accepting the entire world as God's handiwork. We live among clues, like rescuers sifting through pieces of stained glass shattered by a bomb, and only with a blueprint or some memory of original design can we begin to connect the shards, to assemble them into a pattern that makes sense of our world.

"Nature and supernature are not two separate worlds, but different expressions of the same reality. To encounter the world as a whole, we need a more supernatural awareness of the natural world."

Yancey invites readers to join him on a journey of discovery. He challenges us to tune into "rumors of another world" and connect the seen with the unseen. He promises that the grace-filled result will be a life of beauty, purpose, freedom, and faith.

Hardcover: 0-310-25217-2

Pick up a copy today at your favorite bookstore!

What's So Amazing About Grace? Visual Edition

Philip Yancey

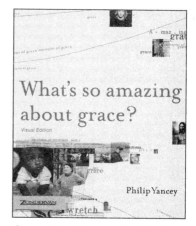

A stunningly innovative visual edition of this award-winning book—designed to appeal to spiritual seekers and visually oriented readers.

Philip Yancey's *What's So Amazing About Grace?* won the Book of the Year Award in 1998 and has sold over one million copies since it was first published in 1997. Now this innovative visual edition uses the life-transforming content of Yancey's message and makes it accessible to a whole new audience. This visually rich book takes portions of the text of the original book and illustrates the themes and messages with provocative full-color photography and graphic illustrations.

The creators of this visual edition designed it with the needs of contemporary postmodern readers in mind: both spiritual seekers and the younger, more visually oriented readers of today's culture. By combining Yancey's engaging style with striking images that enhance and illuminate the message, this unique book enables readers to "experience grace" as they interact with the powerfully imaginative format.

With deep personal honesty, Yancey paints true portraits of grace's life-changing power as he searches for its presence in his own life and the life of the church. He explores grace—God's love for the undeserving—while challenging Christians to become living answers to a world that desperately wants to know: What's so amazing about grace?

Softcover: 0-310-24947-3

We want to hear from you. Please send your comments about this book to us in care of zreview@zondervan.com. Thank you.

ZONDERVAN.com/
AUTHORTRACKER
follow your favorite authors